FIRST EDITION

Congenial Debates on Controversial Questions

Bruce N. Waller
Youngstown State University

PEARSON

Boston Columbus Indianapolis New York San Francisco Upper Saddle River
Amsterdam Cape Town Dubai London Madrid Milan Munich Paris Montréal Toronto
Delhi Mexico City São Paulo Sydney Hong Kong Seoul Singapore Taipei Tokyo

Editorial Director: Craig Campanella
Editor in Chief: Ashley Dodge
Executive Editor: Susan Hartman
Editorial Project Manager: Reena Dalal
Director of Marketing: Brandy Dawson
Executive Marketing Manager:
  Kelly May
Marketing Coordinator: Jessica Warren
Marketing Assistant: Paige Patunas
Media Editor: Thomas Scalzo

Production Project Manager:
  Romaine Denis
Creative Director: Jayne Conte
Cover Designer: Suzanne Behnke
**Editorial Production and Composition
  Service:** Aishwarya Dakshinamoorthy,
  PreMediaGlobal
Interior Design: Joyce Weston Design
Cover Printer: Courier Westford
Printer/Bindery: Courier Westford

Credits and acknowledgments borrowed from other sources and reproduced, with permission, in this textbook appear on the appropriate page within text.

Many of the designations by ma nufacturers and seller to distinguish their products are claimed as trademarks. Where those designations appear in this book, and the publisher was aware of a trademark claim, the designations have been printed in initial caps or all caps.

Library of Congress Cataloging-in-Publication Data

Waller, Bruce N., 1946–
    Congenial debates on controversial questions / Bruce N. Waller.
      p. cm.
    Includes index.
    ISBN-13: 978-0-205-92425-7
    ISBN-10: 0-205-92425-5
  1. Discourse ethics—Textbooks. 2. Social ethics—Textbooks. I. Title.
    BJ1025.W33 2014
    170—dc23

                                              2012037963

10 9 8 7 6 5 4 3 2 1

ISBN-10: 0-205-92426-3
ISBN-13: 978-0-205-92426-4

TABLE OF CONTENTS

PREFACE

Congenial Debates on Controversial Questions: That seems an impossible dream in the current age of harsh and hostile encounters between deeply divided and profoundly distrustful opponents. Whether in legislative halls, dorm rooms, blogs, bars, or rallies, respectful debate too often gives way to personal antagonism, shouting matches, and slogans. In fact, people are often reluctant to discuss deeply controversial issues—like abortion, capital punishment, immigration, and same-sex marriage—for fear that friendships and relationships will be strained or even broken. Yet all of us have friends and family members, not to mention fellow citizens, who disagree with us on these issues, and often feel just as strongly about them as we do. Unfortunately, we tend to discuss these questions only with those we are confident will agree with us: on blogs devoted to one side of a controversial question, among friends whom we know are "on our side," and at rallies where we all march under the same banners and slogans. As a result, we usually hear only *one* side of these questions—the side we are already convinced is right. Thus we rarely or never encounter the strongest arguments from the other side, nor do we gain the benefit of hearing forceful critiques of our own arguments and views. We come to believe distortions and misrepresentations of opposing views, because we rarely talk with people who actually hold those views and who are in a position to correct our errors concerning those views. Distortions are taken for reality, weak arguments are believed to be strong, positions become more deeply entrenched, and divisions grow deeper and uglier.

Congenial Debates on Controversial Questions is not designed to solve the many difficult and controversial questions that face us, nor is it designed to tell you what conclusions you should draw on these issues. These are very difficult and divisive questions, and people of intelligence, insight, and goodwill can be found on both sides of every question. The goal of this book is more modest but still very important: to tone down the rhetoric, reduce the hostility, avoid the distortions, and facilitate honest thoughtful *respectful* consideration of these critical questions. The people who disagree with you on these issues are not demons, nor are they out to destroy you, your country, or your morals. On at least *some* of these issues (unless you live a very narrow and insular life), some of your best friends hold views that are in direct conflict with your own; and while these friends may be a little strange, they are *not* moral monsters. If you approach controversial questions with an open mind and a willingness to *listen* to those who oppose you and *honestly* consider their actual views and their genuine reasons for those views, then you will not lose any friends in the course of these discussions; who knows, you might even find some new friends. An even wilder idea: You might discover that you want to seriously consider changing some of your own views.

Congenial Debates on Controversial Questions contains a number of special features:

- Introductory material on critical thinking, to enhance cooperative critical thinking and avoid the destructive fallacies that promote acrimony rather than insight.
- A chapter on distinctly *un*helpful approaches to ethical issues.

- A chapter on major theoretical approaches to ethics, with the focus on specific perspectives and techniques that each theoretical system can contribute to understanding controversial social issues.
- Every chapter notes strawman distortions on *both* sides of the controversy.
- Every chapter emphasizes points of *agreement* among those holding conflicting views.
- Each chapter contains numerous open-ended thought questions that encourage students to examine issues from new angles and perspectives.
- Each chapter concludes with an annotated list of additional resources, including books, articles, and websites.

I am deeply indebted to many people whose conversations helped me with every chapter of this book—particularly those who hold views in conflict with my own, and who helped me to understand their positions and their reasons better, who rescued me from misunderstandings and distortions I had held about their views, and who proved that even the strongest disagreements can be conducted in an atmosphere of friendship and respect. Special thanks to my departmental colleagues Mustansir Mir, Deborah Mower, Gabriel Palmer-Fernandez, Linda "Tess" Tessier, Alan Tomhave, Mark Vopat, Victor Wan-Tatah, Chris Bache, Brendan Minogue, Tom Shipka, Jeff Butts, Julie Aultman, Walter Carvin, Lou D'Apolito, Nancy Dawson, Martina Haines, Zoreh Kermani, Jeff Limbian, Vince Lisi, Sarah Lown, Bernie Oakes, Brad Pace, Joe Schoenberger, Donna Sloan, Arnold Smith, Linette Stratford, Andrew Stypinski, and Richard White; and to my friends in Youngstown and around the country who have helped me with not only the controversial issues discussed in this book but many other issues as well: Homer Warren, Charles Singler, Howard Mettee, Jack and Chris Raver, Alan Belsheim, Jerry Lanier, Steve Peck, Phil Pendleton, Alan Parnell, Tom and Judy Henricks, John and Gregg Sullivan, Lia Ruttan, Robert Weaver, Nawal Ammar, Paul Sracic, Fred Alexander, Lauren Schroeder, and "Luke" Lucas. Very special thanks to Mary Dillingham, our fabulous departmental administrator, who makes the department run with amazing efficiency, and is cheerful in all weathers; and to her very able student helper, Gina Ponzio. Thanks also to Zac Robbins who read through a number of chapters and suggested excellent examples, particularly of strawman fallacies. My students at Youngstown State University inspired this book, and every semester they provide conclusive proof that even the most controversial questions can be intelligently and fairly and congenially discussed and debated among people of the widest variety of ethnic, economic, and cultural backgrounds and the most divergent of political and social views. Youngstown has its charms, though its rust-belt charms are not always obvious. But few philosophers have enjoyed better or more congenial colleagues than those in my department of philosophy and religious studies at Youngstown State University, and after more than two decades of teaching here I cannot imagine a more interesting and enjoyable and satisfying group of students than those who have filled my classes at Youngstown State University. My greatest debt is to my family: my wife, Mary, who is a constant warm support as well as a wonderful source of knowledge for anything related to psychology; my sons, Russell and Adam, who have discussed many of these issues with me, always insightfully, and who are my greatest source of joy and pride; and my lovely daughter-in-law, Robyn, who is not only an excellent philosopher but also a delightful person. And of course Bruno the wonder dog, who often waited patiently for his walks in the park while I finished one last paragraph.

CONFRONTING CONTROVERSIES AND REMAINING FRIENDS

Chapter Outline

There are many difficult and divisive ethical issues: abortion, capital punishment, immigration, same-sex marriage, and euthanasia to name only a few of the hot-button controversies that divide countries, communities, and even families. These are hard questions needing careful examination, thoughtful discussion, and serious debate. Sadly, it seems that the more serious the question, the less likely that it will be seriously examined. Consider the controversy over abortion: There are lots of marches and rallies, many catchy slogans—"it's not a choice, it's a child"; "if men could become pregnant, abortion would be a sacrament"—and plenty of billboards and websites and bumper stickers promoting one side or the other. But there is very little thoughtful discussion of the abortion issue: Pro-lifers attend their rallies, read their literature, and post on their blogs; and pro-choicers attend competing rallies, read a separate literature, and visit different blogs. When the two sides come into contact, there is a police line between them, both sides shout harsh insults, and the news media seek out the most extreme voices. If pro-lifers visit a pro-choice blog, or vice versa, it is not with the purpose of intelligent discussion, but only to post vitriolic messages that condemn their opponents as moral monsters: hit-and-run attacks, which the posters may then boast of with their fellow believers. If—as often happens—you are having dinner with staunchly pro-life Sarah and fervently pro-choice Rachel, there is likely to be an agreement (spoken or unspoken) that abortion will *not* be discussed. Sad experience has taught us that when friends with opposite opinions discuss abortion, the dinner party is likely to be very unpleasant: Congeniality disappears, hostility deepens, and friendships dissolve. Rachel and Sarah are much more likely to shout at one another across a police barrier than thoughtfully discuss the question of abortion.

It has always been difficult to have respectful, thoughtful discussions of divisive ethical and social issues. Those on one side of the issue read the *New York Times*; on the other, the *New York Daily News*; one side watches Fox News, the other watches MSNBC. The internet revolution—and the amazing advances in personal communication overall—has made the divisions even deeper. We hoped that such marvelous sources of information and communication would facilitate understanding, and in many cases that has happened; but in the case of the abortion controversy, the hope has been in vain. Rather than promoting better understanding, the internet has made it easier for those with extreme views to find and reinforce one another, to talk only among themselves, and to never hear a discouraging or dissenting word. In this hothouse atmosphere, distortions are circulated, repeated, celebrated, and ultimately accepted as indisputable truth. The more extreme the opinion, the more likely it is to gain an audience and ultimately a following. Anyone expressing doubts is swiftly ostracized from the company of true believers. Extreme opinions and gross distortions flourish while intelligent discussion disappears.

Why Are Debates So Angry?

Why have positions become so divided and discussion so acrimonious? We shouldn't exaggerate: It was worse in the late 18th century, and in the 19th and early 20th centuries, racism and anti-Semitism and religious bigotry openly flourished. While we have the tragedy of a member of Congress shot in 2011, we should remember that in the middle of the 19th century, a member of Congress was beaten almost to death by another member, on the floor of the House during a session of Congress.

Still, the atmosphere is unpleasant, and constructive dialogue seems rare. There are probably many factors, but several stand out. First, the internet and expansion of the media have made it easier for people to talk only with those who narrowly agree with them, hardly ever hearing a challenge to their beliefs. You can get your "news" and opinions exclusively from sites that are absolutely in agreement with your views, and almost everyone who posts on that site will share your opinions. Opponents of those positions are attacked and their views distorted because no one is around to set the record straight. Second, there is the great expansion of "talk radio," in which the most abusive and extreme voices often command the largest audiences and the most advertising money. Third, newscasts are often brief and shallow, and compete for viewers by focusing more on entertainment than on careful news gathering or careful analysis: The lead story is more often determined by how striking or graphic the accompanying video is, not by whether the story is genuinely newsworthy. Drivel about "celebrities" often takes precedence over events of worldwide significance. During the people's uprising in Libya, at the same time that the Ivory Coast was sliding into a brutal civil war, something else occurred: A television comedian, Charley Sheen, went into a megalomaniac rant during an interview. Perhaps you can guess which of these events most American newscasts considered most "newsworthy." When political debates are covered, the news teams gravitate to those making the loudest and angriest and most extreme statements, and people soon learn that such extremism is the best way of getting their voices on the nightly news. At a town hall meeting, the person screaming insults is much more likely to get television time than the person asking quiet but important questions. And finally, the enormous amounts of money required to fund campaigns make it tempting for people to demonize their opponents in order to frighten potential contributors into parting with contributions: "President Obama is setting up death squads to kill Grandma—send money to prevent this tragic development"; "American flags are being banned from California classrooms— sign this online petition to stop this attack on American patriotism," and "please use your credit card to make an immediate contribution so that we can take swift action against this outrage."

The Six Rules for Talking Together

There are deep and genuine conflicts in our society. Some see same-sex marriage as a fundamental human right, while others regard it as a moral abomination. Some see a woman's choice concerning abortion as a basic right, while others see it as an almost unparalleled evil. Some see capital punishment as fundamental to genuine justice, while others regard it as a relic of barbarism. Rather than considering how to settle or resolve those deep disputes, the more immediate question is: How can we *talk with* one another about these questions?

1. Listen Carefully

There is no magic formula for turning heated conflict into respectful discussion, but there are some things that can reduce the heat and hostility and make genuine discussion—and *respectful* disagreement—more likely. The first step is the most difficult: *Listen* to those who disagree with you. That's not easy. You may not like their tone of voice; you probably will not like what they say; and you probably think you already know all their arguments anyway. It's not easy, but it is absolutely essential if you want to have a genuine discussion with someone who disagrees with you. First, people *like it* when someone really listens to them. One of the most common complaints that spouses make to marriage counselors: "He (or she) never *listens* to what I have to say." A very common complaint from patients: "My doctor never takes the time to talk with me and *listen* to what my symptoms and problems really are." If you want to bring joy to your grandfather when you visit him, take the time and make the effort to *listen* to his stories. If you want to raise happy and well-adjusted kids, *listen* to their adventures and troubles and questions. One of the most common complaints women make about men: "I was telling him about a problem I have, and he immediately told me what I should do to solve it; I wasn't asking him to tell me what to do, I can figure that out for myself; I just wanted him to *listen* to my problem." So if you want to have a genuine discussion with someone who takes a view that is in conflict with your own, *listen* carefully and respectfully to what the other person is saying. That obviously doesn't mean that you must *agree* with the other person; but you can show respect for that *person*—you are a *person* worth listening to—even if you deeply disagree with that person's views.

Listening carefully is essential for several reasons. First, if you are actually listening, the person with whom you are talking will not have to shout to gain your attention, and the discussion can occur at a conversational level. Second, by carefully listening you lay the groundwork for a *respectful* discussion: If you show respect by listening carefully, it is more likely that the other person will also show respect for you. It doesn't always work, of course; but it's more likely to work than shouting and ignoring what the other person says. Third, if you wish to grapple honestly with the issues that divide you, you must understand the *real* views and arguments of the person with whom you are talking. For any deeply divisive issue on which you hold strong opinions, it is likely that you have heard accounts of the opposing view *primarily* from those who agree with *you*, and not from those who *dis*agree with you. If you attended a demonstration concerning abortion, you spent your time there demonstrating and talking with those who *share* your views; you did not discuss the question with those who were demonstrating in favor of the other side. And if you recently read an article arguing about capital punishment, it is much more likely that you read an article *supporting* your view rather than one opposing it (those on opposite sides tend to read different magazines and visit different websites). Anything you believe about your opponent's views and arguments probably came from those who strongly disagree with those views and arguments, and thus may well include some inaccuracies. If you want an honest and respectful discussion of the issues, you cannot start from a fundamental misunderstanding of what the other person believes. Fourth, you must listen carefully in order to recognize any distortions or misunderstanding of your *own* position by your opponent. Once you and your opponent correct all the misinformation, you may discover that the differences between you are not quite so large as you had both supposed. So you must *listen* carefully to the position and arguments of the other person, so that you can talk together about what is *really* at issue (rather than talking past each other, about positions that neither of you actually hold). Fifth, it is important to listen honestly and openly to opposing views, because there is always the possibility that your own views are *wrong*, and need to change. Unless you are infallible—and unless you are resolved never to change your mind about anything so long as you live—then remaining open to *changing* your views is valuable.

2. Avoid Labels

The first rule in promoting honest discussion is: Listen carefully. The second rule is important in its own right, but is also essential for genuine careful listening. When examining opposing views and talking with those who hold opposing views, *avoid labels*. Once you *label* someone, it is easy to stop listening: "Oh, he's a liberal, I know what he thinks about that"; "she's a conservative, so she obviously believes this."

Texas Governor Rick Perry is a conservative who doesn't care much for science, especially the science that offers evidence of climate change; Michelle Bachman is a conservative who wants to abolish the Environmental Protection Agency (she believes that businesses and industries will regulate themselves to prevent harmful pollution, because that will increase their long-term profits). But there are other conservatives who want strict environmental regulation, on the grounds that conservatives should be very cautious about anything (including severe pollution) that might cause great changes in the social framework, and who believe we should proceed with great caution in making irreversible changes (including irreversible climate and environmental changes). *Maybe* it is an error to be extremely cautious concerning environmental and climate issues when we are not completely certain of all the causes, but it is always better (these conservatives believe) to *err* on the side of *caution*. And of course there are many excellent scientists who hold very "conservative" political views. So what is the *conservative* view on environmental issues? *The* conservative environmental position does not exist; rather, there are many different views held by a wide variety of conservatives.

What is the "conservative" position on capital punishment? Many would suggest that it is pro capital punishment, while liberals oppose capital punishment. But in fact, many of the strongest opponents of capital punishment are staunchly conservative: They fear giving government the power over life and death, and they are profoundly distrustful of the government's ability to get things right (and execute the right person). What is the "conservative" position on drug legalization? Many leaders of the conservative movement—such as William Buckley—have been strong advocates for legalizing drugs, believing that the government has no business deciding what drugs you should or should not use. That is a matter for personal decision, not government interference; and government efforts to ban drugs make government too big and too powerful. In 2011, Ron Paul, a conservative Texas Republican, cosponsored a bill with Barney Frank, a liberal Massachusetts Democrat, to open the way for states to legalize the sale and use of marijuana. Should drugs such as marijuana be legalized? That is a controversial question, with interesting arguments on both sides; but you will not gain a better understanding of those arguments by attaching a "liberal" or "conservative" label to them, but only by examining carefully what the arguments really are.

What about rights for homosexuals, such as the right to serve openly in the military? "Liberals" typically support such rights, while "conservatives" oppose them; but Barry Goldwater, generally regarded as the leader of the modern conservative movement, was a fervent believer in the rights of homosexuals—and heterosexuals—to be free of government interference in their private lives, and he was a forceful advocate for gay soldiers: "You don't have to be straight to be a good soldier," Goldwater insisted; "you just have to shoot straight." Furthermore, a "conservative" on one question may be a "liberal" on another: Many Catholics (including the Pope) take the "conservative" view in opposing all abortions while supporting the "liberal" view in calling for the abolition of capital punishment. So think hard about the issues and the arguments, and avoid the easy labels and snappy slogans that stultify critical thought.

3. Reject the Strawman Fallacy

If you listen carefully and avoid misleading labels, then you are less likely to fall for a fallacy that is very common but particularly destructive: the notorious *strawman* fallacy. A *fallacy* is simply an error or mistake or trick that occurs often in arguments. The strawman fallacy is the fallacy of distorting or exaggerating or *misrepresenting* an argument or position in order to make it more vulnerable to attack.

Strawman fallacies occur with depressing regularity when hot-button social issues and political topics are being debated. During the debate over health care reform, some of the opponents of universal health care claimed that those favoring universal health care wanted to set up "death panels," which would evaluate every senior citizen entering a hospital and decide whether that person should be treated or instead be killed. That's a horrifying idea indeed: As soon as you turn 65, you face a death threat every time you walk into a hospital. That *is* a vile policy, and obviously *no one* proposed it: certainly not the people who favored universal health care. Instead, the actual proposal was that doctors be *paid* for the time spent discussing *living wills* with patients. A living will is simply a document that most people *want* to have on file (no one is *required* to have one); it specifies what sorts of treatments you do and do not want if you should reach a point at which you can no longer make such decisions (e.g., if you are comatose). You can specify that you want to receive very aggressive treatment, or you can specify that you want to be resuscitated and placed on a respirator (if needed in order to breathe) but *not* given feeding tubes, that you want to be resuscitated but *not* placed on a respirator if you cannot then breathe on your own, or that in the case of heart failure you do *not* want to be resuscitated. That is, you can specify exactly what *you want* in the way of treatments. These are sometimes complicated decisions, and people often want to consult with their doctors as they make their decisions ("How long could I live on feeding tubes?" "If I refuse a respirator and am allowed to die, would sedation prevent my suffering?" "If I were placed on a respirator, what would my chances be of eventually being able to breathe without a respirator?"); and the health care proposal allowed doctors to bill for Medicare payments when they spent time talking with patients about their living wills. The bill obviously did *not* set up death panels; to the contrary, it increased patient control over their own free choices by making it easier for them to prepare living wills. But a policy that subjects all senior citizens to the decisions of *death panels* is an easier target to attack than the real policy; and so this strawman distortion is an easier target than the real position.

If you are arguing against a position, it is always easier to attack a strawman distortion than the real thing. Suppose Rhonda favors the legalization of marijuana. That's an interesting position, and worthy of honest debate. "Rhonda wants to give marijuana samples to school children, and have marijuana advertised on children's television; if she had her way, Big Bird and the Cookie Monster would be pushing marijuana along with the letter of the day." That *would* be a terrible thing: No one wants marijuana being marketed or sold to children. But of course that strawman distortion is much easier to attack than Rhonda's real position: that marijuana should be legalized and (like tobacco and alcohol) carefully regulated and restricted.

Perhaps the most famous strawman distortion was provided by Reverend Pat Robertson, the "televangelist" who founded the Christian Coalition. In one of his fund-raising letters, Robertson attacked the Equal Rights Amendment, which was then under consideration by state legislatures; the proposed amendment would have protected women from job discrimination and guaranteed women equal rights with men. It's hard to argue that discrimination against women is good, and so it was difficult to come up with strong arguments against the Equal Rights Amendment; but that did not deter Reverend Robertson, who gave this description of what the Equal Rights Amendment was *really* promoting: "The feminist agenda is not about equal rights for women. It is about a socialist, anti-family political movement that encourages women to leave their husbands, kill their children, practice witchcraft, destroy capitalism and become lesbians." Certainly it is a lot easier to find arguments against killing children and destroying capitalism than it is to find arguments against equal rights for women; and that is why the strawman fallacy is a popular trick.

The strawman fallacy flourishes where everyone supports the same agenda; thus it flourishes in groups and in blogs that allow comments only from those who support a specific view. In that setting, it is easy to believe the worst about your opponents, and it is easy to attribute extreme views to them—and because there is no one present to challenge those views, the views get repeated and entrenched and firmly believed. But as satisfying as it may be to attribute extreme and outlandish views to those who disagree with you, it is fatal to serious intelligent discussion. In particular, if you use strawman arguments when talking with those who hold opposing views, you forfeit any hope of changing their opinions. After all, your opponents *know* what their real views and arguments are, and they are unlikely to be convinced by an attack on views they do *not* actually hold. If Marie's position is that the legal drinking age should be lowered to 18, and Arthur argues in response that it would be a terrible mistake to allow alcohol sales to children in elementary school—"Marie thinks junior high students should have double martinis with their school lunches"—then clearly Marie will not be influenced to *change* her views by an argument against a position she does not hold, an argument that is *irrelevant* to her actual view. If you really want to engage in serious discussion about tough issues, it is essential to listen carefully to your opponent's actual views and actual arguments. Then you can focus on what is genuinely in dispute, not on some strawman distortion that has no relevance to the discussion.

Strawman fallacies corrupt discussion and increase animosity on both sides: If I believe that what you *really* want is to set up a death panel to kill grandma, I am likely to see you in a very unfavorable light; and if you hear me attributing such absurd strawman distortions to *you*—though you obviously do not hold such a view—that will give you grounds for doubting both my integrity and my intelligence. Thus the use of strawman fallacies makes respectful serious debate almost impossible. Another fallacy leads to the same result: the *ad hominem* fallacy.

4. Avoid the Ad Hominem Fallacy

The fourth rule for promoting respectful discussion of controversial issues is one of the most basic: Avoid the *ad hominem* fallacy like the plague. The ad hominem fallacy is as simple as it is common. It is committed when someone attacks the *source* of an argument in an attempt to refute or discredit the argument. If Joan gives an *argument* in favor of capital punishment, you must look closely at Joan's argument, but *not* at Joan herself. It doesn't matter whether Joan is drunk or sober, cruel or kind, sane or insane, consistent or hypocritical. If you discover that last year Joan was opposed to capital punishment, but now she is running for governor and wants to look tough on crime and so now she is arguing in favor of capital punishment, that does *not* change Joan's argument. It might legitimately convince you not to *vote* for Joan, if you conclude that she takes whatever position she thinks is politically convenient; but that is not a reason to reject Joan's *argument*. Even if Joan herself is hypocritical, her *argument* may be good. Or suppose you discover that Joan is being *paid* to give her argument, because she is employed by some capital punishment advocacy group. That doesn't change anything. Whether she is arguing for money or out of deep conviction, her *argument* remains the same. (If you discovered that it was *false* that Joan was being paid for her argument, and *false* that she had changed her views about capital punishment, that would not suddenly make Joan's argument *better*: It's the same argument, no matter what we learn about Joan.) If I give you an *argument* for why you shouldn't drink and drive, then my argument may be an excellent argument even though

I have a long history of driving under the influence of alcohol. In that case, you might correctly conclude that I'm a sleazy hypocrite, but my *argument* may still be a powerful argument, no matter how vile the arguer. "Bruce is a drunk and a hypocrite, so his argument against drinking and driving must be bad." That commits the ad hominem fallacy. When considering arguments, you must judge the *arguments themselves*, and not the source of the arguments. Of course it is perfectly legitimate to criticize someone's *argument*: When Joan gives her argument in favor of capital punishment, you can attack her *argument* with all guns blazing (you can point out factual errors in her argument, note inconsistencies *within* the argument, show that some of the key points Joan makes are *irrelevant* to the question of capital punishment). Attacking Joan's *argument* is fine; but attacking *Joan* in an attempt to discredit her argument commits the ad hominem fallacy.

Ad hominem arguments are sometimes legitimate and useful. If someone is giving *testimony* (not argument), then attacks on the person *testifying* are relevant, and *not* fallacious. If Joe *testifies* that he saw Arnold run out of the convenience store carrying a gun, then it is important and relevant to know that Joe is a notorious liar, that Joe has a long history of severe delusions, that Joe has a terrible drug problem that makes him extremely unreliable, that Joe hates Arnold because Arnold stole his girlfriend, that Joe is being "paid off" by the district attorney in exchange for testifying against Arnold (the district attorney has promised to drop the drug dealing charges against Arnold if Arnold will testify against Joe). And if I am thinking of investing some money with Bernie Madoff, it would certainly be legitimate and relevant for you to tell me that Madoff is a crook, and *not* someone I should entrust with my money. And if Juan is thinking of riding with me on a long drive across the state, it is important for you to inform Juan that I have an extensive history of drunk driving and have been involved in seven auto accidents during the past three months. So ad hominem attacks are often legitimate; but when they are used against *arguments*, they are irrelevant and fallacious.

Like the strawman fallacy, the ad hominem fallacy is particularly destructive if you are trying to engage in serious, thoughtful discussion of controversial questions. "You must be a fascist," "You must love the Taliban," "Anyone who holds your view is just stupid": These are not effective paths to serious reflective examination of tough issues.

5. Be Wary of Golden Mean Solutions

Fifth, avoid "golden mean solutions." When dealing with deep disputes, it is tempting to suppose that if we "meet in the middle" we will come close to the correct conclusion. Sometimes a compromise, "middle-of-the-road" position may be best; but in many cases, one of the more extreme positions may be right. The most famous *compromise* solution in American history was the Missouri Compromise, which allowed slavery to continue in the South, banned it in the North, and required that Northerners assist in the capture and return of any slaves who escaped from the South. It was a *compromise* between those who wanted to abolish slavery and those who wanted to preserve slavery; but it was also a position that allowed for the continuation of a terrible moral wrong. Abolition was an extreme position, but in this case, the extreme position was the only legitimate one.

There is a second reason for questioning golden mean solutions: It is often very hard to *find* the middle position. In fact, we can represent almost any position as "moderate." Consider the dispute over capital punishment: What is the "middle ground," the "golden mean," in that controversy? "We should not go to the terrible extreme of torturing condemned prisoners to death; but on the other hand, we shouldn't go to the other extreme of abolishing capital punishment altogether. The right approach is to retain capital punishment, but make it as painless as possible." "We should not *kill* people in the name of justice: That's a barbaric extreme. But of course I'm not suggesting that we do away with all punishment for serious crimes. The right approach is to abolish capital punishment, but keep very long prison sentences." Those are two golden mean solutions that reach *opposite* conclusions: In the first case, keeping capital punishment is moderate; while in the second case, abolishing capital punishment is moderate. The moral of the story: No matter what position you favor, with a little ingenuity it is easy to present it as the *moderate* position between two extremes. So just because something is offered as a *compromise* or *moderate* position, that is not a reason for thinking it's correct. The compromise position *may* be correct; but just because it is *moderate* is no *reason* for thinking so. The truth is *not* always in the middle.

6. Look for the Positive

Finally, try very hard to appreciate the best arguments for views you oppose, give them a fair hearing, and recognize any genuinely good points and attractive features in positions you reject. That doesn't mean you should be wishy-washy and indecisive; there is certainly nothing wrong with holding deep value convictions that do not shift with the tides and trends and fashions. And it does not mean that you should never regard a view as profoundly and thoroughly morally *wrong* (the 19th century views of those who supported slavery and the 20th century views of those who promoted racial segregation contain not even a glimmer of goodness); but for *most* of the value controversies we currently encounter, there is at least something positive to be said for both sides. If you see no virtue whatsoever in the opposing position, perhaps you are looking at some strawman distortion rather than the real position.

Genuine Value Disagreements

This book does not aim at solving all the disputed issues facing us. The divisions on many issues are deep and genuine, and in some cases it may be impossible to reconcile the profoundly different values held by various groups: Some disputes may not have a solution. Or perhaps they do. That's a question you must decide for yourself. But consider, for a moment, this issue of *value pluralism*. Are there competing values that *cannot* be brought into any objective order? Or can *all* values ultimately be arranged in a harmonious whole? We value allowing parents to raise their children and shape their values; but should we allow parents to indoctrinate their children into systems of racial and ethnic hatred? Should we allow small children to be dressed in Ku Klux Klan robes, and taught to chant racist slogans? We believe that parents should be able to teach their religious beliefs to their children; but if those beliefs include the doctrine that women are "sinks of iniquity," who are inherently inferior to men and who must accept roles of acquiescence and subordination, should we allow children to be shaped into such a belief system? Of course it *is* possible to bring these questions into a clear order: We could insist that our religious practices trump all other considerations, and no view inconsistent with such religious views can be tolerated. That will certainly place values in *order*, but it will do so by *eliminating* values most of us hold dear (such as the values of freedom of thought and freedom of religion— after all, if my religion insists that only *my* God is worthy of worship, then adherence to that religion means refusing to tolerate other religious practices in our society). Or we could say that you are free to teach your children whatever you wish, so long as those teachings promote tolerance; again, that will bring the values into a clear *order*, but at the cost of eliminating freedoms that some people cherish (including the right to teach my children that my religion is the *only* true religion).

One of the famous poetic lines from Walt Whitman is "I am large, I contain multitudes"; and our society contains many multitudes. That is not necessarily a bad thing. In the right conditions, it promotes the best and most creative thinking. Jazz and classical music are very different; but when composer and vibes player John Lewis took both seriously, the result was a remarkable new sound for the Modern Jazz Quartet. The music of the Caribbean and the African-American music of the deep South were quite different, but they joined to form Zydeco. Not every fusion is quite so successful: I once heard a Hank Williams country song—"I'm so Lonesome I Could Cry"—played as a polka, and it took several years off my life. And in any case, simply combining competing views, or seeking some compromise position between them, is not always a good way of dealing with these issues. Sometimes no compromise is possible; and even when compromise *is* possible, that is no reason to suppose that the compromise is *right*. So don't look for easy solutions or "happy mediums"; but do look hard at the arguments, try to understand and appreciate opposing views, and *try* to keep discussions and even deep disagreements cordial. You might find that some of your *own* views cannot really stand up to careful critical examination; and in cases where you remain convinced that you are right and the opposing view is *wrong*, you will have a much better chance of changing the minds of others if the discussion is respectful and congenial. Even the best arguments in the most congenial setting won't always convince your opponents to change their views; but strawman fallacies and ad hominem abuse have no chance at all.

A Case Study in Congenial Conflict Resolution

The Humane Society is an advocacy group for the interests of animals. The society has long worked to prevent cruelty to animals, including pets, race horses, greyhounds, and farm animals. For many years, there has been a battle between the Humane Society and the United Egg Producers, an industry group that represents some 80% of all the egg farmers in the United States. In fact, the suffering of egg-laying chickens in "battery cages" has long been a notorious example of how animals suffer on "factory farms." A battery cage is approximately the size of a filing cabinet drawer, and 8 to 10 hens are housed in each one. Because they are so tightly packed (each chicken having less than the space of a standard sheet of typing paper), the hens are unable to move freely, and cannot stretch or flap their wings, ruffle their feathers, ground scratch, or preen; in fact, they can hardly even turn around. Being deprived of natural movement, the hens often develop harmful abnormal behaviors. In addition, because the hens are deprived of movement their bones often become weak, resulting in painful bone breakage. Before being placed in the battery cages, hens are beak-trimmed using a heated blade that causes severe pain. After approximately 18 months in a battery cage, the hen's egg laying rate declines; she is then pulled from her cage, stuffed in a shipping crate, and dies hanging by her legs on a chain. Because egg production is such an obvious cause of suffering for the animals involved, it has long been a target of protests from the Humane Society and other organizations. The United Egg Producers—on behalf of its membership—has struggled against such attacks, emphasizing the efficiency of its egg-farming methods and fearing that changes in its production methods would make egg production too costly and ultimately unprofitable.

While the Humane Society is sometimes attacked as being unconcerned with the needs of farmers and with wanting to eliminate all animal farming, egg farmers have often been attacked as having no concern with the suffering of their hens; the deep and long-term conflict produced animosity that often resulted in strawman distortions and ad hominem attacks. Thus it was a surprise to everyone when Gene Gregory (president of United Egg Producers) and Wayne Pacelle (president of the Humane Society of the United States) agreed to meet and talk about their concerns and goals (Pacelle has described his relationship with Gregory as "adversaries; some might say bitter adversaries"). When they actually sat down together and talked about their values and interests, they discovered that even these traditional adversaries could find common ground. The result was an agreement that both groups would jointly lobby Congress to pass a law that would phase out the hated battery cages, and require that new cages be significantly larger (large enough for the hens to easily turn around and move around and spread their wings), that the cages would have perches to provide the chickens more natural roosting areas, and that cages would also include "nest boxes" (small dark boxes in which the chickens could lay their eggs, which chickens strongly prefer for egg laying). Instead of a patchwork of state and local laws that the egg producers would find almost impossible to follow, there would be uniform standards that the producers could understand and that—while still costing egg producers millions of dollars—would allow them to remain competitive and stay in business. Instead of trying to fight for improvements on a state-to-state basis (and often in states where it would be all but impossible to pass reforms), the Humane Society gets national standards that will significantly reduce the suffering of egg-laying hens.

It should be noted that not everyone approves: some because it does not go far enough (and would block states from passing more stringent reforms); others because it is a first step toward government concern with animal suffering on factory farms. But while this may not be a perfect solution to the problem, there is no question that it significantly reduces the suffering of egg-producing hens—particularly in states that would be very unlikely to pass laws requiring more comfortable cages—while also giving clear guidelines for egg farmers that enable them to remain in business.

Obviously not every meeting of adversaries will be as successful as the meeting between the Humane Society and the United Egg Producers; in some cases, there may be no way of finding common ground. But when people actually listen to one another respectfully, put aside the strawman distortions and ad hominem attacks, and sincerely try to understand the other side's concerns and arguments, then common ground may be discovered where it was least expected. (Information for this case was drawn from an article by Dan Charles of National Public Radio, at http://www.npr.org/blogs/thesalt/2012/01/26/145900751 /ex-foes-stage-coop-detat-for-egg-laying-chickens.)

Questions for Reflection

1. Do you have friends who hold views on issues of social morality—such as abortion, church-state relations, or capital punishment—that are fundamentally different from your own? If so, do you ever discuss your deep differences, or do you avoid those topics?

2. Think of your own view on some controversial topic; did you reach that position thoughtfully and critically? Or did you feel a strong immediate gut reaction in favor of the view you support, and then think carefully of ways to *justify* that view? That is, are the reasons you would

give in support of your views the product of genuine deliberation, or are they rationalizations for a view held on deep emotional grounds?

3. Is there any major social or ethical issue on which you have *changed your mind* in recent years? If so, what led you to change your mind? Was there a specific argument? Or what?

4. Is there any major social controversy in which *you* believe one of the *extreme* positions to be correct? Any controversy on which your own view is more moderate?

5. Do you have any friends or family or acquaintances who strongly *agree* with your own view on some major social issue (such as abortion) but strongly *disagree* with your position on some *other* issue (such as capital punishment)?

6. Have you ever had a friend (or lover) who once *shared* your view on a major social issue (such as abortion, capital punishment, or immigration) and later (during your friendship/relationship) *changed positions* on that issue? If so, did that change have any effect on the relations between you?

7. Listening isn't easy, but practice helps. Find someone in your class who holds a view that is directly opposed to your own view on one of the 14 controversial issues discussed in this book (e.g., if you favor abolishing capital punishment, find someone who favors capital punishment). Then *take turns* listening to each other, with *no interruptions* (not even for questions)—and without sighing or grimacing or shaking your head or in any other way showing disgust or disagreement. Each person gets to present his or her *reasons* for favoring or opposing capital

punishment, *without interruptions*. After both of you have presented your best arguments, each person writes out the main points of the *other* person's arguments as *accurately* as possible (again, with *no* comments or negative evaluations), and then gives it to the other person to "grade" on how *accurately* the listener summarized the arguments, without distorting or misrepresenting them and without ignoring important argument points. Keep in mind, this is not an exercise in determining how *strong* the arguments are; rather, the point is to *correctly understand* the other person's arguments and position, no matter what you happen to think of them.

8. This book obviously does not cover all the important social issues now being debated. For example, there is the ongoing controversy between those who favor stronger gun control against those who despise any restrictions on the right to bear arms, and the controversy between those who want stronger air pollution regulations and those who believe there is already too much government regulation of air quality. Consider your *own* view on those controversies, and then list several strawman distortions that opponents have *falsely attributed* to those who hold your view. Second—and this is much harder—list some strawman distortions that *you* (or those who side with you) have attributed to your opponents. (And don't say you have *never* used strawman arguments. No one is above temptation, and in the heat of argument, the temptation to bash your adversary with a convenient strawman is sometimes too strong to resist.)

Additional Resources

For more detail on examining arguments and cooperative critical thinking, as well as on the strawman fallacy and both fallacious and legitimate uses of ad hominem arguments, see Bruce N. Waller, *Critical Thinking: Consider the Verdict*, 6th ed. (Upper Saddle River, NJ: Pearson, 2012). For an excellent and extensive discussion of ad hominem arguments, see

Douglas Walton, *Ad Hominem Arguments* (Tuscaloosa, AL: University of Alabama Press, 1998). Deborah Tannen, *The Argument Culture: Stopping America's War of Words* (New York: Ballantine Publishing, 1998), examines factors that cause disagreements to become more heated, and some ways of preventing such animosity.

MYSEARCHLAB CONNECTIONS

1. Deborah Tannen, *The Argument Culture*, p. 12. Deborah Tannen is a professor of linguistics at Georgetown University. Much of her work (including her book, *The Argument Culture*, from which this passage is drawn) focuses on how language can be used to increase hostility as well as to promote cooperation and understanding. In this passage, she notes the strong tendency to frame our social issues in warlike or competitive language. If instead of framing our severe drug problem as a "war on drugs" we conceptualized it as a "search for workable solutions," would we be likely to approach the problem differently?

2. Deborah Tannen, *The Argument Culture*, p. 243 in Diestler. When we are in an adversarial framework, we tend to assume that there are two opposing sides to an argument; Deborah Tannen counsels that sometimes it is useful to challenge that assumption.

3. Deborah Tannen, *The Argument Culture*, p. 354. Deborah Tannen notes that when we are engaged in adversarial argument, and eager to *win* an argument, it is very difficult to listen carefully to the views and arguments and concerns of our opponent.

4. "Changing a Man's Mind." This is a reminder of the importance of genuinely appreciating and understanding the views of those who oppose our arguments and beliefs.

5. Gerry Spence, "The Lock," pp. 411–412. Attorney Gerry Spence demonstrates the value of seeking common ground as a starting point for discussion and argument.

6. *Coffee and Philosophy*, Waller, "Ad Hominem Arguments," pp. 3–6. This dialogue discusses both legitimate and fallacious uses of ad hominem arguments.

7. Manitoba Justice, *The Inquiry Regarding Thomas Sophonow*, "Jailhouse Informants." Thomas Sophonow spent four years in prison after he was wrongfully convicted of the brutal murder of a young woman who was working in a Winnipeg doughnut shop. After it became clear that Sophonow was innocent of the crime for which he had been imprisoned, the Justice Department of the province of Manitoba carried out an extensive investigation into why this miscarriage of justice had occurred, and how such mistakes could be prevented in the future. The inquiry found that one of the key factors in this wrongful conviction was reliance on the false testimony of "jailhouse informants" (jailed inmates who offer to testify against other prisoners in exchange for such benefits as reduced charges, reduced sentences, or better treatment during their term of imprisonment). Several sections of *The Inquiry Regarding Thomas Sophonow* describe the character of some of the jailhouse informants who provided false testimony that helped convict Sophonow, and also describes in general terms the problems with relying on jailhouse informants. The ad hominem attacks on the character and reliability of such jailhouse informants are relevant and legitimate, and do *not* commit the *ad hominem* fallacy.

8. *Report of the Kaufman Commission on Proceedings Involving Guy Paul Morin*, Chapter 3, sections A–D, "Jailhouse Informants" (Ontario Ministry of the Attorney General). Another notorious case of wrongful conviction was the case of Guy Paul Morin, who spent eight years imprisoned in Canada's only "supermax" prison for the rape and murder of an eight-year-old girl who had been his next door neighbor. The

wrongful conviction of Morin—which involved police misconduct, serious mistakes in the crime lab investigations, and perjured testimony by jailhouse informants— was profoundly disturbing to Canadian citizens, and it resulted in an extensive investigation and report by a commission headed by Fred Kaufman, a former judge of the Quebec Court of Appeal. As in the Sophonow case, the Kaufman Commission found that the use of jailhouse informants played a major part in this wrongful conviction. The extensive examination of the jailhouse informants and their testimony— and the deals they received in exchange for their testimony—is chilling (and it led to strong restrictions on the use of jailhouse informants in Canadian courts); as in the Sophonow case, the ad hominem attacks on the jailhouse informants who aided in the wrongful conviction of Paul Morin are a legitimate use of ad hominem argument.

9. Deborah Tannen, *The Argument Culture*, p. 352. As Deborah Tannen notes, the conditions of adversarial argument provide fertile ground for the growing of strawman distortions and misrepresentations.

10. *Coffee and Philosophy*, "Straw-Man Fallacy," pp. 10–12. This is a discussion, in dialogue form, of the temptations and dangers of the strawman fallacy.

11. *Holland v. Illinois*, 493 U.S. 474 (1990). In this case, Daniel Holland was convicted of several criminal offenses in Cook County, Illinois. He appealed his conviction on the grounds that, by use of peremptory challenges, blacks were unfairly excluded from the jury that convicted him. The majority of the U.S. Supreme Court upheld Holland's conviction, on the grounds that the right to be tried by a jury that represents a fair cross-section of the community does *not* mean that the actual jury must be a fair cross-section, but only that the group from which potential jurors are selected must be a fair cross-section; and in particular, that there is no requirement that the actual jury mirror the makeup of the community, and that the important thing is only that the jury be impartial. Writing for the minority, Justice Marshall argued that the majority had attacked a strawman position: the question is not whether an actual jury must "mirror" the makeup of the community from which it is drawn, nor whether the jury members are impartial, but whether the jury is seated in a way that is free of prejudice and discrimination.

12. *Bowers v. Hardwick*, 478 U.S. 186 (1986) was a famous case involving two Georgia men who were charged with sodomy under a Georgia law, which made sodomy a crime punishable by up to 20 years imprisonment. (Under the Georgia law, heterosexuals engaging in consensual oral sex could also be imprisoned for 20 years; but in practice, the law seemed to be aimed only at homosexual behavior.) In the majority opinion (which upheld the law) the U.S. Supreme Court ruled that the Georgia law was *not* unconstitutional, because the U.S. Constitution does not recognize "a fundamental right to commit homosexual sodomy." In dissenting from that majority ruling, the minority argued that the majority had attacked a strawman position: no one was claiming that the U.S. Constitution recognizes a right to commit homosexual sodomy; rather, the Constitution recognizes a fundamental right of *privacy*, and a right to be free of government control and interference in one's private life. (In 2003, in the case of *Lawrence v. Texas*, the U.S. Supreme Court reversed itself, and overturned *Bowers v. Hardwick*, on basically the same grounds that Justice Blackmun had urged in his dissent in *Bowers v. Hardwick*.)

2

DUBIOUS APPROACHES TO THINKING ABOUT ETHICS

Chapter Outline

This book examines controversial ethical issues: abortion, capital punishment, and euthanasia, for starters. When we think of important ethical questions, those are the issues that spring to mind. There are also larger, more theoretical ethical questions: questions concerning the nature of ethics itself, and the right *procedures* to follow in dealing with specific ethical questions. In the course of examining ethical disputes, it will sometimes be useful to look at those issues from several angles: turning the questions this way and that, considering them from various approaches. To make that easier, it will be helpful to have available some of the distinctive *methods* that have been proposed for dealing with questions of ethics. In this chapter, we'll start with some methods that are *not* very helpful; in Chapter 3, we'll look at some ethical models that might prove more useful.

Egoism

The first rather *un*helpful approach to ethics is egoism. Before delving into egoism, it is essential to make a few distinctions. "Egoism" is used for a number of very different views. The first distinction is between *psychological* egoism and *ethical* egoism.

Psychological egoism is not really a claim about ethics; rather, it is a claim about a universal characteristic of the human species. It is the claim that all humans always act selfishly, for their own individual interests. Whether that is good, bad, or indifferent is not the issue for psychological egoism. Psychological egoism is an interesting, dramatic, and robust claim about all humans and all human behavior; but when examined carefully, it has little to recommend it other than its boldness. Perhaps some people act selfishly all of the time, and certainly all of us act selfishly some of the time. But do all of us act selfishly all of the time?

We are all aware of some selfish behavior—if you yourself have never committed or personally observed a selfish act, think of Bernie Madoff, and Ken Lay of Enron infamy, and a whole host of sleazy Wall Street investment firms and mortgage brokers who looted the savings and pension funds and home mortgages of thousands of people. But most of us can also think of some distinctly *un*selfish acts: the firefighters who lost their lives rushing into the collapsing Twin Towers, the medical personnel who donate their time and expertise to the work of Doctors Without Borders, a passing stranger who risked her life to pull a child from a burning car or a raging river, a friend who gave up a beach trip to help you move into your new apartment. Perhaps someone would dispute those examples, claiming that they are actually *selfish* acts: The firefighters were hoping to get promotions and win honors, the doctors are seeking glory and adventure rather than sincerely wanting to help others, the heroic stranger wanted to get her face on television, your friend was helping in hopes that you would "return the favor" next week when he makes a bigger move to a nearby city. That seems a remarkably cynical view: Certainly *some* people who pretend to be acting altruistically are actually acting selfishly (beware of the used car salesman who "generously" gives you a cup of coffee); but that is far from showing that *everyone* who appears to be acting generously is really motivated by selfishness. Even if one or two of the firefighters who risked and lost their lives in the Twin Towers were motivated by hope of reward, it is much more likely that *most* if not all of them were driven by a deep and genuine desire to save the lives of strangers, or perhaps to do what they regarded as their duty. The doctors who volunteer their time and talents typically get neither press coverage nor honors, and they work in bleak areas; if they have any motivation other than healing and helping others, it is not readily apparent. And while some "friends" are actually seeking their own advantage, some genuine friends are concerned only with the welfare of the friend they are helping.

One way of making psychological egoism more plausible is to expand it into biological considerations, and speak in terms of "selfish genes." In that sense, one might say that we (meaning everyone) always act in such a way as to promote our genetic fitness. Thus a mother lion or mother human may sacrifice herself to protect her offspring. But even if we count the mother's self-sacrifice as biologically "selfish," it is doubtful that we can support the claim that *all* behavior is actually selfish. After all, there have been many cases in which people risked or even sacrificed their lives to protect friends to whom they were not related. And many people have risked or given their lives in order to promote their principles, their ideals, or their religious views: Think of civil rights workers who lost their lives in the struggle against racism, fire fighters who rushed into the collapsing Twin Towers in an effort to save the lives of strangers, doctors and nurses who venture into dangerous war-torn regions to save the lives of civilians injured in the fighting.

The most common way of making psychological egoism seem plausible is by turning it into a *definitional*, rather than an empirical, truth; that is, by redefining *selfishness* in such a way that *selfish* is expanded to cover all possible behavior. This is a way of *saving* a claim by turning it into an *empty* claim: The claim is true by special definition, but it no longer has any real content. The claim that *everyone* is always selfish is a strong claim: It makes a real claim about all members of the human species. It may not be a very plausible claim, but at least it does make a genuine claim. How does that claim deal with what seem clear counterexamples, such as the firefighters who lost their lives, the friend who helps with no thought of self-benefit, the doctors and nurses who toil anonymously to save the lives of those in impoverished countries or in disaster areas, or the woman who saves a small child and drives away long before the television cameras arrive? The psychological egoist has a ready answer: All those people *really* were only seeking their *own* pleasure and benefit, because they find personal *pleasure* in helping or rescuing others. The problem with that psychological egoist answer is that it is too easy. It changes the meaning of *selfish* in such a way that *nothing* could qualify as *un*selfish behavior. After all, if someone takes satisfaction in the good of others, or finds joy in helping others, we do not usually count that as selfish. When someone asserts that the woman who saves the life of a small child—strictly from concern for the child, and with no thought of reward or recognition—is acting selfishly, then that *changes* what we mean by *selfish*. If I risk my life to save the child from a raging river because I spot a winning lottery ticket clutched in the little tyke's grimy fist and I hope to get at least half the winnings from that ticket, then that might well be counted a selfish act. But if you rescue the child, strictly because you are concerned for the child's welfare and without hope of reward or publicity, and then you find the rescue a very satisfying result, that is not what we would normally count as a selfish act, unless, of course, one is using a very special definition of *selfish* that makes all acts done for *any* motive count as selfish.

If you are a person who genuinely finds joy in helping others, and does so not for any other reward or benefit, then we do not think of you as a selfish person. "Gina constantly and cheerfully helps others, with no thought of financial benefit or public honors or even reward in heaven; she does it just because she really enjoys helping others, and she finds deep satisfaction in making others happy and relieving their suffering; she is a really *selfish* person." Such a claim would strike us as absurd, and we would conclude that the person making such a claim does not really understand the meaning of *selfish*. Of course everyone has a *motive* for his or her acts; but if that motive is the good of someone else, and one finds satisfaction in promoting the good of others, then that is not a selfish act. If the psychological egoist insists—due to a special definition of *selfish*—that it *is* a selfish act done for one's *own* self-satisfaction, then the most effective challenge to that claim is in the form of a question: What would you (the psychological egoist) *count* as a genuinely unselfish act? The psychological egoist is supposed to be making a claim about the world; namely, that all humans in the world are selfish. That is a real claim about the world; it could be true, or it could be false. If it is *impossible* for it to be false—if nothing and no evidence could possibly count against that claim—then the claim is not really a claim about the world, but instead an empty claim that is true by definition. If I say that "All bachelors are unmarried," that is certainly true; but it is true not because of something about the world and the bachelors who live in the world; rather, it is true because of the definition of *bachelor*. So if the psychological egoist claim that "everyone is selfish" is a *real* claim about the world and the people in it (and not a claim that is true because of a special definition of *selfish*), then the psychological egoist must be able to say what would count as a counterexample, what would count as a genuinely *un*selfish act. The way psychological egoists redefine *selfish*, their claim that everyone is "selfish" is always true, but it is always true because it has been emptied of any real significance.

The more interesting question is not psychological egoism, but *ethical* egoism: the view that people *ought* to do what is in their own narrow interests. If you believe in psychological egoism but reject ethical egoism, then you believe that people always act selfishly, but that at least sometimes that selfish behavior is ethically wrong; if you believe in ethical egoism but reject psychological egoism, then you believe that people always *ought* to act selfishly, but sometimes people do not act selfishly and thus do not do as they ought to do; and if you believe in *both* psychological egoism *and* ethical egoism, then you hold the very cheerful—but quite implausible—belief that people *always* act precisely as they *should* act (that is, people always act selfishly and thus always act virtuously).

Ethical egoism comes in two varieties. The most commonly advocated is *universal* ethical egoism, which asserts that *everyone* ought to act strictly for his or her own best interests. In contrast, *individual* ethical egoism is the view that I ought to act exclusively for *my* best interests, and everyone else should also strive to serve *my* interests (rather than their own).

Individual ethical egoism is a view that is rarely advocated, though it appears to be held by a number of people: for example, those who enriched themselves while plunging millions into terrible losses, including losses of homes and life savings and retirement pensions, and those who release hazardous wastes that cause enormous suffering, including many childhood cancers, while increasing the profits of those who do the dumping. Perhaps some people are closet individual ethical egoists, but few of those openly *advocate* that position; that is, if Joe is an individual ethical egoist—who believes that the right thing for *everyone* to do is whatever is best for *Joe*—then Joe is likely to present himself as proposing plans that benefit *everyone* (after all, Joe will have no qualms about lying in order to gain greater benefit for himself; to the contrary, if by lying and harming others Joe can gain greater benefit for himself, then Joe—as an individual ethical egoist—would be morally *obligated* to harm others and lie to them). Stephen Colbert has created a marvelous comic persona who openly and eagerly promotes his own well-being and strongly encourages others to adopt policies that will benefit and celebrate Stephen Colbert. And the characters on "It's Always Sunny in Philadelphia" often seem to be cheerfully open individual ethical egoists; though even they sometimes pretend to be concerned for others in order to enlist their aid or support (e.g., the character played by Danny DeVito manifests great concern for his daughter's welfare—for the first time ever—but only because he fears he will have no one to care for him in his old age, and hopes to convince his daughter to take on that role).

Individual ethical egoism is such a repulsive view that it is usually just dismissed—it is not so much an ethical theory as a sad psychological disorder. Brian Medlin's swift dismissal of individual ethical egoism expresses the views of most people who consider the theory: "I'm a philosopher, not a rat-catcher, and I don't see it as my job to dig vermin out of such burrows as individual egoism" ("Ultimate Principles and Ethical Egoism," *Australasian Journal of Philosophy*, 1957).[1] If you can actually contemplate living a life of deep deception and selfishness, with no genuine concern or affection for anyone else, and consider it an attractive life, then there is probably no argument that could cause you to reject your views. But such a person is classified by psychologists as a sociopath, and very few sociopaths enjoy happy lives. In fact, as a species we are best adapted for close cooperative social living (banishment is a terrible punishment; solitary confinement is even worse, often resulting in severe and permanent psychological damage if it continues for an extended period, as in "supermax" prisons). We are also well-adapted for detecting cheaters and deceivers (if we could not, our cooperative social structures would have been toppled, and a very different species would have evolved). And so an individual ethical egoist will have to be very skilled and very thorough in practicing deception. The best way to do that is to *never* let anyone close, never let anyone really get to know him or her. If the individual ethical egoist *does* become close to someone, it will be *only* for his or her own selfish gratification, and that is not a good basis for a deeply satisfying relationship.

Universal ethical egoism is basically the idea that everyone *should* look out for number one; that is, everyone should pursue his or her *own* interests, and not worry about others. Having distinguished this view from *psychological* egoism (and from *individual* ethical egoism), the question then becomes: *Why* should everyone seek their own individual interests, without regard for others? Even if it were true that everyone *does* seek his or her own narrow interests—and we have already seen reasons to think that psychological egoism is false—that would not give us any reason to think that everyone *should* do so; after all, one might believe that psychological egoism is true, but ethically unfortunate (in the same manner that *if* we discovered that ethnic prejudice was an ineradicable element of all humans, we would be sad at discovering that such a deep moral flaw is a universal characteristic of the human species). So *why* should we suppose that universal ethical egoism is the right view?

If we set aside the common confusion between psychological and ethical egoism, there are three reasons why egoism is sometimes favored. First, the belief that if everyone pursues his or her own ends, this will work out best for everyone. Perhaps there is something to be said for a brutally competitive market economy (though it tends to crash, especially if not carefully regulated: People get caught up in various schemes that lead to enormous bubbles, monopolies, market manipulation, cheating—including insider trading—and fraud); but even *if* such a market economy worked efficiently, it would be a mistake to equate our entire moral lives with markets. For a start, if we had been left as infants to thrive or die, we would all have died very young indeed.

Second, there is the "social Darwinist" idea, long since rejected in biology but still reverberating in popular thought. In this view, it is only through severe competition—in which the losers are eliminated—that the species improves. Social Darwinism is wrong in many ways, but to mention only a few: First, Darwinism does not suggest "progress," but only successful adaptation to an environmental niche. Second, in a changing environment, maintaining the greatest possible degree of genetic diversity is the best chance for species survival. The distinct disadvantage of one group may become a strong advantage when the environment changes: For example, think of the physically weak but mathematically-gifted individual ill-suited for life on the California frontier, but very well-suited for life in the Silicon Valley; and the individual who has natural genetic resistance to a deadly future plague might turn out to be much better adapted—and better equipped to sustain the human species—than the current healthiest and strongest. And third, for a social species—especially a species that lives in the very complex social environment of 21st century human society—one's capacity for cooperative enterprise may be more valuable than a capacity for individual competitiveness.

A third reason for belief in universal ethical egoism is its power to boost fragile egos: If only I weren't weighted down by all these dead burdens I am supporting, I would soar like an eagle. It can be found in Ayn Rand as well as in Friedrich Nietzsche, and accounts for much of their charm. Ironically, it provides an excuse for those who insist they need no excuses, and who claim to stand entirely on their own: They would achieve great things, if only they were not held back by the burden of the weaker and needier. Rand's novels are fiction, in which the good guys triumph through unrestrained greed; in nonfictional reality, unchecked greed—as manifested in the robber barons of the 20th century and the Wall Street manipulators of the 21st—results in widespread financial disaster, requiring years if not decades for recovery. As utopian fiction, universal ethical egoism may have appeal; sober reality paints a much more depressing picture.

Relativism

Like psychological and ethical egoism, relativism comes in two main varieties: One is a claim made by sociologists, and is not really an ethical issue, while the other is indeed an ethical thesis. The sociological claim is called sociological relativism, and it is interesting but not very controversial. It is simply the claim that different cultures often have different systems of values. The details of those different systems have been the subject of careful anthropological and sociological research, but the general fact of cultural value differences is commonly known. If you examine cultures in Mumbai, Stockholm, Peking, and Dallas, you find significant differences, and those differences will include differences in values. In some cultures, religious conformity and uniformity is a very strong value, while others value religious freedom and diversity; in some cultures, homosexuality is regarded as a terrible moral wrong that may be punished by death, while in others, homosexuality is considered a perfectly acceptable part of a rich sexual mosaic; in some cultures, oral sex is considered an abomination, while in others, it is not viewed as an ethical issue at all; in some cultures, respect for elders is one of the most basic moral principles, while in other cultures, elders are unceremoniously pushed aside; in some cultures, the eating of meat (or certain varieties of meat, such as pork) is regarded as morally repulsive, while in others, it has no moral significance.

The study of different cultures and their substantial differences—including differences in values and ethical views—is a fascinating subject, but in itself it has few ethical implications. (If in the process of *studying* a culture the researchers undermine, destroy, or misrepresent the culture, *that* is obviously an ethical issue.) In contrast to sociological relativism, what is usually called *cultural* relativism makes a very substantive and controversial ethical claim: that all values are culturally relative and that the *right act* is always the act that is approved by the *culture* in which the act occurs.

It is perfectly legitimate and indeed commendable to adopt some of the cultural practices of the culture in which you are a guest. If the culture regards shaking hands as offensive and aggressive, then it is probably a good idea to refrain from shaking hands, and instead adopt the form of greeting of that culture (such as bowing). If the favored style of dress in that culture is very modest, then—whether you are a man or woman—it shows basic respect and consideration to refrain from wearing your cutoffs and tank top and flip-flops. However, if the culture engages in practices you find morally objectionable, civility and respect do *not* require you to participate: If you are a nondrinking vegetarian visiting Texas, you are not required to eat large platters of barbecued beef washed down with Lone Star beer.

While respect for other cultures is generally a positive thing, cultural relativism—the belief that whatever values are approved by a culture are morally legitimate in that culture—is much more problematic. In fact, it has so many problems that it is difficult to take seriously as an approach to ethics. The first basic problem with cultural relativism is the problem of deciding the range and dimensions of various cultures, and what should be done when cultures interact or overlap. In fact, most of us are members of *several* cultures, and those cultures are not always consistent. If you grew up in an isolated Southern Baptist subculture in rural south Louisiana, then your culture taught you that dancing is sinful and alcoholic beverages evil; however, you were also part of the larger culture of south Louisiana, in which community dances—with a fiddle, guitar, accordion, and lots of good red wine—are regarded as wholesome family and community fun. When you venture into the larger U.S. culture, you encounter an aggressive consumer society—with its emphasis on acquisitiveness, "getting ahead," and harsh individual competitiveness—with values quite different from those of the more cooperative, relaxed, and sharing culture of your native region. You are a member of all three cultures, but those cultures have distinctly different *conflicting* values.

An even more serious problem for cultural relativism is that cultures can be *awful*. A culture that allows and even promotes slavery is not a good culture for anyone, whether inside or outside of that culture. The British philosopher Bernard Williams gives a very clear statement of this flaw in cultural relativism:

> [A] mild form of relativism is expressed by "when in Rome do as the Romans do." I must say that this piece of advice has always seemed to me very bad. For one thing, some things done by Romans—perhaps not so much now, but in earlier times—were pretty beastly. Even apart from that, the Romans may not like you doing what they do. Moreover, you may not be very good at it.[2]

If an "honor culture" values deadly duels to avenge trivial affronts, these are cultural values that are not worthy of respect. If a culture grossly mistreats all members of an ethnic group—as Irish were treated in many parts of the United States in 19th century, as the "untouchables" were treated in India, as those of African descent were treated for centuries in the United States—then that culture is perpetuating a terrible wrong, and anyone who interacts with that culture has an obligation to resist those practices, not join them.

There is a third serious flaw in cultural relativism: From the perspective of cultural relativism, all efforts at moral reform of a culture must be morally *wrong* (because the values of every culture are morally correct for that culture). Thus the civil rights workers who risked—and sometimes lost—their lives in the struggle to reform the racist culture of the deep South were morally bad, as were the abolitionists of the previous century. Women who struggled for women's rights were struggling for a moral wrong. When Mother Jones led marches to end the exploitation of children in dangerous factory and mining work, she was marching for reform of commonly accepted cultural practices; thus those marchers were morally mistaken.

Finally, it is doubtful that cultural relativism is even a consistent form of relativism. Its basic principle seems not be a *relativist* principle at all, but a universal absolute: All cultures should be honored and their principles and practices followed by those living within the culture. According to that principle, you (whoever you may be, and in whatever circumstances) should always follow the rules and principles and values of the culture in which you are living. That is a *universal* (rather than a relative) principle that applies universally across all cultures. And it is a universal principle that has very little to recommend it.

Cultural relativism is a difficult ethical view to defend, and it is more likely to confuse than clarify our understanding of ethical controversies. But it does not follow that cultural relativism has been of *no* value. To the contrary, those who have argued for cultural relativism have probably performed a valuable service, even if we conclude that the theory they champion is wrong. The value in cultural relativism is in its strong insistence that we should not be too quick to judge and condemn the practices and values of other cultures. When cultures have different practices from our own, it is too easy to make shallow judgments from our own limited perspective, and fail to understand the complexity of other cultures and the way their values and practices and institutions actually function.

Consider, for example, the Amish culture, and its rejection of various technological advances that most of American society regards as wonderfully valuable. A refusal to adopt certain types of labor-saving devices—indeed, a prohibition against their use in that society (such as the Amish rejection of combine harvesters)—may appear to be an unreasoning rejection of anything new; but when examined more closely, it is based on a deep valuing of shared work as a means to promoting community ties and social bonding. Use of a combine harvester would make it possible for one worker, working alone, to harvest an entire field; but that increase in efficiency comes at a price. The price is the lost opportunity for collective cooperative work, when the entire community comes together, works together, eats together, and joins in shared work. Families gather first at one family farm to help their neighbors with the harvest, and then the family that was helped goes to the farms of other families and joins in their shared labor. The rejection of combine harvesters is not a rejection of progress or efficiency, but instead a deep valuing of shared community labor. The Amish are willing to accept many improvements (such as more efficient stoves and improved plows); but they consider those new products very carefully, and weigh them in the balance of their primary values. When seen in that larger context, the Amish culture is not arbitrarily rejecting "progress," but preserving important values that we may well wish we had found better ways of preserving in our own more isolated lives.

Cultural relativism has serious problems as an ethical theory. However, given the importance of deeper understanding of complex cultures that differ from our own, some sociologists and anthropologists are reluctant to completely dismiss cultural relativism. Instead, they champion a position known as "anti-antirelativism." It might seem that anti-antirelativism is simply the same thing as relativism; it is not. In the United States, in the 19th and early 20th centuries, there was strong anti-Catholic feeling. Most Americans were Protestant, and were deeply suspicious of both the elaborate Catholic rituals and the new immigrants who practiced the Catholic religion. One might consistently reject the teachings of the Catholic Church while also believing that the strong anti-Catholic feeling is a dangerous religious prejudice. In that case, one would be anti-antiCatholic, but not pro-Catholic. Likewise, one might believe that the rejection of relativism is too often based in a shallow intolerance of cultures different from one's own; in that case, one would be opposed to an uninformed and thoughtless anti-relativism; that is, one would be an anti-antirelativist, without being a cultural relativist.

It is always tempting to suppose that one's own culture is the ethical ideal, and that any culture that differs from it is inferior and ought to be reformed. This uncritical "cultural imperialism" has caused tremendous harm, as "reformers" have blundered in with little understanding of the values they are challenging or the complex elements of the culture they are threatening. The anti-antirelativists serve an important role by reminding us to be sensitive to the purposes and benefits of practices that may initially seem alien or even repulsive to us, and on closer inspection turn out to be beneficial. Indeed, a major goal of this book is to encourage people to look more closely at positions and perspectives that initially may seem alien or even morally repulsive, and try to appreciate any positive elements those views might have to offer. So while cultural relativism has serious problems, anti-antirelativism may have benefits.

Divine Command Theory

Ethical egoism and cultural relativism have little to offer as methods of investigating ethical issues. The same conclusion can be drawn concerning theological voluntarism, or the "divine command" view of ethics. Think for a moment of a moral rule: Don't murder. We may disagree on many things, but most of us would agree that a rule against murder is a good moral rule. And of course it is a rule that is favored by most religions; it is, for example, one of the Ten Commandments, common to Jewish, Christian, and Muslim beliefs. According to those religious traditions, it is a rule—a commandment—laid down by God. So if you are a believer in the Hebraic/Christian/Muslim God, ask yourself for a moment: Did God command us not to murder because God (in His wisdom) knew that murder is wrong, and thus gave us this good commandment? Or is murder wrong *only* because God commands us not to do it? (On the latter view, if God had commanded us to murder others at every available opportunity, then murder would be a virtue, not an evil.) The *second* position—murder is wrong *if and only if* God commands us not to murder—is theological voluntarism: the divine command view of ethics.

As an approach to careful critical examination of ethical issues, the divine command theory has serious problems. In fact, such a view makes critical examination of ethical issues impossible. From our human perspective—the only one available to us, assuming there are no deities reading this book—a divine command morality must look arbitrary, almost capricious. If God commands that slavery is good, then slavery is good; if God commands that liberation of slaves is good, then abolition is good. But there is no possibility of *examining* whether slavery is a terrible wrong, and *why* it is a terrible wrong. If God commands the abolition of slavery *because* slavery is wrong, then we can examine and understand what makes slavery a terrible moral wrong. But if slavery is wrong *only* because that is God's command (or slavery is *right* because God approves it), then there is no space for our critical moral judgment. And indeed, there is no space for critical moral judgment concerning our own religious views.

Consider the religion of your childhood, the religion your parents follow and into which you were initiated. As a thoughtful, reflective, autonomous adult, you do not just *accept* whatever your parents believe; rather, you examine it for yourself and draw your own critical conclusions. So if you accept (or reject) the religion of your parents and your childhood, on what grounds did you make that judgment? One of the most important was probably your own *moral* judgments: I reflectively approve of this religion, because of its deep moral teachings that we are all brothers and sisters, that we are all equal, that we have strong obligations to help those who are in need. Or, I rejected the religious views of my family because I simply could not believe that a just God would demand that women be subordinate to men; or because my childhood religion condemned homosexuality as sinful, and it seemed morally wrong to condemn people for a deep personal sexual orientation that they did not choose. But of course if the divine command theory is right, such moral reflection makes no sense: If God condemns homosexuality, then homosexuality is wrong; but if God had condemned heterosexuality instead, then heterosexuality would be morally wrong.

Not only does the divine command theory of ethics block careful reflection about our own moral views, it makes it impossible to honestly consider views that differ from or oppose our own: They are opposed to God's commands, so at best they are gravely mistaken; more likely, they are satanic. Under the best of circumstances, it is difficult to have a congenial and respectful discussion of controversial ethical issues; when one side accuses the other of promoting evil and the powers of cosmic darkness, it becomes impossible. And finally, even if one is dedicated to the divine command theory, there will be problems in determining exactly what God commands: One day Yahweh is commanding not to kill, the next day He is commanding that everyone be put to the sword—men, women, and children—and spare not one. And remember, you cannot use your own moral judgment to determine what rules God *really* commands ("God wouldn't *really* order genocide, that would be morally terrible") because there can be no moral judgments independent of God's commands. Just as cultural relativism leaves no room for ethical inquiry and reflection, so also theological voluntarism blocks any genuine ethical examination. God commands it and that settles it; and the question of whether that command is ethically legitimate cannot arise (nor can one claim that *because* it is bad, it could not really be God's commandment; under the divine command theory, such a claim would be nonsensical, because there can be *no* standard of ethical goodness apart from God's commands).

None of this is to say that religion should play no part in ethical considerations. For many people, it plays a very valuable part, and in many cases, religion has enlarged our ethical perspective: pushing us to extend our moral concern beyond our family and community to embrace those of other nations and ethnic groups, and in some cases even to those of other species. That is not to say that religion has always been a good thing. It has been used to justify the mindless brutality of the Crusades, to promote the burning of witches and the torture of heretics, to defend slavery and approve the subordination of women and promote anti-Semitism and stir up hatred of homosexuals. Reflecting on the darker elements of religious history, we may be inclined to agree with the pithy statement by Blaise Pascal (a devoted Christian): "Men never commit evil so fully and joyfully as when they do it for religious convictions." But that should not blind us to the fact that religion has also promoted good: the deep Muslim tradition of caring for the least fortunate, the use of Christian and Jewish scripture to inspire the American civil rights movement, and the profound Hindu teachings of religious tolerance.

If you are absolutely certain about God's commandments, and absolutely certain that those commandments come from God (and not from some self-appointed spokesperson for God), and absolutely committed to the rightness of following God's commandments no matter *what* God commands, then you will not find it either possible or worthwhile to reflectively consider opposing views. But such a view deprives you of your status as an autonomous, free person; indeed, it deprives you of your status as a moral agent. Mindless allegiance to rules you dare not question or examine may save you the trouble of thinking for yourself, but it also exposes you to the danger of abjectly following "moral rules" that are in fact morally vile. Religious doctrine has, after all, been the justification for many acts that most of us would regard as among the most abominable: for slavery;

genocide; the most vicious forms of racism; the murder of homosexuals; the subjugation of women; the torture and execution of those who dissent from the dominant religious beliefs; and the torture, imprisonment, and killing of scientists whose discoveries challenged the prevailing orthodoxy. Adamantly refusing to subject your basic principles to careful questioning and critical examination runs terrible ethical risks.

Religion can play an important role in deepening our commitment to our ethical principles. For most of us, the obligation to help those in need is an ethical principle we acknowledge and affirm; but when that principle is placed in the context of organized religious teachings and ritual—for example, when we join together to celebrate the teaching of Jesus that when we feed the hungry we are also feeding Jesus himself ("when you have done it unto the least of these, you have done it unto me")—then that commitment can be deepened, and further strengthened as we affirm that principle with songs and chants. But this is a valuable process *only* if we have good reason to believe that the ethical principles we are affirming and celebrating are genuine (after all, religious rituals can also be used to celebrate the torture of heretics and brutal wars of conquest); and it is precisely that reasoned examination that the divine command theory renders impossible.

Questions for Reflection

1. In Saudi Arabia, American servicewomen were not allowed to drive. Was that a legitimate acquiescence to cultural belief, or a violation of the rights of the women soldiers?

2. If you go to a professional golf match, there is great emphasis on showing respect for all the players, and doing nothing whatsoever to distract them from playing their very best. When a player is about to tee off or is trying to sink a long putt, there is a call for quiet in the vicinity of the player; spectators stop talking, and other players stand still and are careful to stand away from the person making the shot so as not to distract that golfer. Even if you are a dedicated fan of a particular golfer who is battling to win a tournament, it would never occur to you to shout at a rival to cause that player to miss a shot. Contrast that with an NFL football game: the fans of the home team make deafening noise—encouraged by cheer leaders and even some of the home team players—in an effort to confuse the opposing quarterback and make it difficult for the quarterback to communicate with the other players. When the opposing field goal kicker is ready to attempt the winning field goal, the fans in the end zone that kicker is facing wave arms and banners, and scream at the top of their lungs, in an effort to make the kicker miss. If you shout to distract a rival to your favorite golfer, you will be escorted away from the tournament and treated as beneath contempt by other spectators. If you shout loudly and ring cow bells to distract an opposing quarterback, you are embraced by the other spectators as a true fan. Why this striking difference in sports cultures? If someone insisted that one of the cultures is clearly *better* than the other, would you consider that plausible, or nonsense?

3. In the United States, abortion was once widely condemned, and was also illegal. Now abortion is widely accepted (though of course a minority fiercely oppose elective abortions). If you were a dedicated cultural relativist, at what point would you think abortion has changed from wrong to right? When a majority of U.S. citizens favored legalized abortion? When the Supreme Court ruled in *Roe v. Wade*? Or when?

4. You and your group of college friends may count as a *subculture*: You have your own expressions, values, ways of interacting, style of

dress, cultural rules, and prohibitions. Can you think of any aspect of your subculture that an *outsider* might regard as negative and harmful, but that has genuine value *within* the subculture, and loss of which would damage the subculture? That is, when you think of your *own* group, can you see any application for anti-antirelativism?

5. Theological voluntarism—the divine command theory of ethics—was motivated by two factors. One, some people had difficulty imagining that there could be any source for ethics other than rules given by some unquestionable authority; that is, they believed that it was impossible to find any ethical guidelines for ourselves, and unless the rules are imposed externally, there would be no ethics at all. There are still people who believe this; for example, Richard Halverson, the former chaplain of the U.S. Senate, insisted that the only possible morality was an absolute morality imposed by an all-powerful God, and without such externally imposed standards, we would fall into ethical chaos:

> Abandoning an absolute ethical moral standard leads irresistibly to the absence of ethics and morality. Each person determines his own ethical/moral code. That's anarchy. Humans become their own gods and decide, each in his own way, what is good and what is evil. Evil becomes good—good becomes evil. Upside down morality! Good is ridiculed! Evil is dignified!

> *Source:* Richard C. Halverson, *We the People* (Ventura CA: Regal Books, 1987).

In Chapter 3, we'll look at a number of ethical theories that offer moral rules and moral guidance without appealing to divine authority. In any case, few people now believe that in the absence of divinely directed arbitrary moral rules there could be no morality.

The second basis for theological voluntarism is more interesting. Traditionally, some people have thought that if there were any principles of right and wrong *independent* of God, then this would distract from God's majesty; indeed, that it would reduce God's absolute freedom. For if there were principles of good and bad independent of God, then God—as a good, virtuous, morally perfect God—would be required to *follow* those rules; and almighty God, in His terrible omnipotence, cannot be bound by any rules. Which view of God do you find more *plausible* (this, of course, is a question you may answer even if you are an atheist or agnostic): one in which an omniscient God perfectly *recognizes* the moral rules and follows them *because* they are morally right; or a God that makes up moral rules, without any possible standard for whether they are wrong or right other than the fact that they are *willed* by God? Which view of God do you find more *attractive*?

Additional Resources

Ethical egoism was promoted by Bernard de Mandeville in *The Fable of the Bees, or Private Vices, Public Benefits* (London, 1723). Mandeville's book is better written and more cogently argued than the more popular contemporary defense of ethical egoism by the novelist Ayn Rand in *The Virtue of Selfishness* (New York: New American Library, 1961). The classic critique of ethical egoism is by Bishop Joseph Butler, *Fifteen Sermons upon Human Nature* (1726). An excellent critique (among many) of psychological egoism is C. D. Broad, "Egoism as a Theory of Human Motives," in *Ethics and the History of Philosophy* (New York: Humanities Press, 1952). Hugh LaFollette has a very good online discussion of psychological egoism in "The Truth in Psychological Egoism," at www.etsu.edu/philos/faculty/hugh/egoism.htm. Good brief accounts of egoism are Kurt Baier, "Egoism," in *A Companion to Ethics*, Peter Singer, ed. (Oxford: Basil Blackwell, 1991); and Elliott Sober, "Psychological Egoism," in Hugh LaFollette, ed., *The Blackwell Guide to Ethical Theory* (Oxford: Blackwell, 2000). For arguments against ethical egoism, see (among many) Laurence Thomas, "Ethical Egoism and Psychological Dispositions," *American Philosophical Quarterly*, 17 (1980); Christine Korsgaard, "The Myth of Egoism," *The Lindley Lectures* (Lawrence, KS: University of Kansas Press, 1999); Kurt Baier, *The Moral Point of*

View (Ithaca, NY: Cornell University Press, 1958); and James Rachels, "Two Arguments against Ethical Egoism," *Philosophia*, 4 (1974). Thomas Nagel's superb book *The Possibility of Altruism* (Oxford: Clarendon Press, 1970) might also be useful in this context. Jesse Kalin defends ethical egoism in "Two Kinds of Moral Reasoning," *Canadian Journal of Philosophy*, 5 (1975). There are also two good anthologies devoted to ethical egoism: *Morality and Rational Self-Interest*, edited by David Gauthier (Englewood Cliffs, NJ: Prentice-Hall, 1970); and *Egoism and Altruism*, Ronald D. Milo, ed. (Belmont, CA: Wadsworth, 1973).

Anthropologist Ruth Benedict, in *Patterns of Culture* (New York: Penguin, 1934), was a major advocate of cultural relativism. Mary Midgley, *Heart and Mind* (New York: St. Martin's Press, 1981), offers a well-crafted critique of cultural relativism. For a more sophisticated version of relativism, and a defense of that view, see Gilbert Harman, *Explaining Value and Other Essays in Moral Philosophy* (Oxford: Clarendon Press, 2000). For a clear and fascinating debate on moral relativism versus moral objectivism by two outstanding contemporary philosophers, see Gilbert Harman and Judith Jarvis Thomson, *Moral Relativism and Moral Objectivity* (Oxford: Blackwell, 1996). Russ Shafer-Landau includes a clear critique of egoism and relativism in *Whatever Happened to Good and Evil?* (Oxford: Oxford University Press, 2004); another extensive critique of relativism is offered by John. J. Tilley in "Cultural Relativism," *Human Rights Quarterly*, 22 (2000). Hugh LaFollette defends rational relativist ethics in "Moral Disagreement and Moral Relativism," *Social Philosophy and Policy*, 20 (1994).

For very interesting anthropological examinations of relativism, see Elvin Hatch, *Culture and Morality: The Relativity of Values in Anthropology* (New York: Columbia University Press, 1983); and an excellent article by Clifford Geertz, "Anti-Anti-Relativism," *American Anthropologist*, 86, no. 2 (June 1984), as well as his *Available Light: Anthropological Reflections on Philosophical Topics* (Princeton, NJ: Princeton University Press, 2000). Good anthologies on relativism include Michael Krausz, *Relativism: Interpretation and Conflict* (Notre Dame, IN: University of Notre Dame Press, 1989); and Paul K. Moser and Thomas L. Carson, *Moral Relativism: A Reader* (New York: Oxford University Press, 2001).

Plato's *Euthyphro* (available in many translations and editions) is the classic critique of theological voluntarism. Kai Nielsen's *Ethics without God* (London: Pemberton Press; and Buffalo, NY: Prometheus Books, 1973) is a powerful contemporary argument against basing ethics on religion. A sophisticated opposing view—which argues for the importance of religious considerations in ethics—is found in George N. Schlesinger, *New Perspectives on Old-Time Religion* (Oxford: Clarendon Press, 1988). Jonathan Berg gives a brief argument for how ethics might be based on religion in "How Could Ethics Depend on Religion?" in Peter Singer, editor, *A Companion to Ethics* (Oxford: Blackwell, 1991); and Philip L. Quinn develops a detailed defense of theological voluntarism in "Divine Command Theory," in Hugh LaFollete's superb anthology, *The Blackwell Guide to Ethical Theory* (Oxford: Blackwell Publishers, 2000).

There are two excellent anthologies on the divine command theory of ethics: P. Helm, editor, *Divine Commands and Morality* (Oxford: Oxford University Press, 1981); and G. Outka and J. P. Reeder, Jr. Editors, *Religion and Morality: A Collection of Essays* (Garden City, NY: Anchor/Doubleday, 1973). An excellent online discussion of theological voluntarism can be found in an essay by Mark Murphy in the online *Stanford Encyclopedia of Philosophy*; go to http://plato.stanford.edu/entries /volunarism-theological/. Lawrence M. Hinman has an interesting presentation on "Divine Command Theories of Ethics," at http://ethics.sandiego.edu/presentations /theory/DivineCommand/DivineCommand2.ppt.

Endnotes

1. "Ultimate Principles and Ethical Egoism," Australasian Journal of Philosophy, 1957.
2. Bernard Williams, "Relativism, History, and the Existence of Value," p. 106 in Joseph Raz, *The Practice of Value*, edited by R. Jay Wallace (Oxford: The Clarendon Press, 2003).

MYSEARCHLAB CONNECTIONS

The *Ethics Updates* website is a superb source for fascinating material on a wide range of issues in ethics, both theoretical and applied. It can be found at http://ethics.sandiego .edu. For excellent material on egoism and relativism, go to that site and under "Ethical Theory" click on Ethical Egoism as well as Ethical Relativism.

3

Some Useful Ways of Approaching Ethical Questions

Chapter Outline

Chapter 2 dealt with some well-known but *un*helpful approaches to ethics. In contrast, there are a number of theoretical approaches to ethical questions that have proved very helpful. Useful as these various approaches may be, they can also come into conflict. In fact, there are long-standing controversies among ethicists over which of these approaches is most valuable. Kantian duty-based ethics is very different from the utilitarian approach to ethics that focuses on beneficial consequences, and both of those differ significantly from social contract models. From the perspective of care ethics, all three of the former are fundamentally mistaken. There are still other approaches to ethical theory, which bring new competing candidates into the mix.

Ethical theory is a useful and fascinating subject, full of interesting arguments and deep divisions. But rather than taking sides, we'll look for the best elements of each theory, and for the insights and perspectives each theoretical approach offers. The hope is that *each* of the theories might offer a perspective that will prove useful in understanding some of the most basic and intractable ethical conflicts we now face. There is an ancient Hindu parable concerning a group of blind men, and their encounter with an elephant. One touches a leg, and pronounces that the elephant is very like a tree trunk. Another touches an ear, and insists the elephant is similar to a fan. Still another touches the tail, and declares the elephant to be quite like a rope. A fourth touches the side of the elephant, and decides that an elephant is similar to a wall. If they can work together, each appreciating the insights of the others, they will gain a better understanding of elephants than if they bicker with one another about which one is right and why all the others are wrong. I'm not claiming that every ethical theory contains some element of basic ethical truth. Maybe one of the theories is far superior to all the others. Perhaps one of the theories is right, and the others are fundamentally wrong. Maybe they are all wrong. Those are questions for a course on ethical theory. The claim of this chapter is only that each theory offers an interesting *approach* to questions of ethics, an interesting perspective, and perhaps some interesting and helpful *techniques* for gaining a clearer view of some basic ethical disputes. We'll look for what *each* of the theories can contribute to our ways of seeing ethical disputes from helpful angles, and for any useful tips they can offer for *resolving* ethical disputes—or if not resolving the ethical disputes (and given the depth and strength of some of those disputes, *settling* the disputes may be rather ambitious), at least promoting a more congenial and insightful discussion of our differences.

Which of these theories or approaches you find most useful is up to you. Perhaps you will favor a thoroughgoing utilitarian position, and resolve every ethical issue you confront in terms of the greatest happiness for the greatest number. Maybe you will find the Kantian line more plausible, and conclude that utilitarian consequences should have no influence whatsoever in deciding right and wrong. Or possibly you will decide that one technique is particularly helpful when dealing with ethics on a more personal level, while another works better in dealing with issues of social policy. But however you decide to use these techniques, they may give you useful ways of probing deeper into tough moral questions, enlarging your perspective on those questions, and appreciating the opposing views of others.

Ways of Thinking about Ethical Issues: Would You Like It If Everyone Did That?

One of the great ethical guides was formalized by the 18th century philosopher, Immanuel Kant. He formulated the principle thus: Always act in such a way that you could will your act as a universal law. That is, you should always act in such a manner that you could will that *everyone* would act in exactly that way, that your act could be established as a universal law that all would follow. For example, you are thinking of selling your old car, and you know that the transmission is near death. You could sell it for a good price if you lie about the condition of the car. Should you lie and pocket the cash? If you do so, you are treating the person who buys the car as not worthy of respect, not worthy of fair treatment. Could you genuinely will that others treat you as merely a means to their ends, as someone not worthy of respect and fair treatment? No. You cannot genuinely desire that you—an autonomous person who has his or her own goals and is capable of reason—should be treated as in such a mean-spirited manner. Or if that is hard to grasp, think of it this way: How would you like it if someone played such a dishonest trick on your dear old trusting mother, or on your best friend? You cannot genuinely wish that everyone treated others merely as means to their selfish ends, with no consideration for the other person's inherent value. And since the person you are thinking of cheating is—just like you—a person with goals and interests and moral capacities, it would be fundamentally *inconsistent* to suppose that it is alright for you to cheat that person, but *not* alright for others to cheat you (or your mom or your friend).

Though Kant gave the principle a formal statement—always act in such a way that you could will your act as a universal law—the principle is a common one, and has been stated in various ways. It is sometimes called the "golden rule": Do unto others as you would have them do unto you. When stated in the negative it is called the "silver rule." As Confucius phrased it: "Do not do to others that which we do not want them to do to us." The ancient Greek philosopher Thales offered the silver rule in an interesting form: "Avoid doing what you would blame others for doing." This version emphasizes the impartial *detachment* that the rule demands of us: Think of how this act you are contemplating would look to you if you were a detached observer. If you saw someone do this act to someone else, would you blame the person for doing the act? If so, then you should not do it yourself. The famous Jewish teacher Hillel stated the most memorable form of the silver rule. When asked to sum up the teachings of the Torah, he replied: "That which is hateful to you, do not do to your fellow. That is the whole Torah; the rest is the explanation; go and learn." The Muslim tradition includes a clear statement that combines the golden and the silver rules: "The most righteous of men is the one who is glad that men should have what is pleasing to himself, and who dislikes for them what is for him disagreeable." Obviously the application of the golden and silver rules requires at least some degree of sophistication: The child who presents his snake-phobic mom a lovely harmless snake is trying to follow the golden rule—I would be delighted if someone gave me a snake, so I should give one to mom—but hasn't quite mastered the details. And though a tour of Bellingrath Gardens might bore you to tears (you might find it hateful), it does not follow that you should not take your flower-loving dad on such a tour.

So one good guide when considering ethical issues is a simple one: Look at the act you are considering, and then consider it from a more detached perspective: Would you be hurt (or pleased) if someone did this to *you*? Another way of approaching it: When you are considering an act, *enlarge* it so you can see it more clearly. That is, think of it *universally*, think of whether you believe this would be a good *policy*. If everyone started doing what you are contemplating, would you consider that a good thing?

Kant insisted that we must think *universally*—in terms of universal principles—when considering ethics. He also insisted that we must think *rationally*: that feelings and emotions have *absolutely no place* in determining whether an act is right or wrong. Some people think Kant placed too much emphasis on *universal* laws, and gave insufficient attention to particular personal relationships (such as relations among friends and family). That's an issue we'll be looking at again. But many people dispute Kant's insistence that *feelings* must have *nothing* to do with our ethical decision making; indeed, many insist that feelings are the essential element of all ethical conduct. But whatever you think about the relation of reason and emotions in ethics, few people would deny that in the current debates over controversial ethical issues (such as abortion and euthanasia and capital punishment), feelings have sometimes run amok. You may not agree with Kant that feelings must be totally banished from ethical decision making, but it is clear that holding our passions somewhat in check and leaving room for quieter reflective rational discussion might be a good step in dealing with some of the toughest ethical decisions. Even if feelings are of prime importance to ethical decision making, that does not mean that we should allow heated and antagonistic feelings to overwhelm reasonable discussion. Passion is great—as very few college students need to be reminded. But passionate feelings are not *always* the best guide, and sometimes passion should be subjected to reasonable restraints—a fact that most of us have learned from sad experience. Whatever you conclude about the overall value of reason as compared to feelings, Kant's basic principle—when considering an act, try looking at it from a larger *universal* perspective, as if it were to be made a universal law—is often a very useful approach to questions of ethics.

An Impartial Observer

Adam Smith is best known today as an economist, but in the 18th century, he was famous for his writings on ethics. Smith believed that ethics must ultimately be based on our *feelings*. That is a view that has been held by a number of philosophers, as well as many psychologists, but it remains controversial. Immanuel Kant despised the claim that ethics is based in feelings. He insisted that ethics must be based in pure reason (and many philosophers, before and after Kant, have maintained that reason is the *only* legitimate grounds for genuine ethical behavior). The long-disputed question of whether ethics should be based more on feelings or on reason is not a debate we'll pursue here. But whatever you think about the proper role of feelings in ethical judgments, it is clear that feelings are powerful, that they play a large part in the ethical judgments of many people, that feelings can be very positive (your mother's deep love for you is one good example; your deep feeling of attachment to your best friend is another; the mutual affection you share with your "significant other" or "main squeeze" is a third), and that feelings can often lead us astray (the profound passion that blew your ship of love straight onto the rocks is an obvious but painful example). And while most of us have learned that our passionate feelings can get us into serious trouble, it is also important to note that our deep *moral* feelings are sometimes badly misguided. In the past, many people *felt deeply* that it was morally wrong to associate socially with Irish immigrants, or Italians, or with whatever ethnic group had recently arrived in the country; that it was morally wrong to marry outside one's race; that it was morally wrong for women to hold any position of authority; that it was morally wrong to suffer a witch to live. There is no doubt that many people had strong feelings on those subjects, and that they considered those feelings reliable moral guides; but from a larger perspective, it is easy to recognize those vile feelings as expressions of racism, sexism, and ignorant bigotry rather than reliable guides to good conduct. Feelings are important, and they can be good (though they can also be very bad); so the question is, how do we sort them out? "Just follow any strong feelings you happen to have" is not much help as a guide to moral behavior (and probably not a very good guide to your love life, for that matter).

So how *do* you use your feelings as a guide? Not by trying to eliminate all your feelings. You probably wouldn't be successful, and that's probably a good thing. Those who lack all feelings tend to be sociopaths, who do horrible things to others (apparently serial killers often suffer from an incapacity to feel empathy for others). And a distinguished neuropsychological researcher, Antonio Damasio, believes that when the brain is damaged in such a way that feelings are blunted or destroyed, the capacity for moral behavior is often lost as well. A better way to deal with feelings is by trying to get a bit of *perspective* on your feelings. Our immediate feelings are often hot and powerful, and sometimes sweep us away, and (especially when we mix them with alcohol) they may push us to do things impulsively that we later regret. But we also have feelings when we see *others* do kind or cruel acts. If you observe someone beating a child, or torturing a kitten, your feelings of condemnation are aroused; and if you see someone perform a heroic rescue, or relieve the suffering of a child, your feelings of moral approval well up. Our feelings of condemnation are aroused when we are purposefully harmed by another; but they are also aroused—perhaps to not quite the same intensity, but still aroused—when we see someone else harmed. And this capacity for empathetic feelings can be used to gain a clearer perspective on our own behavior. Adam Smith recommended that when you are trying to decide what act is right, ask yourself how you would react if you observed someone else act toward another in the way you are considering; that is, take the perspective of the *detached observer* toward yourself, and see what feelings are aroused. While that may not be an absolutely reliable guide to which feelings are morally worthy, the reflection required to carry out this process may help in gaining a better perspective on our feelings—a perspective that is not quite so dominated by unruly passions. The waitress who got your order confused is an easy target, and it may feel good to vent your anger on her; after all, she screwed up, and she deserves it. But if you step back, and ask yourself how you would respond to watching someone in a position of power abusing someone in a weaker position—abusing someone who is tired and overworked, and who made a mistake any of us could make—then you may gain a different and better perspective on what (from the immediate perspective) seemed like a venting of righteous wrath.

The Veil of Ignorance

Looking at an issue from the perspective of the "impartial observer" is one way of trying to gain a clearer view. John Rawls, a 20th century political philosopher, proposed a way of thinking of ethical issues that gives an even more detached and broader perspective: When trying to decide what policy is right, consider it from "behind the veil of ignorance." That is, imagine yourself as one in a group of "disembodied souls" who will soon be embodied as humans and placed on Earth to form a community, and your group is drawing up a set of rules and principles for the new community that will be formed (when you are all "embodied"). All of you are "behind the veil of ignorance," because you are *ignorant* of who you will be when you are embodied in this new community. You know you will be a human, and so you will have all the standard human needs and desires (for food, water, and oxygen, obviously; but also for housing, medical care, protection from attack, social relations, interesting activities, and so on). But beyond that, you are ignorant of any details of who you will be: You don't know your gender or ethnic group, whether you will be bright or dull, strong or weak, grumpy or gracious, industrious or lethargic, able-bodied or disabled; you don't know what religion you will favor, if any; you don't know your tastes in music or literature, your favorite hobbies, your political views, your sexual orientation. In that situation—where you are meeting together to legislate the rules for this new community, without knowing whether you will be a deeply religious white man who is rather lazy, hates sports, and loves reading romance novels, or an agnostic black woman who is highly energetic, a fabulous athlete, and a wonderful physicist, or whatever—what rules would you favor for the community in which you will soon be living? Would you favor rules that exclude women or blacks from positions of authority, and reserve the best educations and best jobs for white males? That might be tempting, if you could be sure you would be a white male; but because you might wake up in this new community as a black woman, and be excluded from important opportunities, it would be foolish for you to adopt such a rule. Or maybe you would like a rule that only a specific religion could be practiced and taught in this community, and all others would be banned. Sounds peachy, if you could be sure that the favored religion was your own religion; but as much fun as it might be to ban all those religions that disagree with your own, you must consider how awful it would be to be a believer in one of the banned religions. Because you might awaken in this new community as a believer in one of the banned religions, you would not find it desirable to allow only one religion and persecute all others. So one way of thinking about ethical issues and ethical principles is to imagine yourself behind the veil of ignorance, and from that perspective ask yourself what rules you would favor. The rules you would favor from that perspective—stripped of all your special interests and biases and prejudices—would be rules that are *fair*, rules that are *just*.

Both Feelings and Principles

On the question of whether feelings or reasoned principles are the best guide to answering questions in ethics, philosophers tend to line up on either side of the debate, with no common ground. But some have tried to bridge that deep divide, arguing that the best approach to ethics is a careful *combination* of both feelings and reasoned principles. One of the most insightful proponents of this approach is Jonathan Bennett, who champions it in a philosophically famous article entitled "The Conscience of Huckleberry Finn."

Perhaps you have read Mark Twain's great novel, *Adventures of Huckleberry Finn*. If not, you certainly should. It is a rather dark novel, and does not paint a particularly pretty picture of human nature or human behavior. It is also remarkably funny, though the humor sometimes has a sharp edge; and it is a powerful attack on slavery, racism, and bigotry in all their ugly forms. There are really two heroes of the novel, both rather improbable heroes, both with significant strengths as well as genuine weaknesses: Huck Finn, of course, who is "lighting out for the territories" to escape a violently abusive alcoholic father, and also to escape the efforts of those who wish to "civilize" him; and Jim, a slave who is escaping in search of his freedom, and in hope of ultimately securing the freedom of his beloved wife and children. The two join forces, and become friends as they make their perilous raft journey along the broad river.

At one point in the novel, Jim expresses his deep appreciation to Huck for helping him escape, calling Huck his best and only friend: "Jim won't ever forgit you, Huck; you's de bes' fren' Jim's ever had; en you's de *only* fren ole Jim's got now." At that point, Huck starts to feel profoundly guilty, knowing that he is helping a slave to escape. To make matters worse, Jim tells Huck that he hopes to buy his wife and children out of slavery, but if the owner won't sell, he will steal them away to freedom. Huck feels more and more miserable: Here is this escaped slave, "which I had as good as helped to run away," and the slave was "coming right out flat-footed and saying that he would steal his children—children that belonged to a man I didn't even know; a man that hadn't ever done me no harm." So with his "conscience" bothering him, Huck resolves to follow his principles against theft of property, and turn Jim in to the slave catchers. But when he has an opportunity to do so, his concern for his friend overpowers his commitment to principle: Huck tricks the slave catchers and helps Jim escape.

In this case, Huck's feeling of friendship overcomes his commitment to principle, and we are delighted with the result. Huck's deep feeling of friendship for Jim is powerful enough to overcome the enormous system of brutal racism that forbids *friendship* (a relation among equals) between a white man and a black man, and it is a positive feeling well worth celebrating. In contrast, Huck's *principle* (that humans can be mere property, with no rights whatsoever) is loathsome. Any time a commitment to principle runs contrary to our deepest feelings, that is good grounds for subjecting that principle to deep questioning. (If my *principle* is that everyone must take care of themselves, and no one should help those who are less fortunate, then when my deep sympathy for some hungry homeless person runs counter to my principle, that is an indication that perhaps the principle should be reevaluated.) But that does not mean that my feelings should always overwhelm my principles. My feeling for my endangered friend may prompt me to provide an alibi, even though I know my friend committed a crime; but when an innocent stranger is sent to prison for the crime my friend committed, this may be a time when principled honesty should win out over strong feelings of friendship. Suppose that you have become director of the university's tutoring center, in charge of hiring tutors, and you are selecting tutors from among many applicants. If one of the applicants for math tutor is your best friend, but a very weak mathematician, and the other applicant is a stranger who is superb at math and an excellent tutor, then your feelings may incline you to select your friend, but clearly this is a case in which your principles should overcome your feelings.

Ethical judgments often involve a difficult balancing act between principles and feelings, and it is essential to keep *both* feelings and deliberation in healthy working order. That's a difficult task. Huck Finn gets so worn out by the process that he resolves to quit worrying about it: "I reckoned I wouldn't bother no more about it, but after this always do whichever come handiest at the time." But the result is that Huck never subjects his principles—including the principle that slavery is legitimate—to serious scrutiny. Huck has a good heart, so "doing whatever comes easiest" may usually work out alright; but what would happen if Huck encountered an escaped slave who was not quite so warm and engaging as Jim?

Many people had—sadly, some people still have—a deep visceral reaction against people of other races or ethnic groups, and a deep moral horror of marriage between such groups. Growing up in a rural community in the 1950's segregated South, I vividly recall the deep feelings of moral revulsion that many whites felt against eating in the same restaurants with blacks, or drinking from the same water fountain, or attending the same schools; and any argument in favor of ending racial segregation was decisively ended with the assertion: "But that could lead to marriage between blacks and whites," a prospect that most whites regarded with such deep emotional horror that it ended all discussion. There is no doubt that people profoundly *felt* that interracial marriage was a terrible moral wrong; but I trust that you would agree that the moral wrong was in that *feeling*, which was the product of centuries of racial oppression: In order to justify the cruel and unjust treatment given blacks, it was essential to believe that they were somehow deeply inferior, or even that they were cursed by God and deserved such treatment. Recognizing the vile source of that feeling destroys its legitimacy as a moral guide. So feelings are important in ethics; but as Jonathan Bennett puts it, that does not imply that we should "give our feelings a blank check." Feelings can and should be subjected to careful scrutiny, and if they are worthwhile then they can withstand such scrutiny. But *principles* can also be terribly wrong (e.g., the *principles* that witches should be killed and escaping slaves should be apprehended). Reason may reveal the flaws in those principles, but a troubled emotional reaction may provide an important stimulus for subjecting even our deepest principles to serious examination. Finding the right balance between feelings and principles is a difficult task—but you never imagined that ethics would be easy, did you?

The Greatest Pleasure for the Greatest Number

What is the right thing to do? *Utilitarians* recommend that we worry less about rules and principles: The right act is simply the act that produces the *best consequences*. And what consequences do we want to produce? More pleasure and less suffering. Isn't that what we all want, whether Ashanti traders or Canadian farmers or Pakistani physicians? Or beagles or hamsters, for that matter.

That is the *utilitarian* approach to ethical questions. Some despise it as a celebration of swinish pleasure over noble virtue, but that is a gross misrepresentation of utilitarianism. Utilitarian ethics does *not* direct us to selfishly and thoughtlessly seek the most immediate pleasures. To the contrary, utilitarians counsel that we should be very careful in deciding what act is right. We're off to dinner; what will bring us pleasure? Let's start with a couple of vodka martinis; then we'll have the biggest steaks in the house, french fries slathered in cheese sauce on the side, a bottle of cabernet with that; double chocolate cheesecake for dessert, accompanied by a nice orange liqueur; we'll finish with port wine and cheese, and we'll have a couple of brandies—maybe three or four—when we're done. There is no doubt that such a grossly excessive meal can bring pleasure. After the third brandy, you are likely to feel considerable pleasure and absolutely no pain. But the pleasure will be comparatively brief, and the eventual pain (the hangover and heartburn) of much greater duration—especially when we factor in the pain of an early heart attack, as well as the pain (which utilitarians insist must be part of the calculation) of the Angus steer that was castrated and ultimately slaughtered for our dining pleasure. Furthermore, the joys of inebriation are strictly incompatible with the joys of reading your ethics textbook—and even if reading an ethics textbook is a very modest pleasure, it still must be entered into the calculation. The pleasures from overeating and excessive drinking may be genuine pleasures, but even a rough utilitarian calculation tells us that seeking such pleasures is not the best way to maximize pleasure and minimize suffering. So whatever its strengths or weaknesses, utilitarian ethics is not an ethics that celebrates selfish gross short-term pleasures at the expense of deeper values and wider considerations.

Still, some maintain that the utilitarian emphasis on pleasure turns ethics upside down. In Immanuel Kant's view, "The goal is not to be happy, but to be worthy of happiness." And as the great 20th century philosopher Ludwig Wittgenstein once said: "I don't know why we are here, but I'm pretty sure it is not in order to enjoy ourselves." And many contemporary feminist philosophers have objected that utilitarians treat the *impersonal marketplace* as the key to ethics, and that the utilitarian calculation of maximizing pleasure and minimizing suffering leaves no room for special personal relationships. Contrary to the impersonal utilitarian model, ethics and the nurturing of ethical character begin at *home* in our special personal relationships of care and affection. Only that foundation in family and friends allows ethics to be *extended* to impersonal relationships: Utilitarian ethics starts from the wrong end. Finally, there seem to be some values that cannot be placed in a utilitarian calculation without destroying them. Consider your closest and deepest friendships: If you start to *calculate* whether a friendship produces the greatest possible balance of pleasure over pain—"My old friend Joan has become rather depressed since the breakup with her lover; she's not as much fun; maybe I should drop her as a friend"—then you have never really understood what it means to have or be a friend. If you think of friendship in that way, you are not really thinking of friendship at all, but instead of a mutually beneficial temporary alliance. That is not to say that friendships or even loves can never prove false, and be rightfully abandoned: If the person you thought was your friend is instead only a manipulator, then that person was not really your friend, and cutting ties with that person does not mean you are abandoning a friend. According to the old blues song, "nobody knows you when you're down and out," and "when in your pocket, you don't have a penny, then your friends, you don't have any"; but if that's the case, you didn't have any friends when you were prosperous, either. If you are thinking of dumping your "own true love" in the hope of doing better, then you have never experienced love at all. That doesn't mean that "love can never die," as fairy tales and romance novels might claim; but it does mean that love can't be placed in a calculus of benefits and detriments.

Utilitarian ethics has its contemporary champions, but it also has a wide range of fierce critics. Whatever its strengths or weaknesses as a *general* ethical theory, utilitarian calculations can be quite useful when we are examining questions of social policy. In dealing with these larger questions, the impersonal calculating character of utilitarianism has some distinct advantages: It makes clear that some policies may provide benefits to a few, but at the expense of significant harm to others; and it can show us that a policy that may provide limited benefits is not as useful as a policy that provides wider long-term benefits. Consider, for example, a policy of passing a 1% tax on all annual income *above* $3 million in order to provide health care for all children. If your annual income is $4 million a year, that means you would pay an extra tax of $10,000 annually. That will have little impact on the very wealthy: They will still have their Fifth Avenue penthouses, their Miami Beach condos, and their Lake Tahoe ski lodges (maybe they'll have to buy slightly smaller yachts); but it will make a tremendous difference to the children who formerly suffered without health care. Perhaps there are other reasons why such a tax would be a bad policy; but at the very least, utilitarian calculations can show us quite clearly the powerful social impact of some of our policies and practices. So one useful tool when considering a controversial issue: Ask what policy would (by our best calculations) produce the greatest overall balance of pleasure over suffering; that is, what policy would maximize pleasure and minimize pain for all concerned?

Taking a Narrower Perspective: From the Marketplace to the Family

Much of contemporary ethics developed to guide *impersonal* relationships: relationships in the market, the legislature, the courtroom. Those are certainly important places for ethical guidance. All of us wish that the predatory lenders and the Wall Street manipulators who drove the world economy to the edge of disaster had tempered their greed with some ethical reflection. But there is sometimes a tendency to see impersonal marketplace ethics as encompassing the *whole* of ethics. That is, it is often tempting to emphasize *impersonal* marketplace ethics to such a degree that the *personal* elements of ethics become invisible.

When we focus on impersonal social contracts or impersonal reason or impersonal utility calculation, it is easy to forget that there were some essential *personal* steps that came earlier. Before we reason about a social contract or take the stance of an impartial observer or calculate utilities, we must be shaped as *moral persons* who take moral considerations seriously. That requires a lengthy and laborious nurturing process that traditional ethical theory has too often ignored. To see the importance of this personal process, imagine life *without* it. Without the lengthy early support of our family and community, none of us would be capable of entering into impersonal ethical deliberation. Without such support, none of us would be capable of ethical behavior. Without such support, none of us would have even survived. Children who do not experience affectionate nurturing care often grow up emotionally troubled with reduced ethical capacities. The care doesn't have to be perfect: Few of us had perfect families, and few of us will be perfect parents to our children. But without at least some degree of affectionate home and family nurturing, few if any would be equipped for the ethics of the impersonal marketplace and social contract.

Personal ethics—the ethics of affection and caring—offers another valuable perspective on ethical issues. When we are taking the *im*personal perspective of the impartial observer or the utilitarian pleasure calculator or the universal rules of Kantian ethics, individual characteristics and personal relationships tend to disappear. Yet when we actually look at our lives and loves and relationships, we realize that these personal commitments are among the most important and meaningful elements of our lives, and the essential foundation of more impersonal abstract ethical theorizing. Your relationship with your parents and children is not one of contract, nor even of reciprocity; certainly it is not one of impersonal choice. If you care for your children out of a sense of impersonal duty, that may be better than nothing, but it is far from the ideal for developing emotionally secure children. Your affection for your children is unconditional. Shakespeare said it best: "Let us not to the marriage of true minds admit impediments; love is not love which alters when it alteration finds." It is an "ever-fixed mark, that looks on tempests and is not shaken." If I deal badly with you in the marketplace, you would be foolish to deal with me again. If you own a restaurant, and the bakery that has supplied you with good baked products for a decade has problems and starts sending you lousy bread, you will switch to another bakery. But if your child or your friend has problems, that is a very different matter. If I drop a friend because the friendship is no longer useful or advantageous (my friend has lost her job, and is no longer useful for networking; or my friend becomes depressed, and is no longer quite as much fun), then I have no grasp of genuine friendship. Of course friendship and affection can end: If you discover that your "friend" is merely manipulative or your lover proves falsehearted or your spouse turns out to be violently abusive, then the basis for any genuine friendship or affectionate relationship is eroded; but that is very different from dropping friends or family members because they are no longer quite as charming or useful.

Personal relations with our friends and family are very different from relations among independent contractors who seek mutual advantage. Personal relations are not governed by utilitarian calculations, and are not based on universal rules. If you go to visit your friend in the hospital because "duty demands it," or because you have calculated that the visit will produce "the greatest balance of pleasure over suffering," then your relation of "friendship" is a pale imitation of the real thing. When we consider our ethical relations with friends and lovers and family members—some of our most valuable relationships—it is clear that not all ethics can be dealt with in abstract impersonal universal terms: The personal details of our personal relationships are important elements of our ethical lives, and they do not fit easily into Kantian or social contract or utilitarian calculations. So as we consider the large questions of social ethics, it is important to leave room for consideration of special relationships among friends and family.

Do I Really Want To Be That Sort of Person?

The ethical guides considered so far have been guides to what acts I should or should not do. There is a different way of looking at questions of ethics that moves the focus from acts and policies to persons and characters. Rather than asking what *act* you should or should not do, ask yourself instead: Do I want to be the sort of *person* who does this type of act? If you are considering cheating on an exam, or lying to your lover, or neglecting a friend who needs your help, then ask yourself: Is this the sort of character I really want to have? Do I want to be a person who does not keep his promises, who does not help her friends, who cannot be trusted? Do I really want to live a life of hypocrisy, pretending to be something I'm not? I might get away with it; but do I really want to *be* that sort of person? And don't tell yourself that it's only for the moment, and when you are more prosperous or after you graduate or when you have more time, *then* you'll change. "It's true that I lie when it's convenient, but I'm not really a liar; it's true, I sometimes cheat on my lover, but I'm not really an unfaithful person; it's true I'm rather stingy with others, but deep down I'm really a very generous person." That makes as much sense as claiming that "I never do any running, but deep down I'm a great marathoner." What you practice is what you become; the way you act is what you are. To pretend otherwise is to add self-deceit to your other faults. So when you are considering an act, ask yourself: When I think about the sort of person I am becoming, the sort of character I am developing, is this really the sort of person I want to be? When I look at myself carefully and reflectively, is this a person I genuinely approve?

The virtue theory approach is usually directed at individuals: The key question is not what *act* I should or should not do, but what sort of *person* I want to be and become. But virtue theory can be expanded to deal with a larger range of social issues, issues concerning our society or country. For any policy or program we are considering, we can ask: What sort of *society*, what sort of *country*, do we genuinely value? Suppose that the American Founding Fathers had asked themselves, honestly: What sort of country do we really want these United States to be and become? It is difficult to imagine that they could have answered: "Well, we think the practice of slavery would make this country better." Not only would such an answer mock the ideals of "liberty and justice for all" that the country claimed to follow; but also, careful consideration of the long-term effects of slavery on a society or country would have made very clear the terrible costs. Slavery entrenches the idea that manual labor is demeaning (fit only for slaves); it brings out the worst in those who hold positions of absolute power over their fellow human beings (as evidenced by the long history of rape and brutal savagery toward slaves); it places in society a large group of fellow humans who have been brutally mistreated and have observed the mistreatment of their parents and grandparents and children (a group of people who have good reason for wanting retribution against their fellows and are thus feared); it creates the obvious absurdity of enslaving men and women of African descent who in talent and ability were fully the equal of their "masters," and who often became skilled workers; it promotes the development of an "honor" society, in which small slights are avenged by death. It is sometimes said that the measure of a society is how well it cares for its weakest and most vulnerable members, particularly the elderly and small children. Thus from a virtue ethics perspective, an affluent society might ask itself: Do we really want to be a society in which small children lack health care, or live in dangerous rundown housing? Do we really want to be a society in which some elderly must choose between buying food and buying medications?

Can We Agree to Disagree?

Robert Frost speaks of "the road not taken," the attractive path not followed, and the person he did not become. Walt Whitman, in *Song of Myself*, wrote: "I am large, I contain multitudes." Probably that is a feeling shared by most of us. I am a person who wants to run free, with no deep personal attachments, a rolling stone who gathers no moss; and I am also a person who wants a profound and unshakable committed personal relationship with someone who is very special to me. I want to be a drifter, free as the breeze, drinking tequila with a dark stranger in a Mexican bar tonight, meditating with Tibetan monks tomorrow, surfing in Australia the day after; and I want to have the security and joy of deep commitments and strong community ties, with a family and true friends whom I love and who love me. "Psychics" make profitable use of this ambivalence, reading your "deepest secret desires": "You are deeply committed to your friends, but sometimes you wish you could be free of all ties and commitments. You work hard at your job and your studies, but sometimes you are tempted to throw it all away and strike out for unknown lands." It's an easy way to make a buck, and it doesn't require any special powers.

So we sometimes find in ourselves values that are in conflict, genuine values that cannot be reconciled. It is hardly surprising that we discover the same thing when we look at the various elements of our society. We value "rugged individualism," the "self-made man," the tough resilience that doesn't ask for help from anyone. Yet we also admire acts of generosity and kindness and helping those in need. When Jesus of Nazareth described his true disciples, he did not mention any religious memberships or essential doctrines; instead, he insisted that his true disciples were those who fed the hungry, helped the homeless, cared for the sick. Most of us, however strongly we profess belief in "rugged individualism," also find those teachings of care for the less fortunate a very important element of morality. We all recognize that we ourselves were not "self-made," and that we needed—and still need—lots of support in order to gain success: the support of our families, our teachers, our community, our culture.

Teresa makes a remarkable new discovery that leads to a major new drug treatment for bone cancer, and she did it with "no help from anyone." But of course Teresa was nurtured by her family for many years as a child and adolescent, she was taught in schools that received public funding, and she carried on a research tradition that was developed and refined by generations of scientists who went before her: Teresa did not invent the scientific method, nor did she discover for herself all the biological and chemical knowledge that made her discovery possible, nor did she build the advanced technology (including computers) that propelled her research forward. One might also mention the system of police and medical care that protected her from disease and crime and the free society that made it possible for her to safely pursue her own research project. Some people will want to put more emphasis on Teresa's genuine personal accomplishment—"she did it herself, she deserves all the credit and all the benefits that come from her discovery"—while others will be more attentive to the multitude of people, present and past, who contributed the essential foundations and conditions for Teresa's research. It's good to give special recognition to those who make special contributions to the good of society; it's also good to recognize that when anyone makes a special contribution, that contribution could not have happened without the work of less heralded bakers and firefighters and candlestick makers, and credit also belongs to the much larger society.

We want freedom to pursue our own paths, stupid and destructive though they might be; we also want to protect people from hazards. So we require people to wear seatbelts when they drive, but we allow them to go hang gliding and mountain bike racing—much more dangerous activities than driving without a seat belt. We want freedom to follow our own values; but we worry when there is no common core of values that unifies our culture. We believe everyone should be free to use their own resources as they wish; but we also insist that some of those resources be used to guarantee a decent minimum living standard for all members of our society.

It is possible that these may be genuine value conflicts, a genuine plurality of values that cannot be reconciled or ordered. We shouldn't decide that too quickly: Perhaps there really is a reliable ranking order that can eliminate any real conflicts. But there is also the possibility that no such objective ranking can be found, and genuine conflicts may remain. If so, it is important to consider that often this is a conflict over the appropriate ordering of values that we all share, but that we rank differently. Even the most rugged of Western cowboy individuals see the value of lending a helping hand; and those most committed to the value of mutual social support understand the appeal of being able to go your own way, and "doing it for yourself." The two may not be able to agree on how to order those values, and which values take precedence; but that doesn't mean that they must view one another as implacable enemies. There may be deep value conflicts that cannot be settled and value disputes that will endure. If that is the case, both sides will be better off understanding the strongest points of their opponents rather than distorting opposing views and treating opponents as moral monsters.

We are a very diverse society, in a world of diverse societies. Such diversity is generally a source of great strength and creativity, though it can be and often is a source of deep conflict. Unless we wish to *force* everyone to give vocal and behavioral agreement to a single set of values—a policy favored by the medieval Roman Catholic Church, and more recently by Taliban fundamentalists—then we will remain a wonderfully diverse society, with many values and many ways of life. Learning to live with disagreements, dissents, and uncertainty is not easy. Avoiding the temptation to demonize those who disagree with us is the first step in such learning. Learning to live with—and even appreciate—values that are different from our own is the very valuable second step. When we have value disagreements, the possibility of genuine *value diversity* reminds us that those with whom we disagree may actually *share* many of our values even though they order them somewhat differently.

The various ethical approaches and guides are not an easy ticket to ethical answers; indeed, applying the techniques may well lead to *different* answers. These are ways of trying to gain better perspective on questions, of viewing ethical disputes from new angles. If you are looking for simple rules to guide all your ethical considerations, I'm afraid you looked in vain in this chapter. If that's what you want, there are plenty of sources that will give you all the answers: politicians, self-help books, moral guides, and religions both old and new. There is no shortage of people absolutely certain of all the ethical answers, and who are perfectly willing to supply them for you—sometimes for cash, other times in

exchange for your complete allegiance. But if you prefer to draw your own critical conclusions rather than mindlessly accept doctrines, then these are some helpful ways of
proceeding. For some questions, many of us will not reach a settled conclusion even for
ourselves. But if we examine the questions carefully, by our own lights, in the absence of
distortion and deception and recrimination and personal attacks, then we will have taken
significant steps toward intelligent and congenial and cooperative examination of some
very important questions—and in our contemporary atmosphere of slogans, distortions,
and insults, that would be a major accomplishment. Respectful critical discussion won't
always lead to a resolution of our conflicts—but it has a better chance than strawman
distortions and ad hominem abuse.

Questions for Reflection

1. Every year, thousands of people visit Arches National Park, in Utah. They stand in awe of the amazing rock structures and the desolate beauty of the deep canyons and sheer cliffs. Three centuries ago, most Europeans would have had a very different reaction. They would have gazed upon a desolate scene of disorder and chaos. Rather than a sense of magnificent austere beauty, they would have viewed the scene with disgust, eager to return as swiftly as possible to civilization and its order and regularity. They might have said: "A proper English formal garden, with every shrub and flower precisely ordered and arranged: now *that* is beautiful, not this wild disorder of rocks and cliffs." So if you find the Utah canyons and cliffs and deserts beautiful, you have a very *different* sense of beauty than that of 17th century Europeans. If people can have such dramatically different senses of what is beautiful, might they also have very different senses or "intuitions" or "feelings" of what is moral and immoral? If so, is that a problem for theories that rely on such feelings?

2. Is loyalty to moral principles a virtue? For example, if we say that Joe has *never wavered* in his commitment to the moral principles he believes in, is that loyalty to his own moral principles *in itself* a virtue? (Racism is surely a morally bad moral view; but is a wishy-washy racist worse than a steadfast racist?)

3. A few years ago, the Canadian Bar Association was formulating a new code of ethics. One of the issues it was considering was whether lawyers should be barred from sleeping with their clients. The code of ethics for doctors and psychologists prohibits sexual contact between professional and client/patient; should lawyers adopt the same principle?

   The Canadian ethical code for lawyers requires that lawyers must always keep their clients' interest paramount. Also, lawyers acknowledge that sometimes clients are deeply dependent on their lawyers, and very vulnerable; so there may exist a significant imbalance of power between lawyer and client. With those points in mind, members of the Canadian Bar Association considered four options. One, they could simply ignore the issue in the new code of ethics. Two, they could prohibit sexual relations in which the lawyer "takes advantage" of the client by exploiting a difference in power. Three, they could prohibit sexual relations except when a consensual sexual relationship already exists *prior* to the lawyer/client relationship. Or four, they could prohibit *all* sexual relations between lawyer and client.

   Which of the four options (or perhaps some other) would you recommend? In making your recommendation, were you helped by one of the "ethical guides" discussed in this chapter, such as virtue theory or utilitarianism or the detached observer perspective? Perhaps by a combination of those methods?

3. Jesus taught that when someone strikes us, we should "turn the other cheek"; that when someone harms us, we should forgive and not seek vengeance. In "honor" cultures and traditions,

if someone strikes you or insults you, your personal honor demands that you strike back (at its most extreme, your personal honor would require that you challenge the other person to a deadly duel). Is this a case of cultures having intractable value differences? If Jesus were attempting to convince members of an honor culture to change their ways, which of the ways of approaching ethical issues do you think would be most effective?

4. Players in the popular World of Warcraft (WoW) internet game often form "guilds" or groups that join together in mutual defense and to attack other groups. One dedicated member of such a guild died (in real life, not in the game), and the members of her guild decided to hold a memorial service for her within the game that she loved. They announced the planned memorial on a WoW open forum, and one of the members of her guild logged into her account and placed the deceased woman's character at her favorite game site, a lake. Other game characters from her guild came by the lake site to pay their respects and honor their gaming friend. Members of a rival guild, on learning of the planned memorial, organized a "bombing attack" on the memorial service, thus destroying many of their rivals and winning kill points.

Those game players who had participated in the memorial service were outraged, and accused the rival guild of being underhanded and disrespectful. Was the attack on the memorial service unfair? Was it morally wrong? Was it a violation of a "gaming social contract"?

Suppose you have a friend—in real-life—who is a member of rival guild in WoW. One day he leaves his laptop in the library while he goes to lunch, and you open his WoW account, move his character to a vulnerable location, and destroy him. Would that be unfair? Would it be morally wrong?

5. Suppose that you are trying to decide what you should do in a particular case; for example, you are deciding whether to purchase a term paper off the internet and submit it as your own work. Would it be more helpful to think about that question in terms of whether the *act* is right or wrong, or in terms of what effect this act would have on the sort of *character* of which you would approve or disapprove?

6. "All ethical issues have a correct solution, even though it is often difficult to determine what the correct solution is." Do you agree with that claim? Of the various ethical approaches discussed in his chapter, which ones would agree with that claim, and which ones would disagree?

Additional Resources

Among Kant's classic works on ethics are *Groundwork of the Metaphysics of Morals*, trans. H. J. Paton, as *The Moral Law* (London: Hutchinson, 1953); *Critique of Practical Reason*, trans. L. W. Beck (Indianapolis: Bobbs-Merrill, 1977); and *Religion within the Limits of Reason Alone*, trans. T. M. Greene and H. H. Hudson (New York: Harper and Row, 1960). Excellent works on Kant's ethics include Lewis White Beck's *A Commentary on Kant's Critique of Practical Reason* (Chicago: University of Chicago Press, 1960); and Onora O'Neill, *Constructions of Reason: Explorations of Kant's Practical Philosophy* (Cambridge: Cambridge University Press, 1989). A fascinating brief challenge to Kant's ethical system is Rae Langton's "Maria von Herbert's Challenge to Kant," which can be found in Peter Singer, ed., *Ethics* (Oxford: Oxford University Press, 1994).

Many outstanding contemporary philosophers follow (to at least some degree) the Kantian tradition in ethics. A small sample includes Kurt Baier, *The Moral Point of View* (Ithaca, NY: Cornell University Press, 1958); Marcia W. Baron, *Kantian Ethics Almost without Apology* (Ithaca, NY: Cornell University Press, 1995); Stephen Darwall, *Impartial Reason* (Ithaca, NY: Cornell University Press, 1983) and *Philosophical Ethics* (Boulder, CO: Westview Press, 1998); Alan Donagan, *The Theory of Morality* (Chicago: University of Chicago Press, 1977); Christine Korsgaard, *Creating the Kingdom of Ends* (Cambridge: Cambridge University Press, 1995) and *The Sources of Normativity* (Cambridge: Cambridge University Press, 1996); and Thomas Nagel, *The View from Nowhere* (New York: Oxford University Press, 1986). Kantian ethics can seem cold and austere. For a more engaging experience of Kantian ethics, try some essays by Thomas E. Hill, Jr., who is clearly a Kantian, but writes with grace, charm, and clarity on a variety of ethical issues. See his essays in *Respect, Pluralism, and Justice: Kantian Perspectives* (Oxford: Oxford University Press, 2000); and *Human Welfare and Moral Worth: Kantian Perspectives* (Oxford: Oxford University Press, 2002).

David Hume has two classic works on ethics and emotions (though both works also contain much more). The first is *A Treatise of Human Nature*, originally published in 1738. A good edition is by L. A. Selby-Bigge (Oxford: Clarendon Press, 1978). The second is *An Inquiry Concerning Human Understanding*, originally published in 1751. A good edition is L. A. Selby-Bigge's *Hume's Enquiries*, 2nd ed. (Oxford: Clarendon Press, 1902). Kai Nielsen's *Why Be Moral?* (Buffalo, NY: Prometheus Books, 1989) is a very readable defense of nonobjectivist ethics based in emotions.

Mencius was an ancient Confucian philosopher whose writings promote a very early version of the moral sense theory; see *The Book of Mencius*. Sentimentalism (a view that relies heavily on the emotions for ethical guidance) was a major ethical theory in the 17th and 18th centuries; among its major advocates were Lord Shaftesbury (Anthony Ashley-Cooper), in *An Inquiry Concerning Virtue, or Merit*; Francis Hutcheson, in *An Inquiry into the Original of Our Ideas of Beauty and Virtue*, and *An Essay on the Nature and Conduct of the Passions and Affections, with Illustrations upon the Moral Sense*; and Adam Smith, *Theory of Moral Sentiments*. Among contemporary advocates of various forms of sentimentalism are Simon Blackburn, in *Spreading the Word* (Oxford: Clarendon Press, 1984), *Essays in Quasi-Realism* (New York: Oxford University Press, 1993), and *Ruling Passions* (New York: Oxford University Press, 1998); Allan Gibbard, in *Wise Choices, Apt Feelings* (Cambridge, MA: Harvard University Press, 1990); and Elizabeth Anderson, *Values in Ethics and Economics* (Cambridge, MA: Harvard University Press, 1993). A good examination of contemporary sentimentalism, and the challenges it faces, can be found in Justin D'Arms and Daniel Jacobson, "Sentiment and Value," *Ethics*, 110 (2000): 722–748.

The classic utilitarian writings are Jeremy Bentham, *An Introduction to the Principles of Morals and Legislation* (London: Henry Frowde, 1823) and John Stuart Mill, *Utilitarianism* (London: Longmans, Green and Co., 1863). Perhaps the most influential contemporary utilitarian, and certainly one of the most readable, is Peter Singer. His *Writings on an Ethical Life* (New York: HarperCollins, 2000) is the work of a philosopher

thinking carefully about ethical obligations, and also striving to live his life by the right ethical standards. Whatever one thinks of Singer's views (he holds very controversial positions on abortion, animal rights, the obligations of the affluent toward those who are less fortunate, and euthanasia, and has been the target of more protests than any other contemporary philosopher), not even his fiercest critics deny that Singer is an outstanding example of someone who takes ethical issues and living ethically very seriously. Singer's *Writings on an Ethical Life* shows a dedicated utilitarian wrestling honestly with serious ethical issues. See also Singer's *Practical Ethics* (Cambridge: Cambridge University Press, 1979) for his views on a variety of ethical issues.

For a critique of utilitarian ethics, see Samuel Scheffler, *The Rejection of Consequentialism* (Oxford: Clarendon Press, 1982). An excellent debate on utilitarian ethics can be found in J. J. C. Smart and Bernard Williams, *Utilitarianism: For and Against* (Cambridge: Cambridge University Press, 1973). There are several good anthologies that examine a wide range of consequentialist and utilitarian views, including Amartya Sen and Bernard Williams, eds., *Utilitarianism and Beyond* (Cambridge: Cambridge University Press, 1982); Samuel Scheffler, *Consequentialism and Its Critics* (Oxford: Clarendon Press, 1988); Philip Petit, *Consequentialism* (Aldershot, Hants: Dartmouth, 1993); Brad Hooker, Elinor Mason, and Dale E. Miller, *Morality, Rules, and Consequences: A Critical Reader* (Lanham, MD: Rowman & Littlefield, 2000); and Stephen Darwall, *Consequentialism* (Malden, MA: Blackwell, 2003). A very good online source for a survey of contemporary consequentialism/utilitarianism is the work of Walter Sinnott-Armstrong in the online *Stanford Encyclopedia of Philosophy*; go to http://plato.stanford.edu/entries/consequentialism.

The classic sources for social contract theory are Thomas Hobbes's *Leviathan*, John Locke's *Second Treatise on Government*, and Jean-Jacques Rousseau's *Social Contract* (*Du Contrat Social*). Hobbes's *Leviathan* is available from Bobbs-Merrill (Indianapolis: Bobbs-Merrill, 1958); it was originally published in 1651. Locke's *Second Treatise on Government* was originally published in 1690; an accessible edition is from Bobbs-Merrill (Indianapolis: Bobbs-Merrill, Library of Liberal Arts, 1952). Rousseau's *Social Contract* was originally published in 1762; it can be found in an edition edited by R. Masters (New York: St. Martin's Press, 1978).

Discussions of social contract theory include Jean Hampton, *Hobbes and the Social Contract Tradition* (Cambridge: Cambridge University Press, 1986); and

P. Riley, *Will and Political Legitimacy: A Critical Exposition of Social Contract Theory in Hobbes, Locke, Rousseau, Kant, and Hegel* (Cambridge, MA: Harvard University Press, 1982).

David Gauthier's version of contractarian theory can be found in *Morals by Agreement* (Oxford: Oxford University Press, 1986) and *Moral Dealing* (Ithaca, NY: Cornell University Press, 1990). For discussion and critique of Gauthier's theory, see Peter Vallentyne, editor, *Contractarianism and Rational Choice* (New York: Cambridge University Press, 1991).

Probably the best-known philosophical book of the late 20th century presented an updated version of social contract theory: John Rawls, *A Theory of Justice* (London: Oxford University Press, 1971). Among the many critical examinations of Rawls' theory are (from a libertarian perspective) Robert Nozick, *Anarchy, State, and Utopia* (New York: Basic Books, 1974); (a feminist critique) Susan Moller Okin, *Justice, Gender, and the Family* (New York: Basic Books, 1989); and (from an egalitarian perspective) G. A. Cohen, *Rescuing Justice and Equality* (Cambridge, MA: Harvard University Press, 2008). See also the recent study by philosopher-economist Amartya Sen, *The Idea of Justice* (Cambridge, MA: Harvard University Press, 2009).

Russ Shafer-Landau, in *Moral Realism: A Defense* (Oxford: Clarendon Press, 2003), critiques the general constructivist approach to ethics, including social contract ethics. A strong critic of the social contract tradition is Martha C. Nussbaum, in *Frontiers of Justice: Disability, Nationality, Species Membership* (Cambridge, MA: Harvard University Press, 2006). Other critics include Carole Pateman, *The Sexual Contract* (Stanford: Stanford University Press, 1988); Virginia Held, *Feminist Morality: Transforming Culture, Society, and Politics* (Chicago: University of Chicago Press, 1993); and Eva Feder Kittay, *Love's Labor* (New York: Routledge, 1999). Good online sources for material on social contract theory include *Stanford Encyclopedia of Philosophy* at http://plato.stanford.edu/entries/contractarianism; and "The Internet Encyclopedia of Philosophy" at http://www.ut.edu/s/soc-cont.htm.

The classic source for virtue ethics is Aristotle's *Nicomachean Ethics*. Perhaps the most influential contemporary book on virtue theory is by Alasdair MacIntyre, *After Virtue* (Notre Dame, IN.: University of Notre Dame Press, 1981). An excellent exposition of contemporary virtue theory is found in Edmund Pincoffs, *Quandaries and Virtues* (Lawrence: University of Kansas Press, 1986). An intriguing brief case for virtue theory is presented by novelist and philosopher Iris Murdoch in *The Sovereignty of Good* (New York: Schocken Books,

1971), though Murdoch's work encompasses a great deal more than just a defense of virtue theory. Other influential accounts of virtue theory include Philippa Foot, *Virtues and Vices* (Berkeley: University of California, 1978) and *Natural Goodness* (Oxford: Oxford University Press, 2001); Michael Slote, *Goods and Virtues* (New York: Oxford University Press, 1984), *From Morality to Virtue* (New York: Oxford University Press, 1992), and *Morals from Motives* (Oxford: Oxford University Press, 2000); and Rosalind Hursthouse, *On Virtue Ethics* (Oxford: Oxford University Press, 1999). An excellent critical review of recent versions of virtue theory is found in David Copp and David Sobel, "Morality and Virtue: An Assessment of Some Recent Work in Virtue Ethics," *Ethics*, 114 (April 2004), 514–544. An interesting discussion of virtue theory was prompted by Steven M. Cahn's very brief essay, "The Happy Immoralist." Cahn's essay, together with replies and comments by a number of writers (including several virtue theorists), can be found in *Journal of Social Philosophy*, 35, no. 1 (Spring 2004), 1–20.

Good anthologies on virtue ethics include Roger Crisp and Michael Slote, *Virtue Ethics* (Oxford: Oxford University Press, 1997); and Stephen Darwall, *Virtue Ethics* (Oxford: Blackwell, 2003). Good online discussions can be found in the "Stanford Encyclopedia of Philosophy," at http://plato.stanford.edu/entries/ethics-virtue; in "The Internet Encyclopedia of Philosophy" at http://www.iep.utm.edu/v/virtue.htm; and in Lawrence Hinman's *Ethics Updates*, at http://ethics.acusd.edu/theories/Aristotle/index.html.

Carol Gilligan, *In a Different Voice: Psychological Theory and Women's Development* (Cambridge, MA: Harvard University Press, 1982), had a powerful impact on the contemporary development of care ethics. Lawrence Kohlberg's account of his research on moral development (which prompted Gilligan's book) is in *The Philosophy of Moral Development: Moral Stages and the Idea of Justice* (New York: Harper and Row, 1981). The Gilligan/Kohlberg work has been extensively discussed; see articles by Kohlberg and Owen Flanagan in *Ethics*, 92, no. 3 (April 1982), 499–528; and in *Ethics*, 97 (1987), 622–637; see also Owen Flanagan and Kathryn Jackson, "Justice, Care, and Gender: The Kolberg-Gilligan Debate Revisited"; and Lawrence Blum, "Gilligan and Kohlberg: Implications for Moral Theory," *Ethics*, 98 (April 1988), 472–491. Nel Noddings's work has been influential in both philosophy and education; see her *Caring: A Feminine Approach to Ethics and Moral Education* (Berkeley: University of California Press, 1984); and *Educating Moral People: A Caring Alternative to*

Character Education (New York: Teachers College Press, 2002). Annette C. Baier is a clear and cogent writer on this topic, and is particularly insightful in placing care ethics in a larger philosophical perspective. See her *Moral Prejudices* (Cambridge, MA.: Harvard University Press, 1994). Among the best advocates of care ethics is Lawrence A. Blum, *Friendship, Altruism and Morality* (London: Routledge & Kegan Paul, 1980). Viginia Held's edited collection, *Justice and Care* (Boulder, CO: Westview Press, 1995), is an excellent collection of essays on the subject. A very good and wide-ranging anthology is Eva Feder Kittay and Diana Meyers, editors, *Women and Moral Theory* (Totowa, NJ: Rowman & Littlefield, 1987). Other good anthologies are Mary Jeanne Larrabee, *An Ethic of Care: Feminist and Interdisciplinary Perspectives* (New York: Routledge, 1993); James P. Sterba, *Controversies in Feminism* (Lanham, MD: Rowman & Littlefield, 2001); and Samantha Brennan, *Feminist Moral Philosophy* (Calgary, Alberta: University of Calgary Press, 2002). Online, see the feminist ethics entry (by Rosemary Tong) in the *Stanford Encyclopedia of Philosophy* at http://plato.stanford.edu/entries/ feminist ethics; and in "Ethical Updates" see the Gender and Ethical Theory section at http://ethics.acusd.edu/ theories/Gender/index.html.

Among early advocates of value pluralism is William James, in "The Moral Philosopher and the Moral Life"; the essay (which first appeared as an 1891 lecture) can be found in William James, *The Will to Believe* (New York: Dover, 1960). Perhaps the best-known contemporary advocate of value pluralism is Isaiah Berlin (whose value pluralism shades into his political pluralism); see his *Four Essays on Liberty* (Oxford: Oxford University Press, 1969). One of the strongest contemporary monistic opponents of value pluralism is Ronald Dworkin, in *Sovereign Virtue* (Cambridge, MA: Harvard University Press, 2000) and *Justice for Hedgehogs* (Cambridge, MA: Harvard University Press, 2011). There are a number of interesting essays on pluralism—with special attention to the pluralistic arguments of Isaiah Berlin, and including a critique by Ronald Dworkin—in *The Legacy of Isaiah Berlin*, edited by Mark Lilla, Ronald Dworkin, and Robert B. Silvers (New York: New York Review of Books, 2001).

MYSEARCHLAB CONNECTIONS

Go to *Ethics Updates* at http://ethics.sandiego.edu. Under "Ethical Theory," you can find excellent material on several topics discussed in this chapter: Aristotle and Virtue Ethics, Gender and Moral Theory, Justice, Kant and Deontology, and Utilitarianism.

The *Stanford Encyclopedia of Philosophy* is a wonderful source for almost any topic in philosophy, including ethics. It is at plato.stanford.edu. See the articles on "Kant's Moral Philosophy," "Original Position" (on John Rawls), "Scottish Philosophy in the 18th Century" (the section on "Smith and Moral Sentiments"), "Consequentialism," "Virtue Ethics," and "Feminist Ethics."

ABORTION

Chapter Outline

There is probably no contemporary issue that generates deeper or more acrimonious dispute than abortion. Across the picket lines, the rhetoric is heated to an incendiary pitch. "It's not a choice, it's a child." "If men could become pregnant, abortion would be a sacrament." Pro-life demonstrators carry placards of bloody fetuses, and accuse their opponents of being nothing less than mass murderers. Pro-choice demonstrators claim their opponents are trying to deprive women of the right to control their own bodies, and equate those who oppose the right to legal abortions with rapists. Is there any way to get beyond such deeply hostile views?

This is an issue on which compromise is possible, but few on either side find it satisfactory. For example, we could pass laws that abortions are allowed only in the first trimester or only to protect the life and health of the mother or only in cases of rape or incest. But while political deal-making may result in such compromises, those positions do not establish any common ground and leave both sides profoundly dissatisfied.

Adversaries in the abortion debate tend to demonize one another, attributing the worst possible motives to those on the other side. But when they actually get to know one another, often they find their opponents are not as vile as they had supposed. Some who have yelled insults at pro-choice vs. pro-life rallies have found themselves joining hands to oppose capital punishment, or protest against a war, or even to work together in a homeless shelter. After all, some of the most spirited opponents of abortion unite with the most ardent pro-choice advocates on the question of capital punishment.

Strawman Distortions

If we attend a rally in which pro-lifers are confronting pro-choicers, it is not difficult to find some nasty folks on both sides of the picket line: There will be some on the pro-choice side who are only out for political gain, some who believe they should not be obligated to or inconvenienced by anything or anyone, perhaps some men who see abortion as an easy way to avoid any unpleasant consequences—such as child support payments—for their irresponsible behavior. On the other side, we find a few people who really do not want women to have control of their own bodies, some who would like to ban birth control as well as abortions, and even a few drawn to the opportunity for violence and murder in a "righteous" cause. But there are many other people on both sides. It is a strawman distortion to characterize all those on the side you oppose as wanting to deny women their basic rights or as caring only for fetuses and nothing for babies or (on the other side) as eager to murder babies.

Consider some of the common strawman fallacies that occur in the debate over abortion. For example, it is sometimes claimed that pro-choice people see abortion as a desirable form of birth control. But whatever one thinks of abortion, no one regards it as a desirable form of birth control. No one likes abortions; can you honestly imagine a woman wishing to become pregnant so she can have an abortion? And can you imagine anyone finding abortion preferable to the ease of taking birth control pills? Abortions occur when the alternatives seem even worse.

A second strawman distortion: Pro-choicers believe parents should always be allowed to kill their children. Whatever one's view of abortion, there is an obvious difference between abortion and infanticide: You can't offer a fetus/*un*born child for adoption. Pro-choice advocates believe that the rights of women to control their own reproductive systems are essential for the autonomy and dignity of women; after birth, that question is removed, for the child is no longer occupying the mother's body.

On the other side of the picket line, it is sometimes claimed that pro-lifers want to subjugate women. That is a strawman distortion. Even if some members of the pro-life movement hold such despicable views, it is obvious that most members of the pro-life movement do not. In fact, some pro-life advocates regard access to elective abortion as a means of protecting abusive *men*, rather than a promotion of the woman's right to control of her own body. Men want to enjoy unprotected sexual encounters with none of the responsibilities. When their partners become pregnant, men pressure them to have an abortion (to avoid the burden of child support payments or to avoid alerting their wives to their philandering or to avoid harm to their reputation in the community—think of the wealthy boss who pressures his vulnerable and underpaid secretary to have an abortion after their "consensual affair" results in a pregnancy).

Now we come to some claims that are more difficult. These are views held by a substantial number of pro-life advocates, especially some of the leaders of the movement; but they are not held by a majority—or even a significant minority—of those who consider themselves pro-life and against abortion. So if we attribute these views to *all* (or even *most*) pro-lifers, we are indulging in a strawman attack. First, the claim that pro-life advocates want to end not only abortions but also contraception. Many (obviously not all) Catholics oppose abortion; but while church leaders may condemn contraception, very few members of the church are convinced by that condemnation. Rachel Jones, the lead author of a 2011 study by the Guttmacher Institute, found that Catholics and evangelical Christians are just as likely to use the pill and other artificial methods of contraception as anyone else. Some strong advocacy groups who oppose abortion do also oppose contraception: the officials of the Catholic Church, the American Life League, the Family Research Council, for example. But to suggest that the pro-life position must be coupled with opposition to contraception is to set up a strawman target. Second, most—not all, of course—of those who are pro-life believe that in the case of rape, a woman should have a right to abortion, and an even higher percentage of pro-lifers believe that abortion is morally acceptable when it is necessary in order to save the life of the mother. But there are clear exceptions. In Brazil, a nine-year-old girl was raped and impregnated by her stepfather. Doctors concluded that if the pregnancy were allowed to continue, she would die (her uterus was too small to carry a fetus to term). In March of 2011, the pregnant child was brought to a hospital in Recife, in northeastern Brazil, where an abortion was performed to save her life. The Catholic Archbishop (with the Pope's approval) condemned the abortion, and excommunicated the girl's mother as well as the medical team who performed the abortion. In Phoenix, in 2009, St. Joseph's Hospital performed an abortion for a mother of four, after concluding that the mother was likely to die of pulmonary hypertension if the pregnancy continued. Bishop Thomas Olmsted (with the approval of the United States Conference of Catholic Bishops) excommunicated Sister Margaret McBride, an ethicist at the hospital, for approving the abortion; and withdrew its ties to St. Joseph's Hospital. So clearly there are those who believe that abortions cannot be allowed to save the mother's life, not even if the mother is a victim of child rape. But few in the pro-life movement agree with that position, and attributing such a view to all (or the majority of) pro-lifers is setting up a strawman opponent.

What Is the Common Ground?

There are those who appear to believe that "life begins at conception and ends at birth"— that is, those who are zealous in insisting that the fetus not be destroyed, but who are apparently indifferent about whether the newborn child has decent housing, health care, and nutrition. They vehemently oppose abortion, but also oppose efforts to provide access to good prenatal care for all pregnant women. With such people, it is plausible to suppose that they are more interested in restricting the rights of women than in genuinely caring for the child, whether the child is born or "unborn." But the claim that *all* pro-lifers are like that is a strawman fallacy that blocks real consideration of the issues. Certainly there are those in the pro-life movement who are committed to preventing abortions and *also* committed to providing excellent prenatal care for *all* expectant mothers, as well as providing safe and satisfactory housing and good nutritional food and excellent pediatric services for all infants and children. Imagine two enormous rallies at the national Capitol, with pro-choice forces lining one side of the mall and pro-life protesters on the other. Just before both the rallies begin, leaders of both groups appear together on the steps of the Lincoln Memorial, and make this announcement: "We have decided to cancel both of the planned rallies; instead, we are *all* joining together to rally in favor of guaranteed health care for *all* children in the United States." No doubt some people would walk away in anger, but many on *both* sides would stay and campaign for children's health care.

So what might we say to those—some from both sides—who leave? Perhaps there is nothing we could say: It may be that we could find no common ground, no starting point for conversation. But for the moment, let's concentrate on those who *remain*: the pro-lifers as well as the pro-choicers. And there—if we get beyond the slogans and the screaming— we can find important common ground. No matter how steadfastly pro-life or pro-choice you are, you are likely to find some admirable persons on the other side. After all, *both* groups are deeply concerned to protect those who are particularly vulnerable. If you are pro-choice, look beyond the shouting and the signs at some of the people on the other side: What are they campaigning for? (*Not* the ones whose goal is to keep women subordinate and under control; they already left, remember? So look past the stereotypes and the slogans, and look for some of the genuinely admirable people who are on the other side; why are *they* spending their afternoon participating in a pro-life demonstration?) They are deeply concerned to protect the lives of perhaps the most vulnerable in our entire society, those who have no power to protect themselves: the unborn children. Now of course, if you are pro-choice, you probably have a very different view of the "unborn child"; in the first place, you call it a fetus, not an "unborn child." And you probably do not think it qualifies as a *person*: At the early stages, it lacks the nervous system required for minimal consciousness; and even at a later stage, it lacks any level of self-consciousness. Nonetheless, for the pro-life demonstrators, the fetus/unborn child *is* a living and very vulnerable person; and working to protect the vulnerable is something that you—as a pro-choice advocate—can agree is a virtuous pursuit. So even if you believe that the pro-life demonstrators are *wrong* in thinking of the fetus as a vulnerable *person* in need of protection, you can recognize and applaud their *goal* of protecting the vulnerable.

What about the view from the other side? Can the pro-lifer find positive traits in the pro-choice demonstrators? *Not* if all pro-choice advocates favor the killing of all children, whenever a parent chooses to do so; and *not* if the only motive of pro-lifers is the subjugation and control of women. But such demonization of opponents is the problem, not the solution. As a pro-lifer, you may believe that pro-choice proponents are dreadfully mistaken in the way they think of the "unborn child," and you may think that they are promoting terrible wrongs because of that mistake. But what the pro-choicers *want* is something you believe is profoundly important: They, like you, want to protect the rights of a group that has traditionally been mistreated and exploited and denied their basic rights. Women in the United States were denied the right to vote until 1920. In 1966, the Alabama Supreme Court ruled that women could be excluded from juries (for their own good, of course). Many religions continue to treat women as second-class citizens (in the Roman Catholic Church, women cannot be priests, much less bishops or Pope; and Protestant fundamentalist sects rejoice in Paul's instruction to "Let the women learn in silence with all subjection"). Only in the past 20 to 30 years have U.S. laws banned spousal rape (before that, husbands had the legal right to rape their wives). And though it may seem difficult to imagine for most contemporary students, only a few decades ago there was enormous controversy over contraception methods that gave women the power to avoid pregnancy: Contraception was condemned largely *because* it gave women power. There are still places in the world where a woman who is a victim of rape is punished by flogging or even stoning. So just as pro-lifers demonstrate to protect the vulnerable "unborn child," in like manner pro-choice demonstrators aim at protecting the rights of women who have also been vulnerable to oppression. There remain profound differences between pro-choice and pro-life advocates; but if we look past the shouting and the heated rhetoric, we can also find important common ground.

Arguments in Favor of Legalized Abortion

1. A common argument in favor of legal abortions notes that if abortions are made illegal that will *not* stop abortions: Abortions will still be performed, but they will be much more dangerous. Of course the wealthy will have access to safe professional abortions, in sterile settings; but the poor will suffer. Opponents claim—probably correctly—that there would be significantly fewer abortions; and because they regard abortion as so horrible (as the killing of an "unborn" baby), they believe that abortion should be banned, even though some women will be injured and some will die seeking abortions that could have been performed safely in legal clinics. Opponents of abortion regard that as tragic, but that tragedy is unlikely to sway one who regards abortion as a particularly horrible crime. (Perhaps there will be some abortion opponents who see the death of those seeking abortions as just punishment. That is *not* the view of most people who oppose legalized abortions; rather, they regard the death of the mother following a botched illegal abortion as a *double* tragedy, involving the death of both the mother and the unborn child. To claim that pro-lifers regard the death of the woman seeking an abortion as a positive and rightly deserved result is to attribute a cruel straw-man distortion to those who favor banning abortions.) In short, banning legal abortions will cause special suffering for poor women; whether one regards a reduction in the number of abortions as sufficient to *outweigh* that increased suffering will probably depend on whether one is pro-choice or pro-life.

2. A more important pro-choice argument is that the fetus—certainly at the earliest stages of pregnancy, when most abortions occur—is *not* a person, and so a woman having an abortion is *not* causing harm to another person. To the contrary, being denied the right to control her own body—including the right to control her own reproductive system—*would* cause harm to a person (the person whose right to an abortion is being denied). The status of the fetus/unborn child—is it really a *person*?—has been the central question in most of the abortion debate. The question is a difficult and controversial one, and we seem no closer to resolving it today than we were years ago.

   At what point—in the development from fertilized egg to fully developed fetus—does *personhood* occur? St. Thomas Aquinas, probably the greatest of the medieval Catholic theologians, claimed that *ensoulment* occurred after 40 days if the fetus was male, and after 90 days in the case of a female fetus. But that seems rather arbitrary (not to mention sexist). Because trying to draw a line seems arbitrary, most pro-lifers insist that the person exists *at conception* (and so they fiercely oppose the "morning after" pill that prevents the fertilized egg from attaching to the wall of the uterus, because that fertilized egg—that embryo—is just as much a person as the newborn baby or a six-year-old child). But for most people, it is hard to regard a fertilized egg—this tiny, almost microscopic clump of cells—as a full person. In approximately one-third of cases in which an egg is fertilized by a sperm cell, the resulting embryo fails to attach to the uterus wall, and does not develop further. The woman will never even know that an embryo was present, and it would seem incredibly strange to suggest that when the embryo fails to attach, the woman has suffered the "death of a child." But if we observe the embryo (after it has attached to the uterus wall) continue its gradual development, we never observe any clear line marking the stage of becoming a *person*. Any line we draw will be arbitrary; until, that is, we reach birth, at which time the *baby* is detached from the mother, and can live independently of the mother (and will do so, if it is adopted). That is *not* an arbitrary line, for it is the line that marks the point at which the fetus/unborn child is *not* occupying space within the mother's body, and the continued existence of the baby does *not* depend on the mother.

In short, this pro-choice argument insists (as Judith Jarvis Thomson puts it) that "a fetus is no more a person than an acorn is an oak tree." Or to use another image, a tadpole is not a frog. The embryo in its early weeks is far from being a real human baby (in fact, it cannot at that stage be distinguished visually from the embryo of a dog, much less from that of a chimpanzee). No doubt in many cases it will *grow* into a baby, but it is not at that point an "unborn child," any more than the acorn is an "untrunked tree."

3. The most important pro-choice argument is based on the fundamental *right* of women to control something so intimate and personal as their own reproductive systems, their own *bodies*. To *force* women to carry a fetus for nine months is to claim that ultimately women should *not* have control of their own bodies.

   Probably the best-known argument of this type was developed by Judith Jarvis Thomson, in her *violinist* argument. Thomson asks you to imagine awakening one morning in a hospital room, with a large double tube in your arm that is attached to a bedside pump, and another double tube running from the pump to another bed and attached to a man who appears to be sleeping. As you are trying to get your bearings and decide whether this is all a bad dream, a doctor walks into your room: "I'm glad you're awake. Look, last night a terrible thing happened. You were drugged, then kidnapped and brought to this hospital room and hooked up to this pump and through the pump to the fellow in the other bed. That guy is a famous violinist, and he has suffered acute kidney failure. His kidneys can no longer remove the impurities from his blood, and there is no kidney transplant available for him; he has a rare blood type, and unfortunately kidney dialysis machines do not work on that blood type, and so this great violinist was approaching death. This nefarious group, the Society of Music Lovers, somehow got access to medical records, and discovered that you are the uniquely perfect blood match for the violinist, so they drugged you, brought you here, and hooked you up to the violinist. Now his blood is flowing into your body, being purified by your good healthy kidneys, and then returned purified to the violinist. You are keeping him alive! Without you, he would soon die. We want you to understand that we had nothing to do with all of this, and we think it was dreadfully wrong for these people to kidnap you and hook you up to the violinist without your consent. But the problem is, now that you are hooked up to the violinist, we must require that you *remain* hooked up; because if you unhook yourself, the violinist would die, and we cannot allow that. As soon as we are able to build a dialysis machine for the violinist's special blood type, then we'll transfer the violinist to that machine, you will be unhooked and free to go. But until that time, you must stay hooked up to the violinist, whether you like it or not." What would your response be? Most people insist that it is *wrong* to *force* someone to remain hooked up to the violinist. It might be *nice* of you, even noble of you, to remain hooked up to the violinist so that he can live; but no one has the right to *require* you to stay hooked up: No one should be able to forcibly control what happens to your body.

Thomson offers this elaborate example to argue that in cases of rape, even if we *concede* that the fetus is a full *person*—just as the violinist is a person—and that the fetus/person will die if the woman unhooks herself (if the woman has an abortion), women should still have the *right* to an abortion: Just as you should have the right to unhook yourself from the violinist, even though by doing so the violinist will die. This is a *limited* argument for the right of abortion. In the violinist case, you were kidnapped, you did not voluntarily do anything to be hooked up to the violinist, and you never gave consent. The analogous case is one in which a woman becomes pregnant as a result of rape: She certainly never consents or does anything voluntarily to "hook herself up" to the fetus. So if you believe that you have a right to unhook yourself from the violinist although that will cause the death of the violinist, then you must also conclude that a woman who was a victim of rape has a right to unhook herself from the fetus/unborn child, *even if* we count the fetus as a full person. So (Thomson argues) the right to an abortion is based on the woman's right to control over her own body, and that right takes precedence even if one believes that the fetus is a person. If the pregnancy is the result of *consensual* sex, then further argument would be needed to establish the right to an abortion. But since many who oppose abortion insist that abortion is wrong even in the case of rape, this is an important argument. Furthermore, Thomson's argument shifts the focus *away* from the traditional dispute about whether the fetus is or is not a person, and instead makes the debate about the rights of the *woman* to control of her own body.

Arguments against Legalized Abortion

There is really only one argument against abortion: Abortion is the purposeful killing of a human being, the murder of a person. (Secondary arguments depend on that first argument: For example, abortion weakens respect for life and leads to the breakdown of society. That claim depends on the starting point that abortion is a terrible wrong.) Is this clump of cells—this very early fetus, or even earlier embryo—a human being? It is indistinguishable from the fetus of many closely related species; there is no brain stem; if there is any consciousness, it is at the level of animals such as a paramecium. But then the argument becomes: It will *develop* into a human person. True; and an acorn will, in the right conditions, develop into a mighty oak tree; but the acorn is not an oak tree, nor is a tadpole a frog. Preventing a *potential* human being from becoming an existent human being is another matter: Every time a healthy young woman and a healthy young man refrain from sexual relations (or use contraceptives), they are preventing the development of a potential human being; but if we prohibited such restraint, the world population problem would be a lot worse than it is now.

This is an intractable issue, and one that no examination of biological evidence will resolve. That is why many pro-life advocates insist on drawing the line at conception: Otherwise, any point selected will seem arbitrary. (That is why they oppose not only the "morning after" pill, but also any birth control device that prevents a fertilized egg from attaching to the uterus wall and thus developing into a fetus.) But in fact very few people—even fervent pro-lifers—regard a fertilized egg that fails to implant in the womb as a human baby. After all, it is estimated that one-third of fertilized eggs will fail to implant (even without using any form of contraception); and few of us regard the loss of those fertilized eggs as the death of a child.

- -

At some point—some inexact and indefinable point—the fetus *does* become differentiated into a brain, arms, legs, and heart. At some point, there is very little difference—except in location—between a newborn baby and a well-developed fetus (indeed, in the case of premature births, the fetus at a later stage may be more developed than the premature newborn). Now the arbitrary shoe is on the other foot: If it is arbitrary to determine when the developing fetus becomes a real human being, or a real person, then surely it is also arbitrary to decide when a well-developed infant (whether newborn or in the womb) is a person. When does one become a genuine person? Some argue that this occurs only through extensive socialization. Abandoned infants do not develop into persons; indeed, if they are fed and protected, but given no other care or affection, they tend to become more like animals than human children. But this argument cuts both ways: It would seem to allow infanticide, and that is not a direction that pro-choice advocates want to pursue.

This leads to a slippery slope argument: If we do not draw a strict line, then there will be no way to prevent infanticide. Indeed, we can even enlarge the argument: Unless we draw clear lines, then there is no stopping point, and any abominable behavior will be allowed. But in this case, there *is* a clear stopping point: birth. It is not an arbitrary point. Whatever the developmental status of the fetus/unborn child, or the newborn, or the newborn socialized infant, at *birth* the infant can be separated from the mother, and the mother can go her separate and unburdened way by giving the infant up for adoption. Until that time, the mother bears the burdens of a pregnancy—and if it is an unwanted pregnancy, that is a substantial burden indeed: She loses the control of her own body and of what happens within her own body.

Even if one argues that there is no clear line of fetal development marking when the fetus becomes a *person*, it does not follow that the fetus does not become an unborn child or person at some stage of development. There is no clear line between day and night (that is why we speak of twilight), but it does not follow that there is no difference between night and day. Whatever the problem in drawing a clear line, there is a difference between a tiny embryo and a fetus/unborn child of seven months' development. An acorn is not an oak tree; but an oak sapling, while it is not a mighty oak, is no longer an acorn. Whatever one thinks about the abortion question, and no matter how strongly one believes in the right of women to control their own bodies, no one can honestly regard an abortion at seven months as the equivalent of taking a morning after pill (to prevent the uterine attachment of a possible fertilized egg). Even if one insists that a woman must have the *absolute* right to control over her own body, if a woman has an abortion at seven months because her advanced pregnancy would interfere with her fun on a beach vacation, one might well conclude that the woman has done something *wrong*. So even if there are significant problems with the claim that the embryo is a person from the moment of conception, and even if we cannot specify a clear point prior to birth when a fetus becomes a person, it does not follow that the fetus/unborn child *never* has a right to moral consideration.

Have you in fact taken on some obligation to a potential fetus/infant by entering into unprotected sexual relations? The male in this passionate encounter may indeed have monetary support obligations that can be legally enforced; but that is very different from the obligation to be pregnant for nine months. Even an easy pregnancy will play hell with your marathon training, and a difficult pregnancy can involve substantial hospital stays and long periods of bed rest (not to mention the fact that giving birth can be rather unpleasant). So if that is an obligation, it is a very substantial one. Of course some women speak with great fondness of the experience of being pregnant and giving birth, and there is no doubt that it is sometimes a profoundly satisfying and wonderful experience; but not everyone experiences pregnancy in that manner, and if it is an *unwanted* pregnancy, the chances of it being an uplifting experience are substantially reduced. Furthermore, there is a great difference between a longed-for pregnancy that one embraces and approves, and a pregnancy that one is forced to carry to term against one's wishes because no alternative is allowed.

Where Do We Stand?

So what *is* the common ground where *most* pro-lifers can agree with *most* pro-choicers? First, the rights of women should be respected: Women should have equal rights with men; women should *not* be subject to rape or sexual abuse or sexual harassment. Second, everyone agrees that abortion should be *minimized*. Pro-lifers want to ban abortions, while pro-choicers want to keep abortion legal but find ways to prevent women from being in the position of having an unwanted pregnancy. So both pro-choicers and pro-lifers have a strong interest in policies that would greatly reduce the number of unwanted pregnancies. Thus both groups share the goal of preventing unwanted pregnancies that might lead to abortions (and of course, even if abortion were criminalized, abortions would still occur to end unwanted pregnancies).

Preventing unwanted pregnancies divides into two parts: First, *preventing* unwanted pregnancies, by means of effective birth control measures. In 2012, the United States Congress dramatically cut funding for Planned Parenthood because some members of Congress opposed the small number of abortions performed at some Planned Parenthood clinics. But the funding cut also meant that Planned Parenthood would not be able to provide contraceptives and family planning counseling to tens of thousands of women, as it has in the past. The result will be a substantial increase in the number of unwanted pregnancies, leading to a substantial increase in the number of abortions. Second, both groups share the goal of preventing *unwanted* pregnancies, by establishing sufficient support systems for pregnant women—support through readily available prenatal care, health care for both children and their mothers so that the family is not overburdened by health costs, good child care facilities so that working women can continue their jobs; in short, providing support that prevents women from seeking abortions due to harsh economic conditions. A woman might very reluctantly have an abortion because she fears that the costs associated with having another child would place severe hardships on her, her family, and her other children. Sincere pro-lifers and pro-choicers share a commitment to making sure that women are not economically coerced into having an abortion.

Third, whether you are pro-life or pro-choice, you agree that it is very important that pregnancies do not result in severe birth defects, and that extremely premature deliveries (which often involve the death of the infant) be avoided. Therefore both sides should agree that excellent prenatal care should be readily and conveniently available for *all* women: Whether pro-life or pro-choice, everyone agrees that it is a tragedy when a pregnant woman cannot get access to good medical care, resulting in a difficult or premature birth that may cause substantial and lasting harm to the newborn, the loss of a baby the mother wanted to deliver, and harm or even death to the woman giving birth.

That's a large and important range of agreement between pro-choice and pro-life supporters. Even with this surprisingly large area of common ground, basic and important differences remain: differences over the status of the fetus/unborn child and differences over the rights of the woman in relation to any rights enjoyed by the fetus/unborn child.

Those are difficult and significant issues, and disagreement on those issues is likely to endure. But when we step back from the slogans and harsh rhetoric, and look at the people who disagree with us on this issue and their *actual* beliefs, then even if we never reach full agreement we may at least stop demonizing our opponents.

There is no common ground among those who think it is wonderful to murder children and those who want to deny women all rights to control over their bodies and their lives; persisting in such strawman distortions and slogan-stereotypes blocks intelligent discussion of this serious question. People in the pro-choice movement do *not* want to murder babies: They want to protect the right of women to control their own bodies. Those in the pro-life movement do *not* want to deny women the right to control their own bodies: They believe that the unborn child's right to life is a *stronger* right than the woman's right to control her own body (but they do not deny that women have such a right). The remaining differences are deep and genuine. But if we work side by side to guarantee good health care for children and good prenatal health care for all women, then we shall be more likely to appreciate the good in those with whom we have an honest disagreement.

Questions for Reflection

1. Fertility clinics often produce more fertilized eggs than can be implanted, and some pro-life advocates oppose these clinics for precisely that reason. But whatever the right or wrong of such fertility procedures, it is clear that there are many such fertilized eggs in storage that will never be implanted. Some abortion opponents regard these fertilized eggs as persons (persons who will die if they are not implanted), while supporters of legalized abortion think it absurd to treat a fertilized egg in a test tube as a *person*. Set that issue aside for a moment. Whatever one's belief about the legitimacy of fertility clinic procedures and the personhood of the many fertilized eggs now preserved in clinics, there appears to be *one* thing that *everyone* agrees on: No woman should be *required* to implant a fertilized egg in order to save the life of that "person." Perhaps it would be a virtuous act if someone *volunteered* to implant a fertilized egg and carry it to term. But we all *agree* that it would be wrong for anyone to require a healthy young woman who is not pregnant to have a fertilized egg implanted in order to save the life of that fertilized egg. (Of course in this case, the woman in whom the fertilized egg is forcibly implanted is not related to either of the biological parents, but for opponents of legalized abortion that is irrelevant: The right of the fetus to life does not depend on the woman being biologically related. If a surrogate mother—who had agreed to carry the fetus of another couple—chose to abort that fetus, the opponents of legalized abortion would consider that just as wrong as the biological mother choosing abortion.) Is it true that *all* of us—whether pro-choice or pro-life—would agree that such forced implantations would be wrong? If so, that is at least *one* area of agreement between the two sides; is there any way to *expand* that limited area of agreement? That is, if we think carefully about that case, and the *agreement* we find there, does it lead to other points of agreement?

2. Many fertilized eggs naturally fail to implant (not counting those that fail to implant because of birth control devices such as IUDs). If one holds the view that personhood begins at conception, should this be regarded as a terrible tragedy? Is it the moral equivalent of a terrible disease that kills an equal number of babies before their first birthday?

3. If a politician votes to ban abortion while also voting to cut funding for prenatal care for impoverished women, is that fundamentally hypocritical?

4. Rape is a terrible crime. As many people have noted, it is not really a crime of passion, but a

crime of brutal power and domination, in which the demeaning of the victim and the assertion of absolute power over the victim is the primary goal. (The most graphic and horrifying illustration of this is in the systematic rape of women of other tribes in Africa, or of other ethnic groups in the Balkan region. The point was not only to brutalize and humiliate the victims of rape, but to show absolute power over a rival group or tribe.) Traditionally many pro-life advocates have made an exception for victims of rape; but many other pro-life advocates insist that no such exception should be allowed (they agree that rape is a terrible crime, but insist the unborn child should not be punished for it). On the other hand, many pro-choice advocates see policies that would deny abortions to victims of rape as furthering the crime: first the rape, and then being forced to carry and give birth to the offspring of the rapist. Can one consistently hold a pro-life view while allowing abortion in at least some cases of rape?

5. Suppose that medical science reaches a point at which a fertilized egg can be placed in a large container and nurtured for nine months until it is full term and ready for "birth." Any woman who becomes pregnant, but does not wish to continue with that pregnancy, could have the fertilized egg or fetus or "unborn child" removed and placed in such a container, with no harm to the life prospects of that individual (and suppose that research has shown that those who came to term in such a container are just as physically and psychologically healthy as those who came to term inside the womb). Would such a development eliminate the question of abortion? That is, would the availability of such a technology do away with the abortion controversy, or would some part of the controversy remain? If you are pro-choice, would the above-mentioned scenario—assuming it is available to all, at no cost—deal with the problem? Would it be legitimate to *require* every woman choosing an abortion to place the fetus in such a container?

Additional Resources

A classic argument against abortion is offered by Don Marquis, in "Why Abortion Is Immoral," *Journal of Philosophy*, 86 (April 1989). Bonnie Steinbock responds to Marquis in "Why Most Abortions Are Not Wrong," *Advances in Bioethics*, 5 (1999): 245–267.

The most famous and widely reprinted prochoice essay is Judith Jarvis Thomson, "A Defense of Abortion," *Philosophy and Public Affairs* 1, no. 1 (1971): 47–66, which contains her famous "violinist" example. See also Thomson's "Abortion" in the *Boston Review*, 20, no. 3 (Summer 1995), together with several replies and Thomson's rejoinder.

One issue that often arises in the abortion debate is the relation between abortion and infanticide. Mary Anne Warren, in "On the Moral and Legal Status of Abortion"—originally appearing in *The Problem of Abortion*, ed. Joel Feinberg (Belmont, CA: Wadsworth, 1984), it was reprinted in expanded form in Thomas Mappes and David DeGrazia, ed., *Biomedical Ethics* (New York: McGraw Hill, 1996)—suggests criteria of personhood according to which fetuses do not qualify as persons. Robert F. Card critiques Warren's view in "Infanticide and the Liberal View on Abortion," *Bioethics* 14, no. 4 (2000): 340–351, and Warren replies to

Card—in the same issue of *Bioethics*—in "The Moral Difference between Infanticide and Abortion: A Response to Robert Card." The most comprehensive study of the various questions related to the status of the fetus/unborn child is Bonnie Steinbock's *Life before Birth: The Moral and Legal Status of Embryos and Fetuses*, 2nd ed. (New York: Oxford University Press, 2011).

Among the anthologies on abortion are Susan Dwyer and Joel Feinberg's *The Problem of Abortion*, 3rd ed. (Belmont, CA: Wadsworth, 1997). Another anthology that stresses comparing competing views on a number of issues related to the abortion controversy is Charles P. Cozic and Stacey L. Tipp, *Abortion: Opposing Viewpoints* (San Diego, CA: Greenhaven Press, 1991). An anthology edited by William B. Bondeson, H. Tristram Engelhardt, Jr., Stuart F. Spicker, and Daniel H. Winship, *Abortion and the Status of the Fetus* (Dordrecht, The Netherlands: D. Reidel Publishing, 1984), contains very interesting articles concerning the physical and moral status of the fetus, and a fascinating historical introduction by H. Tristram Engelhardt, Jr. An anthology edited by Louis J. Pojman and Francis Beckwith, *The Abortion Controversy: 25 Years after Roe vs. Wade*, 2nd ed. (Belmont, CA: Wadsworth, 1998), is a good collection;

the first article—by Sidney Callahan (who is pro-life) and her husband, Daniel Callahan (who is pro-choice)—is "Breaking through the Stereotypes," and it is very good at examining the common ground between the opposing views.

Bryan Hilliard, *The U.S. Supreme Court and Medical Ethics* (St. Paul: Paragon House, 2004), provides a clear analysis of the key Supreme Court cases related to abortion.

Ronald Dworkin's *Life's Dominion: An Argument about Abortion, Euthanasia, and Individual Freedom* (New York: Alfred A. Knopf, 1993) treats the issue very carefully, showing respect for both sides of this deeply contentious issue. Frances Myrna Kamm's *Creation and Abortion: A Study in Moral and Legal Philosophy* (New York: Oxford University Press, 1992) is another excellent and thoughtful book on the subject. Laurence Tribe's *Abortion: The Clash of Absolutes* (New York: W. W. Norton, 1990) is the work of a distinguished legal scholar who seeks common ground on the question. Chris Meyers, *The Fetal Position: A Rational Approach to the Abortion Issue* (Amherst, NY: Prometheus, 2010), analyzes many of the popular arguments on both sides of this controversial issue. Christopher Kazcor offers arguments against abortion without appealing to religious beliefs in *The Ethics of Abortion: Women's Rights, Human Life, and the Question of Justice* (London: Routledge, 2010). An interesting debate on the subject can be found in Michael Tooley, Celia Wolf-Devine, Philip E. Devine, and Alison M. Jaggar, *Abortion: Three Perspectives* (New York: Oxford University Press, 2009). Rosalind Hursthouse, "Virtue Theory and Abortion," *Philosophy and Public Affairs*, 20 (Summer, 1991): 223–246, is a very careful analysis of the abortion question from the perspective of a distinguished philosopher in the virtue theory tradition.

For a superb and evenhanded resource on the abortion controversy, including many links to other sites as well as to videos, recorded radio discussions, and a wide variety of full text articles, go to Ethics Updates at http://ethics.sandiego.edu/.

MYSEARCHLAB CONNECTIONS

In the "Stanford Encyclopedia of Philosophy," at plato.stanford.edu, see the entry on "Feminist Perspectives on Reproduction and the Family." Also, go to Ethics Updates at http://ethics.sandiego.edu, and under "Applied Ethics" click on "Abortion" for a remarkably rich range of resources, including links to all the major U.S. Supreme Court cases on the subject.

CAPITAL PUNISHMENT

Chapter Outline

Though most countries have abolished capital punishment, it remains an issue of intense controversy. Even in the countries that have done away with capital punishment, there are many people who wish to restore it. The United Kingdom ended capital punishment decades ago, but a significant majority of the British population favor it, and some British politicians are attempting to make restoration of capital punishment a campaign issue. Canada banned capital punishment in 1976; current polls indicate that a majority of Canadians think the death penalty is sometimes appropriate, but they do *not* want it reinstated. In the United States, popular opinion concerning capital punishment shifts and swings: A 2011 poll indicated that 61% of people favor capital punishment (though when asked whether they would prefer capital punishment or a sentence of life without parole, the percentage favoring capital punishment drops substantially); in 1966, only 42% of U.S. citizens favored capital punishment, while in 1994, the number was 80%.

The fact of mistaken convictions has led many conservatives to oppose the death penalty. An argument posted on the *Common Sense Conservative* blog states the grounds for conservative opposition to the death penalty:

The horrible truth about capital punishment is that a mistake is a mistake forever. It cannot be remedied. . . . This inability to correct a mistake is what should turn every conservative against the death penalty. We conservatives deeply believe that human fallibility reaps constant mistakes. Our entire suspicion of (and, indeed, hostility to) government and government programs rests on our knowledge of that fallibility. How, then, can we assume, in the sole instance of those sitting in judgment on capital cases, that fallibility is suspended? (Posted May 7, 2009, by Administrator in Conservative Principles)[1]

These are the same reasons that convinced Richard Viguerie (a leading fund-raiser for conservative causes) and Roy Brown (the 2008 Republican nominee for governor of Montana and a staunch conservative) to call for an end to the death penalty. Of course there are also conservatives who support the death penalty, along with a number of liberals. The point is that this is an issue—like most issues—that is not helpfully discussed in terms of easy political labels.

There is no doubt that capital punishment can bring out the worst in people. Drunken parties sometimes occur outside the walls of the prison, reaching a crescendo of revelry at the moment when the condemned is put to death. These are a revolting spectacle, equally repugnant to those on both sides of the question of capital punishment. Supporters of capital punishment regard the taking of a life as a serious and solemn occasion, one that should prompt sad remembrance of the crime victim, sadness at the brutal path taken by one of our fellow humans, and serious reflection on the awesome importance of the laws violated: violations so serious that death seems the only adequate means of acknowledging the importance of that law. A spectacle of drunken partying demeans the victim, the condemned, and the dreadful seriousness of the law and its majesty. From the abolitionist perspective, such gross revelry is a graphic reminder of the callous cruelty that the death penalty can sometimes encourage.

Strawman Distortions

The first distortion flows from the fact that drunken "execution parties" sometimes occur near the execution site. If an opponent of capital punishment claims that such revelry is representative of those who favor capital punishment—"advocates of capital punishment take perverse joy in dragging the condemned to the execution chamber and taking his life, and throw parties to celebrate this brutal act"—that is a strawman distortion. Obviously there are people who think drunken celebrations are an appropriate response to the execution of a condemned prisoner, but that is certainly not the view of most people who favor capital punishment. To the contrary, advocates of capital punishment are just as likely to find such behavior repulsive as are abolitionists. Supporters of capital punishment do not view capital punishment as a cause for celebration, but as a sad necessity. Obviously they believe that capital punishment is just and right, but they would prefer that no criminals ever acted in such a way that their brutal acts demanded (from the perspective of capital punishment supporters) the penalty of death.

Furthermore, proponents of capital punishment do *not* favor widespread use of capital punishment. In the past, many crimes were punishable by death: Youthful pickpockets were hanged in London, horse thieves were strung up in the American West, poachers—who took game from a rich landowner's estate to feed a starving family—were often executed. Some contemporary cultures favor the death penalty for adultery, blasphemy, and a host of other "crimes." In the United States, a group of Christian fundamentalist "Dominionists" wants the United States to be governed as a Christian country in accordance with ancient Biblical law. It favors the death penalty for adultery, blasphemy, and disobeying one's parents. But to represent the views of capital punishment proponents in our society as if they favor such wholesale use of the death penalty is to represent their views in a distorted strawman form.

There is no shortage of strawman distortions in the capital punishment controversy. Not much more than a century ago, children guilty of theft were hanged in public spectacles; but no serious contemporary supporter of capital punishment favors the execution of children, or the execution of shoplifters or pickpockets. "Capital punishment advocates want to hang children who shoplift a pair of designer jeans": That makes a nice strawman punching bag, but it doesn't address the real issue. (Of course there *are* people who favor capital punishment for children—including U.S. Supreme Court Justices Scalia and Thomas—but they are *not* representative of most of those who support capital punishment.) In the past, executions often involved horrific torture. In the heat of outrage over a hideous crime, someone may say that "hanging is too good for him" and contemplate methods of execution that would "match the crime," but few of those who support capital punishment want the condemned to be tortured. Of course even the most humane forms of execution will involve some very severe psychological distress. Imagine being strapped down on a table awaiting execution by lethal injection at a precisely designated hour, or the night you would spend anticipating such an event at dawn. But psychologically horrifying as that may be, it is quite different from the purposeful infliction of suffering through torture.

The other side of the capital punishment debate also takes cheap shots at a few favorite strawmen. The most obvious is the claim that opponents of capital punishment believe that murderers should be "allowed to run free." But obviously "allowing murderers to run free" is *not* the only alternative to capital punishment. Advocates of capital punishment sometimes claim that capital punishment abolitionists "care more about murderers than their victims." But you can oppose capital punishment while feeling profound sorrow for those who have been the victims of murder.

What Is the Common Ground?

When we get past the strawman distortions, we find more common ground than might be supposed. First, *everyone* in the debate has an interest in controlling and minimizing crime, particularly the brutal murders that some would punish with death. There is serious disagreement about whether capital punishment is helpful or harmful in meeting that goal, but there is no disagreement about the goal itself. Second, no one wants innocent persons put to death; that is, we all agree that *if* there is to be capital punishment, we should do everything possible to make sure that we do *not* mistakenly execute someone who is in fact innocent and was wrongly convicted: Whatever our views on capital punishment, we all regard the deliberate execution of an innocent fellow citizen as a dreadful thing indeed. Third, we agree that *if* there is to be capital punishment, it should be used for only the worst crimes (we should not execute shoplifters nor even armed robbers if their crimes do not involve murder). Fourth, both abolitionists and advocates agree that the purposeful state execution of a human being is a serious and somber occasion, and both groups detest the spectacle of drunken partying that sometimes occurs near the execution site. And finally, we all agree that when we witness or hear about a brutal crime, we *feel* a strong desire for retribution. Whether we favor or oppose capital punishment, when we watch the evening news and hear the story of a small shopkeeper being brutally murdered as he pleads for his life, then we *feel* a desire to see the murderer "get what he deserves" in the form of death.

So there are important points of agreement, but the capital punishment controversy remains. Putting aside the strawman distortions, what are the real arguments?

Arguments in Favor of Capital Punishment

1. Probably the most common argument in favor of capital punishment is the *deterrence* argument: The threat of capital punishment *deters* potential murderers from committing murder, and so reduces the number of murders committed. That is a good basic *utilitarian* argument in favor of capital punishment: By causing the suffering of those executed, we prevent more suffering overall (many who would have otherwise been murdered are spared because would-be murderers are deterred). In its rawest form, as a straight utilitarian argument, this argument has some problems. Suppose we could deter murders by trumping up charges against some poor friendless homeless person, and then executing him with much fanfare and publicity. This *might* have a positive deterrent effect (the sacrifice of this one homeless person might prevent many murders); but most of us would find this an appalling policy. So whatever the merits of the deterrence argument, it cannot be a *straight* utilitarian argument: There must also be some element of justice involved (the executed person must *justly deserve* such punishment). But the basic question for the deterrence argument is a simple one: Does it work? Does the threat of capital punishment actually prevent murders that would otherwise have been committed?

Louis Pojman insists that it does, and he offers the following dramatic example:

> Imagine that every time someone intentionally killed an innocent person he was immediately struck down by lightning. When mugger Mike slashed his knife into the neck of the elderly pensioner, lightning struck, killing Mike. His fellow muggers witnessed the sequence of events. When burglar Bob pulled his pistol out and shot the bank teller through her breast, a bolt leveled Bob, his compatriots beholding the spectacle. Soon men with their guns lying next to them were found all across the world in proximity to the corpses of their presumed victims. Do you think that the evidence of cosmic retribution would go unheeded? (Pojman, 2005)[2]

Well, yes, that would deter some potential murderers. But we would get the same effect if murderers were immediately paralyzed, or if the Earth suddenly opened and murderers were plunged into an inescapable dungeon (the cosmic equivalent of life without parole). Pojman treats this as evidence for the deterrent effect of capital punishment, but it could easily be turned to show that the deterrent effect of a long prison sentence would be just as effective as capital punishment. Any deterrent effect seems to depend more on certainty than severity.

Whatever the deterrent effect of an omniscient God zapping every murderer with lightning, the real question is whether the death penalty—in its most effective real-world form—is a *better* deterrent than some other penalty (such as lengthy incarceration). No matter how effective our police force, not every murderer will be apprehended; and in many cases, the murderer is not apprehended until long after the murder was committed. The fact is, we don't know whether capital punishment has any deterrent effect: It is not something we can test by running a controlled, double-blind experiment. But such evidence as there is for the deterrent effect of capital punishment is very thin. After all, the United States is the only Western industrialized nation that practices capital punishment, and its murder rate remains many times that of nations that have abolished capital punishment; and in the United States,

states that have abolished capital punishment—such as Vermont and Maine—have much lower murder rates than do the states that carry out the greatest number of executions—like Texas, Virginia, and Florida. But of course there are many other differences between Texas and Vermont, other than their justice systems; and it is impossible to say whether one of those other differences might be the key causal factor influencing the murder rate.

2. While the deterrence argument remains the most popular, supporters of capital punishment have turned toward an *expressivist* justification of capital punishment: Capital punishment is necessary to adequately *express* the deep revulsion society feels for the most awful crimes. As a society we need to express our moral outrage at the most brutal and vicious crimes, and adequately expressing outrage for such horrific crimes requires the *ultimate* punishment of death. Confining someone to prison for a long term or even a life time does not express moral outrage with the awesome power of the death penalty. If we as a society want to keep our most important principles alive and strong, we must *show* our deep allegiance to those values. When someone commits a terrible crime against a member of our society, a violation of our most basic values, it is essential that the society actively express outrage at that violation. Capital punishment is the appropriate *expression* of our shared outrage at the most horrific acts. Capital punishment must be reserved exclusively for those special awful acts, but it must be available as a means of expressing our ultimate outrage.

This is an interesting and sophisticated defense of capital punishment, which avoids controversies about deterrence: Whether capital punishment deters or not, it is essential that capital punishment be available for the deepest societal expression of moral outrage. But the argument prompts several questions. First, is capital punishment really the only adequate means of expressing our outrage over a terrible crime? Most other Western countries manage to express sufficient outrage without the use of the death penalty. But more importantly, does the use of capital punishment really express what we want to express? In the course of an execution, we set the precise time of a person's death, then we totally incapacitate that person—the person is strapped to a gurney, absolutely helpless, unable to move—and finally we kill the person. Perhaps such a process does express society's rage over the person's crimes, but it also expresses the total power of the state over the individual. When tyrants carried out executions, they wanted to demonstrate their absolute power over anyone who might challenge them, but that is not a message that fits with our democratic values. In a democracy, the state is not supposed to be an overwhelming power that leaves individual citizens helpless and awed before its majesty and might.

3. There is no doubt that we *feel* a strong desire to see those who commit the most horrific crimes punished severely. If you witness or hear of a brutal murder—the shopkeeper gunned down in front of his family, the child abused and then murdered, the old woman who is beaten to death during a robbery—you probably have a strong feeling that the murderer should be killed: "String him up" is a deep and almost universal reaction. But while strong feelings can be valuable, not to mention enjoyable, they are not always a reliable guide. We can think of many cases in which people had strong *feelings*—that marriage between races was wrong, that women holding positions of power was evil, that oral sex was an abomination—that now seem profoundly misguided. I have a strong *feeling* that the person who just cut me off in traffic should be thrown off a high cliff into a lagoon filled with jelly fish and crocodiles; but on further reflection, that feeling does not seem a reliable guide to ethical behavior.

When we are considering the strong *feeling* that there should be severe retribution against those who cause great harm, we must be especially cautious. This powerful feeling that we should *strike back* against harms runs very deep, but it is not particularly careful about its targets. When we are hurt—whether harmed directly or distressed by the observation of severe harm to others—we feel a strong desire to strike back at *something*: at the source of the harm, if that target is available but otherwise at whoever happens to be handy. When two rats are placed in a cage and given shocks, they immediately attack one another. Perhaps you saw the movie *Analyze This*, in which a psychologist (Billy Crystal) is trying to help a mob boss (Robert DeNiro). On one occasion the mobster has become quite angry at a rival mobster who attempted to kill him, but the rival mob boss is not accessible and the mobster is feeling extremely angry and frustrated. The psychologist offers this advice: "You know what I do when I'm angry? I hit a pillow. Just hit the pillow, see how you feel." The mobster immediately pulls a pistol and fires several shots into the pillow. When the psychologist recovers from shock, he asks: "Feel better?" "Yes, I do," the mobster replies. And he does. A cartoon strip shows a man at work being yelled at by his boss, the man comes home and yells at his wife, the wife yells at the little boy, who then kicks the unoffending dog. It's a little funny, because we all recognize the tendency; but a lot sad, because that strong desire to strike back at *something* is the source of great trouble. Unscrupulous prosecutors know that the strikeback feeling is powerful; that is one reason why—in the most terrible cases, where we should be most careful about convicting the right person—it is so easy to get a wrongful conviction. The evidence against the defendant is weak, but a terrible wrong was committed and the jury wants *someone* punished. So even if we believe there is something valuable in the strong feeling that the murderer deserves death, that claim will have to rest on something more than just the strength of the feeling. That something more must be a judgment that such punishment is *just*.

There is, certainly, a visceral desire for blood when we witness severe harm; perhaps it is not rational, but we are not purely rational creatures. This is a desire felt by almost all of us, whether we wish to abolish or preserve capital punishment. Recognizing and acknowledging that common desire may keep capital punishment abolitionists from treating advocates as monsters. All of us think some desires are good, while others are not. This is a difference over what desires should be *satisfied*, rather than over what desires we happen to *have*. Remembering this is to remember that there is more common ground than we might imagine when we chant slogans and wave signs.

4. The most fundamental argument for capital punishment is that *justice* requires it. Without capital punishment, the "moral order" remains unbalanced. This is a powerful poetic image, but giving it solid substance proves difficult. There is certainly a strong *feeling* that justice demands retribution. But when it comes to arguments for *why* justice demands death, the arguments are thin: It is "just obvious," or "God's law" requires it, or "the majesty of the moral law" demands it. "Justice requires it"; but *why* does justice require it? There is a visceral desire to see murderers killed; if the "justice" argument adds anything to that, it is not obvious.

When we seek *arguments* for why justice demands that murderers be executed, the justification often turns to religious principle: God requires that he who sheds blood shall have his blood shed. But that is religious faith, not argument. Immanuel Kant claims that justice *requires* capital punishment, independent of any benefits to society. Kant imagines a case in which we are living on a very remote island, and someone in our society commits a murder.

Kant insists that even if everyone on the island decides to disband the society and move away, we cannot just leave the murderer marooned there (where he cannot harm anyone); before we leave, the murderer must be killed, otherwise "the blood will be on the people" who failed to execute the killer. And indeed, that would be a terrible thing: We all become the moral equivalent of murderers if we fail to execute a murderer. But *why* that should be so is never clear.

Maybe the problem is that such justice—the murderer deserves death—is so basic that it is *more* basic than any argument that could be given in its support. That is, we just *know* that murderers deserve to be executed, and that principle is clearer and more obvious to us than any argument that could be given either for or against it. Certainly almost all of us *feel* the desire to see brutal murderers killed; but is that feeling a genuine moral insight (a profound moral intuition) or merely a strong emotional reaction that should be handled very cautiously? Jack and Jill both feel the strong desire to see a brutal murderer executed; both recognize that many strong feelings are *not* good moral guides. Jack reflects on this feeling, regards it as part of a deep desire to strike back at *something* whenever he is distressed, and decides that it is an unworthy feeling that should be controlled and rechannelled. Jill reflects on this feeling, continues to feel that there is something basically right about it, and supports capital punishment. Perhaps at that point we have reached the limits of argument; but that at least may be a point at which we can agree to disagree, without demonizing one another.

Arguments against Capital Punishment

1.   Among arguments against the death penalty, the one that has recently received the most attention concerns the danger of wrongfully executing an innocent person. This was not always a prominent argument against capital punishment: People generally believed that our justice system rarely convicted the innocent, and that sufficient safeguards were in place to prevent such terrible miscarriages of justice. That belief has been severely shaken by the number of wrongful convictions that have been discovered by DNA testing. Through examination of DNA evidence, dozens of wrongfully convicted persons have been freed from prison, well over a dozen from death row. Because in the majority of cases no DNA evidence is available for further testing, there are almost certainly many more innocent persons who remain on death row but without the evidence to free them.

Because so many past convictions have been overturned by later examination of DNA evidence, many people have started to look more closely at our system of justice and its problems. The picture is not a pretty one. Every student who has taken an introductory psychology course knows the unreliability of the eyewitness testimony that has sent thousands to prison. In addition, there is the problem of "jailhouse informants": Prisoners awaiting trial who offer to testify against a defendant if their own charges are reduced or dropped. If I am in jail, charged with distribution of drugs, and I see on television that a fellow prisoner has been charged with a brutal murder, then I gather some information about the murder (through watching television news or reading the newspaper or asking a friend on the outside to search out some details); I call the district attorney's office and tell them that the prisoner recently confessed the murder to me while we were eating lunch, and *if* my drug charges were reduced to simple possession I would be willing to go into court and swear that the prisoner confessed to me. Everyone involved (except the jury) knows that I am being paid off with reduced charges in exchange for my lying testimony; but it goes on every day in our system of "justice." In fact, in well over half of the cases in which DNA testing proved the innocence of a death row inmate, a jailhouse informant testified against the defendant (this is a uniquely U.S. problem: Other countries either reject such testimony altogether or—like Canada—allow it only in very limited circumstances). When we add in the desire of a jury to "see someone punished" for a terrible crime, and the fact that the defendant typically has the services of a severely overworked public defender (and sometimes a grossly incompetent public defender—there are several capital cases in which the defense attorney slept through portions of the trial), then it is not difficult to understand why there are so many mistaken convictions.

Mistaken convictions are a problem even without the death penalty: It is a terrible thing when innocent people spend years or even decades imprisoned for crimes they did not commit. But at least there is a possibility of *partially* righting the wrong that was done. If you are now being freed after ten years in prison for a crime you did not commit, we cannot give you back the ten years you lost. However, we can apologize and compensate you to some small degree for the wrong you suffered. If we executed you, then the apology is not much help. Perhaps we can place some flowers on your grave, but that will be cold comfort. Imprisoning an innocent person is a terrible miscarriage of justice, but the execution of an innocent person is particularly awful. When the state carries out a wrongful execution—on behalf of all of us—we all seem demeaned and corrupted by that act. Given the high number of mistaken convictions, wrongful executions are an inevitable element of the death penalty.

There are two responses to this argument against capital punishment. One is to call for a moratorium until the problems with our justice system are fixed. But in fact we are not getting any closer to preventing wrongful convictions; to the contrary, we are probably becoming worse. Resources for public defenders, already woefully inadequate, are being cut rather than increased. And rather than banning or severely restricting the use of jailhouse informants, the U.S. Supreme Court has ruled them legitimate. If we are going to have a moratorium on capital punishment until we are confident that wrongful convictions are extremely rare, that will be a very long moratorium indeed. The second response is that wrongfully executing the innocent is indeed bad, but not so bad that it should cause us to give up capital punishment. After all (so the argument goes), many legitimate and important acts carried out by the state occasionally involve the deaths of innocent persons: When we send a fire truck or ambulance or police car rushing to an emergency, innocent people are sometimes killed in traffic accidents. That does not imply that we should stop sending fire trucks; rather, we take what precautions we can, and continue the practice, knowing that it will occasionally result in innocent deaths. That's an interesting argument by analogy; is it convincing? One problem is that there is no real alternative to sending fire trucks rushing to a fire: If they stop at every traffic light, they will arrive too late to be effective. There is an obvious alternative to capital punishment: life imprisonment. But the deeper problem is that there is something profoundly different about a traffic accident in which an innocent person is accidentally killed in a collision with a fire truck, and the deliberate ritualized state killing of an innocent condemned prisoner. Both may involve terrible mistakes, but the second is a mistake of a very different magnitude that involves every member of the society in a terrible and irreversible wrong.

2. The second argument against the death penalty is that the death penalty is administered *unfairly*: It is arbitrary, based on bias, and often capricious. Even if you believe that the death penalty itself is fundamentally right and just, the way it is carried out is so unfair that it should be suspended.

The fact that the death penalty is *not* assigned in a just and equitable manner is obvious. Think of the old but accurate joke about capital punishment: "Why is it called capital punishment? Because those with the capital avoid the punishment." Wealthy people sometimes commit murders, but they *never* wind up on death row. In fact, it is very difficult to find anyone on death row who could afford to hire a private attorney; it's impossible to find anyone on death row who could afford to hire the best legal talent. It may be true that people in poverty are more likely to commit capital crimes than are people who are wealthy; but the poor don't commit almost *all* the capital crimes, yet the poor make up almost the entire population of death row. In addition, there appears to be a substantial element of racism in who gets the death penalty. Blacks are more likely to wind up on death row than are whites who commit similar crimes, but the real disparity comes when we look at the race of the victim: Those who murder whites (whatever the race of the murderer) are much more likely to receive the death penalty than are those who murder blacks. Gerald Heaney, a former appellate judge, summed up the problem thus:

> Imposition of the death penalty is arbitrary and capricious. The decision of who will live and who will die for his crime turns less on the nature of the offense and the incorrigibility of the offender and more on inappropriate and indefensible considerations: the political and personal inclinations of prosecutors, the defendant's wealth, race, and intellect; the race and economic status of the victim; the quality of the defendant's counsel; and the resources allocated to defense lawyers. (EPCM USA newsletter, March 2003)[3]

Or as U.S. Supreme Court Justice Ruth Bader Ginsburg sums it up: "People who are well represented at trial do not get the death penalty."

It is impossible to argue that the death penalty is carried out in a just and evenhanded manner. The evidence of bias and arbitrariness is overwhelming. But does it follow that we should eliminate the death penalty? It is possible to argue that we *should* impose the death penalty, but only after we are certain that everyone (rich and poor, black and white, educated and illiterate) gets genuinely equal justice. That would require that *everyone* accused of a capital crime should have top notch legal talent and enough monetary resources to put on a genuine defense, and that the case be tried before an unbiased jury. Waiting for that to happen would mean a permanent end to the death penalty. The other reply to this argument is to admit that it *is* unfair that only the poor (and the poorly represented) are in fact subject to the death penalty, but insist that those poor people who commit terrible crimes still justly deserve execution, even if many others who *also* deserve execution (but who have the wealth to hire a good lawyer) manage to avoid it. That is, the fact that some who deserve execution are *not* executed does not change the fact that those who *are* executed for their crimes justly deserve it. That is the argument put forward by Louis Pojman, a leading supporter of the death penalty. Pojman recognizes that the system is unfair, and that the poor are executed while the rich escape punishment. He recommends a drastic change that would perhaps even the playing field: expanding the category of capital punishment so that some rich corporate executives are also subject to capital punishment:

> Perhaps our notion of treason should be expanded to include those who betray the trust of the public: corporation executives who have the trust of ordinary people, but who, through selfish and dishonest practices, ruin their lives. . . . My proposal is to consider broadening, not narrowing, the scope of capital punishment, to include business personnel who unfairly harm the public. The executives in the recent corporation scandals who bailed out of sinking corporations with golden, million-dollar

lifeboats while the pension plans of thousands of employees went to the bottom of the economic ocean, may deserve severe punishment, and if convicted, they should receive what they deserve. (Pojman, 2005)[4]

It's an interesting idea; but if we stop all capital punishment until the execution of some super wealthy CEO who has pillaged the savings and pensions of thousands of people and caused more overall misery than most murderers, that will be the end of capital punishment.

3. Another argument against capital punishment concedes that those who commit terrible murders may *justly deserve* to be executed, but argues that we as a society should not descend to the level of murderers when we carry out punishment. That does not mean that when the state, after a trial and in accordance with the law, carries out an execution, it is simply doing the same as the murderer. "Murder is murder, and it's wrong whether carried out by an individual or by the state." That may be a good slogan, but it's a bad argument. The state carrying out an execution may or may not be right, but it is not murder (just as the state imprisoning someone for his or her crimes is very different from you locking someone in your basement). Still, when we as a country carry out an execution—so this argument goes—it tends to coarsen us, it brings us down toward the level of those we execute. Perhaps murderers rightly deserve execution, but the cost to our own decency and humanity is too great. This is essentially just an extension of an argument that was used to eliminate the more repulsive forms of brutal execution, in which the condemned ultimately died in screaming maddened agony. We may very well *feel* that someone who tortures a small child to death justly *deserves* to be tortured in turn. Maybe such torture would be justified, rightly deserved. But whether justified or not, most of us do *not* want our country engaging in judicial torture on our behalf. And for many people, the same principle applies to capital punishment: Deserved or not, we do not want to be a people who descend to that level. It's not clear, however, that this argument will really convince anyone who sees capital punishment as *just*. On that view, carrying out an execution is not *descending* toward the violent level of the murderer, but is instead *ascending* toward genuine justice. While this argument is likely to capture some of the feelings of abolitionists, it is unlikely to be persuasive for their opponents.

4. Yet another argument against capital punishment is that it may actually *promote* violence, by teaching that violence—in the form of killing the condemned—is a solution. Larry Mattera endorses this argument:

> If violence is objectivated institutionally as an expression of a society's collective political will to justice, institutions of violence will necessarily become formative of society. The more profoundly a society comes to rely on institutionalized violence as an instrument of its political purpose, the more tightly will institutionalized violence entangle society and the more formative of societal identity violence will become. (quoted at http://www.capital-punishment.us/2010/11/larry-mattera.html)[5]

That is certainly a possibility, and it makes a good counterweight to the argument that violence will *increase* if we do not have capital punishment to keep it in check. But plausible as that may seem, it is not the sort of question that we can answer by what *seems* plausible. The question of whether "institutionalized violence" in the form of capital punishment will produce a culture of violence is a difficult question to answer, but it is a question more suited to sociological and anthropological analysis than to speculation. Certainly it seems plausible that cultures that institutionalize violent practices, such as capital punishment, would become more violent: The culture institutionalizes the lesson that violence is a solution to problems. But whether that causes increased violence in the society is not a question that can be answered without empirical investigation, and at this point, there is no conclusive proof one way or the other on that issue.

5. Perhaps the greatest problem with capital punishment is that it gives us the false impression that by executing the murderer we have solved the problem. Of course some will say that the immediate problem *is* solved: The executed person will commit no more murders. But that blinds us to the fact that the larger underlying problems have been ignored. The conditions that shaped the condemned individual toward a life of violent crime remain in place, and are even now shaping those who will follow the same murderous path. Killing a condemned prisoner is easy; fixing the problems that led this prisoner to a life of crime is much harder.

We know a great deal about the conditions that shape people toward violent crime. James Gilligan—the medical director of the Bridgewater State Hospital for the criminally insane and director of mental health for the Massachusetts prison system as well as head of the Center for the Study of Violence at Harvard Medical School—has done extensive research on the causes of violence. He concluded that the basic factor triggering violent behavior is a deep sense of shame or disrespect, and he discovered several key systemic factors that cause such a violence-provoking sense of shame:

> [T]he social and economic system of the United States combines almost every characteristic that maximizes shame and hence violence. First, there is the "Horatio Alger" myth that everyone can get rich if they are smart and work hard (which means that if they are not rich they must be stupid or lazy, or both). Second, we are not only told that we can get rich, we are also stimulated to want to get rich. For the whole economic system of mass production depends on whetting people's appetites to consume the flood of goods that are being produced (hence the flood of advertisements). Third, the social and economic reality is the opposite of the Horatio Alger myth, since social mobility is actually less likely in the U.S. than in the supposedly more rigid social structures of Europe and the U.K. As Mishel, Bernstein and Schmitt (2001) have noted:
>
> Contrary to widely held perceptions, the U.S. offers less economic mobility than other rich countries. . . .
>
> Fourth, as they also mention, "the U.S. has the most unequal income distribution and the highest poverty rates among all the advanced economies in the world. . . ." The net effect of all these features of U.S. society is to maximize the gap between aspiration and attainment, which maximizes the frequency and intensity of feelings of shame, which maximizes the rates of violent crimes. (James Gilligan, 2001, pp. 44–45)[6]

Those are substantial problems, and fixing them—in order to bring the murder rate in the United States in line with that in other Western countries—would take enormous effort. By focusing on capital punishment, we avoid serious examination of the deeper causes and tougher problems that lead to violent crime. In particular, so long as the focus is on the specific *individual* who is to be executed, we avoid looking at the larger social issues that cause our society to suffer a very high rate of violent crime.

Where Do We Stand?

The question of capital punishment remains deeply contentious, but in the midst of that continuing controversy there is substantial common ground. First, everyone agrees that reducing the number of murders would be a good thing. Second, there is disagreement about whether capital punishment deters or promotes murder, but we agree that there are certainly some *other* things society could be doing to reduce violent crime (e.g., promoting more avenues for achievement for those who currently lack the skills to achieve economic success in our society). Third, whether you believe that capital punishment should be abolished or you believe that justice requires the most extreme penalty for the most extreme crimes, everyone has an interest in making sure that the people who are executed are actually guilty, and that innocent persons are not wrongly killed. Thus everyone has an interest in making sure that the accused have excellent representation (the notorious Texas cases of murder defendants being represented by lawyers who were drunk or asleep through much of the trial are equally offensive to proponents and opponents of capital punishment), that jailhouse informants not be allowed to give perjured testimony, and that lineups are conducted fairly. Fourth, whether you favor or reject capital punishment, you share an interest in making sure that the punishment is *not* arbitrary and capricious: that the determining factor is the actual guilt of the condemned, not the biases of juries and prosecutors or the incompetence of defense attorneys.

This is not an issue we will soon resolve: If you see justice as demanding blood, and someone else sees capital punishment as fundamentally unjust and barbaric, then the basic disagreement will remain. But that disagreement notwithstanding, when the strawman distortions are put aside, there is substantially more agreement than might be supposed.

Questions for Reflection

1. In ancient Greece and Rome, condemned prisoners were allowed to take their own lives (in the case of Socrates, by drinking hemlock), and usually given a significant space of time in which to carry out the "self-execution." In the modern United States, condemned prisoners are totally immobilized, and executed at a specific time; and for several days prior to the scheduled execution, they are placed on a "death watch" by prison guards, to make sure they do *not* take their own lives prior to their scheduled time of execution. Whatever your views on capital punishment, so long as capital punishment *is* carried out, would it be better to give the condemned prisoner a pill (perhaps a cyanide pill or some other swift and deadly potion) that the prisoner could swallow at any point during, say, a 48-hour period of execution? (Of course if the prisoner chose not to take his or her own life, the prisoner could wait for the end of that period and have the executioner carry out the process through lethal injection or some other method.) Would this be a more humane method of execution? Would it be better? Would it be more *expressive* of the values that capital punishment is supposed to express?

2. Many conservatives wish to minimize the power of the state ("social" conservatives take a different view; they want the state to be deeply involved in many of the personal aspects of our lives, such as enforcing criminal laws against private homosexual behavior). Would one who holds the traditional conservative view (favoring a minimum state—the government is best which governs least) be more likely to oppose capital punishment?

3. The classic argument for capital punishment is retributive: Blood deserves blood, those who commit murder deserve to die, and justice is not

done when a murderer is allowed to live. The retributive view is stated plainly by Igor Primoratz:

> Capital punishment ought to be retained where it obtains, and reintroduced in those jurisdictions that have abolished it, although we have no reason to believe that, as a matter of deterrence, it is any better than a long prison term. It ought to be retained, or reintroduced, for one simple reason: that justice be done in cases of murder, that murderers be punished according to their just deserts. (Igor Primoratz, 1990)[7]

Many people (including, of course, Primoratz) regard that as a clear and certain truth. But what is the basis for the claim that murderers *justly deserve* to be executed? Is it a gut feeling? A matter of religious faith? Or what?

4. Walter Berns—a supporter of capital punishment—insists that "the criminal law must be made awful, by which I mean 'inspiring or commanding profound respect or reverential fear.' It must remind us of the moral order by which alone we can live as *human* beings, and in America . . . the only punishment that can do this is capital punishment." Assuming that the death penalty does command reverential fear, is that an appropriate goal for a *democratic* society to have toward its laws?

5. The murder of a homeless drifter is a horrible event, as is the murder of a loving mother. The latter will likely have a much more moving "victim impact" statement, yet surely the murder of a drifter is just as serious a crime. Are victim impact statements legitimate during the sentencing phase? The fact that a victim was tortured to death surely is relevant; is the fact that the victim had beautiful friends or a charming family (in contrast to the friendless drifter) a relevant consideration? An unemployed young man uses a gun to rob a convenience store; during the robbery, he panics and shoots the clerk. If we are deciding whether the murderer deserves the death penalty, does it matter whether the clerk is a beautiful and popular young woman who is working nights to pay for college, or a homeless drifter with no friends?

6. When you were small, you told your family that "When I grow up, I want to be an astronaut (or teacher or baseball player or scientist or maybe a pilot or train engineer or firefighter or doctor)." Your family smiled, and said, "That's fine, Sweetheart." But what if you had said, "When I grow up, I want to be an executioner"? Your family would have been deeply troubled, and perhaps would have taken you to a child psychologist. Even those who support capital punishment do not want their children growing up to be executioners. Does that have any significance for the question of the moral legitimacy of capital punishment? Of the various ethical approaches considered in Chapter 3, which one would be most likely to consider that significant? Which one would be most likely to consider it *in*significant?

Additional Resources

The U.S. Supreme Court has been involved in many death penalty cases, most of which have deeply divided the court. Many of the most articulate statements of opposing views on the death penalty have occurred in the divided opinions of Supreme Court justices. Justice Scalia, in his minority opinion in favor of the death penalty for a mentally retarded defendant (536 U.S. *Atkins v. Virginia*, 2002), stated that, "The fact that juries continue to sentence mentally retarded offenders to death for extreme crimes shows that society's moral outrage sometimes demands execution of retarded offenders." On the opposing side, see Justice Thurgood Marshall's statement, in *Gregg v. Georgia*, 428 U.S. 153, 1976: "The death penalty, unnecessary to promote the goal of deterrence or to further any legitimate notion of retribution, is an excessive penalty forbidden by the Eighth and Fourteenth Amendments"; and the famous statement by Justice Harry Blackmun (who had cast earlier votes in favor of allowing capital punishment) in which he resolved that capital punishment cannot be made fair and should be abolished:

> From this day forward I no longer shall tinker with the machinery of death. . . . I feel morally and intellectually obligated simply to concede that the death penalty

experiment has failed. It is virtually self-evident to me now that no combination of procedural rules or substantive regulations ever can save the death penalty from its inherent constitutional deficiencies. The basic question—does the system accurately and consistently determine which defendants "deserve" to die?—cannot be answered in the affirmative. (*Collins v. Collins*, 1994)

All of these cases can be found at www.oyez.org. For further study of key Supreme Court death penalty cases, a good source is Barry Latzer, *Death Penalty Cases: Leading U.S. Supreme Court Cases on Capital Punishment* (Woburn, MA: Butterworth-Heinemann, 1997). Another good book on the U.S. Supreme Court and the death penalty is Michael Meltsner, *Cruel and Unusual: The Supreme Court and Capital Punishment* (New Orleans, LA: Quid Pro Books, 2011). John D. Bessler takes a very careful look at the death penalty views of the original framers of the U.S. Constitution, in *Cruel and Unusual: The American Death Penalty and the Founders' Eighth Amendment* (Boston, MA: Northeastern University Press, 2012).

Robert Bohm has written a good textbook on capital punishment, which is now in its fourth edition: *Deathquest: An Introduction to the Theory and Practice of Capital Punishment in the United States* (Cincinnati, OH: Anderson Publishing, 2012). See also his recent book examining the death penalty through interviews with a wide variety of people most closely involved with it: *The Ultimate Sanction: Understanding the Death Penalty Through Its Many Voices and Sides* (New York: Kaplan Publishing, 2010).

Franklin E. Zimring and Gordon Hawkins, *Capital Punishment and the American Agenda* (Cambridge: Cambridge University Press, 1986), place capital punishment within a world setting and draw the historical and sociological background for use of capital punishment in the United States. Bruce N. Waller places the issue of capital punishment in the larger context of philosophical theories for the justification of punishment, in "From Hemlock to Lethal Injection: The Case for Self-Execution," *International Journal of Applied Philosophy*, 4, no. 4 (Fall 1989): 53–58. David Garland views the death penalty from a sociological perspective, in *Peculiar Institution: America's Death Penalty in an Age of Abolition* (Cambridge, MA: Harvard University Press, 2010).

Michael A. Mello has been a defense lawyer involved in death row cases for many years; his very readable book on the subject is *Dead Wrong: A Death Row Lawyer Speaks Out against Capital Punishment* (Madison: University of Wisconsin Press, 1997).

A particularly interesting book that examines the death penalty in light of the many mistaken convictions that have been overturned (many involving prisoners on death row) is Barry Scheck, Peter Neufeld, and Jim Dwyer's *Actual Innocence* (New York: Doubleday, 2000). Elizabeth A. Linehan has written an excellent essay on the risk of "Executing the Innocent," and its implications for the issue of capital punishment. It is available online at www.bu.edu/wcp/Papers/Huma?HumaLine.htm.

For debates on the death penalty, see E. Van den Haag and J. P. Conrad, *The Death Penalty: A Debate* (New York: Plenum, 1983) and Louis P. Pojman and Jeffrey Reiman in *The Death Penalty: For and Against* (Lanham, MD: Rowman & Littlefield, 1998). For a fascinating debate that places the issue in a much larger context, see Jean Hampton and Jeffrie Murphy, *Forgiveness and Mercy* (Cambridge: Cambridge University Press, 1988).

Among the many anthologies are Hugo Adam Bedau, *The Death Penalty in America*, 3rd ed. (New York: Oxford University Press, 1982); J. Feinberg and H. Gross, eds., *Punishment: Selected Readings* (Belmont, CA: Dickinson, 1975); Carol Wekesser, ed., *The Death Penalty: Opposing Viewpoints* (San Diego, CA: Greenhaven Press, 1991); Robert M. Baird and Stuart E. Rosenbaum, *Punishment and the Death Penalty: The Current Debate* (Amherst, NY: Prometheus Books, 1995); James R. Acker, Robert M. Bohm, and Charles S. Lanier, *America's Experiment with Capital Punishment* (Durham, NC: Carolina Academic Press, 1998); and Austin Sarat, ed., *The Killing State: Capital Punishment in Law, Politics, and Culture* (New York: Oxford University Press, 1999).

For arguments opposing capital punishment, see Stephen Nathanson, *An Eye for an Eye? The Morality of Punishing by Death* (Totowa, NJ: Rowman & Littlefield, 1987); Charles Black, *Capital Punishment: The Inevitability of Caprice and Mistake*, 2nd ed. (New York: W. W. Norton, 1976); and Thomas W. Clark, "Crime and Causality: Do Killers Deserve to Die?" *Free Inquiry*, February/March 2005: 34–37. The pro capital punishment view can be found in Walter Berns, *For Capital Punishment: Crime and the Morality of the Death Penalty* (New York: Basic Books, 1979); and Ernest van den Haag, "In Defense of the Death Penalty: A Legal-Practical-Moral Analysis," *Criminal Law Bulletin*, 14 (1978): 51–68.

Excellent anthologies on the more general issue of punishment are Robert M. Baird and Stuart E. Rosenbaum, *Philosophy of Punishment* (Buffalo, NY: Prometheus, 1988); and Jeffrie G. Murphy, *Punishment and Rehabilitation*, 2nd ed. (Belmont, CA: Wadsworth, 1985).

The Ethics Updates website has good material on both punishment in general and the death penalty in particular, including links to other sites, full-text online articles, video discussions, and audio recordings of relevant radio programs; check particularly the link to excellent resources provided by the documentary series *Frontline*. Go to ethics.sandiego.edu/Applied/Death Penalty. The Death Penalty Information Center is an excellent resource with facts about capital punishment, recent news stories related to capital punishment, and an extensive list of relevant publications; it can be found at www.deathpenaltyinfo.org. Religioustolerance.org has substantial material on capital punishment; go to http://www.religioustolerance.org/execute.htm.

Endnotes

1. Posted May 7, 2009, by Administrator in Conservative Principles.
2. Louis P. Pojman, "Why the Death Penalty is Morally Permissible," in Debating the Death Penalty: Should America Have Capital Punishment, edited by Hugo Adam Bedau and Paul G. Cassell (New York: Oxford University Press, 2005).
3. Gerald Heaney, EPCM USA Newsletter, March 2003.
4. Louis P. Pojman, "Why the Death Penalty Is Morally Permissible," in Debating the Death Penalty: Should America Have Capital Punishment, edited by Hugo Adam Bedau and Paul G. Cassell (New York: Oxford University Press, 2005)
5. Larry Mattera, qtd. at http://www.capital-punishment.us/2010/11/larry-mattera.html
6. James Gilligan, Preventing Violence (New York: Thames & Hudson, 2001), pp. 44–45.
7. Source: Justifying Legal Punishment by Igor Primoratz. Amherst NY Humanity Books, 1989.

MYSEARCHLAB CONNECTIONS

Go to *Ethics Updates* at http://ethics.sandiego.edu, and under "Applied Ethics" click on "Death Penalty & Punishment." You will find a rich range of resources; particularly note the links to the *Frontline* documentaries, the NPR "Talk of the Nation broadcasts," and Hugh LaFollette's interviews.

The "Death Penalty Information Center" at www.deathpenaltyinfo.org contains an abundance of material.

An interesting Canadian case is *United States v. Burns* (2001), in which the United States asked that a person wanted on murder charges in the United States, who had been captured in Canada, be returned to the United States for trial (with the possibility that if found guilty, the prisoner might be executed). The Canadian Supreme Court refused to permit the extradition, due to Canadian rejection of the death penalty. The case can be found at http://scc.lexum.org/en/2001/2001scc7/2001scc7.html. Among the most important U.S. Supreme Court cases on the death penalty are: *Furman v. Georgia*, 1972, which led to a four-year moratorium on the death penalty in the United States; *Gregg v. Georgia*, 1976, which reaffirmed the Supreme Court acceptance of the death penalty; *McCleskey v. Kemp*, 1987, in which the Supreme Court refused to consider racial disparities as a violation of the "equal protection" requirement; *Thompson v. Oklahoma*, 1988, which ruled against executing anyone aged 15 or under at the time the crime was committed; *Stanford v. Kentucky*, 1989, which permitted the execution of children ages 16 or 17 at the time of the crime; *Penry v. Lynaugh*, 1989, which permitted the execution of the mentally retarded; *Herrera v. Collins*, 1993, which ruled that new evidence that a prisoner sentenced to death is actually innocent is not sufficient reason for a new trial or to halt execution; *Atkins v. Virginia*, 2002, which ruled that mentally retarded defendants could not be executed; and *Roper v. Simmons*, which ruled that those under the age of 18 at the time they committed a crime could not be subject to the death penalty. All of these cases can be found at the Oyez Project at the IIT Chicago-Kent College of Law; go to www.oyez.org, where you can read the entire cases, listen to the oral arguments before the Supreme Court, and find a transcript of the oral arguments.

6

EUTHANASIA

Chapter Outline

Euthanasia is sometimes referred to as "mercy-killing," but that name obscures a very important distinction: the distinction between *active* euthanasia and *passive* euthanasia. *Active* euthanasia is the controversial question: Is it morally acceptable to *cause* death by administering lethal drugs to a patient who is suffering and *chooses* a quicker and less painful death? Obviously this requires the free choice of the patient. If a patient who has not chosen to die is administered a lethal drug, that is not active euthanasia; it's murder.

In contrast, *passive* euthanasia involves *allowing* someone to die—stopping treatment or stopping some element of treatment—when aggressive medical measures could prolong the patient's life. For example, a patient might choose to stop dialysis treatments, which will lead to the patient's death; or a patient might refuse a respirator, or ask to be taken off a respirator, though the patient cannot breathe without a respirator; or a patient might refuse antibiotics, choosing to die from pneumonia rather than from the lengthier and more painful process of bone cancer; or a terminally ill patient might choose the "do not resuscitate" option, requiring that if his or her heart stops, the hospital staff will *not* take aggressive measures to start the heart beating again.

If we were having this discussion in 1950, the question would be whether it is ever acceptable to allow a patient to die when further medical treatment could extend life;

that is, whether it is permissible to allow a patient suffering from a very painful untreatable cancer to die more swiftly from untreated—but treatable—pneumonia. That question of passive euthanasia is no longer controversial. Two factors have caused the general acceptance of passive euthanasia. First, there is much more emphasis on the rights of patients to make their own treatment decisions: the rights of patients to exercise *informed consent*.

Informed consent has become such an important and widely accepted ethical and legal principle in our society that it is difficult to recall it is also a comparatively *recent* principle. Throughout the first half of the 20th century, informed consent was certainly not a recognized ethical principle. To the contrary, informing patients of their actual condition was regarded as a severe ethical violation: Doctors considered it wrong to tell patients that they were suffering from a fatal disease, and often considered it wrong to tell patients anything whatsoever concerning their medical conditions. The motive behind keeping patients in ignorance may have been generous—"If Joe knows he has cancer, he will be miserable; better to give him a few more months of ignorant bliss"—but the results were disastrous. In the first place, it involved treating patients as children: The truth has to be kept from patients, because they can't handle it. And of course if they don't know their condition, then obviously they can't make informed choices about what treatments to have (or not have), and so the decisions must be made for them by the doctor: The patient is being treated as a child who is incompetent to make his or her own decisions. There were other problems. If the doctor lies to a patient, then others—who may not wish to be involved in the deception—will be drawn into the process. Nurses will not be able to answer the patient's questions honestly, and family members (if they know the truth) will have to lie to their loved one. Because lying is unpleasant, people may avoid the patient, and that may lead to isolation of the patient at a time when the patient needs special support from both family and medical staff. If the patient is denied knowledge of a fatal disease, the patient is also denied the opportunity to decide how to live the remaining period of his or her life: denied the opportunity to reconcile with an estranged brother or sister, decide what to do with his or her small business, pursue the lifelong dream of seeing the Grand Canyon. Furthermore, if physicians commonly lie to patients, then patients will have deep doubts about anything doctors tell them: "Dr. Jones said I was fine, and the pain in my stomach was just indigestion; but I know doctors never tell patients the truth about their conditions, so maybe it really is the same stomach cancer that killed my father." And finally—and perhaps most importantly—not being honestly informed deprives patients of a sense of control, and causes much more worry than it prevents. If I am told that I only have indigestion when it is really an untreatable cancer, then as my condition deteriorates there will be a constant series of terrifying surprises. If instead I know what is happening, and can predict and anticipate what will occur over my remaining weeks or months, I will have a much stronger sense of control, and be much less likely to sink into depression. I can't control the course of my disease, but I can *predict* the stages, and I *can* control various aspects of my treatment (such as pain medications). Those small elements of control will make a tremendous difference in my psychological well-being during the closing chapter of my life.

In sum, we now believe that if you don't want medical treatment, or you refuse a specific medical treatment, that is *your free choice*, and you have a basic *right* to make that choice and the right to accurate honest information in making your own decision. No competent adult should be *forced* to undergo any unwanted medical treatment or procedure. If you do not want heart surgery (though your doctor strongly recommends it), that is your choice; and if you do not want antibiotics or do not want to be placed on a respirator or do not want feeding tubes, then you have a right to make that choice for yourself. You also have a right to make those choices in advance—through a living will—in case you become so incapacitated (perhaps slip into a coma) that you can no longer make choices for yourself. In fact, the law makes it very clear that patients have a right to know their medical conditions and a right to make their own decisions concerning medical treatment. A doctor who fails to keep a patient fully informed, or who does not gain the *informed consent* of a patient before carrying out a medical procedure, is in violation of the law, in violation of medical ethics, and in violation of American Medical Association (AMA) principles. Your doctor may tell you that bypass heart surgery is essential for you: Without the bypass surgery, you are almost certain to suffer a fatal heart attack. But the decision to have or *not* have that surgery—assuming you are a competent adult—belongs to *you*, and no one else. If you choose not to have medical treatment that would extend your life (if you choose passive euthanasia), that is your right.

There is a second reason for the general acceptance of passive euthanasia: extraordinary advances in medical treatments. A few decades ago, the medical community struggled to keep patients alive as long as possible, but with very limited success. For the severely ill or injured, usually all medical efforts to extend life were of little benefit. If you stopped breathing, physicians could try to resuscitate you; but even if that worked briefly, the next time you stopped breathing, all efforts would probably be in vain. If you were long-term comatose, the hospital might be able to give you sufficient nutrition and hydration to keep you alive for at most a few weeks. Times have changed. A respirator will keep you artificially breathing and a heart pump will keep your blood circulating; flexible tube-feeding can keep you adequately nourished for many years; dialysis machines will purify your blood when your kidneys fail, and antibiotics will keep you free of infection. People can and *do* survive for years, even decades, in a permanently vegetative state. Their bodies—through artificial processes—remain alive, long after they have lost all consciousness.

Suppose you suffer a severe brain injury or stroke, and you permanently lose all cognitive abilities: You have no awareness of those around you, no ability to reason or speak or respond. Would you choose to spend years hooked to a respirator being tube-fed, with no consciousness? Not so long ago no one had to make that choice. The best medical efforts could not keep your body functioning in that state for very long; an infection or massive organ failure or inadequate nutrition would soon cause your death. But now *everyone* is faced with that decision: If you were severely injured in an auto accident or a skiing accident, or you suffered a sudden severe stroke, what sort of treatment would you want, and what sort of treatment would you *not* want? Many people sign living wills, or give explicit instructions to their families or close friends about exactly what they would or would not want in the way of medical treatment. Thus an elderly person might decide that he or she has lived a full life, but health problems are becoming steadily more severe, and "if I should have a heart attack and lose consciousness, I do *not* want to be resuscitated." Or someone might carefully instruct a friend: "If I have lost consciousness, or suffered severe brain damage, and there is little or no chance that I will ever be restored to consciousness, then I do *not* want to be placed on a respirator and I do *not* want tube-feeding; if I am already on a respirator, when it is determined that I am in a permanently vegetative state, I want to be sedated, *removed* from the respirator, and allowed to die." That's *your choice,* and the law guarantees you the right to make that choice (and to specify what you want done if you are ever so incapacitated that you can no longer exercise choice). If I am on a respirator, and I *know* that I will die without the assistance of that respirator, I have the right to be taken off the respirator; and I have the right to continued careful and respectful treatment during my dying (e.g., dying of oxygen deprivation is likely to be painful, so I can ask for sedatives that will remove the discomfort from that process, even if that requires sedating me into unconsciousness).

Perhaps you would consider it wrong to "give up" and accept death: You're a fighter, and you want to continue your struggle to live, no matter how unpleasant and painful life should become. That's your choice, and you have every right to make that choice. I may consider it foolish, and it may not be the choice I would make, but that doesn't matter: You have the right to make your choice, just as I have the right to make my choice to *not* receive treatment (refusing a respirator or dialysis, rejecting antibiotics, or deciding against heart surgery). If I choose not to take antibiotics to treat my pneumonia or I demand to be taken off a respirator or I reject dialysis to deal with my kidney failure, then I am choosing to stop treatment and die. That is a case of passive euthanasia: You, as my physician, do not directly cause my death; my disease or injuries cause my death; you are only allowing me to die (in this case, you don't really have any choice in the matter: the choice to refuse or stop treatment is *mine*).

So when it comes to the question of euthanasia, there is a very large area of agreement: No competent adult should be forced to have treatments against his or her wishes; every competent adult should have the right to give or withhold informed consent to any medical treatment. Every competent adult has the right to honest information, and all the information he or she desires, at the appropriate explanatory level, in making those decisions. And patients should not be punished for making decisions their physicians may not agree with (e.g., physicians should not threaten to abandon patients if they do not follow the physician's recommendation).

The right to refuse life-sustaining treatment is well established, and so controversy over passive euthanasia has disappeared. The current controversy is over active euthanasia (or physician-assisted suicide). The debate is not over whether patients should have the right to refuse treatment and be allowed to die. The question is whether patients have a right to *hasten* their deaths, and obtain medical help in that hastening process. The Netherlands has long allowed active euthanasia; several years ago, the state of Oregon (in a statewide referendum) approved physician-assisted suicide for terminally ill patients. That brings us to another distinction that must be noted: the distinction between *active euthanasia* and *physician-assisted suicide*. In the Netherlands, there is little concern with whether the doctor prescribes a lethal drug that the terminally ill patient then takes (physician-assisted suicide) or the doctor injects the terminally ill patient (at the patient's request) with a lethal drug. But in Oregon, the former would be legal while the latter is not. In the Netherlands, both would be considered under the category of active euthanasia, and the Dutch see little difference between a patient requesting that the physician mix a lethal dose and give it to the patient to take, and a patient requesting that a lethal dose be administered by the physician. The crucial question is not whether the doctor or the patient administers the lethal drug, but whether it is done as a result of the patient's *free choice*. If a patient is suffering from throat cancer, and cannot swallow, then instead of giving the patient a lethal dose to swallow the physician administers a lethal injection. The Dutch simply classify both as active euthanasia. In the United States, the distinction between physician-assisted suicide (in which the physician provides the lethal dose but the patient must actively take it) and active euthanasia (in which the physician prepares and *administers* the lethal drug) is considered very important. In the remainder of this discussion, I will use the term *active euthanasia* in the broader sense, as *including* physician-assisted suicide; but of course you might still conclude that physician-*assisted* suicide is legitimate, while active administration of lethal drugs by a physician is wrong.

Strawman Distortions

The debate over active euthanasia is a passionate one, and both sides occasionally stoop to distorting the arguments and impugning the motives of their opponents. Those who favor active euthanasia want to kill off old people to save money (or even grosser; this is the first step toward extermination of "undesirables"). The strawman nature of such accusations is obvious. If you were facing a terrible brain disease that would cause you great agony, destroy your cognitive capacities, and reduce you to the state of a miserable wailing infant for the weeks prior to your death, would you find the *option* of a swifter death appealing? Even if your religious or moral convictions prevent you from availing yourself of that option, it is easy to see that many people would find it desirable. And since all of us face death, and we are all aware that some diseases are terrible and debilitating, it is not surprising that many people find an optional escape route desirable. Whether we favor or oppose active euthanasia, all of us recognize that there are legitimate motives for wanting to legalize active euthanasia; thus there is no plausibility to the attribution of vile motives, and certainly no evidence that such motives exist. All advocates of active euthanasia agree that there must be very careful regulation of its use, with clear evidence that the choice for active euthanasia is the patient's free uncoerced choice. If there is some moral monster who wants to "eliminate undesirables," that person would be better served by a policy that involves much less scrutiny and supervision. Furthermore, such a moral monster would find active euthanasia a poor method, for it involves waiting around for the victims to develop terminal illnesses and thus become suitable candidates for euthanasia. In any case, this strawman distortion requires little scrutiny to see its falsity.

On the other side of the active euthanasia controversy we find the strawman claim that those who *oppose* active euthanasia wish to impose their religious views on everyone, undermining the freedom of those who have different views and denying them religious freedom. Certainly there are some people who oppose active euthanasia on religious grounds, believing that it is wrong for anyone to "play God" by hastening death: Humans belong to God, and only God can decide when their lives should end. But most of those opposed to active euthanasia do not oppose it on religious grounds; rather, they fear that—primarily because of financial burdens on the sick person and his or her family—some people will feel pressured to choose active euthanasia against their real wishes.

What Is the Common Ground?

Whether you fiercely oppose or strongly support active euthanasia, there is a large area of underlying agreement. First, *no one* should be compelled to accept active euthanasia, and *no one* should be *pressured* toward active euthanasia. If your continued medical treatment is driving your family into bankruptcy, will result in your beloved spouse losing his or her home due to medical expenses, and is eating away all the funds that were saved for the college education of your children, then certainly you will feel pressured to stop the enormous medical costs that are bankrupting your family and threatening their futures. You are likely to feel that pressure, even if everyone in your family insists that you should not worry at all about the costs. Indeed, if your loving family insists that they are more than willing to bankrupt themselves in order to extend your life for another month, that might well cause you to feel even greater obligation not to cause the financial suffering of those you love and who love you so deeply. Yet that is precisely the problem that confronts many people in the United States who are dealing with terminal illness: The cost of their treatment is astronomical, and the financial burden they are causing their families is crushing. So perhaps from that we can find some *additional* common ground that both sides can favor: No one should have to worry about financial burdens in dealing with illness. That is, we should have (at the very least) a stop-loss program that will prevent families from being bankrupted by catastrophic medical expenses. That is not a problem in any other Western industrialized country, where health care is considered a basic right and no one has to pay out of pocket for health care.

Where else is there agreement? Everyone generally agrees that each competent adult should have control of his or her own body. (Of course if you are healthy, we try very hard to prevent you from committing suicide; but that is because we believe that those who wish to commit suicide are suffering from severe depression or other mental problems that make them incompetent to decide what happens to them.) If you wish to risk your life hang-gliding or mountain-climbing, that's your choice. Furthermore, there is agreement that having control, and a sense of control, is a good thing (most of us regard it as inherently good; and we know that when people *lose* a sense of control, severe depression often follows).

Most would also agree that the state has a legitimate interest in the welfare of its citizens, though exactly how far that legitimate interest extends is often a matter of controversy. Everyone agrees that the state has an interest—indeed, a strong obligation—to protect its citizens from murderers and terrorists and thieves. Almost everyone would agree that the state has an obligation to protect its citizens from such dangers as toxic chemicals and dangerously defective products: If you are selling cars in which the brakes frequently fail, the state should stop such sales; if an industry is discharging high levels of lead into the air we breathe, or dangerous levels of mercury into the water we drink, then the state has the right and the obligation to prevent such harmful activities. Does the state have the right to prevent or discourage or limit dangerous activities its citizens voluntarily choose? Riding motorcycles is very dangerous, but few of us believe that the state should outlaw that activity. On the other hand, most of us believe that the state can legitimately require that motorcyclists pass a test (and get a special license) to show that they are reasonably competent riders and knowledgeable about proper safety procedures. So there are limits to what the state should do to protect its citizens (it should not ban motorcycle riding) but the state does have an interest in protecting the welfare of its citizens (it can require motorcycle riders to obtain a special license before they ride). What about requiring motorcyclists to wear a helmet, in order to protect them from severe head injuries? On that issue, we get much less agreement: Some states require helmets, others do not; some people regard helmet laws as a legitimate safety requirement, while others regard such laws as an illegitimate infringement on individual choice. Exactly where active euthanasia fits in this debate (Is a ban of active euthanasia a legitimate exercise of state authority to protect its citizens?) remains in dispute. That the state has *some* legitimate interest in protecting its citizens is generally agreed.

Finally, everyone agrees that *if* active euthanasia is permitted, it should be very carefully regulated. For example, there should be some waiting period between the request for active euthanasia and carrying out that process: If you wake up a bit grumpy from your afternoon nap and start yelling at the nurse that you wish you were dead, we do *not* want the nurse to immediately jab you with a lethal injection. At the very least, there should be a psychological evaluation to make sure you are competent.

Arguments against Active Euthanasia

1. The greatest concern with active euthanasia is that it will *lead* to cases in which active euthanasia is practiced on people who do not freely choose it. This is a concern that troubles some who ultimately support active euthanasia, and troubles others who would support active euthanasia policies in the right circumstances but *not* under the U.S. system in which medical costs often fall heavily on individuals and their families.

There are two ways that an active euthanasia policy might lead to the euthanasia of persons who have not freely chosen euthanasia. The first is that individuals may fear that they are becoming a financial burden on their families because of the extraordinarily high cost of medical care. Even affluent families can be financially devastated by a lengthy illness and hospitalization, and sick persons may be deeply concerned that medical costs will leave their loved ones destitute. In such circumstances, an individual who might prefer to fight for a few more weeks or months of life could well decide to end his or her life more quickly, to avoid burdening family members with staggering medical costs and debts.

There are two points to note about this genuine problem. First, in Western industrialized countries, this problem can arise only in the United States. In other countries—in Canada or France or Australia—medical care is considered a universal right, and individuals and their families are not burdened by medical costs. However, it is a very real problem in the United States, where medical costs are one of the leading causes of bankruptcy, and a few weeks in a hospital intensive care ward can wipe out very substantial savings accounts (and even if one is not hospitalized, a full round of some recently developed outpatient cancer treatments can cost well over $100,000).

Second, this is not a *special* problem for active euthanasia, but a problem that runs much deeper. The burden of enormous medical costs is not so likely to result in active euthanasia as in passive euthanasia (which, as noted earlier, is widely accepted). Because of the enormous costs of hospitalization or special cancer treatments or organ transplants, patients—fearing the burden that will be placed on their loved ones—might decide not to pursue aggressive treatments, instead opting to let the disease take its course; even though the actual preference of the patient is to fight the disease with every resource available. This sad fact does not persuade us to deny patients the right to refuse treatment, and thus does not block passive euthanasia; that being the case, it is difficult to count it as a strong objection to active euthanasia, since active euthanasia would be much less common in these circumstances (most patients who choose not to pursue further treatments would allow the disease to take its course, perhaps in a hospice setting).

The crushing weight of medical costs is one possible way that patients might feel pressure to accept active euthanasia when they do not really want it; a second way that active euthanasia might expand beyond patients who *freely choose* active euthanasia is in dealing with patients who have become comatose. In those circumstances, patients obviously cannot choose anything, including active euthanasia; but if active euthanasia becomes acceptable, there might be some danger of medical personnel concluding that this person would really prefer to die—"if this patient could choose, that is what he would want"—and thus administering active euthanasia without the patient's choice. Though such an extension of active euthanasia is possible, it does not seem likely, for a variety of reasons. First, such a procedure would violate the law, and any medical professional participating would not only be in danger of losing his or her license to practice medicine, but also be subject to both civil suits and criminal penalties. Second, living wills—in which patients give explicit instructions concerning what medical procedures they do and do *not* want should they lose the capacity to choose—are becoming much more common. If a comatose patient has completed a living will requiring that in the event that he or she becomes permanently comatose, then no nutrition, hydration, or artificial respiration should be supplied; death through passive euthanasia will soon follow, preventing any need for active euthanasia. In addition, *if* we limit active euthanasia to physician-*assisted* suicide—in which the *patient* must actively take the lethal dose that the physician prepares—that would eliminate the possibility of nonconscious persons who have not chosen euthanasia being killed. If we fear this expansion of active euthanasia, such a restriction could block it.

2. A second objection to active euthanasia is that allowing active euthanasia would destroy a valuable clear line that regulates medical practice: Physicians must never aim at death. The first problem with this objection is that the line is not quite as clear as we might suppose. For many years, pain management for terminally ill patients was very poor; not because effective means of pain management did not exist, but because physicians feared that adequate doses of such drugs might hasten the death of the patient and so were reluctant to prescribe sedatives sufficient to control severe pain. In recent years, the medical community—under great pressure from patients and the public to provide adequate pain relief for terminally ill patients—has placed much greater emphasis on effective pain management for terminally ill patients. As a result, physicians have become more willing to prescribe larger doses of sedatives for pain relief. One well-known side effect of such sedative doses is that respiration slows, and by slowing the respiratory rate death is hastened. But even in Catholic hospitals—which are adamantly opposed to any form of active euthanasia—this practice is approved, on the grounds that although it hastens death, the drugs are prescribed for the *purpose* of relieving pain, *not* for the purpose of causing death. Whatever one thinks of that distinction, obviously the clear line that blocks physicians from any treatment that aims at death is not quite as clear as it once was.

Second, the fact that this is part of medical tradition does not carry much weight. Centuries of medical tradition required that physicians never tell patients their condition, but instead keep all such information a secret. But the principle of *informed consent*—every patient has the right to full honest information concerning his or her condition as well as the available treatment options and their benefits and risks—is now a basic requirement of medical ethics as well as a fundamental principle of medical law. Both patients and medical professionals agree that rejecting the earlier tradition produced ethical, psychological, and medical benefits. So the fact that something is part of long medical tradition is not a point in its favor.

Finally, asserting the value of this clear line against aiming at death begs the question concerning the value of active euthanasia. The question at issue is whether in some special circumstances, when a terminally ill patient has freely chosen a swifter death, is it legitimate for physicians to aid the patient in dying? Is it legitimate for physicians to aim at death for the patient who desires it? If that is valuable, then the clear line blocks what the patient genuinely prefers rather than protecting patient interests.

3. For many people, the rejection of active euthanasia is based on deep religious principle. Catholic doctrine condemns active euthanasia, and for those holding such religious beliefs, active euthanasia is clearly wrong. But religious doctrines carry little weight in the larger pluralistic society in which people hold a variety of religious views (ranging from fundamentalism to atheism). The right of the religious believer to reject active euthanasia is absolute, but that right does not extend to forcing religious beliefs and doctrines on others.

   One prominent religious argument against active euthanasia is that it involves playing God: Humans, as God's creatures, have no right to determine their time of death; that power should be left exclusively to the Creator. But consider the current use of antibiotics that prevent deaths from infection, transplants and dialysis to treat kidney failure, sophisticated successful cancer treatments, open heart surgery and heart transplants. In light of these welcome medical advances that save and dramatically extend life, it seems strange to object that active euthanasia is playing God. If there is no objection (except among small Christian sects) to playing God by saving and extending life, then there is little basis for playing-God objections to voluntary active euthanasia.

4. Finally, some argue that advances in effective treatment of pain eliminate the need for active euthanasia: Pain can be effectively controlled, and so no one need seek active euthanasia in order to escape unbearable suffering. In addition, patients now have the right to refuse any treatment at any time. Given the right to refuse treatment and the availability of effective pain relief, patients need not fear a long, slow, helpless, and painful death tethered to a battery of machines. Thus the fears that caused people to desire active euthanasia have been lessened, and people can have adequate control over their own dying process without the need for active euthanasia.

Arguments in Favor of Active Euthanasia

1. The most prominent argument in favor of active euthanasia is based on individual freedom: the right of a free competent adult to make his or her own choices (so long as they cause no harm to others). For many people, that includes the basic right to script the final chapter of one's own life narrative. If you wish to "rage against the dying of the light" and use every means available to extend your life as long as possible, that is your right; if, on the other hand, you choose to make a graceful exit from life when your health problems have become overwhelming—if in particular you do *not* want the final chapter of your life to include a period of lying unconscious in a hospital room, in a state of ultimate helplessness—then that is likewise your individual right. In some cases, effective pain control for your disease will require sedating you into unconsciousness: Nothing short of that will block the pain. If you prefer to die in such a state, that is your free choice. But if you detest the idea of slipping into death from an unconscious state, and prefer clear control over your impending death, then that also should be your choice.

2. Another key argument in favor of active euthanasia is that it gives patients—including patients who ultimately do *not* choose active euthanasia—a psychologically important sense of control. If I know that I can always choose to end my life, swiftly and painlessly, then I know I have ultimate control over the course of my illness: It can never reach a level and leave me in a state that I find intolerable.

   Psychologists have long realized that the sense of effective control is very important to us. It is vital to our psychological well-being (if we feel helpless, this often leads to severe depression) as well as to our physical health (those who experience a sense of helplessness are much more vulnerable to infection and other health problems). Furthermore, having a sense of control promotes better participation in treatment and rehabilitation programs, and increases the capacity to endure pain (patients who have control of their pain medication—through a machine that will allow them to self-administer sedatives—use significantly less pain medication). When the patient is unable to control the course of a fatal illness, it might seem that control over the exact time of one's death would seem insignificant. But when control over illness is impossible, the control over other details (such as what one wears, the decor in one's hospital room, the schedule under which visitors are admitted) becomes particularly important to patients; and patients who have a sense of control over such details suffer much less psychological distress than do patients who feel that they have little or no control over their circumstances. Thus the sense of control over one's death—including the choice *not* to request active euthanasia, rather than being deprived of that choice—is an important factor in the psychological well-being of terminally ill patients.

3. Finally, some argue that by legalizing and carefully regulating active euthanasia, we will *reduce* the danger that active euthanasia will be employed carelessly and without the genuine request and consent of the patient. Because it is illegal for doctors in most states and countries to carry out active euthanasia, it is impossible to compile accurate data on how often it occurs. However, there is anecdotal evidence that it does occur—not on a regular basis, certainly, but in some cases in which a sympathetic doctor grants a patient's plea for a drug concoction or an injection that will end his or her life. In cases where the patient is not hospitalized, this may occur with a wink and a nod: "Here are a dozen pills that you can take to control the pain from your illness; this is a very powerful sedative, and it is important that you not take more than one pill every 12 hours, and you must not drink alcohol while you are taking this medication. If you took four of these pills at the same time with a glass of brandy, you would fall into a deep sleep and die within a very short time." In other cases, when the patient is hospitalized and cannot take the pills (perhaps because illness keeps the patient from swallowing anything), the patient's physician—at substantial risk to his or her career—may give in to the patient's desperate pleas and very quietly give the patient a lethal dose. So active euthanasia does occur, but because it is not legalized, it is not regulated.

   Some years ago, an AMA journal published a short note (entitled "It's Over, Debbie") in which an anonymous resident physician at a major research hospital wrote of being awakened in the middle of the night, called to the room of a young woman, "Debbie," who was dying of cancer. She was having severe problems breathing, and was in great pain. The patient's mother was at her bedside, and asked that the physician give her daughter a shot that would kill her and put her out of her misery; the patient, who could not speak,

- -

affirmed the request with a nod and a look of pained desperation. The doctor describes how he drew up a fatal dose, returned to the room, and—after both the patient and her mother nodded their approval—injected the patient with a drug that caused her to lapse into a coma and soon die. Some applauded the doctor's act while many condemned it; but almost everyone agreed that this was a hasty and badly regulated process: The doctor had very little knowledge of the patient's condition (other than what he quickly read on her medical chart), the patient's nod fell well short of a deliberate and informed request that everyone agrees should be an essential element of any program of active euthanasia, and there was no systematic review process to be certain that this was a voluntary and informed request from a terminally ill patient. Legalizing active euthanasia would allow much better and stricter regulation of a process that now occurs secretively.

Where Do We Stand?

First, no one should be pressured to choose either passive or active euthanasia (and that includes not being pressured by fear of financial burdens on one's family). If we agree on that, the implication is that we should be sure that all persons have adequate health care that will *not* overburden them financially, even if they require extensive treatment. A second area of agreement is that patients (especially patients suffering from terminal illnesses) should have access to aggressive pain relief, even if it shortens their lives. A final point of agreement is that end-of-life treatment should be carefully monitored, both to avoid abuse and to ensure that patients have as much control as possible (including the honoring of their living wills, which are too often ignored); and that *if* any form of active euthanasia is allowed, it should be very carefully regulated.

Questions for Reflection

1. Consider your *own* conclusions concerning abortion, capital punishment, and euthanasia. Are your views on these three issues consistent? Is there any conflict among them?

2. Arthur is paralyzed, is suffering from oxygen deprivation and bone cancer, and finds his current and future life intolerable. He cannot move, and his nutrition and hydration come from feeding tubes (he cannot swallow). There is no way that Arthur can participate in physician-assisted suicide, though he can express—through blinking, in answer to questions—his fervent desire to die. In such a case, is the distinction between physician-assisted suicide and active euthanasia still a useful one? That is, *if* someone believes in physician-assisted suicide, would consistency require that that person favor active euthanasia in the case of Arthur?

3. Jane is rapidly moving toward dementia, from her severe early-onset Alzheimer's. Though the disease will eventually kill her (actually, she will probably die of something else before she succumbs to Alzheimer's), it is likely that she will live for many more years. Sadly, almost all of those years will be in a state of severe dementia, in which Jane will not recognize her family members, will have no memory of what happened one minute ago, and will have lost the ability to use language coherently. Jane—who is a superb astronomical physicist, and whose favorite hobby is rapidly solving very difficult crossword puzzles—has a profound horror of losing her intellectual capacities, and despises the idea of living the final chapter of her life in a helpless and demented condition. *If* you favor active euthanasia, should Jane—who is still healthy and competent, but will soon not be—be a candidate for active euthanasia?

4. Would it make sense to say that active euthanasia is acceptable in the Netherlands or Canada, but not in the United States, because in the United States, end-of-life health care is so expensive for the patient and the patient's family?

5. Think of your own view concerning active euthanasia (whether pro or con). Now consider carefully: Is there *anything* you could discover about this issue that would cause you to change your mind? That is, can you think of any item of evidence (which obviously you now believe does *not* exist), the clear proof of which would *change* your position on active euthanasia?

Additional Resources

Ethics Updates provides extensive online resources on the question of euthanasia, including videos, links to other sites, recorded radio discussions, and full text articles taking a wide range of positions. Go to http://ethics.sandiego.edu/. Another good web source is the BBC site on euthanasia; it gives an even-handed summary of both pro and con arguments, as well as information on the status of the debate in the United Kingdom. Go to www.bbc.co.uk/ethics/euthanasia. At www.religioustolerance.org/euthanasia, you can find a good survey of the arguments as well as interesting links.

F. M. Kamm presents a well-crafted argument in favor of euthanasia and physician-assisted suicide: "A Right to Choose Death?" Originally published in *Boston Review*, it is available online at bostonreview.net/BR22.3/Kamm.html (also available at *Ethics Updates*). Margaret P. Battin's "Euthanasia: The Way We Do It, the Way They Do It" is not only an insightful defense of euthanasia, but also a very clear comparison of medical systems in the United States and Europe. The original article first appeared in the *Journal of Pain and Symptom Management*, 6, no. 5 (1991): 298–305; a revised and updated version was published in Bruce N. Waller, *Consider Ethics: Theory, Readings, and Contemporary Issues* (New York: Pearson Longman, 2005). Battin also has an excellent book on the subject: *The Least-Worth Death: Essays in Bioethics at the End of Life* (New York: Oxford University Press, 1994). Robert Orfali's *Death with Dignity: The Case for Legalizing Physician-Assisted Suicide and Euthanasia* (Minneapolis, MN: Mill City Press, 2011) is a very accessible book in favor of euthanasia.

James Rachels's brief paper, "Active and Passive Euthanasia," *New England Journal of Medicine*, 292 (1975), which is widely anthologized, is perhaps the best source for a clear and cogent argument for allowing active euthanasia *if* we approve of passive euthanasia; that is, Rachels argues that if we believe it is alright to stop the treatment of a suffering patient and allow that patient to die (when further treatment would prolong the patient's life and also her suffering), then we should also approve of purposefully *causing* death (perhaps by administering a drug) in order to hasten death and relieve suffering. Rachels' ideas are expanded in his book, *The End of Life: Euthanasia and Morality* (New York: Oxford University Press, 1986).

Dan W. Brock's "Voluntary Active Euthanasia" (*Hastings Center Report*, March–April 1992) is a careful examination of both pro and con points concerning active euthanasia. Brock favors active euthanasia, but not without serious misgivings, and he is quick to acknowledge the strong points made against such a policy.

John D. Arras, "Physician-Assisted Suicide: A Tragic View," *Journal of Contemporary Health Law and Policy*, 13 (1997): 361–389 is a very careful and thoughtful examination of potential problems with allowing active euthanasia within the current U.S. health care system. Edmund D. Pellegrino's "Distortion of the Healing Relationship," in *Ethical Issues in Death and Dying*, 2nd ed., Tom L. Beauchamp and Robert M. Veatch, eds. (Upper Saddle River, NJ: Prentice-Hall, 1996) is a good brief argument against active euthanasia. For a longer examination of the arguments against euthanasia, see David C. Thomasma and Glenn C. Graber, *Euthanasia: Toward an Ethical Social Policy* (New York: Continuum, 1990); and Neil M. Gorsuch, *The Future of Assisted Suicide and Euthanasia* (Princeton, NJ: Princeton University Press, 2009).

Ronald Dworkin's *Life's Dominion: An Argument about Abortion, Euthanasia, and Individual Freedom* (New York: Alfred A. Knopf, 1993) is careful and reflective, and treats all sides on these difficult issues with respect and fairness. His chapter on "Dying and Living" is particularly good in examining the psychological aspects of why some patients would prefer to have the option of active euthanasia.

Susan Wolf's "Gender, Feminism, and Death: Physician-Assisted Suicide and Euthanasia," in *Feminism & Bioethics: Beyond Reproduction*, edited by Susan M.

Wolf (New York: Oxford University Press, 1996), raises doubts about active euthanasia, and offers original insights in a debate where many of the arguments are becoming rather standardized.

Active euthanasia has been openly practiced in the Netherlands for many years, originally as a result of court rulings that authorized it. The Dutch experience with euthanasia has been closely watched, and one of the best sources for examining the issue from the Dutch perspective is a book edited by David C. Thomasma, Thomasine Kimbrough-Kushner, Gerrit K. Kimsma, and Chris Ciesielski-Carlucci, *Asking to Die: Inside the Dutch Debate about Euthanasia* (Dordrecht: Kluwer Academic Publishers, 1998).

An interesting debate on physician-assisted suicide can be found in the *New England Journal of Medicine*, the issue from January 2, 1977: Marcia Angell, "The Supreme Court and Physician-Assisted Suicide: The Ultimate Right," argues in favor of legalizing physician-assisted suicide, while the opposing view is given by Kathleen M. Foley, "Competent Care for the Dying instead of Physician-Assisted Suicide." An excellent debate is found in Gerald Dworkin, R. G. Frey, and Sissela Bok, *Euthanasia and Physician-Assisted Suicide* (Cambridge: Cambridge University Press, 1998); Dworkin and Frey argue for allowing physician-assisted suicide in some circumstances, while Sissela Bok opposes it. *Euthanasia (Opposing Viewpoints)* (Farmington Hills, MI: Greenhaven, 2006), edited by Carrie Snyder, gives pro and con

arguments from a variety of sources on a range of issues related to euthanasia.

There are many good anthologies on euthanasia, including: Bonnie Steinbock and Alastair Norcross, eds., *Killing and Letting Die*, 2nd ed. (New York: Fordham University Press, 1994); Margaret Battin, Rosamond Rhodes, and Anita Silvers, eds. *Physician-Assisted Suicide: Expanding the Debate* (London: Routledge, 1998); Loretta M. Kopelman and Kenneth A. De Ville, eds., *Physician-Assisted Suicide: What Are the Issues?* (Dordrecht: Kluwer, 2001); Robert F. Weir, ed., *Physician-Assisted Suicide* (Bloomington: Indiana University Press, 1997); and Tom L. Beauchamp and Robert M. Veatch, *Ethical Issues in Death and Dying* (Upper Saddle River, NJ: Prentice-Hall, 1996).

An interesting debate on euthanasia, from the perspective of two Canadian authors, Bob Lane and Richard Dunstan, can be found at www.mala.bc.ca /www/ipp/euthanas.htm.

The courts have been heavily involved in disputes concerning euthanasia, as well as issues surrounding the withdrawal of treatment and allowing to die. For more information concerning the key cases, see Bryan Hilliard, *The U.S. Supreme Court and Medical Ethics* (St. Paul: Paragon House, 2004). The full text of the Supreme Court decisions, as well as the arguments before the court, can be found at oyez.com.

Religioustolerance.org has good material on euthanasia; go to http://www.religioustolerance.org /euthanas.htm.

MYSEARCHLAB CONNECTIONS

In the *Stanford Encyclopedia of Philosophy*, at plato.stanford.edu, see the entry on "Voluntary Euthanasia." Also, go to *Ethics Updates* at http://ethics.sandiego.edu, and under "Applied Ethics" click on Euthanasia, where you can find all the relevant U.S. Supreme Court cases on euthanasia, as well as other material. *ProCon.org* has extensive materials on the euthanasia debate; go to http://euthanasiaprocon.org.

7

Same-Sex Marriage

Chapter Outline

When we discuss capital punishment, everyone involved has no doubt that we are discussing an important moral question, with one side insisting that *justice* requires the most severe punishment for the most horrible crimes, while the other side argues that it is morally wrong to kill someone so long as there are other means of protecting society from harm. But when the discussion turns to questions related to sex—in this case, to sexual relations among consenting adults of the same sex, and to the marriage of same-sex couples—then for one side it is an important moral issue, while the other side may not regard it as a moral question at all. Of course those who favor same-sex marriage believe there *is* an important moral issue involved: Homosexuals should enjoy the same rights and freedoms as any other group in society. But for many who favor same-sex marriage, the question of the legitimacy of homosexual relations between consenting adults—the question of how consenting adults conduct their private sex lives—is not a moral issue. The opposition, in contrast, regards private sexual behavior as a very important moral issue. The opposing views are not so much in conflict as not even in contact.

To see this, consider attitudes toward sexual activity generally, without focusing on homosexual relations. Many of the laws under which homosexuals were prosecuted in the past were not specifically laws against *homosexual* relations, but against certain kinds of *sexual* activity (whether engaged in by heterosexuals or homosexuals—though often the assumption was that only homosexual couples would engage in such activities). They were laws prohibiting oral sex and anal sex; and although generally only homosexuals were prosecuted under those laws, the laws as written treated oral sex as a criminal act, whatever the sexual orientation of the couple. Today, these laws strike most people—and certainly most college students—as intrusive, unreasonable, and silly: Whether a couple does or does not engage in oral sex is nobody's business but that of the couple involved. It is not a moral issue at all, but more like a question of taste: If you like anchovies on your pizza, fine; if someone else doesn't, that's also fine. If you and your lover enjoy oral sex, that's fine; if you don't, that's also fine. (It is obvious that there can be some serious moral issues related to sex, including questions of infidelity, deceit, knowingly exposing partners to risk of sexually transmitted diseases, sexual exploitation, and—most obviously—sexual violence and rape. But those are questions concerning the mistreatment of others, and they arise in all avenues of life, though they may well have more profound psychological consequences when sex is involved.)

A similar change is occurring in the attitude toward homosexual relations. Like many social changes, it is occurring most rapidly among young people, and gradually extending throughout society. Two hundred years ago in England people were put to death for engaging in homosexual relations; a hundred years ago, they would have been imprisoned. In the United States, until 2003 a number of states treated homosexual activities as criminal; a Supreme Court decision (*Lawrence et al. v. Texas*, No. 12-102, decided June 26, 2003) was required to banish such laws from all states. The Lawrence case started when Houston police, in response to another inquiry, mistakenly entered the apartment of John Lawrence and observed him and another adult man engaged in a private consensual sex act. The police arrested the two men and charged them with violating a state law against such homosexual acts. The Court ruled that the Texas law is unconstitutional because it violates the Due Process Clause of the U.S. Constitution, which states that no one can be deprived of life, liberty, or property without due process of law. The Court majority held that laws such as the Texas law touch upon

> the most private human conduct, sexual behavior, and in the most private of places, the home. They seek to control a personal relationship that, whether or not entitled to formal recognition in the law, is within the liberty of persons to choose without being punished as criminals. The liberty protected by the Constitution allows homosexual persons the right to choose to enter relationships in the confines of their homes and their own private lives and still retain their dignity as free persons. (*Lawrence et al. v. Texas*, 2003)[1]

Of course, homosexual relations are still punished by death in many parts of the world. In 2009, an evangelical group from the United States went to Uganda to campaign against homosexuality, and the result was a push in Uganda to make homosexual behavior a capital crime.

Certainly it *is* a moral issue if one considers the mistreatment of homosexuals, just as it is a moral issue when anyone is mistreated, gay or straight, for any reason. But the question of homosexuality—like the question of oral sex—is probably not itself regarded as a moral issue by most college students, though it may be by their parents or grandparents. The most common exceptions are students holding fundamentalist or very traditional religious views. The Christian evangelical movement (including groups such as "Focus on the Family") as well as the Catholic Church condemns homosexual behavior as sinful because it violates "God's law." But even among those groups, very few of their members believe that the full range of traditional religious laws (of which the condemnation of homosexuality was only one) should be followed. After all, few of them would approve of parents battering their children to death with stones if the children disobeyed their orders; or the execution of persons engaging in premarital sex; or the killing of anyone eating pork, or touching the hide of a pig; or enslaving those of other ethnic groups; or murdering those who practice other religions; yet all of those rules were part of the same set of religious rules that included the rules prohibiting homosexual relations. And just as most practicing Catholics in Europe and North America have no problem with artificial birth control (though it violates "official Church teaching") likewise an increasing number of Catholics regard homosexual relations as neither a religious nor a moral issue, and thus not an issue on which religious leaders have any authority.

The rapid change in attitudes toward homosexuality has been remarkable. In 1960, an openly gay college student would have faced abuse, and been subject to physical threat as well as arrest. Police regularly entered gay/lesbian bars, ridiculing and beating up the patrons (the famous "Stonewall" riots in New York City were in response to such abuse). Now most universities have clubs for gay and lesbian students, and while open acceptance of gays and lesbians is hardly complete—we seldom get through a prom season without some high school principal becoming unhinged at the prospect of a gay or lesbian couple attending prom together—the atmosphere has certainly changed, and very few college campuses (with the exception of conservative religious institutions such as Brigham Young or Liberty University or Notre Dame) discriminate against gays and lesbians; to the contrary, almost all have programs to make gays and lesbians feel safe and welcome, and to protect them against discrimination or abuse. While the military forces of almost all NATO countries have long since admitted homosexual soldiers, the United States was slow to take that step; it has finally done so, and like its NATO allies has encountered few problems.

But while homosexuality is rapidly losing its status as a moral issue, the question of same-sex marriage remains controversial. And it is on that issue that the most intransigent opponents of homosexual relations—those who still regard homosexual relations as an important *moral* issue—take their stand. Heterosexual and homosexual couples have the same right to their own private sexual lives: That is a settled question, at least as far as the law is concerned. But whether same-sex couples also have the same right to marriage as do heterosexual couples remains a disputed subject, both legally and morally.

Same-sex marriage is not an issue that can be labeled conservative or liberal. Outstanding leaders of the conservative movement in the United States have been among the most outspoken advocates of the rights of gays and lesbians, including the right to serve in the military. Barry Goldwater, longtime Arizona Senator and widely regarded as the "father" or the American conservative movement, spoke out forcefully against all forms of discrimination against homosexuals:

> The conservative movement, to which I subscribe, has as one of its basic tenets the belief that government should stay out of people's private lives. Government governs best when it governs least—and stays out of the impossible task of legislating morality. But legislating someone's version of morality is exactly what we do by perpetuating discrimination against gays. (*Washington Post*, June 10, 1993)[2]

More recently, in 2010, Theodore B. Olson—a leading conservative in the Republican Party who served in both the Reagan and Bush Sr. administrations—published an article in favor of legalizing same-sex marriage, in which he wrote:

> Same-sex unions promote the values conservatives prize. Marriage is one of the basic building blocks of our neighborhoods and our nation. At its best, it is a stable bond between two individuals who work to create a loving household and a social and economic partnership. We encourage couples to marry because the commitments they make to one another provide benefits not only to themselves but also to their families and communities. Marriage requires thinking beyond one's own needs. It transforms two individuals into a union based on shared aspirations, and in doing so establishes a formal investment in the well-being of society. The fact that individuals who happen to be gay want to share in this vital social situation is evidence that conservative ideals enjoy widespread acceptance. Conservatives should celebrate this, rather than lament it.[3]

Once we have gotten beyond labels and distortions, what is the same-sex marriage controversy really about? Some people see marriage as a morally bankrupt institution, and oppose any form of marriage. They view marriage as contracting relationships that should not be contracted or institutionalized, with contracts that imply ownership rather than free commitment. But that is not the issue here, where those on both sides have a positive view of marriage. Also, there are some who regard homosexuality as an abomination, and want to build their religious doctrines into the criminal law. But that is a fringe movement, which wishes to turn the United States into a theocracy and impose harsh religious laws and strict religious observances on everyone. Such people exist, but they are comparatively rare, and attributing such views to those who oppose same-sex marriage would be a gross strawman distortion.

So what does the question of same-sex marriage really involve? On the one side, it concerns the desire of many gays and lesbians to participate in a societal institution that (its problems notwithstanding) still has enormous power and significance in our social lives. A civil union is better than nothing, but it is certainly not the same as marriage. When did you last receive a "civil union" invitation, or hold a shower for your friends planning a civil union? On the other side, there is the same recognition of the great social and symbolic importance of marriage, and a desire to preserve such basic social institutions from change. Experiment with lots of social programs and policies, fine; but be very cautious about making fundamental changes in basic societal institutions. When you change one of these basic structures, it is difficult to know what else you might be throwing out of balance. There is cautious wisdom in the institutions that have endured through many cultural and societal changes.

Strawman Distortions

One prominent strawman in the same-sex marriage debate is fear of "the homosexual agenda." When examined closely, that "agenda" is simply the desire to be treated like everyone else, with the same rights against discrimination in employment and housing, the right to adopt children, and to marry. That is, the "homosexual agenda" is a movement to claim the same rights that other minorities who have suffered oppression and discrimination have campaigned to gain. The goal of enjoying the same rights that others enjoy is not the goal of taking over the world.

The second strawman is the claim that same-sex marriage is an "attack on marriage." There are those, both homosexuals and heterosexuals, who believe that the institution of marriage is outdated, treats a personal relation as a property matter, and should be abolished; but obviously that is not the position of those same-sex couples who campaign for the right to be married. You do not campaign for participation in a policy or institution that you wish to destroy.

On the other side, those who *oppose* same-sex marriage are not proposing that we turn back the clock to a time when gays and lesbians were persecuted, imprisoned, and even executed. Of course there *are* people who hold such views, as noted earlier; but to characterize all who oppose same-sex marriage as having such views is to set up a strawman.

What Is the Common Ground?

In this debate, both sides see marriage as a good thing, worth having and worth preserving. One side wishes to extend participation in this desirable institution to same-sex couples, while the other side wants to exclude them from marriage.

Everyone agrees that religious groups should be able to maintain their own views on this issue. No one wishes to require Catholics or Southern Baptists to perform same-sex marriages. For many years, the Catholic Church refused to marry couples if one member of the couple was not Catholic and did not agree that any children from the marriage should be raised as Catholics. Whatever one may think of that policy, it was within the rights of the Catholic Church to place that limitation on the marriages it would perform. But that was not a restriction on such couples getting married; they still enjoyed that right, though they could not get married in the Catholic Church. Marriages between Catholics and non-Catholics were legal, and recognized by the state; but that did not mean that the Catholic Church was required to recognize or perform such marriages. The same applies to same-sex marriage.

Arguments against Same-Sex Marriage

1. Probably the most common argument against same-sex marriage is that such marriages confer legitimacy on homosexual relations, and homosexual relations are morally wrong. Perhaps homosexual relations should be *tolerated*, but society should not give homosexuality its blessing by allowing same-sex marriages. This argument, obviously, requires as a basic premise that the practice of homosexuality is morally wrong. But what grounds are offered for the moral wrongness of homosexuality? First are the religious arguments: Writings considered sacred by some

religions—particularly passages from the Hebrew Bible—condemn homosexuality. But as already noted, the same section that condemns homosexuality also commands stoning children who disobey their parents, approves of slavery, and sentences to death anyone who eats pork: rules that few people would take seriously as moral guides (it is not difficult to imagine what the judgment of the courts would be if you stoned your child to death and attempted to justify the murder on the grounds that the child had disobeyed you). But even if one can establish that some religious groups and their sacred texts condemn homosexuality, that provides no reason for a secular democratic state to forbid it. Of course, if the state is a theocracy—such as Iran—that is a different situation. But for states that are not under the control of a specific religion and its religious authorities, the status of a rule as a religious law for some specific religion or sect carries no weight in showing that the state should adopt that religious principle as law. Second, there are arguments that homosexuality is immoral because it is "unnatural." But establishing that homosexuality is unnatural will be quite a challenge; after all, we know that homosexual behavior is not uncommon among other species (our close relatives, the bonobo, apparently have no qualms whatsoever about homosexual relations). And even if one could somehow establish that homosexuality is not "natural," it would be difficult to move from there to the conclusion that homosexuality is wrong. There are many behaviors that are widespread and seemingly *natural*—such as brutal attacks on any group of outsiders who stray into our territory—that we certainly believe to be wrong; and from the other direction, there are many acts that seem quite *un*natural—such as turning the other cheek when someone strikes us, and forgiving those who harm us—that some respected religious teachers have taught as morally desirable behavior.

2. A second argument against same-sex marriage does not rest on the claim that homosexuality is a moral wrong; rather, it counsels that we should be very cautious and slow in making any changes to our basic social institutions. Those institutions have proved their worth over a long period, they have served as basic foundations for a working society, and they have connections and intricacies that we may not fully understand. Changing them is inherently perilous, and should be done slowly and cautiously, if at all. Instead of tampering with our traditional institution of marriage between men and women, we might consider civil unions for same-sex couples, examine carefully how that change works out over a number of years, and only then consider the possibility of making a major change in one of our most basic social institutions.

This is a difficult argument to answer: not because it is so strong, but because it is so vague. Changing our institution of marriage to allow same-sex marriages *might* result in some *unknown* terrible consequences. That sort of argument is offered whenever reforms are proposed: Our voting procedures have never allowed women to vote; we should proceed very cautiously, and not rush into radically changing this cherished policy because it might lead to terrible consequences. The same arguments were offered against allowing women to serve on juries, and against abolishing the institution of slavery. If this argument is to be taken seriously, those who claim that there are unknown perils lurking in any reform of our current practices must be more specific about what those perils are and why they are likely to occur. Of course some people insist that the terrible consequences just *are* the legalized marriages of same-sex couples; but that argument spins in a circle.

3. At least one slippery-slope result that is sometimes mentioned as possibly resulting from same-sex marriage is pressure for other forms of marriage, such as polygamous and polyandrous (group) marriages. In fact there have been and are some people who advocate for such marriages, as well as for "open" marriages in which monogamy is not required. (It seems strange to hear people who cite Biblical grounds against same-sex marriage worrying about polygamous marriage, since polygamous marriage was clearly approved by the same Hebraic religious sources that condemned homosexual relations; but that's another question.) But most of those advocates for polygamous and polyandrous marriage have been heterosexual, rather than homosexual. One argument given by many supporters of same-sex marriage is that entering into such socially recognized public formal marriage relations is more likely to promote and strengthen long-term *monogamous* commitments between partners. Perhaps there is some slippery slope that slides from same-sex marriage to polygamy; but those who make that claim have offered little evidence for the existence of such a slope, much less showing that the slope is slippery. There have been many major changes in the United States: the abolition of slavery, guaranteeing women the right to vote, legalizing artificial methods of birth control. In each case, opponents of those changes predicted disasters that did not occur. Guaranteeing to same-sex couples the right to marry would also be a significant change, as everyone agrees; but to use that as an argument against same-sex marriage requires some *evidence* that this will be a change that produces *bad* results, and that last crucial element of the argument is missing.

4. A fourth argument against same-sex marriage claims that if same-sex marriage were approved, then religious groups that are opposed to homosexuality—that regard homosexual relations as sinful—would be compelled to conduct same-sex marriages. But of course the legalization of same-sex marriage does not imply that any religious group would be required to permit same-sex marriages in its religion or give its religious approval to same-sex marriages. When the Supreme Court ruled that interracial couples had the right to marry, some churches continued to oppose interracial marriages. They remained free to refuse to perform such marriages, and even to condemn them in their teachings; but they were not free to forbid them. The Catholic Church can continue to exclude women from its priesthood, but cannot forbid women to take positions of authority outside the church. If the Catholic Church wishes to continue to condemn homosexual relations and reject same-sex marriage, it is free to do so and to promote that position among its followers. But it is something altogether different to allow the Catholic Church to compel everyone to follow that religious doctrine.

5. Finally, a fifth argument claims that same-sex marriage is part of the "homosexual agenda," which demands that society not merely tolerate but give its full blessing to homosexuality; and that means that individual citizens who disapprove of homosexuality (on whatever religious or nonreligious grounds they base that disapproval) would have their right of conscience violated. In the first place, there is no "homosexual agenda"; but there is certainly a powerful anti-homosexual agenda that works hard at preventing homosexuals from enjoying the same basic rights of private association and nondiscrimination that other people enjoy. What gays and lesbians campaign for is simply the same rights that others have. Those who consider homosexuality sinful have every right to hold that view, and indeed to promote it (just as racists have a right to their views, and persons who believe women should never hold positions of authority have a right to their views, and religious

bigots have a right to their views); but while groups and individuals have the right to believe that women should always be subservient and never hold positions of authority, they do not have the right to oppress women and deny women employment opportunities and voting rights and protection from abuse and violence and all the other rights enjoyed by citizens. The "homosexual agenda" pushes for exactly those same rights for homosexuals. *Not* the right to have everyone approve of their views and behavior (no one has such a right), but the right to live their private lives as they wish, to be protected from violence, to be protected from discrimination in housing and employment. Not special rights, but equal rights. And guaranteeing the right of same-sex couples to marry in no ways implies that everyone in the society gives their blessings to such marriages. One of our most cherished freedoms is the freedom of religion: You are free to be a Roman Catholic, an Orthodox Jew, a Mormon, or an atheist; but that does not imply that Roman Catholics must approve of Mormon theological principles, or that—because people are free to hold atheistic beliefs—Mormons must give their blessing to atheism. Just because the society recognizes and protects your right to be an atheist or a Baptist or a Wiccan, that does not imply that atheists approve of Baptist views, or vice versa. And if society recognizes and protects the rights of homosexuals to enter into same-sex marriages, that would not imply that everyone in society approves of same-sex marriage, or of homosexuality.

Arguments in Favor of Same-Sex Marriage

1. The fundamental argument in favor of same-sex marriage is one of basic rights. Marriage is deeply valued in our society: Marriage proposals are often carefully planned, occurring in places of special significance to the couple (announced on the scoreboard at a sports event and cheered by the crowd or in a favorite restaurant or at a cherished picnic spot or on a favorite ski lift or romantic beach); families devote enormous energy and substantial money to celebrate marriages, friends and family gather from distant places, extensive plans are made, the festivities often stretch over several days, and marriage ceremonies are often regarded as among the most important and joyful occasions in the lives of the married persons as well as their families. Marriage is celebrated in different ways in different cultures, but every human culture includes the recognition and celebration of marriage. Not everyone values marriage, of course; but for those who do, marriage and the marriage ceremony are of profound importance. To deny couples— because of their sexual orientation—the right to marry is comparable to denying persons the right to a job or to eat in a restaurant or to attend a school or live in a particular neighborhood because of their race. It is denying persons the right to something of great value—the right to publicly celebrate and commit to a marriage relationship and enjoy the legal and societal benefits of marriage—because of something about those persons over which they had no control. You no more *choose* your sexual orientation than you choose your race or gender. To deny your rights on an arbitrary basis—whether of gender, race, or sexual orientation—is fundamentally unfair.

2. Many gay and lesbian couples stay together over long periods, through thick and thin, through sickness and health, in deeply committed and profoundly satisfying relationships. It is sometimes suggested that allowing same-sex marriages would destabilize our institution of marriage; in fact, that institution has already lost a great deal of its

stability: Better than one-third of marriages in the United States end in divorce, and many marriages that continue are certainly not models of stability. Of course, many gay and lesbian relationships also fall apart; but such relationships face special disadvantages: Because marriage is not allowed, there is no socially recognized process for couples to make a deep public commitment to one another, a commitment celebrated with one another and recognized by friends and family, by the community, and by the state. If we value marriage, and want to support and sustain stable enduring relationships, then extending the right of marriage to gay and lesbian couples is a positive step in that direction. If we want to encourage stable lasting relationships among gay and lesbian couples, we cannot do so by denying them the right to marry. Rather than undermining marriage, same-sex marriage is more likely to have a stabilizing effect on a shaky institution.

3. Marriage benefits are important, and it is wrong to deny gay and lesbian couples those benefits. Some of the benefits *may* be available through civil unions, but marriage is a much clearer and more certain way of protecting such rights. The rights that attach to partners in civil unions are still being defined, while those for married partners are securely established. There have been too many sad cases when a partner in a long-time and devoted lesbian or gay relationship was denied admission to her or his partner's funeral; or when the family denied the partner of a dying or very sick (and unconscious) person the right to visit in his or her hospital room, or to have any voice in making medical or funeral decisions for a long-term partner. Your in-laws may despise you, but they have no right and no power to exclude you from your spouse's hospital room; without the right of marriage, such basic rights are jeopardized, or at the very least are left uncertain.

Where Do We Stand?

It was not until 2003 that the U.S. Supreme Court declared laws criminalizing homosexual relations to be unconstitutional: a basic violation of the right of individual privacy. Justice Kennedy, who wrote the majority opinion, stated as follows: "Liberty presumes an autonomy of self that includes freedom of thought, belief, expression, and certain intimate conduct." And concluding his opinion, Justice Kennedy made clear the importance of a right of privacy:

> The petitioners are entitled to respect for their private lives. The State cannot demean their existence or control their destiny by making their private sexual conduct a crime. Their right to liberty under the Due Process Clause gives them the full right to engage in their conduct without intervention of the government. (*Lawrence et al. v. Texas,* 2003)[4]

But it is worth noting that the Supreme Court decision was by a narrow margin, and justices such as Scalia denounced the decision as signing on to "the so-called homosexual agenda." The rights of gays and lesbians to live their private lives as they wish remains controversial, though clearly—especially among younger people—belief in the rights of homosexuals to live as they wish is gaining strength. But marriage is a different step. Many people are reluctant to allow any change whatsoever in such a basic and long-standing institution (though changes in divorce laws have already made significant alterations in traditional marriage); and while many are supportive of the rights of homosexuals to live their private lives as they wish, marriage brings homosexual relations into a much more public sphere. For several years, the U.S. armed services followed a "don't ask/don't tell" policy for gay and lesbian soldiers: You could serve in the military, so long as you kept your sexual orientation a secret; that is, you could serve in the military, so long as you didn't let anyone know who you really are, so long as your sexual orientation was not public. It was not a very satisfactory policy for anyone, and has finally been dropped, allowing gays and lesbians to serve in the military without restriction and without secrecy. In some ways, the current controversy over same-sex marriage is similar to the debate over don't ask/don't tell. There is growing consensus that homosexuals should be able to live their private lives as they wish, so long as those lives are private; but marriage is an open and public process that brings our relations into the open and makes our commitments public. That is why many oppose same-sex marriage; and that is why many gays and lesbians regard same-sex marriage as of utmost importance.

Questions for Reflection

1. If you are involved in a heterosexual relationship of some duration, then even though the question of marriage may not have come up, it is probably lurking somewhere in the background. Will this relation continue beyond college? My parents are visiting campus this weekend; if I invite my lover to have dinner with my parents, will that imply anything about this being a more permanent relationship? Is this really a person I might want to marry? If you and your lover belonged to a group for whom marriage was not a legal possibility, would that change your current relationship in any way?

2. Some opponents of same-sex marriage claim that changing the legal status of marriage to allow same-sex marriages would be a *change* in the marriage tradition, and that any such change opens the way for other changes: polygamous and polyandrous (group) marriages, for example. Supporters of same-sex marriage argue that the opposite result is more plausible: No doubt there are some gays and lesbians who support polygamous and polyandrous relationships, just as there are some heterosexuals who favor such relationships; but those gays and lesbians who want to be *married* are interested in making public and legal long-term monogamous commitments to each other, and thus

they would *strengthen* the tradition of marriage as a stable committed monogamous relationship. Which side of this argument do you find more plausible?

3. In 2003, *Commentary*—a journal promoting conservative views—published a number of articles by conservatives on both sides of the same-sex marriage debate. Sam Schulman contributed an essay opposing same-sex marriage, and one of his arguments was that basically homosexuals suffer no special harm by being denied the right to marry: "The social status of homosexuals is no better and no worse than that of anyone else who lives in an unmarried condition."[5] Is that claim true?

4. The question of same-sex marriage (and generally the question of the rights of homosexuals, such as the right to serve openly in the military, and to live their private lives as they wish so long as they do not harm others) is an issue that drives a deep wedge between the two groups that make up the conservative movement in the United States. Barry Goldwater—regarded as "Mr. Conservative" by many conservatives, the former Republican nominee for president, and a leading conservative theorist on the "libertarian" side of the conservative movement—campaigned vigorously for the rights of homosexuals to serve

openly in the military, and generally for the rights of homosexuals to lives their private lives as they wish. Economist Milton Friedman was also a libertarian conservative. Andrew Sullivan, a leading contemporary conservative theorist, is a homosexual who argues in favor of same-sex marriage. Ron Paul, a member of the U.S. House of Representatives from Texas, is another leader in the libertarian wing of the conservative movement (in 2011 he sponsored a bill to eliminate the federal laws against marijuana, on the grounds that they are an illegitimate restriction on the rights of individuals and states to make their own decisions about drug use). On the other side of the conservative movement are the "social values conservatives," who typically campaign for traditional religious values, and who believe that those values should govern not only the public sphere but also the private lives of individuals. Social conservatives oppose same-sex marriage—since it violates traditional religious values—and also deny the right of homosexuals to engage in private homosexual relations.

William Bennett is a contemporary social values conservative, along with Rev. Pat Robertson, Michelle Bachman, Sarah Palin, Rick Perry, and Rick Santorum. The question of homosexual rights and same-sex marriage (along with differences on a number of other issues that libertarians regard as private matters and social conservatives believe should be under restrictive government and/or social control) has caused serious tensions within the larger conservative movement. In 2011, a major convention of the conservative movement (the Conservative Political Action Committee) allowed a conservative (libertarian) gay/lesbian rights organization (GOProud) to attend and participate in the convention; some social conservative groups (such as the Family Research Council, Concerned Women for America, and the Heritage Foundation) were so strongly opposed to the views of this group that they boycotted the convention. On the question of same-sex marriage, is there any way for social conservatives and libertarian conservatives to find common ground?

Additional Resources

An excellent anthology on the issue of same-sex marriage is *Same-Sex Marriage: The Moral and Legal Debate*, 2nd ed., edited by Robert M. Baird and Stuart L. Rosenbaum (Amherst, NY: Prometheus Books, 2004). Another good anthology is edited by Andrew Sullivan, *Same-Sex Marriage: Pro and Con* (London: Vintage, 2004).

Two books that argue in favor of same-sex marriage—from a conservative perspective—are Bruce Bawer's *A Place at the Table* (New York: Simon & Schuster, 1993), and Andrew Sullivan's *Virtually Normal* (New York, Alfred A. Knopf, 1995). Conservative *opponents* of same-sex marriage include Stanley Kurtz, "What Is Wrong with Gay Marriage?" *Commentary*, September 2000; and William J. Bennett, *The Broken Hearth* (New York: Doubleday, 2001).

A very readable book that argues in favor of same-sex marriage is Jonathan Rauch's *Gay Marriage: Why It Is Good for Gays, Good for Straights, and Good for America* (New York: Henry Holt, 2004). William N. Eskridge, Jr. and Darren R. Spedale, in *Gay Marriage: For Better or for Worse? What We've Learned from the Evidence*

(New York: Oxford University Press, 2006), argue that same-sex marriage is much more likely to strengthen than threaten marriage. A vigorous debate on the subject is found in *Debating Same-Sex Marriage*, by John Corvino and Maggie Gallagher (New York: Oxford University Press, 2012).

Evan Gerstmann's *Same-Sex Marriage and the Constitution*, 2nd ed. (Cambridge: Cambridge University Press, 2008) is an insightful study of same-sex marriage in relation to the U.S. Constitution. M. V. Lee Badgett's *When Gay People Get Married: What Happens When Societies Legalize Same-Sex Marriage* (New York: NYU Press, 2010) is an outstanding sociological and psychological study of the impact of same-sex marriage on culture.

On the more general issues concerning homosexuality, see a superb anthology edited by John Corvino, *Same Sex: Debating the Ethics, Science, and Culture of Homosexuality* (Lanham, MD: Rowman & Littlefield, 1997). Another excellent anthology is Robert M. Baird & M. Katherine Baird's *Homosexuality: Debating the Issues* (Amherst, NY: Prometheus Books, 1995).

For a sympathetic approach to homosexual rights, see Richard D. Mohr's *Gays/Justice: A Study of Ethics, Society, and Law* (New York: Columbia University Press, 1988). For the opposing view, see Roger Scruton, *Sexual Desire* (London: Weidenfeld and Nicolson, 1985).

An essay that opposes the legitimacy of homosexual relations—from a "natural law" perspective—is John Finnis's "Law, Morality, and 'Sexual Orientation,'" *Notre Dame Journal of Law, Ethics, and Public Policy*, 9 (1995). One of the best and clearest arguments for the moral legitimacy of homosexual behavior is by John Corvino, "Why Shouldn't Tommy and Jim Have Sex? A Defense of Homosexuality," from *Same Sex: Debating the Ethics, Science, and Culture of Homosexuality* (Lanham, MD: Rowman & Littlefield, 1997).

Michael Ruse offers a powerful critique of the claim that homosexuality is "unnatural," in "The Morality of Homosexuality," in *Philosophy and Sex*, rev. ed. by Robert Baker and Frederick Elliston (Buffalo, NY: Prometheus Books, 1984).

Linda J. Tessier, *Dancing after the Whirlwind: Feminist Reflections on Sex, Denial, and Spiritual Transformation* (Boston: Beacon Press, 1997), combines philosophy, religion, psychology, and poetry into a unique exploration of the rich structure of lesbian relations.

A remarkable online source for more information is Professor Lawrence Hinman's "*Ethics Updates.*" Go to http://ethics.sandiego.edu, and under the applied heading, click on "Sexual Orientation." Suffolk University Law School maintains a remarkably thorough site on same-sex marriage. It reviews the laws in every state and around the world, as well as provides an enormous bibliography on the subject. Go to www .law.suffolk.edu/library/research/a-z/.../samesex .com. The Pew Forum on Religion & Public Life has an excellent site with interesting material on a range of issues related to same-sex marriage at www.pewforum .org/Topics/.../Gay-Marriage-and-Homosexuality. Religioustolerance.org has a good section on same-sex marriage at http://www.religioustolerance. org/hom_marr.htm.

Endnotes

1. Lawrence et al. v. Texas, Supreme Court of the U.S., Decided June 26, 2003
2. Washington Post, June 10, 1993
3. "The Conservative Case of Gay Marriage: Why Same-Sex Marriage is an American Value," January 8, 2010, The Daily Beast, at http://www.thedailybeast.com/newsweek/2010/01/08/ the-conservative-case-for-gay-marriage
4. Lawrence et al. v. Texas, Supreme Court of the U.S., Decided June 26, 2003
5. "Gay Marriage - And Marriage" by Sam Schulman, Commentary Magazine, Nov. 2003

MYSEARCHLAB CONNECTIONS

Ethics Updates at http://ethics.sandiego.edu (under "Applied Ethics" click on "Sexual Orientation") has good material; look especially at the "Talk of the Nation" programs. The Pew Forum on Religion and Public Life is also an excellent resource; go to http://www.pewforum.org/Topics/Issues/Gay-Marriage-and-Homosexuality.

IMMIGRATION

Chapter Outline

The Statue of Liberty stands in New York Harbor, a beacon of freedom and opportunity to many weary immigrants who risked life and fortune to make the difficult voyage to America. The famous lines by Emma Lazarus, engraved on a plaque at the statue, express the ideal:

> Give me your tired, your poor,
>
> Your huddled masses yearning to breathe free,
>
> The wretched refuse of your teeming shore.
>
> Send these, the homeless, tempest-tost to me.
>
> I lift my lamp beside the golden door![1]

In New York harbor stands the welcoming ideal. On the U.S. border with Mexico stands a much harsher reality: A wall constructed to block immigrants from entering the country, turning away people longing for the same opportunities sought by thousands who arrived by ship at Ellis Island, close by the Statue of Liberty with its pledge to welcome the "masses yearning to breathe free." Of course countries often fail to live up to their stated ideals: The U.S. Declaration of Independence asserts that "all men are created equal," and are "endowed by their Creator" with an inalienable right of liberty; but this same newly independent nation continued the practice of slavery for almost a century. Still, when we find such stark contrasts as a monument welcoming all the "huddled masses yearning to breathe free" and a wall constructed to exclude those same huddled masses, then it is hardly surprising that we find an issue on which there are deep conflicts and strong feelings.

If there is any issue on which alliances split, and people find themselves united with people they usually view from the opposite side of the picket line, it is the issue of immigration. Human rights activists, environmentalists, and labor groups often find themselves on the same side (not always, of course; environmentalists may have special concerns about the harmful effects of burning coal, while labor groups want to protect the jobs of coal miners). And cultural conservatives typically join forces with economic conservatives. But in the controversy over immigration, old alliances fall apart and new ones take shape. Various labor groups have differing views on immigration, but there is general concern that an influx of immigrant labor may drive down wages. There is special concern about illegal immigrants, who have no protection against the most brutal exploitation. They often work for extremely low wages in hazardous conditions, making it more difficult to establish both minimum wage and job safety requirements. Some—not all—environmentalists fear that increased immigration will lead to higher population growth as well as much greater consumption and pollution (individuals living in affluent countries like the United States consume more goods and thus cause greater pollution than those living in impoverished countries). People from both these groups may find themselves in opposition to human rights activists (who are concerned at the desperate plight of those wishing to leave impoverished homelands), with whom they are usually allied.

On the other side, the *social* conservatives express fear that a large immigrant influx will threaten cultural stability and cultural traditions (thus their emphasis on "English only" laws), and that large numbers of illegal immigrants might lessen respect for "law and order." That is not to suggest that social conservatives see nothing attractive in a surge of Latino immigrant populations from Mexico and Central America: Those immigrant groups tend to be more religious and have fewer objections to government endorsement of religion, and their cultures are often strongly intolerant of homosexuality—all qualities that endear them to social conservatives. The *laissez-faire* capitalist (libertarian) conservatives—who want a minimum of government regulation—are more concerned with the idea that people should be able to sell their labor where they wish, and employers should be able to employ anyone they wish (whatever their nationality or citizenship). They also like the fact that desperate immigrants are less insistent that employers follow health and safety and wage regulations. So long as they harvest the wheat, pack the meat, and put roofs on houses, these employers don't care what religion they practice or what language they speak. In fact, perhaps the one thing these two conservative groups agree on concerning immigration is that they do not want a large influx of immigrants—whether legal or illegal—making use of social services such as free medical care or food stamps; both groups—one in the name of rugged self-help individualism, the other in the name of capitalist principle—want to minimize government aid to the poor. If there is any question on which labels like "liberal" and "conservative" are confused and unhelpful, the immigration question is that issue.

As we consider immigration, it is important to keep one sad fact in mind: People rarely emigrate for the fun of it. Of course some affluent Canadians and Americans and Australians and Germans do move to other countries out of pure preference, and not from any sense of desperation. Perhaps because their ancestors were from Sweden or Ireland or Uganda, and they want to go back to the "home country"; or because there is a university in Canada or the United States or Australia where they really want to study, and they wind up "putting down roots" there. Or because they like the cosmopolitan atmosphere of Vancouver or the bright lights of New York City or the café culture of Paris. If you are a college student—poor as you may be—you are already among the privileged; and if you are a Western college student from a family of even modest means, then when you think of the possibility of emigrating, you may view it as a delightful adventure, an opportunity to move to another culture or continent that seems appealing and exciting, and perhaps a better fit with your interests and values and tastes. But emigration for "fun" is a rare exception compared to the desperate expeditions that most experience. For nearly all immigrants—including most of your parents or grandparents or more distant ancestors, perhaps including yourself—emigration is a profoundly disturbing and stressful experience. You leave family and friends, and the land and culture with which you are most familiar and in which you are probably most comfortable (most "at home"). You travel to a land where the culture is alien, the language is foreign, and the people are strangers. Such journeys are rarely undertaken lightly or cheerfully: It is no accident that many folk songs lament the leaving of the homeland, and the longing for the family or lover or culture—or even the mountains and rivers—left behind. Most decisions to emigrate are forced upon emigrants by desperate circumstances: political or religious persecution, war, famine, poverty. Almost all the people who are seeking admittance to a new country are people driven abroad by very difficult conditions. The best estimates place the current number of refugees—people who have fled from their homes because of civil war or violence—at over 40 million people, with many more people living in desperate conditions and facing starvation in their home areas. When those people seek to emigrate, they do not look upon it as a holiday.

Article 13 of the Universal Declaration of Human Rights, passed by the General Assembly of the United Nations in 1948, asserts the freedom to move from one's country, and return to it, as a fundamental human right: "Everyone has the right to leave any country, including his own, and to return to his country."[2] We may consider the "right to leave" as so basic that it hardly needs stating, but that right has sometimes been denied. Many Jews living in the former Soviet Union wanted to emigrate to Israel, but were denied that right. But the much more common problem for the "right to leave" is the problem of where to go. If you are "free to go," but no place will let you in, that is an empty "freedom." That is the fundamental issue in the contemporary debate over immigration: not the freedom to leave, but the freedom to enter. You have the right to leave a country where you are persecuted for your religious beliefs or your political activities or your ethnic identity, and you have the right to leave your country to escape poverty and starvation; but the right to move elsewhere is a hollow right if you are denied entrance to all the "elsewheres."

One of the most contentious issues is the status of "illegal immigrants," particularly questions concerning immigrants who have worked and lived for many years in a country, making a significant contribution through their labor (often difficult and dangerous labor), but who have not become legal immigrants. Even more troubling is the question of illegal immigrants who arrived here as small children, coming with their migrant worker illegal parents, and who have lived here all their lives—often well into adulthood—and have never known any other home or culture.

Strawman Distortions

There are many people who want very tight restrictions on immigration; but they do *not* favor closing immigration altogether, and it is a strawman distortion to attribute such views to immigration opponents. Even those who favor the most restrictive immigration policies typically favor the admission of those who have close relatives who are citizens (some people argue for very restrictive immigration policies on the grounds that once one member of a family is admitted, that will open the door for others; but even they rarely oppose immigration rights for those who have close family members who are already citizens of the country). Furthermore, those who advocate very restrictive immigration policies typically favor the admission of at least some asylum seekers (very few people favor denial of asylum for a person who will face death when returned to his or her home country because he or she is an advocate of women's rights or an opponent of child sexual abuse or a convert to a religion banned in that country). In short, it is a strawman distortion to claim that proponents of more restrictive immigration policies want to eliminate immigration altogether.

Second, while racism and ethnic prejudice have often played a strong role in opposition to immigration, it is a strawman distortion to claim that *all* opposition to more open immigration policies is rooted in prejudice. Prejudice has caused enormous misery, and has proved stubbornly difficult to eradicate. But if we paint all who favor restrictive immigration policies as racists, we avoid taking seriously their concerns and arguments and we make it impossible to honestly examine their position.

On the other side, those who champion more *open* immigration policies do not want to throw open the borders with no restrictions whatsoever. No one is opposed to screening potential immigrants to deny admission to terrorists; and no one is opposed to preventing psychopathic murderers or child sexual abusers or habitual criminals from entering the country. And in fact, even those who favor the most liberal immigration policies insist that immigration should occur in an orderly, systematic manner: Immigrants should be screened and treated for disease, and an orderly immigration process affords the opportunity to help immigrants make a successful integration into their new country (they may need help learning the dominant language, developing skills to enhance their employment opportunities, finding suitable housing, and avoiding those who would exploit them). When we eliminate the strawman distortions that plague discussion of immigration, there will still be much to discuss and debate.

What Is the Common Ground?

What can we all—or almost all—agree on? Imagine (for many of you, perhaps it is not that difficult) that you are 19 or 20 or 21; your family moved to the country where you now live a few years before you were born; you were born in that country, its language is your native tongue, its culture is the only one you have ever experienced, all of your friends are living in that country. Now you discover that your hardworking parents—who worked long hours to make a decent life for you and your siblings—are illegal immigrants. Would it be *fair* to deport you? Even if the country has a legal right to do so, few people would think that a *fair* outcome. And indeed, in most countries (including the United States), people who are born in the country automatically become citizens, even if their parents are not in the country legally. There are a few people who oppose that, demanding that even those who are born here should be denied citizenship and be subject to deportation. But such views strike most people as fundamentally unfair and unjust: When a child is born into a country, the child obviously has no choice about arriving in the country of birth. To be banished from your native land because of some illegal act committed by your parents before you were born strikes most people as an act of wanton cruelty as well as gross injustice. Furthermore, there is general agreement that there should be *some* immigration, as well as agreement that at least *some* screening of immigrants is permissible. But those points of agreement leave enormous scope for debate.

Arguments for More Restrictive Immigration Policies

1. Some who are legitimately concerned about environmental issues worry that by bringing more people into an affluent high-consuming society like the United States, we will increase consumption and worsen the danger of global warming. If the immigrants stayed in Mexico or Guatemala or Bangladesh, they would consume and pollute much less. That claim is probably true, but merely to state it shows its problems. This is not a justification for keeping others out, but a powerful reason to get our consumption and pollution problems under control, not only for our own benefit but for the benefit of everyone in the world. If a country is consuming far more than its share of the world's resources, and producing a disproportionate share of pollution, then that country needs to get its house in order, not prevent others from entering that house.

2. One objection to more relaxed immigration policies is their potential threat to strong social welfare systems. The threat can come from two possible directions: cost and general support. That is, immigrant consumption of social welfare resources can raise those costs to an unsustainable level; and second, a large influx of immigrants—with whom the majority population have little empathy—can undercut general support for a strong social welfare program. While this is an issue for Sweden, and in a different manner an issue for Canada, it is not as much of an issue for the United States. In the first place, the United States has the most meager social welfare program of any Western industrialized country; for example, it is the only such country that fails to provide health care for all its citizens, and indeed not even for all of its children (it has one of the lowest childhood vaccination rates, considerably below that of Cuba and many other Latin American countries). It spends a smaller proportion of its gross national product on social welfare programs (and the bulk of that is for the elderly, who are much less likely to be new immigrants). Furthermore, most economists agree that immigrants, including illegal immigrants, contribute a great deal more to the economic well-being of a country than they cost: Rather than straining social welfare programs, immigrants contribute to their funding.

3. Perhaps the most interesting argument for restricting immigration is the effect of large numbers of immigrants on distinctive and valuable cultures. Most viable cultures are not terribly fragile, but some may be more fragile than others. An Amish country, for example, might well have special concerns that large numbers of immigrants would upset its distinctive culture and way of life. Interesting as this argument is, it obviously has no force against broader immigration policies for countries such as Canada and the United States, which are characterized by a rich and vibrant multiculturalism. In a country where Cinco de Mayo is celebrated by people of every imaginable ethnic group, it is difficult to claim that immigration poses a threat to our culture; to the contrary, it

clearly enriches a culture that prizes its diversity. If the national culture is in fact one of exciting multiculturalism, then it makes no sense to think of it being overwhelmed by an additional tile in that rich mosaic.

Even in cultures that are more homogeneous, there are perils in the argument that immigration must be restricted in order to maintain an existing culture. A legitimate concern that one's culture not be overwhelmed is easily transformed into a right to be intolerant. We should keep in mind that the Irish, Italian Catholics, and Eastern Europeans were all seen as threats to "American culture." Certainly the culture *was* changed, but through being enriched in its music and art and cuisine and in many other more subtle ways. Cultures that cannot survive outside influences are likely to be so fragile that they had little chance of long-term survival under any circumstances. After all, even a culture that severely restricts immigration will feel the impact and influence of many other cultures and belief systems and ideas and styles: through the internet, television, films, books, foreign travel by its citizens, and study abroad by its students. And in fact, few of us really want our cultures to be fixed in stone. Perhaps there are some who long for "the good old days" of the 1950s, when many areas practiced strict racial segregation, women had few professional opportunities, any hint of nonconformity—in clothing or beliefs—was regarded with deep suspicion, and (unless you lived in a major metropolitan area) you were very unlikely to be anywhere near a Mexican, Indian, Thai, or Middle Eastern restaurant. Our culture has undergone significant changes, but most regard the changes as major improvements.

4. Some have argued for a right to restrict immigration on the basis of the right of free association. The "right of free association" has an unsavory history: It was the right claimed by the Augusta National Golf Club (site of the Masters' Tournament) to exclude women and the right asserted in the deep South to exclude blacks from restaurants, theaters, and hotels. (And on the other side of the coin, my right of free association would seem to imply a right to invite others to live in my country.) Even *if* one grants such a right, it is clear that it can be trumped; for example, by the right against being subjected to gender and ethnic discrimination, and perhaps by the right of others to free movement and to asylum and to be free from threat. In any case, this argument has more often appeared on the other side of the issue, as the right of citizens to *invite* others—from outside the country—to live on their property and work in their fields and factories, and it will be discussed further in the next section.

Arguments for More Open Immigration Policies

1. The basic argument for more open immigration policies is that denying immigrants access to wealthier countries denies access to opportunity, which is fundamentally unfair and unjust. Joseph Carens argues that if we condemn the feudal practices that bound peasants and serfs to the land, the contemporary practice of denying access to immigrants deserves the same condemnation:

> Consider the case for freedom of movement in light of the liberal critique of feudal practices that determined a person's life chances on the basis of his or her birth. Citizenship in the modern world is a lot like feudal status in the medieval world. It is assigned at birth; for the most part, it is not subject to change by the individual's will and efforts; and it has a major impact upon that person's

life chances. To be born a citizen of an affluent country like Canada is like being born into the nobility (even though many belong to the lesser nobility). To be born a citizen of a poor country like Bangladesh is (for most) like being born into the peasantry in the Middle Ages. In this context, limiting entry to countries like Canada is a way of protecting a birthright privilege. Liberals objected to the way feudalism restricted freedom, including the freedom of individuals to move from one place to another in search of a better life. But modern practices of citizenship and state control over borders tie people to the land of their birth almost as effectively. If the feudal practices were wrong, what justifies the modern ones?[3]

In medieval times, the feudal lord was born to wealth and privilege and opportunity, while his serfs were born into servitude and denied freedom of movement. The difference between the lord and the serf was an accident of birth, not something earned. Likewise, those of us born into wealthy nations are born to wealth and privilege and opportunity (of course some are born into considerably less wealth and privilege and opportunity than others; but even the child born into relatively unfortunate circumstances in Canada or the United States has enormously greater opportunity than the child born into Somalian poverty), and our fortunate circumstances of birth were just a matter of luck. Others—equally through luck, though in this case bad luck—are born into grinding poverty, and emigration is often their only hope of escaping such poverty.

While emigration to a more prosperous country may have enormous benefits for impoverished families that move, it is not without its problems. In the first place, often it is not the most desperately impoverished who emigrate, but those who already enjoy at least a modest level of prosperity. In India, Pakistan, Uganda, and the Philippines, there are many people who live in poverty; but the excellent students who arrive in Australia and Canada and the United States from those countries are not from impoverished families, but instead from families of comparative wealth, who have been able to give their children excellent preparation for their college studies. The United States and Canada have benefitted from the influx of outstanding doctors and engineers from Pakistan and India, but those highly trained professionals were not living in poverty in the countries they left. The desperately poor in those countries typically do not have the means or the connections to move to wealthier countries. They are left behind, while many of the best educated leave. The resulting "brain drain"—from less prosperous to more prosperous countries—may worsen the plight of those who remain. This problem could be avoided if host countries opened their doors to the impoverished as well as to the well-educated and prosperous; but when choosing between a hungry uneducated family and a family headed by an outstanding physician and her chemical engineer husband, very few host countries favor the former.

2. Another argument in favor of immigration rights is connected with the *basic* right that is a key provision of the United Nations Declaration of Human Rights, and that almost all of us recognize: The right to *leave* one's home country. When East Germany erected a wall to keep its citizens from leaving, that was regarded as an outrage against a universal human right. When the Soviet Union refused to permit Jews to leave—many wished to emigrate to Israel—that was widely condemned. But of course the right to *leave* a country is a hollow right if there is no place to go. When countries close their doors to those seeking to leave their countries of birth, then the right to leave is

severely compromised, if not denied. This seems especially the case if those who are
seeking to leave their country are asylum seekers who are fleeing an oppressive regime
that is threatening to imprison or kill them. One of the saddest stories of World War II
was the story of the ship *St. Louis*. It was commanded by Captain Gustav Schröder,
a German anti-Nazi. It carried 930 Jewish refugees, seeking to flee Nazi brutality. It
sailed on May 13, 1939, and for over a month it searched for a place that would accept
its desperate asylum-seeking passengers, only to be turned away in Cuba, the United
States, and Canada; finally the United Kingdom, France, Belgium, and the Netherlands
accepted the desperate passengers, who faced almost certain death if they returned to
Germany. In 1982, boat loads of Haitian refugees attempted to flee chaos and violence
in Haiti by escaping to the United States, only to have their boats intercepted at sea and
turned back.

3. From the libertarian conservative perspective, the right of the individual to free movement trumps any right of the state to restrict such movement. This is the laissez-faire
   capitalist view: I own this property, I should be able to sell it to anyone who wishes to
   live on it; I own this company, and I should be free to hire anyone I wish (including impoverished persons living in other countries who are so desperate that they will work
   for meager wages in dangerous working conditions). Ironically, the same conclusion—
   in favor of open borders (with restrictions only against terrorists)—is favored by those
   at the opposite end of the political spectrum, who believe that national borders are basically illegitimate. The conservative laissez-faire capitalist position does not, however,
   include any right of citizenship for those brought to this country to work for low wages;
   in fact, it explicitly denies such a right. On this view, employers have a right to hire
   workers from anywhere, but those workers have few if any rights. Harry Binswanger
   is representative of this view: Binswanger considers "American businesses that want to
   hire the lowest cost workers," and insists that "It is morally indefensible for our government to violate their right to do so, just because the person is a foreigner." But the foreigner who is hired has no right to citizenship, nor any right to protection from harsh
   and dangerous working conditions. (If desperately poor foreigners "choose" to work for
   starvation wages in dangerous conditions with no opportunity to gain citizenship, then
   they have the "right" to do so.)

4. A special argument in favor of more open immigration policies concerns how countries should deal with those who have been in the country for some time but are not
   legal residents; that is, the question of whether immigrants who entered illegally should
   be granted citizenship in the country or be expelled. Consider those who have lived in
   a country for years, but who have not met the conditions imposed by the host country
   for "legal" immigration: those who came seeking jobs and fleeing poverty, who stayed
   for many years putting down roots in their communities, establishing their families,
   and working long hard hours in agricultural fields, as hotel maids, in meat-packing
   plants, or for landscaping services.

Have we allowed those illegal immigrants to stay? Of course. If we had actually wished
to deport illegal immigrants, we could have done a major sweep through large farms at
harvest time, picked up the illegal immigrants there and deported them; and we could
have sent agents to surround the enormous meat-packing plants that hire dozens of illegal
immigrants, rounded up all the illegal immigrants working there and sent them out of
the country. Everyone knew that by going through the slaughterhouses, the meat-packing

plants, and the largest farms, we could find thousands of illegal immigrants. But that would have left crops rotting in the fields, it would have forced many of the largest meat-packing plants to close (or pay higher wages and develop safer working conditions), and that would have cost a lot of very powerful people a lot of money. These people love to hire illegal immigrants for their fields and factories, because the working conditions are tough, the pay is low, and the work is hazardous. Illegal immigrants are the perfect employees for such jobs, because they are easily exploited: They cannot complain to the authorities about dangerous working conditions, and when they are injured, the employers can't be sued and don't have to pay for treatment. And if you want to cheat the workers out of their pay, or force them to work in hazardous conditions (in which field workers are exposed to high levels of toxic pesticides, and workers in slaughterhouses and meat-packing plants frequently suffer severe injuries from working at high speed with very sharp cutting tools), the threat of deportation is always hanging over their heads, so the workers cannot complain.

The large farmers and the owners of the meat-packing plants made big profits, and made big contributions to political campaigns, and the immigration authorities found it convenient to look the other way. This large-scale acquiescence means that the workers were actually accepted, even though not officially; and at that point, they acquired *some* rights to remain. When the government quietly accepts people into the country, then it can't legitimately turn around and insist that those people are illegal immigrants. People stay for years, work hard, start families, and become residents, all with the tacit approval of the country in which they live. Even if one believes that there should be major restrictions on immigrants admitted to one's country, it is another matter altogether to banish people who have been living and working and raising families in the country for many years, with the quiet acceptance of the government.

Where Do We Stand?

Immigration is an issue that causes discomfort when we look at it honestly. If I am living in a country that others desire to enter, what right do I have to exclude them? If I am an immigrant or the child of an immigrant—as almost all of us are—what right do I have to close the door behind me? In setting admission standards for immigrants, is it *fair* to give preference to the best educated and most highly skilled workers (who are most *beneficial* to the wealthy country they are entering, but who are also the least desperate)? If a country has allowed people to stay and work and contribute to the economic development of the country, can the country legitimately turn them out? If people have grown up in a country—and are at *home* in that country, whatever their legal status—do they have a right to stay?

On these vitally important immigration questions, it is not easy to say "where we stand," because there are few points on which we all agree. If there is common ground to be found, it is more likely to be *procedural*. Feelings about immigration issues are often very strong, and discussions and debates about immigration often generate more heat than light. We might all find it worthwhile to step back from the issue, and view it from the perspective of the detached observer: When you consider *your* position on immigration, and the immigration laws of *your* country, ask how you would feel about them if you were an independent observer from another country (or another planet): Would they strike you as fair? As selfish? As hypocritical? As just? If you extended the "veil of ignorance," so that you did not know what *country* you would be born in (it might be Canada or it might be Somalia) or what talents you would have or lack, what immigration rules would you agree to? What rules would you consider fair?

Questions for Reflection

1. Two of the strongest arguments in favor of immigrant rights come from perspectives that are usually very much opposed: the laissez-faire capitalist perspective and the human rights perspective. Starting from very different values and assumptions, they reach a similar conclusion: Immigrants should be allowed into countries with almost no restrictions. Are there any less obvious but important *differences* in their position that stem from these dramatically different starting points?

2. If we deny entry to immigrants, do we have a special obligation to make their current situations (in the countries in which they are living) better?

3. If you are reading this book, it is very unlikely that you have been caught up in a civil war or ethnic conflict that destroyed the stability of your country, threatened the well-being and safety of your family, and placed you at significant personal risk. Instead, you have lived in a relatively stable environment. But that was not of your doing; it was your good fortune. Perhaps your family did something to secure your place in the relatively peaceful and prosperous society in which you live; you did little or nothing. By what right can you exclude others?

4. Suppose that you are living in a wealthy country, such as Canada, the United States, or Germany; and you are setting immigration policies for your country. You can establish a policy that will favor highly educated, highly skilled prosperous immigrants—such as doctors, engineers, and accountants—or you can choose an immigration policy that favors immigrants who are in desperate need (victims of drought, famine, civil war) who have much less education and very little money. Which policy would you adopt? Which ethical view (from Chapter 3) would best

support your decision? Which ethical view would *challenge* your decision?

5. You are a citizen of a relatively poor country—such as Honduras or Bangladesh. Your government has developed a program to select, by testing, 100 students each year who will be sent to Canada, the United States, Australia, or Europe for an all-expenses paid college education, with the goal of developing a growing body of highly educated citizens who will held lead the scientific, educational, and economic development of the country; and you were one of the students selected and educated under that program. With your excellent education, you have the opportunity to gain citizenship in a more prosperous country and make a nice income—considerably more than if you returned to your home country. Do you have an *obligation* to return?

6. A number of quite prosperous countries (particularly in Europe) have very low birth rates, and this is causing problems for those countries. The overall population is aging, there is a higher proportion of retired citizens (usually receiving some government financial support as well as government-paid medical care), and fewer productive workers to pay for the increased costs. These countries recognize that to solve the problem they need young immigrants who will come and work in the country. Because the countries are prosperous and the pay is relatively good, many people in poorer countries are eager to move to these more prosperous countries. However, some of the citizens of the prosperous countries do not want the immigrants—the legal, invited immigrants—to become *citizens* and enjoy all the rights of citizens (such as the right to vote and the protections of the Constitution); instead, they favor

offering these young immigrants *guest worker* status. As guest workers, the immigrants could not obtain citizenship, and they could be deported whenever the host country wished (e.g., when the guest workers become too old or too sick to work, or if they are convicted or even *suspected* of a crime, they could be sent back to the countries of their birth); but in most cases, they could remain in the host country as guest workers for extended periods: years, even decades. Because of impoverished conditions in their own countries, many young people will accept guest worker status in order to gain jobs in more prosperous countries. Are guest worker programs morally *legitimate*? Whatever your views on their moral legitimacy, do you see any *practical* problems for countries developing guest worker programs?

7. Imagine that you are a strict and thorough *utilitarian*; what conclusions would you draw concerning immigration?

8. Of the various approaches to ethical questions discussed in Chapter 3, which one would you find most helpful in dealing with the issue of immigration?

Additional Resources

A very good contemporary debate on a range of questions and views concerning immigration is offered by Christopher Heath Wellman and Phillip Cole in *Debating the Ethics of Immigration* (New York: Oxford University Press, 2011). Anthologies that debate immigration issues include M. Katherine B. Darmer and Robert M. Baird, eds., *Morality, Justice, and the Law* (Amherst, NY: Prometheus Books 2007); Carol Swain, ed., *Debating Immigration* (Cambridge: Cambridge University Press, 2007); Brian Barry and Robert E. Goodin, eds., *Free Movement: Ethical Issues in the Transnational Migration of People and of Money* (University Park, PA: Pennsylvania State University Press); and Mark Gibney, ed., *Open Borders? Closed Societies? The Ethical and Political Issues* (New York: Greenwood Press, 1988).

Several people have argued for open borders; that is, for the right of people to move wherever they wish, without restrictions based on national borders. One of the most powerful advocates of that view is Joseph H. Carens, in "Aliens and Citizens: The Case for Open Borders," *Review of Politics* 49 (1987): 251–273. Another champion of that position is Chandran Kukathas, "The Case for Open Immigration," in Andrew I. Cohen and Christopher Heath Wellman, eds., *Contemporary Debates in Applied Ethics* (Malden, MA: Blackwell, 2005): 207–220. Seyla Benhabib, *Another Cosmopolitanism* (Oxford: Oxford University Press, 2006), develops an interesting argument in favor of free movement, along with many other fascinating reflections. One of the earliest statements of that view is by Roger Nett, in "The Civil Right We Are not Ready for: The Right of Freedom of Movement of People on the Face of the Earth," *Ethics* 81, no. 3 (1971).

The argument that states have the right to restrict immigration in order to preserve a distinctive culture can be found in Michael Walzer, *Spheres of Justice* (New York: Basic, 1983); and David Miller, "Immigration: The Case for Limits," in Andrew I. Cohen and Christopher Heath Wellman, eds., *Contemporary Debates in Applied Ethics* (Malden, MA: Blackwell, 2005): 193–206. For a critique of that argument, see Michael Dummett, *On Immigration and Refugees* (New York: Routledge, 2001).

The "freedom of association" argument has been used both by those who advocate for restricted immigration as well as by those who argue that borders should be open for all immigrants. Christopher Heath Wellman argues for the former position, in "Immigration and Freedom of Association," *Ethics*, 119 (October 2008): 109–141. The opposing view (in favor of open borders, argued from the perspective of laissez faire capitalism) is presented by Harry Binswanger, "Immigration Quotas vs. Individual Rights: The Moral and Practical Case for Open Immigration," *Capitalism Magazine* (April 2, 2006).

The most detailed environmental argument against immigration is by Philip Cafaro and Winthrop Staples III: "The Environmental Argument for Reducing Immigration into the United States," *Environmental Ethics*, 31 (2009): 3–28. The authors acknowledge a strong obligation for wealthy countries to reduce pollution and also to aid those who are less fortunate, but oppose allowing large numbers of immigrants to wealthy nations.

Matthias Risse presents a strong argument for much greater openness to new immigrants into wealthy countries, in "On the Morality of Immigration," *Ethics & International Affairs*, 22 (Spring 2008); the full text of the article, together with several replies and Risse's response, can be found at the Carnegie Council website, at http://www.carnegiecouncil.org/resources/journal/22_1/essays/001.html/. The replies are at the same site, at journal22_3.

There are several interesting internet sources for information on immigration. The U.S. Commission on Immigration Reform was dissolved in 1997, but its website still contains a number of interesting papers,

at http://www.utexas.edu/lbj/uscir/. The goal of the Federation for American Immigration Reform is the dramatic reduction of both legal and illegal immigration to the United States; its views can be found at http://www.fairus.org/. The Urban Institute site is wide ranging, with good papers on a variety of topics, including papers concerned with the poverty of immigrant workers and their children, as well as papers on the question of immigrant workers replacing native-born workers; it is at http://www.urban.org=/hotopics.htm#immigration (a 1994 study by Michael Fix and Jeffrey S. Passel, *Immigration: Setting the Record Straight*, can be found at that site).

Endnotes

1. Emma Lazarus
2. Article 13, Universal Declaration of Human Rights (United Nations, 1948)
3. Joseph H. Carens, in "Aliens and Citizens: The Case for Open Borders," *Review of Politics* Volume 49 (1987): 251–273.

MYSEARCHLAB CONNECTIONS

See the entries on immigration, multiculturalism, and citizenship in the *Stanford Encyclopedia of Philosophy,* at plato.stanford.edu.

TREATMENT OF ANIMALS

Chapter Outline

Which would you rather be? A fighting cock, protected and pampered until you meet a relatively swift end in the pit? Or a chicken raised in a battery cage, with no space to turn around, whose beak has been painfully removed, who is crammed into a crate and strung up by its legs in a long line until its throat is slashed: a chicken who never in its entire life gets to walk around, scratch for worms, or do anything else that brings chickens joy. Yet we ban the former, and allow the latter.

It is clear that attitudes toward other species have undergone significant changes. Dog fighting was a popular legal activity in the United States in the late 19th century; it is now illegal in all 50 states, and involvement in dog fighting can and does lead to prison terms, even for popular athletes. "Cruelty-free" cosmetics—which are produced without animal testing—have become a significant part of the cosmetics industry. The number of vegetarians and vegans has steadily increased, though they still make up a very small minority of the population (and a significant part of that group are concerned about improving their own health by eating less meat and fewer animal products, rather than about the welfare of animals). The general attitude toward using animals for food and experimentation has changed comparatively little (in fact, contemporary "factory farming" methods probably cause more pain for animals than did farming methods of a century ago—certainly chickens confined to small "battery cages" for their intense but brief egg-producing lives would probably be delighted to change places with their ancestors who lived in large pens or even roamed free in the barnyard). Nonetheless, there has been a significant change: A century ago, few people would have considered the suffering of nonhuman animals as a moral issue at all (if you were the owner of an animal, what you did with it was your business). In contrast, most people now regard the suffering of nonhuman animals as morally significant, and news accounts of a dog or cat treated cruelly (left in a car to die of heat, left outside to freeze to death) provoke widespread outrage—and may subject the responsible person to criminal penalties for violating animal cruelty laws. True, cruel treatment of pigs or chickens or cattle on factory farms rarely provokes outrage (there is considerable *inconsistency* in the general attitude toward treatment of animals—pigs are quite intelligent, and certainly they are as capable of suffering as are poodles and beagles). Still, there is now widespread belief that the suffering of at least *some* nonhuman animals is morally significant, and that marks a substantial change in attitudes. And as noted in Chapter 1, there has recently been an agreement between the Humane Society and the United Egg Producers to significantly change egg-farming methods (including the elimination of battery cages) to reduce the suffering of chickens involved in commercial egg production; and that marks an important change in the attitudes of both consumers and producers of eggs. (The importance of that shift is indicated by the negative response from a cattle industry spokesperson, who expressed anger that any governmental policies would be adopted for the purpose of "making farm animals happy.")

Questions of animal rights and the ethical treatment of nonhuman animals are very large questions. They go far beyond the question of whether purposeful cruelty to animals is morally wrong; almost everyone (with a few disturbing exceptions) agrees that it is. Animal rights pose questions of the treatment of animals more generally, and especially the animals we describe as "livestock" or "lab animals." Serious questions concerning treatment of nonhuman animals are not confined to the treatment of *cute* animals such as kittens and puppies; they extend to veal calves, pigs, chickens, and laboratory rats. The basic question is simple: Is it morally legitimate to inflict suffering on a nonhuman living creature for human benefit? Or as some people would prefer to pose the question: Do nonhuman animals have a *right* not to be treated in ways that cause them special suffering? Or another possible way of asking the question: Is it morally legitimate for humans to treat individuals of other species in ways that we would consider morally *wrong* if the individual were human? Of the ethical issues we are examining, this is probably the most immediately relevant: It is an issue we confront daily, as we consider what to choose for lunch.

Strawman Distortions

To suggest that those who favor laboratory animal experiments also favor dog fighting would be a gross strawman distortion. On the other hand, those who oppose animal experimentation are *not* terrorists: Even the most radical of the "animal liberation" groups are strongly opposed to harming, much less killing, human researchers. They may try to disrupt research, and take animals out of the labs; and while many believe that is wrong, it is quite different from an act of terrorism that aims at killing large groups of people for political purposes. They do not "care more for laboratory rats than for humans"; rather, they *do care* about laboratory rats, and chimpanzees and cats and dogs and other animals used in experiments. And while the opposing view certainly believes that torturing animals is wrong, they do not regard the suffering inflicted on animals in the course of medical experimentation as wrong (and they do *not* take pleasure in causing pain to nonhuman animals); indeed, they often do not regard it as a moral issue at all. The same is true of those who raise animals for food production. They regard the animals they raise as simply meat, and their goal is to produce as much meat as possible, as economically and efficiently as they can. Genuinely humane methods of producing beef and pork would raise the costs enormously.

Those who oppose the use of laboratory animals in medical and scientific research are sometimes characterized as antiscience: as denying the value of medical research as well as biological and psychological research carried out on laboratory animals. To the contrary, those who oppose using nonhuman animals in such research (inflicting pain on them, and killing them) are typically strongly convinced of the principles of evolutionary biology, and particularly aware that human animals are very similar to the animals on which research is conducted. Chimpanzees are great favorites for research precisely *because* they are so similar to humans, both genetically and behaviorally. It is the *scientific* understanding of how much we have in *common* with other animals that motivates many to question the legitimacy of using other animals in ways that we would regard as terrible moral wrongs if they were done to humans. Those who oppose research on animals are no more "antiscience" than its supporters are "pro-cruelty."

What Is the Common Ground?

While this is a controversial issue, it is clear that we have a large area of common ground. Everyone agrees that animals other than humans can suffer and feel pleasure, and almost everyone believes that abusing animals is wrong. Hunters seek swift kills, and rush to put a wounded animal out of its misery. When we see evidence of abuse of dogs or cats or horses, we are deeply moved and deeply disapproving. Of course there are blood sports, such as fox hunting, bull fighting, and other such activities. But it is significant that a few years ago fox hunting, deep in the British tradition, was banned because of its cruelty to the fox. Mark Twain has Huck Finn describe "tying a can to a dog's tail, and watching it run itself to death" (an amusement for a slow afternoon, which Huck and his friends regard as having the same moral significance as a game of horseshoes). If children of today engage in such a cruel activity, the community becomes profoundly alarmed: In part, because of the concern that children who enjoy torturing dogs and cats sometimes grow up to enjoy torturing humans; but also because the torture of animals is itself regarded as a grave moral wrong. Indeed, even the neglect of an animal typically causes community outrage: When a dog is left outside to freeze to death, this is often a local news story and most people in the community are enraged at this cruel neglect.

Arguments against Animal Rights

1. The most common, but also the weakest, argument against animal rights is the argument from tradition: Humans have killed animals for food and sport for thousands of years, therefore it is right to continue doing so. Merely stating that argument makes its

flaws manifest. Slavery was widely practiced for thousands of years: That is not a reason for thinking slavery is morally legitimate.

2. A second argument against animal rights comes from religion: Ancient texts that some religions consider sacred clearly approve of killing animals for food; some may even imply that the sole purpose of nonhuman animals is to serve human needs. Even for believers in the sacred status of such texts, this is not a strong argument. Those texts were written when living without killing animals for food would have been much more difficult than it is today, and the texts are adapted to that period. Furthermore, the interpretation and understanding of sacred texts can change, along with religious beliefs and traditions: Certainly the Judeo-Christian tradition approves of killing animals, and sacrificing animals in religious ceremonies, and treating nonhuman animals as having no rights. But that tradition also approved slavery, as well as the stoning of disobedient children, those who committed adultery, and anyone who questioned or challenged the religion; and while it did not treat women as nonhuman animals, it certainly ranked them well below men. Thankfully, very few Christians now believe it essential to seek out and kill witches (though it still occurs in some cultures); but that is required by Christian scripture. The question is not whether killing animals for food is part of the Judeo-Christian tradition: It is. The question is whether this should change (perhaps as religious understanding deepens). And while the Judeo-Christian-Islamic tradition approves of killing animals, it should be noted that many other religious traditions (such as the Hindu and Jainist) strongly *dis*approve of such treatment of other animals, emphasizing instead the *unity* of all life (rather than the supposed distinctness of humans from the rest of creation).

3. A third argument is that the human use of animals is natural. Humans have long eaten meat, hunting and then raising animals for that purpose. But what is natural is not always good. It may be "natural" for men to force themselves on less powerful women, or for powerful groups to enslave those they conquer; certainly both were common for thousands of years. That is no reason to think those "natural" tendencies are morally legitimate.

4. The argument concerning "other animals are predators, so why not us" is common, but weak. First, other animals don't have substitutes (tigers cannot switch to a tofu and brown rice diet), but humans do. Indeed, there is no doubt that if humans switched to a vegetarian diet, we would not only be much healthier, but also could significantly reduce pollution and feed substantially more people (producing meat requires much more grain than using the grain directly for food). But even more importantly, in the natural world, predators serve a useful function that ultimately benefits the species that is preyed upon: Sick and weak individuals are thinned out and populations are kept in check (preventing overfeeding and starvation cycles). Human use of animals does not have that effect. To the contrary, humans often breed and raise animals in ways that are clearly damaging to the environment and to the physical well-being of the animal. Consider the commercially bred turkey, which—in response to consumer demand for large portions of white meat—has become slow, clumsy and stupid, and then compare a swift, intelligent, and wily wild turkey with the pathetic creature that is raised in large turkey-farming operations. There are good reasons to be cautious about tinkering with natural relationships in the environment, such as predator–prey relationships (we discovered to our sorrow that eliminating wolves has had bad effects on deer and elk herds, for example). But in the case of factory farming, the tinkering has already

occurred. If we reduce the number of factory farms, this is not a dangerous tinkering with natural predator–prey relationships, but instead would have clear positive effects on our health and our environment.

5. A more substantive argument bases the denial of rights to nonhumans on *differences* between humans and animals of other species. Centuries ago, the dramatic difference between humans and other animals was accepted by almost everyone. But that was before we learned that we are much more closely related to other species than we had supposed, having evolved from common ancestors. In fact, biologists now classify humans as simply one species among the hominids, with humans branching off from the line that led to chimpanzees only about six million years ago—the blink of an eye, in the evolutionary time frame. Rather than marked differences between humans and other hominid species, we find striking similarities. Many of the "distinctive features" that supposedly separate humans from other animals have been found in other species. Chimpanzees can carry out elaborate plans. They can travel a distance to a place where they know there are large stones, select an appropriate large stone, travel back to the place where a rival is resting, and use the stone in a dominance display. Chimps delight in the game of taking mouthfuls of water when human visitors are arriving at their display area, sitting quietly with the water in their mouths until the visitors come within range, and then spewing the water at their targets. They form elaborate long-term alliances in order to hold power in the group. They make and use simple tools. Chimps can consider things from the perspective of others. They can learn and use sign language to discuss things that are not present, even combining signs to form new words (whether this counts as "language" remains a debated subject, but there is no doubt that chimps can communicate a great deal to humans as well as to one another using such signs and that they can use combinations of signs to make new and original "sentences"). They can develop and transmit elements of a culture. All these abilities had been considered as setting humans apart from nonhumans.

In response, those who maintain that only humans have rights may insist that there is one characteristic that sets humans distinctively apart: the ability to reason one's way to abstract moral rules and to follow such rules. A chimp may act as a peacemaker, and do so skillfully and purposefully. But a chimp cannot reason to the abstract *rule* that "reducing hostilities and restoring peace is good," and then follow that *rule* out of a sense of duty. The capacity to rationally derive moral rules and follow them as a moral commitment is uniquely human, and *that* is the basis for human rights. Only humans have this capacity, and therefore only humans have rights.

The capacity for abstract reasoning and rule-following is impressive, but why should that capacity be the essential condition for having rights? Such a capacity might be an essential condition for understanding abstract principles concerning rights; but why couldn't one *have* rights even if one is incapable of formulating those rights in terms of abstract rules? A small child may not have the abstract reasoning ability to formulate a rule that it is wrong to torture or abuse beings that are capable of feeling pain; but it does not follow that the child does not have a *right* not to be tortured or abused (a right that you and I, who are capable of abstract reasoning, can recognize as the child's right, even if the child—the holder of that right—cannot formulate it). In any case, it hardly seems obvious that the ability to formulate abstract principles is the best basis for rights. There are lots of other candidates: Perhaps rights holders are simply those who are capable of suffering or those who are capable of feeling sympathy or those who are capable of cooperative behavior or those who are capable of affection. Abstract reasoning is a wonderful thing, but it is not clear that it is the *only* basis for rights.

There is an even tougher problem for those who wish to use abstract reasoning ability as the unique basis for rights. Psychologists tell us that we actually reason our way to abstract principles much less often than we might imagine. Instead, we typically follow the rules we have taken from our society and culture; and when we reason, we are more likely to be seeking *justifications* for those rules, rather than actually reasoning our way to those rules themselves. But the most serious difficulty is that, sadly, there are some humans who lack the capacity for abstract reasoning: small children, those who have suffered severe brain damage, elderly persons suffering from dementia. But few would say that none of those people have rights. Those who claim that abstract reasoning ability is the basis for rights face a challenge: What about our fellow humans who have lost (or never gained) the capacity for abstract reasoning; do they have *no rights*?

The answer often given is that while these unfortunate individuals lack the capacity for abstract reasoning, they *still* have rights; they have rights, because they are members of the human species, and humans are the right *kind* or *type* of thing to reason abstractly. But if the standard for having rights is the capacity for abstract reasoning, then the fact that some *other* member of my species is capable of abstract reasoning (and thus has rights) is no reason to ascribe rights to me if I am *in*capable of abstract reasoning.

6. There is a final argument for the human use of nonhuman animals for food and research: The human need is so great that we cannot really consider changing our policies regarding animals. Animals are essential for food, and they are essential in medical experimentation to combat the diseases that afflict us.

Though persons who are particularly fond of grilled beef steaks, fried chicken, and double cheeseburgers may have a difficult time imagining how they would survive without meat, it is clear that we could not only survive but flourish without meat. If we all ate meat-free diets (while being careful to get protein from a variety of plant sources that are high in protein), we would have lower cholesterol levels, weigh less, and in general be much healthier. Furthermore—because the production of meat is a very inefficient way of producing food, requiring many times as much grain as would be required to feed people if they directly ate the grain rather than feeding it to animals—we could greatly increase our food supply while reducing damage to our environment.

What about the claim that use of animals is essential for medical research? It is certainly more plausible than the claim that we require animals for food, but still controversial. A few decades ago, it might have been a very strong claim; today, many experimental techniques—computer simulations, in vitro testing, and others—may serve as adequate substitutes for animal testing; in fact, some of these may be more reliable than animal testing (there are many cases in which drugs that caused no harmful side effects in lab animals caused severe problems for humans). But even if it is true that humans can benefit from medical experimentation on animals, it remains an open question whether such testing is morally legitimate. After all, we know that we could benefit even more from running tests on *humans* that we force into testing laboratories; but no one, I trust, believes that the benefits derived from such tests would be morally justified. Thus even *if* it is true that medical testing on animals benefits humans, it would remain an open question whether such testing is legitimate, or is instead a violation of the rights of the tested animals.

Arguments in Favor of Animal Rights

1. The most basic argument for animal rights is the *utilitarian* argument. Actually, utilitarians prefer not to speak in terms of *rights*, but in terms of what act or policy produces the greatest *benefit*: What act will produce the greatest balance of pleasure over suffering for everyone involved? It does not require any detailed utilitarian calculation to recognize the suffering of animals raised in confined spaces and transported in crowded trucks to slaughter houses where the animals spend their last terrifying moments being pushed toward death and to calculate that the pleasures of eating steak or veal or ham or chicken (rather than tofu or some other vegetarian dish) are greatly outweighed by the suffering of the animals involved. This argument struggles with the question of "killing with replacement," noting that if animals are raised in pleasant circumstances, killed swiftly and painlessly, and then replaced, then there will be a greater *balance* of pleasure. While that is a significant theoretical challenge, the painless production of animal food products would be so costly as to all but eliminate them from the marketplace.

2. A second line of argument focuses more on developing *rights* for animals: It is wrong to mistreat a chimpanzee, not simply because it reduces the overall balance of pleasure over pain, but because that individual chimpanzee has a *right* not to be mistreated, just as you have that right. The first step in the campaign for animal rights is an attack on the traditional philosophical view that rights require the capacity for abstract reasoning: more specifically, the traditional view that you have rights *only* if you are capable of reasoning about abstract moral principles, and following those principles *as* principles. On this traditional view, it is not enough for you to comfort me when I am feeling distressed: Dogs and chimpanzees are capable of doing so, and doing so purposefully; rather, you must be capable of comforting me *not* because you feel sympathy for me, but because you recognize the abstract moral principle that it is right to provide comfort for those in distress, and you follow that principle not out of inclination but because you rationally recognize it to be your duty. If that capacity for high-level abstract reasoning is the necessary condition for rights, then only humans—but certainly not *all* humans—have rights. That is a convenient standard if we want to be sure that no animal other than the human animal will have rights; but is that really the standard we find most plausible?

Tom Regan recommends a new standard: An animal has rights if it is capable of recognizing that its life is becoming better or worse. That is a standard that small children who are not capable of abstract reasoning can meet, as well as Alzheimer's patients who have lost the capacity for abstract reasoning; it is a standard that your dog obviously meets (when you return home from school, your dog makes it clear that his or her life has taken a dramatic turn for the better); an Angus steer that is being forced into the slaughter house by electric cattle prods may not have full understanding of how dire his situation is, but he certainly knows that life has gotten worse; and a dog or chimpanzee that is totally immobilized in a restraining harness recognizes that life has taken a downward turn. Or perhaps some other standard for rights might be favored: for example, the capacity to feel sympathy, or perhaps simply the capacity to feel pain. But the point is, when we question the tradition that makes abstract reasoning the sole basis of rights, there is nothing strange about extending the notion of rights to animals that are not members of the human species. In fact, if we believe that a severely demented elderly person—who can no longer recognize members of his or her own family, much less engage in abstract reasoning—is still a holder of *rights*, then it is difficult to suppose that a dog or pig or chimpanzee does *not* have rights: At least, it is difficult to imagine any reasonable standard that would protect rights for a severely demented elderly human while denying them to members of others species.

3. A third argument for animal rights emphasizes the *similarities* between humans and other animals. Evolutionary science makes clear that there is no gap between us and other animals, and both psychological and medical research on nonhuman animals assumes basic similarities between humans and other species. Like humans, nonhuman animals can and do suffer, both psychologically and physically, and their suffering can be extreme. After all, it was through studies on dogs that we gained some of our most important knowledge about the causes of severe depression, and the misery as well as the debilitating effects on physical health that depression can cause; and studies on monkeys gave information concerning the causes and effects of extreme terror as well as despair, both in humans and other animals.

4. One animal rights argument grants the rational superiority of humans, but argues that the imbalance of rationality and power imposes strong obligations. This argument attempts to reverse the argument that because other animals kill and eat animals (indeed, sometimes tigers and crocodiles and sharks kill and eat human animals, and apparently feel little guilt about it), there is nothing wrong with *humans* doing the same. That has always been a rather strange argument. After all, we do not think that because a small child throws a temper tantrum and kicks or bites someone, it is all right for an adult to kick and bite the child. We say that the child "didn't know any better" (*not*, incidentally, that the child has no *rights*, for we would insist that the child has a right not to be kicked and bitten by an adult); but adults, who *do* know better, have an obligation *not* to do the same thing. Likewise, *if* it is wrong to inflict suffering on other animals, then we have an obligation to avoid doing so because we can recognize that it is wrong, and because there is no necessity for us to do so. (The tiger, on the other hand, has no other options: It cannot adopt a vegetarian diet.) And because we *do* have a higher level of understanding and because (due to our high level of intelligence) we *are* capable of living in such a way that we avoid or minimize the harm we cause other animals, we have an obligation to other animals that other animals do *not* have. Humans have the capacity to kill others animals in massive numbers (within a few years, the enormous bison herds of North America were almost entirely destroyed), and we have the capacity—sometimes exercised almost accidentally—to totally extinguish other species (over the last century, humans have caused the extinction of thousands of species), as well as the capacity to protect endangered species. No other animal has such powers for destruction and preservation, and that power carries with it—so this argument goes—a special obligation to use that power and intelligence carefully, cautiously, and justly.

Where Do We Stand?

There is almost universal agreement that cruelty to animals is morally wrong. Exactly what constitutes cruelty may remain a matter of debate (Does confining chickens in battery cages constitute cruelty?), but the fundamental principle is widely accepted. The widespread outrage at evidence of dog fighting is strong evidence of the general acceptance of that principle. Of course that has not always been the case: British fox hunting (in which riders pushed their horses hard so that they could be present at the "kill," when a pack of hounds finally caught the weary fox and tore it to pieces) was banned only in 2005; in the United States, a popular rural sport involved placing a raccoon on a log out in a pond, and then turning loose a pack of hounds to attack it; the raccoon eventually was killed, and in the process, a number of dogs would be badly injured or killed. Now, however, there is consensus that injuring or killing animals for sport or fun is wrong. There is also growing consensus that causing suffering to laboratory animals in order to test a new shampoo or beauty product is unacceptable: "Cruelty-free cosmetics," not long ago a very small niche in the market, are becoming common.

Obviously most people in society continue to eat meat and support the raising of cows, pigs, and sheep for slaughter. And in most cases, people do not want to know the details of how the animals were treated (the treatment of "beef animals" receives significant media attention only when there is a question of whether the mistreatment of animals has resulted in contamination of the meat that goes into our hamburgers). However, when those details become common knowledge, there is often widespread demand that the conditions be improved (though not a demand that the killing be stopped). So we can point to at least two areas of basic agreement: One, that the suffering of nonhuman animals *counts*, it is *relevant*, and it *is* a moral issue. While that may seem too obvious to deserve comment, it should be noted that 150 years ago, many people regarded the suffering of nonhuman animals as not an ethical issue at all; for example, Immanuel Kant believed that there was nothing wrong with torturing an animal. He thought it should be discouraged, because it might lead to torturing *humans*, and Kant certainly regarded *that* as wrong. But considering the torture of animals in itself, Kant saw nothing wrong with it: It was not a moral question at all, any more than taking an ax and destroying a wagon would be a moral issue—unless you were destroying someone else's property and thus harming the human owner. Two, there is growing consensus that it is wrong to inflict suffering on another animal for sport or entertainment. But if the "entertainment" is eating pale veal (which requires raising veal calves in ways that cause them considerable suffering), then there is much less agreement—though when people become *aware* that the methods of producing pale veal involve cruelty, some people change their views.

Medical experimentation is a significantly tougher question. While we know that a wide variety of experiments are not essential (and cruelty-free cosmetics are gaining in popularity), there are some very important medical experiments that involve animals, and the benefits from those experiments are genuine. It is also obvious that at least some of the experimentation could be reduced, and substitutes of various types are available (including computer simulations and in vitro studies); furthermore, animal proxies are often not very helpful (we know, for example, that many things do not cause cancer in laboratory animals but do cause cancer in humans).

In discussing same-sex marriage, it was noted that in some ways this is not a difference between people who regard homosexual behavior as wrong and others who regard it as morally legitimate, but between people who regard homosexual behavior as a moral issue and those who regard questions of sexuality (including oral sex as well as homosexual relations) as not a moral issue at all. A similar distinction may account for much of the problem in reaching common ground concerning the treatment of animals. When we express concern about medical labs that are experimenting on animals, or factory farms that raise animals in painful conditions, the response is often "these animals are *my property*;

mind your own business." And if animals are merely property, like cars or garden tools, then it's nobody's concern but the owner of the property how that property is treated (if you want to leave your shovel and rake outside and let them rust, that's your business). If we are speaking of dogs and cats and horses, then we do not take that attitude: If you treat your dog in a cruel manner, the community does *not* regard that as "just your business"; to the contrary, the community may take the dog away and bring criminal charges against you. But if you run your factory farm in a cruel manner, the community will largely ignore it. Thus there is a deep ambivalence about animals and the treatment of animals, in the larger community as well as in individuals. Our beloved poodle, Bruno, has been a member of the family for almost a decade; everyone in the family would be outraged if someone kicked Bruno. But we feed him hamburger with little thought of the suffering of the beef animals that were raised on factory farms and herded into slaughter houses with electric cattle prods.

Some years ago, the Defense Department proposed a study on the effects of nuclear radiation from an atomic bomb blast. At the time, nuclear weapons were being exploded in above-ground tests. The Defense Department proposed placing a number of dogs—beagles were to be the test subjects—on a remote island near the test site. After the blast, researchers would retrieve the dogs and examine the damage caused to the dogs by intense radiation. Since in the "experiment" many of the dogs were expected to survive for some time before dying from the effects of the radiation, the suffering for the dogs would obviously be great. The American public was outraged, and the protest was so strong that the Defense Department dropped the planned experiment. Instead, it placed an equal number of pigs on the island, and the experiment went forward as planned, with little objection from the public. Of course pigs—highly intelligent animals—suffered in the same way that the beagles would have suffered; but for most Americans, the suffering of dogs is a serious moral issue, while the suffering of pigs is morally irrelevant. This was an "experiment" that could only be done if the suffering of the animals involved was counted as totally irrelevant. After all, we already had extensive data on the terrible effects of intense radiation on *humans*: Atomic bombs had been detonated in two highly populated areas of Japan. There was very little likelihood that the enormous suffering that the test animals endured would result in any significant enhancement of our knowledge.

What should be our attitude toward *important* medical tests on animals? If we begin to see it as a moral issue at all, that will be significant. It won't solve the problem, but at least there would be common ground that there is a problem to solve.

Questions for Reflection

1. You have developed a new medication; should you test it on animals? Don't answer. Instead, consider that question from the perspective of utilitarian, Kantian, care, virtue, social contract, and detached observer perspectives; which one of these is most useful? Do they yield similar or radically divergent conclusions?

2. Two hundred years ago in the United States, many people were somewhat uncomfortable with slavery (and of course slaves were *very* uncomfortable with slavery, but their voices were largely silenced), and a few people were profoundly outraged by slavery; but the majority (of nonslaves) seemed to believe that slavery—while not very pleasant to think about—was deeply traditional, and that slave labor would be very difficult to replace, and so slavery should be accepted without really thinking too hard about it.

When we look back at the general acceptance of slavery, it is difficult for us to imagine how such cruelty could have been so easily accepted by most people in society. Is it possible that two hundred years in the future, people will look back at our attitude toward treatment of nonhuman animals from a similar perspective?

3. Utilitarian arguments have been the most common ethical arguments for reforming our treatment of nonhuman animals; recently, rights-based arguments have also been offered. If you were looking for a *third* approach to arguing for changes in treatment of animals, which of the various approaches would you think the most likely candidate? Virtue ethics? Care ethics? Social contract ethics? Or some other approach?

4. Suppose extraterrestrials arrive on Earth, and they are smarter, much more technologically advanced, and far more powerful than humans. These extraterrestrials find human flesh quite tasty, and they propose to herd all humans onto factory farms and raise us for slaughter. What argument might you make to the extraterrestrials to convince them that treating humans that way would be *morally wrong*? Does your argument have anything in common with the argument that a Hereford cow might give against current treatment of members of her species?

5. Many cultures allow eating dogs, though in the United States, eating dogs is generally regarded with horror and revulsion. One *could* argue that there should be a ban on eating dogs in the United States simply to spare the feelings of all those humans who would be disturbed by seeing restaurants that serve dog; but we usually do not ban practices on that basis (many people are profoundly disturbed by neo-Nazi rallies, but we do not count that as a legitimate reason for banning them). Is there any moral argument that you could give for a special U.S. ban on the use of dogs for human food? There are of course arguments for banning *all* killing of animals for food; but if you do *not* believe that *all* killing of animals for food should be banned, is there any *argument* that you could give for why there should be a specific ban on the killing of *dogs* for food?

6. Animal rights advocates obviously oppose hunting, but the question here is not whether hunting is right or wrong. *Suppose* for a moment that you agree with the views of those who support animal rights; would you, as a *believer* in animal rights, find deer or duck hunting *worse*, *better*, or morally *equal* to factory farming? Would it make a difference whether the hunters were strictly trophy hunters as opposed to hunters who used their kills for food?

7. Many people—hunters included—feel particular disgust at some commercial "hunting preserves," where "hunters" pay to enter a fenced area containing (for example) elk or moose, and using a high-powered rifle at relatively short range simply gun down the animals they choose to kill. *If* you find such practices disgusting, *why* do they disgust you? Is it because this is a special mistreatment of animals? Or is it because it is a corruption of the sport of hunting? Or something else?

Additional Resources

For an excellent, thoughtful, and fair debate on animal rights, see *The Animal Rights Debate,* by Carl Cohen and Tom Regan (Lanham, MD: Rowman & Littlefield, 2001). Cohen presents arguments against animal rights, followed by Regan's arguments in favor of animal rights, and then Cohen and Regan each offer a critique of the opposing view. The arguments on both sides are of very high quality, and it is a model of careful, intelligent, respectful disagreement on an issue that both writers care about deeply. Paul Waldau's *Animal Rights: What Everyone Needs to Know* (New York: Oxford University Press, 2011) is a clear and even-handed examination of many of the issues involved in animal rights and the animal rights movement.

Animal Rights and Human Obligations, 2nd ed., edited by Tom Regan and Peter Singer (Englewood Cliffs, NJ: Prentice Hall, 1989), is a good collection of essays, both pro and con, on the rights of animals. The collection of historical views, ranging from ancient Greece and

Medieval thought up through the modern period, is a strong point of this anthology. Another good collection of pro and con articles, covering a wide range of subjects in the area of animal rights and the treatment of animals, is by Andrew Harnack, *Animal Rights: Opposing Viewpoints* (San Diego, CA: Greenhaven Press, 1996). Harlan B. Miller and William H. Williams, eds., *Ethics and Animals* (Clifton, NJ: Humana Press, 1983), provide a very good collection of philosophical articles by leading philosophers. *The Animal Ethics Reader*, 2nd edition, edited by Susan J. Armstrong and Richard G. Botzler (London: Routledge, 2008), is a wide-ranging collection of excellent essays from a variety of perspectives. Cass R. Sunstein and Martha C. Nussbaum have edited an excellent book that contains interesting views from a number of different approaches, particularly those involved in legal thought: *Animal Rights: Current Debates and New Directions* (New York: Oxford University Press, 2004). Gary L. Francione and Robert Garner's *The Animal Rights Debate: Abolition or Regulation* (New York: Columbia University Press, 2010) is a thoughtful two-person debate.

Peter Singer's *Animal Liberation* first appeared in 1976, and the most recent edition of this classic was published in 2009 (New York: Harper); it is probably the most famous book in the campaign for animal rights. Tom Regan's *The Case for Animal Rights* (Berkeley: University of California Press, 1983) is another modern classic; Regan's more recent essays are collected in *Defending Animal Rights* (Urbana, IL: University of Illinois Press, 2001). Paola Cavalieri's *The Animal Question: Why Nonhuman Animals Deserve Human Rights*, trans. Catherine Woollard (Oxford: Oxford University Press, 2001) is a brief but creative and well-argued case for animal rights. Another excellent defense of animal rights is Bernard E. Rollin's *Animal Rights and Human Morality*, revised edition (Buffalo, NY: Prometheus Books, 1992). Two very good books, whose authors emphasize the close biological links between humans and other animals, are Mary Midgley, *Animals and Why They Matter* (Athens, GA: University of Georgia Press, 1983); and James Rachels, *Created from Animals: The Moral Implications of Darwinism* (Oxford: Oxford University Press, 1991). A remarkable and very readable book that examines both research on teaching chimpanzees American Sign Language and recent attempts to stop the mistreatment of chimpanzees in research settings is Roger Fouts's *Next of Kin: What Chimpanzees Have Taught Me about Who We Are* (New York: William Morrow, 1997); Fouts also has an interesting website

at www.cwu.edu/~cwuchi/. Stephen R. L. Clark, in *The Moral Status of Animals* (Oxford: Clarendon Press, 1977), offers a detailed, powerful, and philosophically complex argument for a radical revision of our view of animals (as well as ourselves). See also Clark's fascinating book, *The Nature of the Beast: Are Animals Moral?* (Oxford: Oxford University Press, 1982), for his argument that the study of animal behavior can enhance our understanding of ethics. Mark Bekoff, a leading researcher on animal emotions, has written a very readable and well-documented book: *The Animal Manifesto: Six Reasons for Expanding our Compassion Footprint* (Novato, CA: New World Library, 2010).

Books opposing animal rights arguments, written from a variety of perspectives, are R. G. Frey's *Interests and Rights: The Case against Animals* (Oxford: Clarendon Press, 1980) and Michael P. T. Leahy's *Against Liberation: Putting Animals in Perspective* (London and New York: Routledge, 1991). Peter Carruthers, in *The Animals Issue: Moral Theory in Practice* (Cambridge: Cambridge University Press, 1992), argues that social contract ethics is the only viable ethical theory, and that nonhuman animals cannot qualify as social contractors and thus have no rights whatsoever; he states in his conclusion that "those who are committed to any aspect of the animal rights movement are thoroughly misguided."

On a subject in which the debate has raged for decades, even centuries, it is difficult to find a new perspective; but novelist J. M. Coetzee manages it brilliantly in *The Lives of Animals* (Princeton, NJ: Princeton University Press, 1999).

The Great Ape Project, an organization dedicated to "including the non-human great apes within the community of equals by granting them the basic moral and legal protection that only humans currently enjoy," has a website that is well worth a visit, at www .greatapeproject.org.

Lawrence Hinman's *Ethics Updates* website has a superb collection of material on the moral status of animals, including many links to other sites; go to ethics .sandiego.edu/Applied/Animals.

The website of People for the Ethical Treatment of Animals (PETA) has lots of resources, and is also entertaining; on my most recent visit to the site (around the holiday season), I watched a "Merry Catmas" video, at www.peta.org.

The *Tom Regan Animal Rights Archive* has a variety of topics and many links; it is at www.lib.ncsu.edu /animalrights/.

MYSEARCHLAB CONNECTIONS

Ethics Updates at http://ethics.sandiego.edu (under "Applied Ethics" click on "Animal Rights") contains a number of links to a variety of websites with material on animal rights. In the *Stanford Encyclopedia of Philosophy*, at plato.stanford.edu, see the entries on "The Moral Status of Animals" and "Environmental Ethics."

POLICE DECEPTION

Chapter Outline

The use of deception is common in law enforcement, and most uses of police deception generate little controversy. I may be upset when a police officer in an unmarked patrol car pulls up behind me, flashes a blue light, and writes me a speeding ticket, but I don't feel morally offended by the process. I know that the police use unmarked cars, and I know that I should not be speeding, and I recognize that one effective way of enforcing the traffic laws is the use of unmarked cars. I want the traffic laws enforced for my own protection, and the protection of my friends and family; and though I am hardly delighted by getting a ticket, I do not feel either deceived or abused. When the police set up a fencing operation, and put the word out on the street that this is a good place for thieves to bring their stolen merchandise, and use this fake fencing business to apprehend thieves and burglars, few object: This is an effective way of apprehending thieves, the deception seems harmless enough, and no one is entrapped or encouraged into committing a crime (those apprehended are already in the business of theft). When the FBI uses an undercover officer to infiltrate a dangerous and violent group—such as the Ku Klux Klan—in order to find out when the group is planning attacks and prevent them, this is a form of deception we applaud: The undercover agent is not inciting violence, but attempting to discover plans for violence and prevent the brutal acts of such hate groups.

Of course we do *not* want state or federal undercover agents infiltrating our book club or joining our peaceful protest movement or becoming undercover agents in our nonviolent political movement. But that is not because we deplore the *deception* involved, but because we firmly believe that the government has no business spying on our nonviolent political or social organization: If our group is not posing a threat to society, then we have a basic right to privacy that the government should not violate. Also, while we have no objection to the police doing undercover work against violent or criminal organizations, we certainly do *not* want government agents *encouraging* people to commit crimes they otherwise would not have committed in order to arrest them. If the police discover that I am eager to sell illegal arms to terrorists, then it is perfectly legitimate for the police to set up a sting operation in which an agent poses as a terrorist wishing to buy arms, and arrest me when I make the sale. But if I have shown no inclination to become an illegal arms dealer, and an undercover agent offers me an enormous sum of money if only I will travel around to various gun shows and buy up a dozen assault rifles, then the undercover agent is not preventing a crime I had already planned but instead inciting and encouraging me to engage in a criminal activity that I had not initiated. And there are some other forms of police deception that we generally agree are *not* legitimate. It is unacceptable for a police officer to lie under oath in order to obtain a conviction (even if Officer Jones is confident that I am the person who burglarized the house, it is *wrong* for Officer Jones to testify that she saw me running out of the house when in fact she did not). And obviously, it is *wrong* for the police—or police crime labs—to fabricate or plant false evidence in order to incriminate me, even if the police firmly believe that I am guilty. If the police are confident I burglarized the Smith home, it is still wrong for the police to take the butt of a cigarette I smoked during interrogation and plant that cigarette at the scene of the crime in order to provide "evidence" that I committed the burglary.

There may be dispute about some details in the above-mentioned cases, but for the most part we agree on those guidelines for when police deception *is*—and is *not*—legitimate. But there is one area of police deception that generates controversy: the practice of using *deception* during the process of interrogation. Suppose that you and a friend have been out for a drive in the summer night to see the stars—your friend saw something online about a possible meteor shower around midnight, and the two of you were out looking for shooting stars. As you drive back into the city, a police car pulls up behind you, lights flashing. When you stop, the police officer orders both of you to get out of the car with your hands up, and he is holding a very dangerous looking shotgun. The two of you are handcuffed, placed in the cruiser, and taken to the police station. You are left alone in an interrogation room, while your friend is taken elsewhere. After a few minutes, two detectives walk into the room and start asking questions. You soon learn that you are a suspect in a very serious crime: A convenience store was held up at gunpoint by two young people who roughly fit the description of you and your friend; and the robbers were seen speeding away in a convertible that looked something like the one in which the two of you were riding. The detective who interviews you is sympathetic, and seems eager to help you.

> You don't really want an attorney, right? That would just make you look guilty, and besides, if you have an attorney, I really can't help you. Look, you've got a big problem. Your friend is over there in the next room claiming he had no idea you were

planning a robbery: He thought you were just going into the convenience store to buy a six-pack, and all of a sudden you pull a gun and threaten the manager—he claims he didn't even know you had a gun—and then you grabbed the money out of the register and took off running, and he panicked and got in the car and drove away. Now, I'm guessing it happened just the opposite way, didn't it? You didn't really want to rob that convenience store; it was all your friend's idea, he had the gun, and you just went along with it. But if you don't tell us about how the crime happened, and fast, your friend is going to pin the whole thing on you, and you'll be in a maximum security prison for a good 10 years, while your "friend" gives evidence against you and takes a walk. Look, we've got plenty of evidence to convict you. There were two people in the back of the store when you guys robbed it, and they got a good look at you, and they're here at the station, and they recognized you when we brought you in. And I shouldn't be telling you this, but we found a gun in the car hidden under the driver's seat, and the boys at the lab tell me they've found an excellent match with the fingerprints we took from you a few minutes ago. It looks bad. But I don't think you were holding that gun during the robbery; I think you probably held it some time earlier, and your prints got on it then. You seem like a nice kid; I would hate to see you in a maximum security prison for the next 10 years. Those are horrible places, and terrible things happen to good-looking young men who wind up there. When you stopped at the convenience store, you hadn't really planned to rob it, had you? There wasn't any premeditation. If you go ahead and confess now, and tell me all about it, I'll do everything I can to keep you out of prison. I've got a son just your age, and I would hate to see him in this kind of trouble; and if he were in this kind of trouble, I'd tell him to do exactly what I'm telling you: Tell us all about it, and let us help you. Otherwise, your "friend" is going to blame the whole thing on you— that's the way it always happens, the one who planned the whole thing blames it on some poor guy who just went along for the ride—and you're going down for armed robbery. How many years is that, Joe? 10 years minimum, and because the gun laws are so strict, there's no way to get early release. 10 years minimum. God, I'd hate to see my kid spend 10 years in that hell hole of a maximum security prison; you're young now, but you won't be young when you finally get out.

So what's going on? Two witnesses have already identified you, they've got your prints on a pistol, your friend is down the hall accusing you of being the gunman in an armed robbery, and you're looking at spending the next 10 years in hell. But these guys want to help you. Maybe if you agree with what they say, they really can get you off with community service. You certainly don't want to spend a decade in prison, come out when you're 30 with a major criminal record.

Nothing in this scenario is out of the ordinary. But of course nothing the detectives told you is true: Your friend *is* down the hall, just as confused and scared as you are, but he hasn't accused you of any crime and is maintaining his innocence. No gun was found, and certainly your fingerprints were not on the nonexistent gun. No witnesses were sitting in the station, identifying you as you walked past. The detective does not have a son your age, and the detective is not eager to help you; to the contrary, the detective is eager to get a confession that will convict you of a very serious crime. And the suggestion that you would be better off talking, and not asking for a lawyer, is absurd. In fact, everything the detective told you is completely false; and in a few more minutes, someone will knock on the door with a very official looking "crime lab report," proving that your fingerprints were in fact on the gun; and they may throw in a written statement from your friend, as well as written statements from the two witnesses who identified you. All of this is common practice in interrogating criminal suspects. In fact, the standard textbooks on interrogating suspects spell out precisely how to use such deceptive methods for obtaining confessions. (Those textbooks also include instructions on how to make the suspect feel completely helpless and dependent on those questioning him.)

Before examining the debate about deceptive practices in police interrogation, it should be noted that in some ways this is a substantial *improvement* in interrogation practices. These deceptive techniques were developed as a means of correcting some major problems in police interrogation methods. In years past, confessions weren't tricked out of suspects; they were beaten out. Rather than trickery, police used rubber hoses and other techniques of causing severe pain while leaving few marks. And the beatings were often accompanied by threats that even worse could happen if the suspect did not confess; and sometimes those were not idle threats, as suspects knew well. As police procedures became more professionalized, and police training improved, the new interrogation techniques were regarded as an important positive step toward a more professional police force.

Obviously police forces have not always lived up to those higher standards. The brutal videotaped 1991 beating of Rodney King in Los Angeles; the horrific 1997 beating and sodomizing of a defenseless Latino prisoner in a New York City police station; the notorious CRASH unit in the Rampart Division of Los Angeles in which police beat and murdered citizens, carried unmarked guns to plant on unarmed suspects they killed, routinely planted evidence, and gathered together to celebrate their killings; the racist brutality of the New Orleans police, which involved a number of murders and such a high degree of corruption that the Justice Department spent years trying to clean up the department, reporting systemic departmental corruption—these are profoundly disturbing contemporary cases of gross abuse of police power, and they do occur. But at least these are terrible *exceptions* to the standards for legitimate police conduct, and they are often prosecuted and police officers dismissed; such practices are no longer the standard accepted practice. But the current approved practice includes use of deception—and falsehood—in the process of interrogation. There is no doubt that this is an improvement; but does it meet the standard for what should be expected of police forces in democratic societies?

The issue of police deception during interrogations is not a "conservative vs. liberal" issue. It might be thought that "law and order" conservatives would favor police deception, and the relaxing of rules in order to catch more criminals; while liberals would be more concerned about individual rights, including the rights of those suspected of crimes. But some "law and order" advocates also place great value on individual freedom, including freedom from deceitful practices (and especially deceitful practices carried out by government officials). These conservatives may be especially concerned about government practices that enhance government power, and deeply disturbed when government procedures result in the wrongful imprisonment of the innocent. After all, imprisoning an innocent person is an extreme and deeply disturbing example of government abuse of power against individual citizens. One of the strongest statements condemning flawed police and prosecution policies that result in wrongful convictions was published in 2011 by Radley Balko, a senior editor at *Reason* (a proudly conservative publication). And while "liberals" have traditionally been more concerned with protecting the rights of accused criminals and preventing miscarriages of justice, there are many liberals who regard police deception during interrogation as a relatively harmless extension of deceptive practices (such as use of undercover agents and sting operations) that almost everyone regards as acceptable. So whatever you conclude about this issue, you will have to reach your conclusion without the use of easy labels and mindless categories.

Strawman Distortions

It is sometimes suggested that those who approve police deception in interrogation approve of police deception throughout the legal process. That is false. No one approves of police officers perjuring themselves on the witness stand, or planting false evidence. Those who are worried about deceptive practices during interrogations may fear that the common practice of deception during interrogations could *lead* to an erosion of police integrity, and thus lead to falsified evidence and perjured testimony. But everyone on *both* sides of the issue *agrees* that perjured testimony and falsified evidence during trials are wrong, and that police officers committing such wrongs should be disciplined or even criminally prosecuted.

On the other side, it is sometimes claimed that those who *oppose* deceptive practices in interrogation are not concerned about convicting criminals and punishing wrongdoers and protecting society. That is also a strawman. We all want to solve crimes and catch criminals; but we want to be sure that we are actually catching criminals, not intimidating innocent citizens into giving false confessions (false confessions that result in the actual criminal escaping punishment, while an innocent fellow citizen is wronged). In April of 1989, a terrible crime was committed: The newspapers and tabloids were filled with stories of youth gangs "wilding." Supposedly the gangs would randomly attack anyone they encountered—in this instance, a young woman who was jogging in Central Park. Five 15-year-old black juveniles were charged with the crime, and under enormous pressure "confessed" to the attack; they were tried as adults, convicted, and imprisoned. In 2002, after they had spent 13 years in prison, a known sex offender confessed to the attack, and his confession was confirmed by DNA evidence; their convictions were vacated, and they were released from prison. The known sex offender—who remained free to commit other crimes, and who might well have been apprehended if the frenzy to convict and condemn the young men had been resisted—was finally arrested. Though this is one of the most famous cases of false confession under police pressure, it is by no means the only one. In approximately a quarter of the wrongful convictions overturned by DNA evidence, the convicted person entered a guilty plea or confessed or made self-incriminating statements.

What Is the Common Ground?

First, there are very few people who do not regard lying as a morally bad practice. Indeed, Immanuel Kant regarded lying as absolutely wrong, and never allowable under any conditions. However, most people believe that in some special circumstances lying is appropriate: lying to slave catchers in order to protect escaping slaves or lying to the Gestapo to save the lives of a Jewish family. The question, then, is whether lying to criminal suspects fits the very special conditions that make lies—which are in themselves a very bad thing—morally acceptable.

Second, everyone agrees that conviction of innocent persons is a terrible wrong. Or at least everyone claims to believe that. In fact, we are painfully aware that conviction and imprisonment of the innocent is a very common event in the United States, and it does not seem to cause great outrage. Literally hundreds of innocent people have been freed from prison as a result of newly obtained DNA evidence, and it is obvious that there are thousands more who were wrongfully convicted but with no DNA evidence available to overturn their convictions and free them from prison. George C. Thomas III, Distinguished Professor of Law at Rutgers University, estimates that thousands of innocent persons are convicted of crimes every year in the United States. But however poorly we live up to our principle that conviction of the innocent is a terrible miscarriage of justice, all of us agree that it *is* wrong. And it is clear that police deception during interrogation is one factor that increases the number of innocent persons who are wrongfully convicted (and particularly the number of people who confess to crimes they did not commit, from fear of receiving an even more severe sentence if they maintain their innocence in the face of what *appears* to be strong evidence of guilt). The disagreement is not about whether police deception during interrogation increases the number of wrongful convictions—it clearly does. The question is whether this is a price worth paying in order to facilitate the interrogation of suspects, some of whom are in fact guilty and might escape conviction if deceptive interrogation techniques were banned.

Arguments in Favor of Deceptive Interrogation Techniques

1. One argument in favor of deceptive interrogation techniques is common, but not very effective: the argument that such techniques are a great improvement over earlier interrogation techniques of beating and torturing prisoners to gain confessions. Everyone agrees that deceptive interrogation techniques are an improvement, but that does not settle the question of whether they are legitimate. It would be like saying that beating prisoners with rubber hoses in order to obtain a confession must be legitimate, because it is better than torturing prisoners on the rack. In a debate over capital punishment, everyone might agree that lethal injection is a more humane execution method than boiling in oil or drawing and quartering; but it does not follow that execution by lethal injection is legitimate. Likewise, the fact that deceptive interrogation techniques are a big improvement over torture does nothing to settle the question of whether deceptive interrogation techniques are legitimate. In order to make such an argument work, one would have to establish that we *must* choose between only two possible alternatives: using deceptive interrogation techniques or torturing suspects to obtain confessions. But no one offers such an argument, because it is obvious that those are *not* the only alternatives. We might ban both deceptive interrogation techniques *and* torture, and rely instead on careful forensic investigation to establish guilt. The last alternative may or may not be as effective as the first two, but it clearly *is* an alternative.

2. An argument developed by Christopher Slobogin is more substantive. Slobogin draws heavily on the analysis of lying given by Sissela Bok, who argues that lying is often very destructive and leads to even more severe problems, and therefore lying should be carefully restricted. One of the scenarios in which Bok believes lying might be acceptable (under careful restrictions) is lying to enemies: enemies who are openly acknowledged

as enemies, and who intend to cause harm. Slobogin suggests that this might apply to police interrogation of suspects. When someone is brought to the police station and subjected to questioning, it is clear that the police suspect that person has engaged in criminal activity and is thus an "enemy" of society; and so the suspect has been "given notice" that he or she is regarded as an enemy, and thus that hostile behavior (including deception) toward the suspect is now authorized.

While this is an interesting and subtle argument, it is not clear that it justifies police deception during interrogations. In the first place, it is not clear that suspects understand that they are being classified as "enemies"; to the contrary, part of the deceptive practice typically involves trying to convince the suspect that at least one of the interrogating officers is a friend who is deeply sympathetic with the suspect, and who has the interests of the suspect at heart. Second, there is an inherent problem in classifying suspects as "enemies." Suspects are not convicted criminals, but *suspects* who are entitled to the presumption of innocence until found guilty. And of course *many* such suspects are in fact not guilty of the crimes of which they are suspected (often the police will interrogate many suspects in the course of their investigations, most and perhaps all of whom are not guilty).

3. A third claim in favor of deceptive interrogation is that it is an essential element of criminal investigation and we cannot do without it. There is no doubt that deceptive interrogation techniques can sometimes be useful. But that usefulness must be balanced against the false confessions they sometimes produce, with the result that investigation stops, an innocent person is convicted, and the actual perpetrator of the crime goes free. Bertrand Russell once described a proposed solution as having benefits: all the benefits of theft over honest labor. The question with deceptive police interrogation is whether honest labor by police investigators could produce most of the benefits we now gain from deception, but without the problems that deception generates. That is a difficult question, and not one that we can settle by careful reflection: We must actually consider what investigatory resources are available to replace the lost advantages of deceptive interrogation techniques.

Clearly the resources available are substantial. Advances in forensic science are made daily, from improved techniques for DNA analysis to better voice identification methods and even improved camera surveillance. If as a society we conclude that deceptive interrogation tactics are unacceptable, we might need to invest more resources in police investigators and police investigation technologies. That is a question of priorities that society would have to weigh. Sufficient investment in more extensive investigation and better crime-solving resources might effectively replace whatever is lost when deceptive interrogation techniques are stopped; whether we are willing to make that investment is another question altogether.

4. A fourth argument is that extending deception to police interrogation of suspects is actually not a very substantial extension. Assume that we accept the need for deceptive undercover operations. If you do not, then this argument cannot get started; but most people agree that undercover operations—against suspected terrorist cells or illegal arms dealers or child prostitution rings—are sometimes legitimate, notwithstanding the deep deception involved. The step from deceptive undercover operations to deceptive interrogation techniques is not significant, so if we accept the former we should also accept the latter. But in the former case, the deception is unavoidable; the question

then goes back to the previous argument. Is the deception in police interrogation really a necessity? Or perhaps more to the point, in the context of this argument: Would it be more difficult for law enforcement to give up deceptive undercover operations than to give up deceptive interrogation of criminal suspects? We have a good idea of the additional investigations that could take the place of deceptive interrogations, but adequate substitutes for undercover investigations are difficult to imagine. Thus from the fact that we approve of deceptive undercover operations, it does not follow that by the same principle we must approve deceptive interrogation processes. If the principle guiding use of police deception is that it should only be allowed when there is no workable alternative, then undercover operations may be consistent with that principle while deceptive interrogations are not.

5. The final and fundamental argument in favor of deceptive practices in police interrogation is a simple one: Such practices work. It is undeniable that deceptive police interrogation practices are often effective in securing evidence of criminal acts and criminal guilt. After all, these are techniques that have been carefully honed and improved, and have proved their usefulness over years of police interrogations. So ultimately the question will be: Do the benefits derived by use of these techniques—benefits in successful conviction of those involved in criminal behavior—outweigh the costs, and could the benefits be gained at less cost? Those are questions that must be weighed in light of the arguments in the following section: arguments opposing deceptive police interrogation procedures.

Arguments against Deceptive Interrogation Techniques

1. Deception is bad; that is, lying to others is bad. Deceptive police interrogation techniques involve lying. This is perhaps such an obvious argument that it hardly needs stating. Nonetheless, it raises an important point that should be carefully noted. Lying is a morally bad, harmful act. For most people, "don't lie" is one of those basic moral rules learned so early and long ago, a rule that now seems so fundamental and obvious, that it is difficult to say exactly *why* it is such a basic and universal rule of morality. Immanuel Kant probably gave the most substantive account of why it is wrong to lie: It involves treating others as merely means to our ends, as mere objects to be manipulated, and it denies and violates their autonomy as reasoning persons who are entitled to make their own decisions based on accurate information. Among contemporary writers, Sissela Bok has given the most detailed and thorough account of the harms that result from lying. She notes that lying (as Kant pointed out) is an attack on the autonomy of the person lied to (if a drug company lies about the dangers and effectiveness of the drugs it sells, you cannot make an informed free decision about whether or not to take that drug). Bok also notes that individuals who start lying often become practiced liars, and their characters change as lying becomes a deeper part of their personality. If you have told a number of lies, you probably realize—even if you are reluctant to admit it—that what was initially a rather difficult process that caused personal discomfort becomes easier and easier as the lies increase; and you may be able to observe disturbing changes in your own personality. Finally, Bok argues that lying by members of a society results in significant harm to that society:

> The veneer of social trust is often thin. As lies spread—by imitation, or in retaliation, or to forestall suspected deception—trust is damaged. Yet trust is a social good to be protected just as much as the air we breathe or the water we drink.

When it is damaged, the community as a whole suffers; and when it is destroyed, societies falter and collapse.[1]

All lying is destructive, but officially sanctioned deception by government entities against private citizens is particularly damaging. In a democracy, lies by the government to its citizens are among the most destructive forces undermining democratic government. If voting citizens are purposefully misinformed by their own government, they cannot effectively exercise control over their government, which makes democracy a sham. Government-approved systems of deception—such as those that occur when members of the public police force systematically engage in deceitful practices of interrogation—also undercut the fabric of social trust. As Margaret Paris notes, "It harms a society when the officers who enforce its laws behave like the worst used car salesmen."[2] Perhaps this harm is one we must bear, in order to deal effectively with the threat of crime; but we should be aware that there is a significant harm involved.

2. The second objection to trickery and deceit in police interrogation is that it can and does lead to conviction of innocent people, often because an innocent person—faced with what seems to be overwhelming evidence of guilt—confesses to a crime that he or she did not commit. Any one of us could be picked up because we happen to resemble someone who committed a vicious crime, wrongly identified by eyewitnesses (a very common problem), lack any strong alibi (especially if you live alone). And if you are a poor college student—who lacks the resources to hire a good defense lawyer and must rely on an overworked public defender's office for your defense—you may easily find yourself in a very perilous situation, innocent though you are. When the district attorney offers to drop the first degree burglary charges and allow you to plead guilty to breaking or entering—with a one-year sentence in a minimum security facility, rather than eight to ten years in a maximum security hell hole—confessing to a crime you did not commit may well seem your best alternative, especially if you are falsely convinced that the police have additional eyewitnesses eager to testify against you (you know that these "eyewitnesses" are *mistaken*, since you have not committed any crime; but you also know that mistaken eyewitnesses can be very convincing to a jury).

3. One of the most significant concerns about the common practice of deception in police interrogation is the possibility that it will lead to other forms of deception. Even if one approves of deceptive police interrogations, there are other areas of the justice system where we want the police to be scrupulously honest. In particular, we do *not* want the police to commit perjury when they testify under oath (we do not want police officers testifying that they saw the defendant run from the burglarized building when they did not), we do *not* want the police encouraging other witnesses to lie, we do *not* want the police planting falsified evidence, and we do *not* want crime labs fabricating false evidence to be used against defendants at trial. Sadly, all of these things have happened on many occasions. In addition to the well-publicized cases of police planting falsified evidence and police crime labs producing falsified reports, the use of "jailhouse informants" is very common. Jailhouse informants are prisoners in jail on various charges who volunteer to give evidence against a highly publicized suspect: "I'll testify about how Jones confessed to me in the exercise yard that he was the one who killed the little girl if you will reduce my drug trafficking charges to simple possession." Everyone involved in the process (except the jury) is well aware that the jailhouse informant is

lying under oath in order to get a reduced sentence or a "get out of jail free" deal. Does the systematic deception that occurs in police interrogations lead to a greater willingness to employ deception (such deception as offering reduced charges deals to jailhouse informants in exchange for their perjured testimony) in order to obtain a conviction at trial? It is impossible to answer that question definitively; but we all know that once we get into the habit of lying, it is difficult to draw the line.

4. A final objection to police deception during interrogations is that it may encourage shoddy investigations: Police focus on proving that the available suspect did it (and gaining a confession from that suspect) rather than seeking out other suspects who might be more difficult to find but who might be more plausible suspects for this crime.

Where Do We Stand?

The police officers who enforce our laws, investigate crimes, and interrogate suspects are *our* police officers. We do not live in a police state, or a tyrannical dictatorship. If the police use deceptive techniques while interrogating prisoners, they are doing so on our behalf, and with our approval; and they are using those techniques on *us*, the citizens of our democracy. Thus it is up to us to decide whether this is a legitimate exception to our general rule against deception. Crime is a serious problem, and the apprehension of criminals is a worthwhile goal. What means we approve for dealing with that problem and meeting that goal is an issue that we as citizens have a responsibility to consider carefully.

We all agree that conviction of the innocent is a terrible tragedy, that finding and convicting those guilty of crimes is important and worthwhile, and that deception is inherently bad. In drawing a conclusion about the legitimacy or illegitimacy of deceptive interrogation techniques, those factors must be weighed in the balance.

Questions for Reflection

1. You are picked up as a suspect in an armed robbery, in which two persons were killed. You happen to be a good match for the eyewitness accounts of the gunman, and indeed one eyewitness—who was in the store at the time of the robbery—confidently picks you out of a lineup, naming you as the gunman who fired the fatal shots during the robbery. During the interrogation, the police claim—falsely—that they have surveillance video that clearly shows you participating in the robbery, that your fingerprints were found on the store counter, that an eyewitness spotted you getting into a car parked near the store and remembered your license plate number, and that one of your friends brought in for questioning has admitted his part in the robbery and is accusing you of being the one who planned and organized the whole thing. A few hours later, the police finish checking out your alibi, and realize that you were playing in an intramural basketball game at the time of the robbery, with dozens of witnesses attesting to the fact that you were nowhere near the scene of the robbery. They apologize, and send you on your way. What effect would this experience have on you, particularly the experience of having your interrogators make false claims about the evidence against you? Would it lessen your own confidence in the integrity of the police? Would it make you less likely to believe police testimony if you were later serving as a juror in a criminal trial? Would it make you less trusting of your government as a whole?

2. If we approve of deceptive police interrogation practices, then we are officially approving of a process that requires some persons—some professional police interrogators—to become

polished and effective liars. They must not only lie about faked claims of evidence, but also lie about their sincere concern for the welfare of the suspect (when they pretend to be concerned to help the suspect get the best deal possible on the charges in return for cooperating, they are actually trying to convince the suspect to confess; or when they pretend that having a lawyer present will be a disadvantage to the suspect, they know that a lawyer would be very advantageous for the suspect). Thus these interrogators are required to become adept not only at lying about evidence, but also in lying about their feelings and concerns. *If* we agree that encouraging people to become effective liars is not a way of encouraging them to become more virtuous—but instead may cause serious long-term character flaws and damage their capacity for expressing honest affection—would that in itself be a reason to ban deceptive interrogation techniques?

3. Undercover operations—in which a police investigator joins a potentially dangerous criminal group (a hate group such as the Ku Klux Klan or a terrorist group or a violent gang) in order to monitor the group's activities and gain evidence to convict the group members of crimes—are inherently deceptive. The undercover officer takes a pledge to uphold the principles of the group he or she is investigating, acts like someone who shares the vile ideals of that group, feigns friendship with members of the group—all of which are false. Though many people have genuine concerns about such undercover infiltrations (there is grave danger that such operations may be used against those who simply disagree with government policies, but who are in no way a violent or criminal threat), it is difficult to imagine that we could completely eliminate such deceptive operations against groups that often pose genuine threats to society and to specific people within the society. Is there a real difference between such deceptive undercover operations and deceptive interrogation techniques? That is, if we approve of the former,

does consistency require that we also approve of the latter? Are there significant dangers to the characters of these undercover operatives?

4. One suggestion for dealing with deceptive interrogation techniques is that we videotape all interrogations, so that the jury could consider whether confessions were genuine and a judge could decide whether a confession was obtained under coercive conditions (and so should not be admitted into evidence). Should videotaping be required? Would that be a solution to the problem?

5. Deceptive interrogation techniques are widely practiced, but there are clear limits. For example, the police cannot legitimately extract a confession from a suspect by use of threats. If a suspect signs a confession while a police officer holds a .38 revolver in the suspect's ear, the "confession" is obviously illegitimate, along with the means of acquiring it. But what about more subtle threats? "If you don't confess, you will be spending the night locked in a group cell, and we'll tell your cellmates that you raped and strangled a six-year-old girl. I hate to think of what those guys will do to you during the night." Would this be a case of coerced confession?

6. *Suppose* that you believe that deceptive interrogation techniques are sometimes legitimate. What *restrictions* would you place on them? For example, almost everyone agrees that a police detective should *not* be allowed to pose as the suspect's court-appointed attorney in order to obtain a confession. Would you allow a police officer to pose as a priest, who encourages the suspect to "confess his sins"? Should police officers be allowed to pose as eyewitnesses who confront the suspect?

7. Consider the question of deceptive interrogation methods from the detached observer perspective, the utilitarian perspective, and the virtue theory perspective. Do the different approaches yield different conclusions? Does one approach seem more appropriate than the others for dealing with this issue?

Additional Resources

Christopher Slobogin offers a strong argument in favor of deceptive interrogation techniques in "Deceit, Pretext, and Trickery: Investigative Lies by the Police," *Oregon Law Review*, 76, Winter 1997; Slobogin's argument is critiqued by Margaret L. Paris in "Lying to Ourselves," in the same issue of the *Oregon Law Review*.

Sissela Bok's *Lying: Moral Choice in Public and Private Life* (New York: Vintage Books, 1978) is an important examination of lying and its effects.

Wesley G. Skogan and Tracey L. Meares, "Lawful Policing," *Annals, AAPSS*, 593 (May 2004): 66–83, review research on police adherence to laws and rules; they note the difficulty in determining the degree to which police are following or violating the rules, and argue that internal processes are the best means of improving compliance. Jerome H. Skolnick and Richard A. Leo, "The Ethics of Deceptive Interrogation," *Criminal Justice Ethics*, 11, no. 1 (Winter/Spring 1992): 3–12, examine the legal history of deceptive interrogation, explore various types of police deception, and warn of its dangers. An essay by Welsh S. White, "Deceptive Police Interrogation Practices: How Far Is Too Far?: Miranda's Failure to Restrain Pernicious Interrogation Practices," *Michigan Law Review*, 99 (2001): 1211–1247, examines deceptive interrogation techniques in the context of false confessions and legal protection for the rights of suspects. Richard A. Leo, *Police Interrogation and American Justice* (Cambridge, MA: Harvard University Press, 2008), examines systematic use of deceit as well as psychological manipulation in police interrogations; it is an extraordinary book that offers a clear look at the current practice of police interrogation. Roger W. Shuy, *The Language of Confession, Interrogation, and Deception* (Thousand Oaks, CA: Sage, 1997), notes ways that deceptive language can influence confessions. George C. Thomas III, "Confessions and Police Disclosure: Regulating Police Deception during Interrogation," 39 *Texas Tech Law Review* 1293, Summer 2007, notes several ways in which deceptive police interrogation can confuse innocent persons, even creating a false memory of a guilty act. Gisli H. Gudjonsson, *The Psychology of Interrogations and Confessions: A Handbook* (Hoboken, NJ: Wiley, 2003), includes fascinating cases and insightful psychological analysis of the interrogation process.

A classic manual for police interrogation, which coaches interrogators in the use of deceptive techniques, is Fred E. Inbau and John E. Reid's *Criminal Investigation and Criminal Interrogation*, 3rd ed. (Baltimore: Williams and Wilkins Co., 1962); this book expands their earlier *Lie Detection and Criminal Investigation*, 3rd ed. (Baltimore: Williams and Wilkins Co., 1953); its most recent edition is *Criminal Interrogation and Confessions*, 5th ed. (Boston: Jones & Bartlett Publishers, 2011). Another standard manual advocating deceptive techniques is Charles E. O'Hara and Gregory L. O'Hara's *Fundamentals of Criminal Investigation*, 7th ed. (2003). An incisive critique of Inbau's manual can be found in Yale Kamisar, "What Is an 'Involuntary' Confession? Some Comments on Inbau and Reid's *Criminal Interrogation and Confessions*," *Rutgers Law Review*, 17 (1963). Fred Inbau gives arguments in favor of deceptive interrogation techniques in "Law and Police Practice: Restrictions in the Law of Interrogation and Confessions," *Northwestern University Law Review*, 52 (1957); and "Police Interrogation: A Practical Necessity," in the *Journal of Criminal Law, Criminology, and Police Science*, 52 (1961). (Inbau's enthusiasm for deceptive interrogation methods may well seem excessive by contemporary standards; however, when evaluating Inbau's work, it should be remembered that when he originally developed his interrogation model in the early 1950s, Inbau was attempting to move police interrogation practices away from methods of violent coercion: Beating and threatening of suspects was not an uncommon interrogation technique, and Inbau was campaigning to abolish that method. Whatever one thinks of the deceptive techniques advocated by Inbau, they are surely an improvement over police torture of suspects.)

Paul Cassell voices doubts concerning false confessions in "The Guilty and the 'Innocent': An Examination of Alleged Cases of Wrongful Conviction from False Confessions," *Harvard Journal of Law and Public Policy*, 22 (1999). Concern about false confessions and the techniques that induce them is voiced by Miriam S. Gohara, "A Lie for a Lie: False Confessions and the Case for Reconsidering the Legality of Deceptive Interrogation Techniques," *Fordham Urban Law Journal*, 33 (March 2006): 791–842; she also examines the law concerning deceptive interrogation techniques. Other good examinations of psychological techniques leading to false confessions are Richard A. Leo and Richard J. Ofshe's "The Consequences of False Confessions: Deprivations of Liberty and Miscarriages of Justice in the Age of Psychological Interrogation," *Journal of Criminal Law and Criminology*, 88 (1998); and Hollida Wakefield and Ralph Underwager's "Coerced or Nonvoluntary Confessions," *Behavioral Sciences and the Law*, 16 (1998): 423–440. Extensive accounts of actual cases of false confessions, and what led to them, can be found in Rob Warden and Steven Drizin, eds., *True Stories of False Confessions* (Evanston, IL: Northwestern University Press, 2009). Psychological examinations of why innocent persons might confess to crimes—especially when confronted with deceptive interrogation techniques like fake fingerprint or DNA identifications—include Richard J. Ofshe and Richard A. Leo's "The Decision to Confess Falsely: Rational Choice and Irrational Action," *Denver University Law Review*, 74 (1997); and two articles by Saul M. Kassin: "The Psychology of Confession Evidence," *American Psychologist*, 52 (1997); and "On the Psychology of Confessions: Does Innocence Put Innocents at Risk?" *American Psychologist*, 60 (2005).

Endnotes

1. Sissela Bok, *Lying: Moral Choice in Public and Private Life* (New York: Vintage Books, 1978).
2. Margaret L. Paris, "Lying to Ourselves," *Oregon Law Review*, Volume 76, Winter 1997.

MYSEARCHLAB CONNECTIONS

Report of the Kaufman Commission on Proceedings Involving Guy Paul Morin, Chapter 3, sections A–D, "Jailhouse Informants" (Ontario Ministry of the Attorney General). Describes the severe problems associated with reliance on "jailhouse informants."

Manitoba Justice, "Jailhouse Informants," *The Inquiry Regarding Thomas Sophonow*. Gives accounts of some the less-than-reliable testimony offered by jailhouse informants that led to the wrongful conviction of Thomas Sophonow.

Manitoba Justice, "Eyewitness Identification," *The Inquiry Regarding Thomas Sophonow*. Describes in detail some of the problems that can arise in eyewitness identification, especially when photo lineups are involved.

JURY NULLIFICATION

Chapter Outline

Jury nullification is probably not at the top of your list of problematic moral issues. Abortion, capital punishment, drug policies—those are the big public moral debates. But the question of jury nullification raises interesting and challenging questions for anyone concerned with social issues and morality.

"Jury nullification" occurs when jury members refuse to convict a person they believe is guilty under the law, *because* they believe that either the law under which the person would be convicted is unjust or this specific application of the law creates an injustice. Those who advocate jury nullification insist that jurors are more than merely "fact finders." In *addition* to weighing the facts of the case (Does reliable evidence conclusively prove that the defendant is guilty under the law?), jurors should also weigh questions of *justice*. First, is the law this person is accused of breaking a *just* law, or is it instead an unjust law under which *no one* should be convicted? Second, even if the law is basically just, is the specific *application* of the law under these particular circumstances really just?

As an example of the first sort, consider a case that occurred in a federal court in California. California had passed laws legalizing the use of medical marijuana (e.g., for use in relieving nausea for those undergoing cancer treatment). Under California law, some people were authorized and licensed to legally grow marijuana for medical purposes. However, federal law still prohibits the growing of marijuana, and does not provide an exception for medical marijuana. In 2002, a licensed California medical marijuana grower, Ed Rosenthal, was charged under federal law with illegally growing marijuana. This was a very serious federal charge, since the amount being grown was substantial. If convicted, the grower could face a long prison sentence. The jury in this federal case found Rosenthal guilty. The jurors believed it was unfair to convict the grower, but—because he was guilty under federal law—they believed they had no choice. When interviewed later, the jurors agreed that jury nullification would have been the right course, because they believed the federal law (because it made no exception for medical marijuana) was unjust.

A clear example of juries refusing to convict when they consider a law unjust occurred in Georgia, in the mid-20th century. In 1941, a seven-year-old girl was killed when she was bitten by a poisonous snake during a "snake handling" ceremony at a rural Georgia fundamentalist church. It was apparently an accident—the snake handling was confined to adults who chose to participate, but one snake escaped during the religious frenzy and bit the child. The case caused outrage across Georgia, and in response, the Georgia legislature passed a law, making it a capital crime to participate in a snake handling religious ceremony. Over the next few decades, a number of people were charged under the Georgia law—and would have been subject to execution had they been convicted. But Georgia juries consistently refused to convict. The jurors would probably have convicted if a child was endangered or injured at such a religious ceremony; but while most people thought that snake handling was very foolish, they did not believe there should be a law against adults choosing to do foolish and dangerous things, and *certainly* no one should be put to death for such an activity. After many cases in which juries refused to convict people who were clearly guilty under the law, the Georgia legislature finally repealed the law.

A second type of case is that of Leroy Reed, who in 1985 was tried in Milwaukee on charges of violating Wisconsin gun laws. In the previous year, Wisconsin had passed a law making it illegal for a convicted felon to knowingly possess a firearm. Reed was a convicted felon who had served several years in prison. He had been released from prison 11 years earlier and had been a law-abiding citizen during the decade following his release. Reed was of borderline intelligence (he read at the second-grade level), and could not find work, though he desperately wanted to work. He spent most of his time watching television and occasionally hanging around the Milwaukee County Courthouse, often watching trials. A fan of detective programs, Reed longed to be a "private detective": He viewed it as a job opportunity in which he could "help people out, like that fellow that comes on the TV, *The Equalizer*." One day he saw an advertisement in a magazine for a correspondence course: Send in a few dollars, we'll show you how to be a private detective, and you will receive a private detective "badge." Reed eagerly sent his money and received his "private detective's badge." He then decided that (like the private detectives he saw on television) he should have a gun. He went to a sporting goods store and bought a cheap .22-caliber pistol. This was *prior* to the Brady Bill, which did not become law until 1994. At the time Reed bought his gun, all he had to do was put his name on a form, together with his date of birth. No one checked the form. (Reed couldn't understand the form, and wrote "2" as his date of birth.)

One day while Reed was hanging around the courthouse, a deputy sheriff asked him for identification. Reed proudly showed the receipt for the pistol he had recently purchased, which had his name on it. The deputy ran a background check on Reed and discovered that he had a felony conviction. The deputy instructed Reed to go home, get the gun, and turn it over to the sheriff's department. Reed did as he was instructed. When he turned the gun in, Reed was immediately arrested. Clearly no one regarded Leroy Reed as a threat to society. The police department did not send a SWAT team to surround his house and demand he surrender his gun; instead, they asked Reed himself to go home and bring the gun back (thus requiring him to carry the gun from his home to the downtown sheriff's office). Furthermore, Reed's motives were entirely innocent: He wanted to find a job, and he wanted to help people. And finally, Reed obviously had no clue that he was violating a recently passed law when he bought a gun. The state law (which made it a crime for a convicted felon to knowingly possess a firearm) was passed long after Reed was off parole. Reed certainly did not learn about the law from reading the newspaper, and he did not watch the news on television. But it was also obvious that Reed had broken the law: He was a convicted felon, he possessed a gun, and he knew he possessed a gun, and those were the *only* requirements for being guilty under that law (the law did *not* require that the person breaking the law know that there was such a law, and it did *not* require that the person know that he or she was violating that law). In this case, the jurors had no objection to the state law: Most of them apparently thought it was a good law. However, most of the jurors believed that *applying* the law was unjust *in this particular case*—applying it to convict a person of very limited intelligence, who was trying to live as a law-abiding citizen, who wanted to work and help people, and who had no idea whatsoever and little chance of discovering that he was breaking the law. Thus the jury decided that even though Reed was guilty under the law (and the law itself was a good law), it was wrong to convict him. The jury exercised their power of jury nullification, and returned a unanimous verdict of not guilty.

If the jury does not believe that the guilt of the accused under the law has been proven beyond a reasonable doubt, then jury nullification is not an issue: Whether the law is good or bad, just or unjust, when there is reasonable doubt that the defendant broke the law, the defendant is entitled to an acquittal. (The case of Casey Anthony—charged with first-degree murder in the death of her daughter, and tried on those charges in the midst of frenzied media attention—was certainly *not* a case of jury nullification. The jury did *not* decide to acquit Casey Anthony because the jurors thought laws against murder were unjust, or because they thought this was a special case in which murder was justified. Rather, they acquitted Casey Anthony because the prosecution clearly failed to prove every element of the crime beyond a reasonable doubt. Casey Anthony was charged with *first-degree* murder; so in order for the jury to find her guilty of *that charge*, the state was required to prove beyond a reasonable doubt that she *purposefully planned* and carried out the murder of her daughter. Perhaps she did; or perhaps Casey's father actually killed the child, and Casey was covering up for him. Or possibly Casey Anthony was negligent in caring for her daughter, allowed her daughter to fall into a swimming pool and drown, and then tried to cover up her crime of negligent homicide. Or perhaps something else happened. But the point is that the prosecution left all those possibilities open, and so *failed* to establish that Casey was guilty of premeditated purposeful killing of her daughter and therefore failed to prove that Casey Anthony was guilty of the crime for which she was being tried. Under those circumstances of reasonable doubt, the jury rightly returned a verdict of not guilty: Unless the defendant's guilt of the *specific charge* is proved beyond a reasonable doubt, the defendant is entitled to a verdict of not guilty. Whatever one thinks of jury nullification, this was not an instance of it.)

A famous case that occurred in the American colonies shortly before the American Revolution strongly influenced American thought on jury nullification. Peter Zenger was a printer who published material critical of the royal governor. At that time, it was a crime under British law (the law that applied to all British citizens, including the American colonists) to publish criticisms of the royal governor. The case was tried in Philadelphia, with a jury of American colonists. Although there was no question that Zenger was guilty under the law, the jury refused to return a verdict of guilty: The jurors refused to convict under a law they considered unjust. The judge was outraged, and insisted that the jury return a verdict of guilty; the jury continued to refuse. The judge ordered the jurors locked up—with no food or water—until they returned a verdict of guilty. After two weeks of confinement, the jury still refused to return a guilty verdict (food and water were slipped to the jury by sympathizers). The judge finally released the jurors, and Zenger was not convicted. The Zenger case was a rallying cry for the colonists, and one of the sparks leading to the revolution. It was also a case that remained in the popular American memory for many decades: A powerful example of courageous jurors refusing to convict a fellow citizen under what they considered an unjust law. This was regarded as one of the main functions of American jury (as it was and remains for British juries): Protecting citizens against unjust laws or unfair treatment, because no one could be convicted unless a jury of his or her *fellow citizens*—not judges, nor legislators, nor nobility—found the defendant guilty and deserving of punishment.

Powerful as the Zenger case was as a symbol of American justice and the power of the people, eventually (in *Sparf and Hansen v. U.S.*, 1895), the U.S. Supreme Court ruled that American juries should *not* reject the law by their verdicts, but were obligated to follow the law even when they considered the law unjust. There were two main reasons for that decision. First is the belief that the law should apply equally and universally: It is unfair for a person in Miami to be convicted under a law and a person who commits the same offense in Orlando be acquitted because a jury in Orlando doesn't approve of the law. All citizens are entitled to the same treatment, and all citizens have a right to be tried under the *same* laws. (Of course the law in Florida may be different from the law in Nevada. For example, prostitution is legal in Nevada, but a criminal offense in Arizona; and so it is legitimate under the law for an act that is a criminal act in Arizona to not be criminal in Nevada; but if the laws of Arizona make prostitution illegal, then—according to this justification—it would be wrong for a person in Tucson to commit the same criminal act as a person in Phoenix, but the person in Tucson go free because the jury doesn't like the law against prostitution, while the person in Phoenix is convicted and goes to jail.)

The second reason why the Supreme Court rejected jury nullification was based on the premise that the United States is a *democracy*, rather than a monarchy or a dictatorship. In 1770, if the American colonists did not like the laws approved by King George, they had no way to change them; but in 1895, if U.S. citizens did not like a law that was passed, then they could vote for new legislators and get the law changed. So—according to this justification—the right way to change a law is not by a small group of jurors rejecting the laws passed by the democratic government, but rather by the democratic process: All citizens vote on their representatives who then pass laws that citizens must all follow. If a small group of jurors can nullify a law that has been passed by a majority of the elected representatives, then the will of the majority—which is supposed to govern people in a democracy—is being thwarted by a very small minority (a group of 12 jurors). That was the second justification for rejecting jury nullification: If you don't like the laws that criminalize marijuana possession, then vote for legislators who will change those laws; but don't undermine the democratic process by refusing to convict people who are guilty under our democratically passed system of law. (There was actually a third reason that the Court broke over a century of precedents and voted against jury nullification—though with a strong dissent from the Court's minority. In the late 19th century, labor movements were struggling to organize factory and mine workers to demand better wages and safer working conditions. The wealthy mine and factory owners were able to pressure state legislatures to pass laws against the organizing of labor, and so when workers tried to organize for better pay and better working conditions, they were often arrested and charged with breaking those anti-organizing laws. However, those laws were unpopular with the majority of citizens, and so juries often refused to convict workers charged with breaking laws they considered unjust. Thus the same mine and factory owners who had pushed for laws preventing labor organizing now exerted pressure on the Supreme Court to rule against the jury nullification that was preventing those laws from being enforced.)

Although the U.S. Supreme Court has ruled against jury nullification, it is clear that American juries still have the *power* of jury nullification; and as the Reed case shows, they sometimes use that power. During Prohibition, juries often refused to convict those charged with sale of liquor, because they thought the law unjust. During the period of the Vietnam War, on several occasions juries refused to convict persons accused of resisting or interfering with the draft process. More recently, Dr. Jack Kevorkian—the "suicide doctor"—assisted several people suffering from debilitating diseases in committing suicide, setting up a machine they could activate to release drugs that would lead to a painless death. Though Kevorkian's acts clearly violated state law, juries generally refused to convict him.

One of the most cherished rights of American, Canadian, and British citizens is the right to a "trial by jury," the right to have one's case tried "by a jury of your peers." If you are accused of a criminal act, then you have a right to have the charges against you decided by ordinary citizens—a "jury of your peers"—who do *not* hold positions in government. That is an important safeguard against excessive government power over individual citizens: The government *cannot* impose criminal penalties against you unless a *jury* of your fellow citizens finds that those penalties are legitimate. (Actually, that is no longer quite true. Under the "Patriot Act," passed in the panic that followed the September 11 attack on the Twin Towers in New York and the Pentagon in Washington, DC., laws were passed that allowed the government to hold you in prison if it *suspects* you of being a terrorist; but that is a striking—and for many people, very frightening—*exception* to the important rule that no one can be subjected to criminal penalties without the judgment of a jury of their fellow citizens.) Of course if you are charged with a criminal act, and you *choose* to have your case heard by a judge rather than by a jury, that is your privilege. But you still have the basic *right* to a trial by jury.

If we continue to value the right of a trial by jury, then the jury will always have the *power* to reach a verdict that the judge and the prosecutor don't like; indeed, the jury will have the *power* to reach a verdict that is contrary to the law and contrary to all the evidence presented. To deny juries that power (to have a rule that the jury is only allowed to reach a verdict that agrees with the verdict favored by the judge) is to destroy the system of jury trials altogether. The right to a trial by jury precisely *is* the right to have a jury of one's fellow citizens make the decision of whether one is guilty or innocent. Thus juries will always have the *power* of jury nullification. That is, juries will always have the power to *nullify* the law in a particular case and to decide that (even though the defendant may in fact be guilty under a particular law) the defendant should not be found guilty (either because the jury believes that the law is unjust or because the jury believes that in this particular case the *application* of the law would be unjust). So the question at issue is not whether juries have the *power* of jury nullification (so long as there are genuine juries, juries will inevitably hold such power); rather, whether juries should *exercise* that power.

Though their motives may differ, some fiercely conservative writers join a number of dedicated liberals in championing jury nullification. Other conservatives and liberals share a deep distrust of jury nullification. Conservative advocates of jury nullification see it as a check on the power of big government: If government passes laws that the people regard as unjust, or as interfering in matters that should be left to individual choice, then jury nullification is a way of blunting the effect of such laws. Many liberals join conservatives in opposing various forms of interference in personal choices (e.g., they may join conservatives in opposing laws criminalizing marijuana), and agree that jury nullification is an appropriate response to such laws. In addition, many liberals oppose restrictions on political speech (such as laws limiting criticism of agricultural products or laws that would criminalize flag-burning) and see jury nullification as a means of countering such restrictions. On the other side, there are many conservatives who find jury nullification a frightening breakdown of "law and order," with juries refusing to follow the "authority" of the judge's instructions. Many liberals fear that jury nullification will result in localized rejection of laws they may regard as valuable and legitimate (such as laws restricting the sale of firearms or banning various forms of discrimination; for example, when states passed tougher laws against spousal abuse, juries in some localities seemed reluctant to convict defendants even when there was solid evidence of such abuse). So this is an issue that divides conservatives just as it causes splits among liberals. Whether you consider yourself liberal or conservative, this is a question that defies labels and requires careful independent thinking.

Strawman Distortions

Those who favor a right of jury nullification are sometimes accused of being anarchists, who reject all government and all rule of law. (A variation on that strawman attack is the claim that those who favor jury nullification favor "mob rule.") But obviously one can believe that the jury should be the final check on the criminal justice system without rejecting the legitimacy of government and the laws passed by the government.

A strawman attack on those who reject jury nullification is that they believe we should simply accept and uncritically follow any laws that are passed. That is false. They believe that if we consider a law unjust, we should work hard to get it changed through our democratic process: by trying to persuade our elected representatives to repeal or modify the law, or by voting into office new legislators willing to change the law. And one can reject jury nullification as a general policy, but still believe that in some extreme cases, one should refuse to follow the law (if the law involves a major violation of human rights, such as the fugitive slave act).

What Is the Common Ground?

Everyone agrees that it would be *wrong* to convict under the fugitive slave act (which made it a crime to aid an escaped slave). Perhaps everyone agrees that we should make our laws more responsive to the actual needs and desires of the citizens, rather than controlled by moneyed interests (thus reducing the felt need for jury nullification). And *almost* everyone agrees that a criminal defendant's right to a trial by jury—guaranteed by the Constitution—is a vitally important right that should not be lost (even those who are strongly opposed to jury nullification do not want to destroy the right to a trial by a jury of one's peers). Everyone agrees that jury nullification should not be based on prejudice—as was the case when all-white juries in the deep South refused to convict people accused of violating civil rights laws or people who had committed assault or even murder against civil rights workers.

While jury nullification to prevent a conviction is controversial, that controversy does not extend to jury nullification to *convict* a person who is in fact *not* guilty under the law. That is, imagine a case in which the defendant is not guilty under the law, but you believe that there *should* be a law against what the defendant did. For example, suppose that in your state someone who sells a used car is not required to reveal known faults in the car, so long as those faults do not pose risk of harm. A used-car dealer sells a sweet trusting old lady a used car that the dealer knows will soon break down, because the transmission is shot. By the time the lady drives her car to her garage, the car will be useless. It will be impossible for her to get the car into gear; and replacing the transmission would cost more than the value of the car. In your state, the law on sale of used cars is "buyer beware": The dealer is under no obligation to reveal that he is selling a worthless car, so long as the car's defects are not likely to be dangerous (this defect will not pose a hazard—with the transmission broken down, the car will not move at all). You and your fellow jurors are rightly appalled at the sleazy behavior of this dealer, and would like to convict him of fraud, or perhaps reckless endangerment. Both charges have been made against the defendant, but the evidence to support those charges is very weak—it certainly does not prove the charges beyond a reasonable doubt. As sleazy as this dealer is, most of us will agree that it would be wrong to convict him of crimes he did not commit, even though that might seem more *just*. That is, some of us may believe that it is wrong to convict someone if the law under which he is charged is an unjust law (that is, some of us may believe in jury nullification in such cases); but that is very different from convicting someone who has *not* broken any law simply because we feel he should be convicted of *something*.

Arguments in Favor of Jury Nullification

1. Obviously, those who favor jury nullification believe it should be used only to prevent injustice. When someone is guilty under the law but the law itself is fundamentally unjust, or if application of the law in *this case* (because of the special nature of the case) would be an injustice, then—according to those who favor jury nullification—one has not only a right to exercise jury nullification, but a *duty*. Even if the laws are passed democratically, that does not change one's obligation to resist unjust laws. If 75% of the citizens voted to ban Catholicism in the United States and impose severe prison sentences on anyone practicing the Catholic religion, that law would be passed democratically, but that would not change the fact that it would be a terribly *unjust* law. So the basic argument for jury nullification is the right and *obligation* to follow one's basic moral principles, and to refuse to support injustice.

If you are a juror when the defendant is on trial for helping a fugitive slave escape from brutal slave catchers (as often happened during the period before the Civil War), then voting as a juror to find the defendant guilty would violate your deepest principles of justice. When you serve on a jury, you do not become a moral cipher: If the laws of your country are fundamentally unjust, then you have a moral duty to work against them, and you certainly do not have a moral duty to support them as a juror. A few years ago, the city of Las Vegas passed a law, making it illegal to give food to homeless people in the city; at that time, a number of people publicly declared that they could not in good conscience follow such a law; and those same people would obviously not feel obliged—or even morally permitted—to find someone guilty who broke such a law.

That does not mean, of course, that jury nullification is *always* legitimate. In a genuinely democratic society, citizens generally have an obligation to follow and uphold the laws of that society, *unless* following and supporting such laws (such as the fugitive slave act) would cause or promote injustice. Thus in most cases, you probably have an obligation to follow and uphold the laws, even if you think they are mistaken. Where the line crosses from *mistaken* law to *unjust* law is difficult to say. But that does not change the fact—according to those who support jury nullification—that we do *not* have a duty as jurors to uphold unjust laws. If we are clear that a law or its application is unjust, then we should not convict the defendant even if the defendant has been proved guilty under the law.

2. For the ordinary citizen—who does not hold political office and who does not have great influence over those who *do* hold office and pass laws—jury duty is the most direct and important governmental role he or she plays. Voting is important, but in most elections, one vote has little effect. But the vote of a citizen-juror is critically important. In most jurisdictions, a jury verdict requires that the jury reach a *unanimous* verdict. Thus if you are serving on a jury, the defendant cannot be found either guilty or not guilty until *you* individually agree with the verdict. If the jury finds the defendant guilty, that can only happen because *you* voted to find the defendant guilty. When Daniel Ellsberg released the secret military documents that became known as "the Pentagon Papers" (documents showing that the government had systematically deceived the American people about the nature and course of the Vietnam War), he violated the law. The jury made it clear that this was a bad law, and that it would be *unjust* to convict Ellsberg under that law. In no other context could 12 ordinary American citizens make such a forceful statement concerning the justice or injustice of governmental rules and behavior. To make jurors strictly *fact finders*—whose only role is to examine the facts of the case, apply those facts to the law *as given by the judge*, and then calculate whether the defendant is or is not guilty under that law (*without* judging whether *justice* is being done)—is to deprive citizens of a uniquely important role they play in their own government.

Arguments against Jury Nullification

1. Jury nullification may be legitimate in the case of Peter Zenger, when the laws were made and enforced by rulers whom the people did not elect (American colonists could not vote in British elections). But (so this argument goes) it is *not* legitimate in a democracy, where the people make the laws through their elected

representatives, and also elect the people who ultimately control the enforcement of those laws (the president or the governor). If you do not believe a law is just, then you should work to have that law changed by *your* Congress (or state legislature); and if those bodies will not change the law, then join with your fellow citizens in electing new representatives who *will* change the law. But in a democracy, it is wrong for a jury—made up of a dozen citizens—to invalidate through jury nullification a law that was passed democratically for *all* citizens, through their democratically elected representatives.

One objection to this argument is that it presents the *ideal* (laws passed for the benefit of *all*—or at least the *majority*—of citizens) as if it were actual. In fact, laws are too often passed not for the benefit of all, and not for the benefit of the majority, but for the benefit of those with the greatest influence and the most resources (Exxon-Mobil, Bank of America, and Walmart obviously have much greater influence on Congress—through their lobbyists and their massive campaign donations—than you do as an individual citizen). Clearly some people (and some corporations) have more power and money than others, and have disproportionate influence on what laws are passed. For example, in Texas a law was passed, making it a criminal act to raise questions about the safety of beef and other food products. (Such laws were ridiculed as "veggie libel" laws, and the majority of Texans thought these laws were not only wrong but also ridiculous; but they were the law in Texas.) This was clearly a law that benefited some very wealthy ranchers and food processors, and jeopardized the safety of all Texas citizens: Those who had reason to think that there was a danger of food contamination were silenced, and could not express their warning. In fact, there was very good reason to think that some food products being sold in Texas were potentially hazardous: The threat of "mad cow disease"—a terrible disease that attacks the nervous system and results in insanity—was a genuine if rare danger, and there were almost no procedures to prevent the virus from infecting cattle that were slaughtered in Texas. But it was a law that was passed "democratically" by the Texas legislature. If a jury refused to convict someone who raised serious public concern about the safety of Texas food products, it is hardly clear that the jury would be going against any "democratic" process, much less that the jury is thwarting the will of the majority.

2. Everyone has a right to be tried under the same law. Persons tried in an area with one set of views should be entitled to the same trial as people tried in a different location. If I am on trial for marijuana possession, I *should* get the same trial in Austin that I would in Dallas. We know that this does not actually happen (if you are arrested for "liberating" a dozen beef animals on the way to the slaughter house and hiding them where the owners cannot recover them, try to get arrested in Austin rather than Amarillo). But it's an important ideal, and jury nullification goes against that ideal. In a democratic society, every law will be more popular in some regions than in others; but they are still laws for the entire country (or the entire state, if it is a state law). As citizens in a democracy, we have an obligation to obey its laws. A federal law requiring a background check before buying a gun will be less popular in Georgia than in Vermont; but citizens of Georgia have the same obligation to follow the laws of the country as do the citizens of Vermont, and it is fundamentally unfair for a defendant in Vermont to be convicted for the same crime that a jury in Georgia nullifies by refusing to convict.

Where Do We Stand?

Even if we stand on opposite sides of this issue, we should be able to respect and appreciate the views of our opponents. After all, both sides agree that not all of our laws are perfect and that some may be fundamentally unjust; and both sides agree that we should work *against* unjust laws. The difference is that those who *oppose* jury nullification believe that those efforts should be devoted to getting the laws *changed* in the legislature or the congress; and those who *support* jury nullification agree that getting the laws changed is a good idea, but they also insist on more *direct* action against unjust laws, by refusing to convict persons charged under them. While that is an important difference in approach, the common ground is much broader than might be supposed at first glance.

Questions for Reflection

1. Current U.S. laws make it a criminal offense to distribute marijuana to others and to possess marijuana for personal use. Suppose you believe those laws are profoundly wrong. Some of you in fact believe that; others do not. Set aside that issue for the moment. *Suppose* that you believe such laws are wrong and are a violation of personal freedom. You don't think they are wrongs on the order of the fugitive slave act, which made it a criminal act to help an escaped slave elude capture; nonetheless, you believe those laws are wrong, and you believe it would be *wrong* to convict anyone of violating that law. You are called for jury service, and the case you are called to hear involves a young man living in a rural area, who grew a few marijuana plants for his own use, and occasionally gave small amounts of marijuana (no more than an ounce) to a few adult friends, never accepting money for those gifts. The young man is charged with production, possession, and distribution of marijuana—serious criminal offenses. As the lawyers are questioning you to determine who should be selected for the jury and who should be excluded, the lawyer for the prosecution asks the following question: "This is a case of a person charged with violating the laws prohibiting the production, possession, and distribution of marijuana. Many people think those are bad laws, and should be repealed. That's not the question before us. Whether you agree with those laws or not, those are *our* laws: They were passed by our elected representatives, and they are the laws of our democratic society. Whatever your attitude toward those laws, can you put aside your personal like or dislike of the laws and, *if* the evidence shows beyond a reasonable doubt that the defendant violated those laws, return a verdict of guilty?" If you answer that question honestly, and say that you would refuse to convict anyone under the current laws criminalizing marijuana, then you will be automatically excluded from the jury; in that case, there is a strong likelihood that the defendant will be found guilty. Because criminal juries require unanimous verdicts, if you are on that jury, you can block any guilty verdict against the defendant. Would it be legitimate for you to lie about your belief in jury nullification in order to serve on the jury? If you answered no, suppose the case were one in which the defendant is charged under the fugitive slave act, and will be subject to criminal penalties for something you regard as virtuous and heroic: aiding an escaped slave's quest for freedom. In that case, would it be legitimate to lie about your views in favor of jury nullification?

2. Could someone consistently hold to a "mild" or "moderate" view of jury nullification? That is, might one consistently hold that jury nullification is right in extreme cases of injustice (such as charging someone under the fugitive slave act) but wrong when the law in question is not so morally vile (such as laws criminalizing

marijuana, if you believe those laws are bad but not morally outrageous). *If* you took this view, would you be able to draw a clear line for when jury nullification is and is not legitimate?

3. The fundamental question concerning jury nullification is the question of the proper *role* and function of the criminal jury. Is the jury strictly a body for fact-finding (the laws are made by the legislature and interpreted by the judiciary; the role of the jury is to take those laws as given by the judge in the case, and determine whether the evidence shows beyond a reasonable doubt that the defendant violated those laws)? Or is the jury the last barrier against state injustice?

4. Private Bradley Manning is accused of leaking classified documents to WikiLeaks, revealing that the country's leaders have been deceiving the American people. To take only one of many examples, in 2009, the mayor of Kabul, Mayor Sahebi, was imprisoned on charges of corruption; the official line from the U.S. government—reported on television and in the newspapers—was that this proved Afghanistan was finally cracking down on corruption. In fact, the mayor was convicted and imprisoned *not* because he was corrupt, but because he was the rare official who was *fighting* corruption and thus getting in the way of the many corrupt government officials who were taking bribes and stealing money. Those in the U.S. State Department knew that, and reported it in their secret cables; but the press and the American people were told exactly the opposite. Suppose it is proved beyond a reasonable doubt that Manning actually leaked those documents, in violation of the law; but you believe that he did so in order to counteract the false information the government was telling its citizens and to provide his fellow citizens with

accurate information. Would that be legitimate grounds for refusing to convict?

5. In cases of civil disobedience, those who commit illegal acts *expect* to be convicted, in order to demonstrate the fundamental *injustice* of the law. Would this be a special case in which believers in jury nullification should convict, even if they also believe that the law is unjust? Or would the jury make a stronger statement against the law by *refusing* to convict?

6. Joe, aged 20, is charged with drinking under the legal age. Suppose that Amy is being interviewed as a potential juror, and she is asked her opinion of the law that denies legal access to alcoholic beverages to those between 18 and 21. In answer to one of the questions, Amy states: "I believe that this is a stupid law that should be repealed; it's not fair; if someone is considered old enough to join the armed forces (or even be *drafted* into the armed forces) and risk his or her life in combat on behalf of his or her country, then that person should have the *rights* of an adult, including the same right to drink alcohol that other adults have. However, I also believe in the rule of law, and although I think this is an unfair and stupid law, I believe people have an obligation to follow the law; so if the prosecution proves beyond a reasonable doubt that the defendant broke that law, I am willing to find the defendant guilty." Almost certainly the prosecution will use one of its peremptory challenges to exclude Amy from the jury that will sit in judgment on Joe. But suppose the prosecuting attorney asks you—the judge—to dismiss Amy for *cause*; that is, to dismiss Amy on the grounds that she will not be able to judge the case fairly. Would you (as judge) agree with the prosecutor, and dismiss Amy for *cause*?

Additional Resources

Sparf and Hansen v. U.S., 156 U.S. 51, October Term, 1895, is the U.S. Supreme Court case in which the Court ruled that judges need not tell jurors of their power to nullify law by judging both fact and law. Justices Gray and Shiras wrote a strong dissent. (This case can be found at www.oyez.org.)

Alan W. Scheflin's "Jury Nullification: The Right to Say No," *Southern California Law Review* 45, 168–226 (1972) is an excellent source for the legal history of jury nullification. An even more extensive study can be found in Clay Conrad, *Jury Nullification: The Evolution of a Doctrine* (Durham, NC: Carolina Academic Press,

1999). Akhil Reed Amar, in *The Bill of Rights: Creation and Reconstruction* (New Haven, CN: Yale University Press, 1998), argues that the U.S. Constitution recognized and preserved the right of jury nullification. An interesting history of jury nullification—which treats jury nullification quite broadly—is Irwin A. Horowitz, Norbert L. Kerr, and Keith E. Niedermeier's "Jury Nullification: Legal and Psychological Perspectives," *Brooklyn Law Review*, 66 (Summer 2001): 1207–1249. Steven E. Barkan, "Jury Nullification in Political Trials," *Social Problems*, 31 (October 1983): 28–44, focuses on the role jury nullification has played in a variety of political trials.

Paula Di Perna, in *Juries on Trial: Faces of American Justice* (New York: Dembner Books, 1984), offers a very readable history of the idea of jury nullification in U.S. and British courts. Another good source is William L. Dwyer, *In the Hands of the People: The Trial Jury's Origins, Triumphs, Troubles, and Future in American Democracy* (New York: St. Martin's Press, 2002), Chapter 5. An outstanding book on the jury and the jury system is Neil Vidmar and Valerie P. Hans's *American Juries: The Verdict* (Amherst, NY: Prometheus Books, 2007).

Richard St. John argues against jury nullification in "License to Nullify: The Democratic and Constitutional Deficiencies of Authorized Jury Lawmaking," *Yale Law Journal*, 106 (June 1997): 2563–2597; another opposing voice is Erick J. Haynie, "Populism, Free Speech, and the Rule of Law: The 'Fully Informed' Jury Movement and its Implications," *Journal of Criminal Law & Criminology*, 88, no. 1 (1998).

An outstanding contemporary defense of jury nullification is offered by Jeffrey Abramson in *We, the Jury: The Jury System and the Ideal of Democracy*, Chapter 2 (Cambridge, MA: Harvard, 2000). Some other defenders of jury nullification include Alan W. Scheflin and Jon Van Dyke, "Jury Nullification: Contours of the Controversy," *Law and Contemporary Problems*, 43 (Autumn 1980): 51–115; and Alan W. Scheflin and Jon Van Dyke, "Merciful Juries: The Resilience of Jury Nullification," *Washington and Lee Law Review*, 48 (Winter 1991). A well-researched and engagingly written book on the importance of independent jury deliberation is John Gastil, E. Pierre Deess, Philip J. Weiser, and Cindy Simmons's *The Jury and Democracy: How Jury Deliberation Promotes Civic Engagement and Political Participation* (New York: Oxford University Press, 2010).

Nancy J. King, "Silencing Nullification Advocacy Inside the Jury Room and Outside the Courtroom," *University of Chicago Law Review*, 65 (1998): 433–501, offers an excellent study of the current law as well as current controversies related to jury nullification. Irwin A. Horowitz and Thomas Willging survey the long and extensive debate on jury nullification in "Changing Views of Jury Power: The Nullification Debate, 1787–1988," *Law and Human Behavior*, 15 (1991). An interesting study that examines the ethical issues surrounding jury nullification is Alan W. Scheflin's "Mercy and Morals: The Ethics of Nullification," in John Kleinig and James P. Levine, eds., *Jury Ethics: Jury Conduct and Jury Dynamics* (Boulder, CO: Paradigm Publishers, 2006).

The Fully Informed Jury Association, or FIJA, is a nonprofit organization that promotes the principle of jury nullification; it can be found at www.fija.org.

MYSEARCHLAB CONNECTIONS

The U.S. Supreme Court ruling against jury nullification is *Sparf & Hansen v. U.S.*, 1895. The majority opinion can be found at http://constitution.org/ussc/156-051a.htm, and the dissenting opinion at http://constitution.org/ussc/156-051c.htm. In 1794, in *Georgia v. Brailsford*, Chief Justice John Jay ruled that jurors have the right "to determine the law as well as the fact in controversy." Chief Justice Jay's 1794 ruling can be found at http://scholar.google.com/scholar_case?case=17662972068346058599&q=georgia+v.+brailsford+1794&hl=en&as_sdt=2,36&as_vis=1.

12

SHOULD ILLEGAL DRUGS BE LEGALIZED?

Chapter Outline

Tobacco has been the cause of millions of death in the United States, but cigarette manufacturers are honored and respected members of society; marijuana has killed few if any, but marijuana growers are despised as "drug pushers" and are imprisoned for lengthy sentences. Tobacco is a much more addictive drug, and also more dangerous and deadly. The "pusher" who tries to hook children on drugs is the stuff of nightmares and political witch hunts; the clever tobacco advertiser who finds ways of making a brand of cigarettes more appealing to underage smokers—for example, by use of flavored tobacco products—is rewarded with huge bonuses and advertising awards.

Wanting to move more drugs toward legal status is usually considered a liberal view, while supporting the status quo is regarded as conservative; but that is not a very useful or accurate distinction. Many conservatives (such as William Buckley) have been bold leaders of the movement to legalize marijuana; while many liberals (concerned with negative health effects of increased marijuana use) have been reluctant to change the marijuana laws. But of course many liberals have also campaigned for legalizing—or at least decriminalizing—marijuana, and often other drugs as well. In June of 2011, Representative Barney Frank of Massachusetts (one of the most liberal members of the House) and Representative Ron Paul of Texas (a longtime archconservative) joined in sponsoring a bill that would end federal regulation of marijuana and allow states to make their own rules (including legalizing, if the people of that state so choose) to control its manufacture and use. "Conservative" and "liberal" are not very useful labels for this discussion.

Strawman Distortions

No one can look at the drug policies of the United States and regard them as rational. But the fact that the current policies are ridiculous does not tell us what the policies should be. Clearly, however, there are some policies that no one wants. Unfortunately, some of those obviously undesirable policy strawmen are falsely attributed to the opposing argument side. First, no one wants to legalize all drugs and allow them to be sold with no restrictions or regulation. Even if we limit discussion to drugs that are already legal, such as tobacco and alcohol, it is clear that we all want them to be regulated. There are serious debates concerning what the legal age for consuming alcohol should be: in the United States, the legal age is 21, while in Canada, Australia, and most European countries, the age is 18. Some people think we should set the U.S. age lower, while others would push the Canadian age higher. But no one believes that there should be *no* restrictions on when people should be able to buy alcohol: No one thinks that six-year-old children should be sitting in bars knocking back vodka tonics. Just as clearly, while some think we should legalize marijuana and others oppose such a move, no one on either side believes that it should be legal to sell or give marijuana to children, or to advertise marijuana to children. So the question is not whether all these drugs should be regulated (everyone agrees they should be); the question is whether there should be carefully regulated *legal* sales of marijuana (and perhaps other drugs, such as cocaine), or whether all sale and use of marijuana should remain a criminal offense.

The second point of agreement (and of potential strawman distortion) is over the *nature* of the drugs (particularly marijuana) that are proposed for legalization. Everyone—on both sides of the legalization issue—agrees that marijuana is not a health food: If you want to stay healthy and run marathons, and you have a choice between smoking marijuana and eating a green salad, choose the latter. There is significant disagreement about how harmful and dangerous marijuana is, but there is no disputing the fact that it is harmful, just as alcohol and tobacco are harmful. So the question is not whether marijuana use is harmful (it is), but whether—like other harmful drugs such as tobacco and alcohol—it should be legal for adults to buy and use that harmful drug. Furthermore, those who want to decriminalize drugs do not propose treating all currently illegal drugs the same. Marijuana might be sold in carefully regulated shops, such as those in the Netherlands; while heroin—a much more dangerous drug—would be available only to registered users, who would be counseled to switch to heroin substitutes and eventually free themselves of their habit.

What Is the Common Ground?

There are many relevant points on which we generally agree. We want to minimize addiction and maximize freedom (though there may be disputes about what counts as freedom). We want to reduce violent crime and reduce the use of dangerous drugs. As a society, we would like to reduce the *costs* associated with dangerous drugs, including the costs of drug enforcement, drug treatment programs, prisons, and drug-related health problems. Finally, almost everyone agrees that people should have access to *accurate* information concerning drugs (the "drug education" programs that are promoted in the schools are clearly ineffective both in providing accurate information and in reducing the use of dangerous drugs). That's a lot of agreement. Our differences are not so much differences in goals, but differences about the best way to achieve those goals. No one (with the exception of the tobacco industry) wants to increase the number of addicts; everyone wants to reduce the amount of violent crime. So those who disagree with us are not monsters who wish to addict small children to heroin, nor are they enemies of personal freedom. Disagreements on this issue can become intense; so it is important to remember that the *agreements* on this issue are more basic than the *dis*agreements.

Arguments against Legalizing Marijuana and Other Drugs

1. Marijuana, cocaine, and the other drugs that are currently illegal are particularly dangerous: For example, contemporary varieties of marijuana are stronger than those available in the United States a few decades ago. Drugs such as heroin, opium, and cocaine are dangerously addictive. We should continue to outlaw those drugs, because of the special dangers they pose.

   But are the dangers that great? Nicotine—the drug in tobacco—is probably a more addictive drug than cocaine or heroin, certainly more addictive than marijuana. And alcohol, as many alcoholics will sadly attest, is also strongly addictive. It's true that *withdrawal* from some of the illegal drugs is particularly unpleasant, but that unpleasantness can be significantly reduced with proper treatment. And withdrawal from tobacco, as well as from alcohol addiction, is both difficult and unpleasant.

   If the question of dangerousness concerns the *behavior* of those taking the drugs, then alcohol is the clear leader, and no other drug is even close. Alcohol is a factor in a high percentage of domestic abuse cases, as well as in crimes of violence such as assault and rape and homicide. If we add the dangerous and deadly driving that occurs under the influence of alcohol, it is clear that use of alcohol poses the greatest threat for others. There is little dispute that if all alcohol drinkers switched to marijuana, there would be much less violence (imagine marijuana being substituted for beer at NFL games; there would be considerably fewer fights among fans). Of course there is the problem of violent crimes—especially crimes of theft and burglary—committed in order to obtain the money to support drug habits. But that is not a result of the drugs themselves causing violence; rather, it is the result of the very high price of the drugs, which is caused by their illegal status.

   Obviously all of these drugs—tobacco, alcohol, marijuana, cocaine, and heroin—pose dangers; thus it is important that people have *accurate* information about the genuine dangers of addiction, and the significant health hazards posed by use of these drugs. But the supposed extreme danger associated with illegal drugs—as compared to legal drugs such as tobacco and alcohol—is a very doubtful foundation for an argument against drug legalization.

2. A second argument is that legalizing marijuana will lead to much greater levels of drug abuse and crime. That is a question for careful research, not one that can be answered by speculation or by "what seems most plausible." But the evidence that exists is against that claim, though the evidence is not conclusive. On the question of increased crime,

it is much more likely that legalizing drugs would greatly reduce crime, and in particular would be a very important step toward reducing the enormous power and brutal behavior of the major drug cartels that operate throughout North and South America, which have had such a terrible impact on Mexico and Colombia—large numbers of murders, corruption of government and police officials, and assassinations of mayors and police chiefs and prosecutors and judges.

Whether legalizing and regulating drugs would increase use of those drugs is a more difficult question. It would seem plausible that a number of people who are reluctant to use *illegal* drugs might be more likely to use them if they were legalized. Of course, some of those users would be switching from one drug (alcohol) to another (marijuana), and so drug use overall would not increase among such users. And because of effective educational programs, use of tobacco—a legal but very dangerous and addictive drug—has substantially declined in the United States during recent years. Use of marijuana has been decriminalized and regulated in the Netherlands, yet that country is reported by the European Monitoring Centre for Drugs and Drug Addiction to have one of the lowest rates of marijuana use in Europe. Though both sides in the debate make bold claims concerning the effects of legalization on drug use, the actual evidence for either side is very thin.

3. Alcohol and tobacco are certainly significant health hazards and cause serious social problems (alcohol is involved in many cases of domestic abuse, is a major cause of automobile deaths, and is often a factor in child abuse and neglect). But alcohol and tobacco are deeply entrenched in our culture; indeed, both alcohol and tobacco—in many forms—have been part of American culture since well before the American Revolution, and they can be found in every corner of America as well as in almost every ethnic group and subculture throughout the United States. So for better or worse, alcohol and tobacco use cannot be eliminated. But marijuana—while it is certainly widely used—is not part of the tradition, and its use is not so deeply entrenched in the culture; and the same applies to other illegal drugs. The fact that some harmful drugs (tobacco and alcohol) cannot be eliminated is no reason to legalize an additional drug—marijuana— that everyone agrees has harmful effects. Even if it proves impossible to eliminate marijuana, keeping it illegal prevents it from gaining a powerful foothold in our culture, and that is worth the effort.

This is an interesting argument, but its strength depends on two difficult questions. First, have some illegal drugs—particularly marijuana—*already* established such a strong presence in our society that efforts to prevent that happening are futile; and second, even if the illegal drugs have *not* established such a strong foothold, *is* it "worth the effort" and the costs of criminalization to prevent such drugs (already widely available in our society) from becoming even more a part of our culture? Answering the second question requires exploring two prior questions: First, how costly—in both monetary and social terms—is the "war on drugs," which keeps the use and sale of such drugs criminal activities? That is a question that will be examined further in the arguments for legalization. The second prior question is, how bad would it be if these illegal drugs were more easily available? If marijuana use were substituted for some of the current consumption of alcohol, that might be an improvement. Of course if addiction to cocaine or heroin soared, that would be a terrible consequence; but if those drugs were carefully regulated (while being decriminalized) and educational programs made people well aware of the risks involved, then the likelihood of a surge in addictions seems low. Educational programs have helped people recognize the health hazards of tobacco and have greatly reduced the number of tobacco users; furthermore, countries that have decriminalized such drugs have not reported a significant increase in the number of people using or addicted to such drugs. Still, these remain important and difficult questions for the debate on drug legalization.

4. Marijuana is a dangerous and damaging drug. It is simply wrong for society to give its blessing to the use of marijuana by legalizing its sale and use. If society gives its stamp of approval to marijuana and cocaine and heroin by removing criminal penalties for their use, then more people will think they are all right and start using them.

It would certainly be a mistake to give a social "blessing" to marijuana, much less to heroin and opium. But by making it legal, society is not giving its blessing to the use of marijuana, any more than it gives its blessing to pornography when it refuses to make that illegal. Tobacco use is legal, but society does not give its "blessing" to the use of tobacco; to the contrary, there are now strong social pressures to reduce tobacco use. Society may regard many activities as foolish or even immoral, while still holding that competent adults should be free to make bad choices for themselves. Most people in society regard smoking as very dangerous to one's physical health, and worshiping Satan as dangerous to your spiritual health; but most also believe that competent adults should be free to make such choices.

5. The "freedom" to use drugs (such as marijuana) is not a real freedom at all; it is not a freedom anyone could genuinely want. The only genuine freedom—the only freedom worthy of our respect—is the freedom to do the *right* thing; and using drugs (whether tobacco, marijuana, or cocaine) that ultimately harm health is clearly not the right thing.

The concept of "freedom" in this argument is not one that many people find attractive. It opens a path to not only criminalizing marijuana, but also tobacco, along with cheeseburgers and French fries—as well as requiring everyone to get at least three hours of exercise every week, and perhaps to worship the "true God." If you are only "free" when you are doing what is "right" (or what society or government believes is right), then forcing you to "do the right thing" is not a violation of your freedom, so there are no restrictions on what we can compel people to do "for their own good." That is like the "freedom" to eat your candy whenever you *properly* wish, so long as you properly wish to wait until after dinner. For most of us, the *freedom* to make and follow our *own choices* (even if society, government, and religious leaders consider them mistaken) is a very valuable element of freedom.

6. A final argument against legalization: We must keep laws criminalizing drugs, because if drugs are made more available through legalization, more people will abuse them. Whether that is true or not (and the evidence is at best mixed), it does not seem to follow that drugs should not be legalized. We make legally available cars with large engines, boats capable of high speeds, casinos that make gambling more convenient, and both alcohol and tobacco (not to mention, of course, guns). In all of these cases, there are people who abuse them (they drive too fast, or they become gambling or alcohol addicts). We typically do not favor paternalistic laws that restrict the freedom of many in order to protect others from their own dangerous behavior. That is not to say that we should not attempt to help those who become alcoholics or problem gamblers or cocaine addicts; but we should not do so by placing severe restrictions on everyone.

Arguments for Legalizing Marijuana and Other Drugs

1. If drugs were legalized and carefully regulated, then we could regulate quality, avoid dangerous additives, and establish standards for potency. (Just as we label alcohol by proof—an ounce of 120-proof liquor has twice the alcohol content of an ounce of 60-proof liquor—so we could label marijuana by similar measures.) That would have significant benefits: Many overdose deaths occur because of the widely varying potency of street drugs, and drug dealers are not always the most scrupulous of merchants, sometimes adding hazardous substances to drugs to increase the volume.

   But there may also be a downside. If drugs are neatly packaged and the contents regulated and inspected, some people who are wary of using illegal drugs might begin to use these reliably labeled drugs. Many people who would be reluctant to buy and consume "moonshine" from an illegal and unregulated still (because of fears that the distilling process might leave high levels of lead or other contaminants in the product) are quite willing to buy an inspected, regulated, and labeled bottle of tequila or vodka. This might lead to increased use, and some of those additional users might become problem users. This danger should not, however, be exaggerated. Those who are reluctant to use illegal drugs because of potential health hazards are unlikely to easily embrace legal drugs that are still recognized to be dangerous, especially drugs such as heroin. And in places where formerly illegal drugs have been legalized and regulated, there has not been a jump in drug use or addiction.

2. The legalization and regulation of currently illegal drugs would significantly reduce crime, including international crime. This is probably the strongest argument for the legalization of drugs. Everyone is aware of the powerful criminal networks that have developed for the production, transportation, and sale of drugs; of the enormous profits that such criminal enterprises collect; and of the corrupting influence this often has on law enforcement officials (police officers accepting bribes to look the other way, sometimes facilitating and protecting drug operations, and in some cases actively selling confiscated drugs). Those effects of criminalizing drugs—like the similar effects from alcohol prohibition—are obvious to everyone. But one very unfortunate side effect of the criminalization of drugs and the resulting "war on drugs" (in which drug enforcement methods become increasingly sophisticated and forceful in trying to stop the flow of illegal drugs) is less obvious and poses even greater dangers. The Global Commission on Drug Policy is a group that came together to study the problem of illegal drugs and possible solutions to the problem; its members include not only former U.S. secretary of state George Shultz and former chair of the U.S. Federal Reserve Paul Volcker, but also former secretary general of the United Nations Kofi Annan, the former presidents of Brazil, Colombia, Mexico, Switzerland, and Brazil, and a number of other well-respected members. In the report they issued in June 2011, they note that:

   > poorly designed drug law enforcement practices can actually increase the level of violence, intimidation and corruption associated with drug markets. Law enforcement agencies and drug trafficking organizations can become embroiled in a kind of "arms race," in which greater enforcement efforts lead to a similar increase in the strength and violence of the traffickers. In this scenario, the conditions are created in which the most ruthless and violent trafficking organizations thrive. Unfortunately, this seems to be what we are currently witnessing in Mexico and other parts of the world. (p. 15)

So as the United States pursued a "war on drugs" with increasingly severe and power-ful resources, the unanticipated result was that the weaker drug trafficking forces were eliminated, and the survivors were those groups that were the most powerful, the best armed, the best organized, the best connected to corrupt officials, and the most violent. The successful groups constantly became stronger and more sophisticated and more ruth-less in order to survive. The result is the very powerful drug cartels that operate in Mexico, which threaten to destroy the entire country. Just as the powerful gangs that distributed illegal liquor in the United States during Prohibition did not suddenly go away when Pro-hibition was repealed, the powerful drug cartels that illegal drugs have funded will not immediately disappear if the drugs they supply are legalized; but eliminating their major source of funding would be an important step in the right direction.

3. With drug legalization, we would have fewer prison inmates and less of the social disruption caused by high levels of imprisonment. It is sometimes argued that very few simple consumers are actually in prison, but that is deceptive. Some are in prison because they refuse to turn in or testify against their suppliers (who may be friends or may be people they fear more than prison); some imprisoned "dealers" are not profes-sional drug dealers, but instead people who buy a pound of marijuana, split it into one-ounce bags, and sell enough of the one-ounce bags to friends in order to pay for the few ounces they themselves use. Others are low-level street dealers, who turn to drug deal-ing as their only means of earning money. Still others are drug couriers—often referred to as "mules"—who transport drugs into the country for those in large drug trafficking organizations, and do so in a desperate effort to escape poverty, or under coercion, or because of threats to their families. Most of the people imprisoned for drug violations are not dangerous hardened criminals; but because of the severity of U.S. drug laws, many of them are serving very long sentences. This is not only enormously expen-sive but also profoundly disruptive to the communities in which significant numbers of their young and middle-aged men are taken from the community and imprisoned.

4. Instead of spending large amounts of money on a failed "war on drugs," legalized mari-juana would be a valuable commodity that could be taxed, resulting in a significant increase in tax revenues coupled with an enormous reduction in costs. This is one of the legaliza-tion arguments emphasized by the Global Commission on Drug Policy. The commission notes that we spend billions of dollars on a "war on drugs" that is a conspicuous failure (its main result has been to escalate the amount of drug violence and the power of drug cartels in Mexico and Latin America) and billions of dollars imprisoning primarily low-level drug operatives (small-time dealers, growers, and couriers); and we lose the billions in tax money that could be collected by regulating and taxing marijuana sales. As the Global Commission points out, the high cost of illegal drugs is due to their illegal status; thus that high cost might be regarded as a "tax" that is collected by drug cartels and drug gangs, and that is used to increase their power and their corrupting influence. The commission argues that we would be better off collecting an actual tax by legalizing the drugs: The tax money could go to government services, rather than to powerful criminal organizations.

Opponents of this argument offer two lines of criticism. First, they say that it is wrong to raise tax money from products that are harmful (whatever the force of this argument, following its logic would require that we no longer tax tobacco or alcohol). The second line of argument is that the savings and tax benefits are illusory: They would be more than balanced out by the increased costs of treatment programs for the larger number of addicts, the costs of social programs for the families that are harmed by drug addiction, and the lost productivity of those who become addicted. This argument, of course, relies on a claim about the effects of legalizing drugs that are currently illegal: the claim that it would result in dramatically increased usage of those drugs and a spike in the number of drug addicts. That claim does not appear to be supported by the evidence (though the evidence is limited): Countries that have tried legalization have not experienced the predicted increase in either use or addiction. Furthermore, by decriminalizing a range of addictive drugs, it is possible for those suffering from addiction to seek and receive treatment, and that might well reduce the number of addicts.

5. Legalizing and regulating drugs takes the manufacture and sale of drugs out of the hands of the secretive criminal underground and brings it into the open; and it also brings transparency to the *use* of such drugs. This openness produces a number of very important benefits. First, the manufacture and sale of these drugs can be carefully *regulated*. (When tobacco and alcohol companies attempt to market to juveniles—through clever advertising practices or through producing products that have special appeal to underage users, such as flavored tobacco products—they face fines, tighter advertising restrictions, and potential criminal sentences.) Currently juveniles are often recruited as low-level distributors of illegal drugs, because they are easily controlled and are subject to shorter sentences when apprehended; with legalization and regulation, distributors would no longer have any reason to use juveniles, and significant reasons not to do so (the same reasons that alcohol distributors have for not hiring juveniles to distribute their products). Sales to juveniles would be more effectively prevented: In an underground illegal enterprise, distributors are very unlikely to check the identification of a customer to determine the customer's age; when sales are legal and regulated, sales to juveniles can result in loss of license, substantial fines, the closing of businesses, and criminal prosecution, and those marketing the legally regulated drugs would have much greater interest in preventing such sales. Products can be accurately labeled (as alcohol content and potency are currently clearly labeled) and regulated, reducing the danger of overdoses from an unusually and unexpectedly pure and potent dose of heroin or cocaine; and the practice of "cutting" drugs with dangerous substances can be prevented. When drugs are legalized, those who are addicted can openly seek treatment and rehabilitation, and those who are using such drugs—and might be candidates for rehabilitation—can be more easily identified. Furthermore, when drug use is no longer criminalized, some of the most serious health issues related to illegal drug use can be dealt with more effectively; for example, drug users who inject drugs need no longer fear arrest if they participate in a needle exchange program, and the practice of sharing needles—and thus spreading a wide variety of dangerous diseases not only to drug users but to their sexual partners—can be greatly reduced.

6. Finally, there is the basic libertarian/classic liberal argument for legalization of such drugs: People should be free to make their own choices, including choices that may cause them personal harm, so long as they do not harm others. If I choose to smoke two packs a day, then I am certainly endangering my health: I greatly increase my chances of developing emphysema, suffering various forms of cancer, having a stroke, and experiencing a variety of other health problems. But so long as I do not smoke in places that would expose others to the perils of second-hand smoke, I should be free to pursue my dangerous and unhealthy habit. It is perfectly legitimate for the government to warn and educate me about the genuine dangers of using tobacco; but it is wrong

for the government to deprive me of the opportunity of making my own choice on this personal question. Likewise, if I choose to use marijuana or cocaine or heroin, then that may be a very bad choice, and the government can legitimately warn me about the risks I am taking; and certainly the government can prohibit me from driving on public highways while using marijuana, because (like driving while intoxicated) that will place others at significant risk. But so long as I am not harming others, and am not choosing under deception (the government can legitimately prevent those who sell marijuana— or tobacco—from claiming that it poses no health hazard), I should be free to make my own choices, whether those choices are wise or stupid.

Ultimately this may be the most powerful argument for drug legalization. It does not depend on data concerning monetary costs or numbers of addicts, but is a simple and straightforward argument. There are two arguments *against* this argument. First, as discussed earlier, this is not *real* freedom (because the only real freedom is in doing what is right and beneficial). Second, harms involved are *not* private harms that do not involve others; after all, if you develop a debilitating disease as a result of your drug use (e.g., your prolonged use of marijuana results in lung cancer), then the costs of your treatment will be borne by others as well as yourself (either through government costs or through costs to your insurance company and increasing insurance rates). Furthermore, your illness may have a profound effect on your immediate family, which will lose your financial support and—in the event of your early death—your emotional support. But this is an argument with impli- cations that few people would wish to accept. After all, if you fail to exercise regularly, you are significantly endangering your health, and increasing your likelihood of suffering a heart attack—which will require expensive treatment and the loss of financial support for your family. But that is not a justification for the government forcing everyone to exercise three hours each week. It is perfectly legitimate for the government to educate people about the *benefits* of exercise, and also to make exercise more easily available (by providing walking and bicycling paths and perhaps by providing tax breaks for exercise equipment and health club memberships); but it would be wrong (most of us believe) for the government to require us to exercise, even though doing so would benefit us, our families, and our society. So unless there is *direct* harm or risk to others (such as from driving intoxicated), society should not forbid me from making stupid choices (such as the choice to use harmful drugs or forgo exercise).

Where Do We Stand?

Whether one wishes to retain criminal penalties for drugs that are currently illegal, or legalize and regulate at least some of those drugs, all agree that the drug problem is a very serious problem indeed. Thousands of people are in prison for drug crimes, resulting in the dis- ruption of thousands of families and enormous costs to society (costs in social support for families with incarcerated family members, the huge costs of drug enforcement programs, and the enormous costs of imprisoning those who violate the drug laws). Many people suf- fer from various forms of drug addiction. The vast amounts of money that flow from the illegal drug trade result in widespread corruption of police and government officials and—as in the case of Mexico—can threaten to plunge an entire country into chaos. All of us have a stake in dealing with this growing problem, and all share basic goals of reducing corruption, addiction, and incarceration. Achieving those shared goals will require honest examination of the facts, more recognition of common goals, and less demonizing of our opponents.

Questions for Reflection

1. Suppose, for the sake of discussion, that alcohol and marijuana are roughly equivalent in health risks; neither is a health food, both can be addictive, and both can cause health problems. Almost everyone agrees that prohibition of the sale and use of alcohol—from 1920 to 1933—was disastrous: It caused widespread disrespect for the law, generated major criminal enterprises and greatly increased corruption in many local governments (with effects that lasted long after the repeal of Prohibition), and lack of alcohol regulation resulted in injuries and even death from the contaminants that sometimes found their way into illegal alcohol. Even those who oppose the use of alcohol rarely believe that we should reinstate the prohibition of alcohol. Do the reasons for opposing prohibition of alcohol also count as reasons for legalizing the sale and use of marijuana?

2. The "conservative" movement in the United States sometimes appears to be a powerful unified force, but in fact it is deeply divided. There are a few points on which most conservatives seem to agree: They oppose taxes, they oppose restrictions on gun ownership, and they generally oppose all social support programs (they tend to believe that everyone should look out for themselves, and that if anyone can't afford health care or housing or food, that's unfortunate, but it's not a problem that government should try to solve). But on many other issues, they are deeply divided. The *libertarian* conservatives insist that no one's freedom should be restricted so long as they are not causing harm to others: If you want to use marijuana, that may damage your health, but that's your free choice; if you want to watch pornography, that's probably not morally uplifting, but you should be free to make that decision and no censorship should be allowed; if your sexual orientation is toward members of your own sex, that is no one's business but that of you and your consenting sexual partner, and that should not restrict you from serving in the military or choosing where to live or deciding whom to marry; no one should feel any pressure to favor any religion, and certainly the state should not support any religious view, since you should be totally free to be an atheist, agnostic, Orthodox Jew, Southern Baptist, Muslim, or Sun worshipper. In opposition to the libertarians, the *social* conservatives emphasize the preservation of "traditional values," including traditional marriage (excluding same-sex marriage), refusal to allow gays and lesbians to serve in the military forces, opposition to changes in the drug laws that would allow the legalization of marijuana, and government and social support of traditional Christian beliefs (through allowing and encouraging prayer in public schools and the placement of religious displays—such as the Ten Commandments—in public buildings).

   The tensions between these two "conservative" groups usually remain in the background, but sometimes bubble to the surface. In 2011, the organizers of a large convention of conservative groups invited a gay conservative group (GOProud) to participate in their convention, which caused some social conservative groups (such as Focus on the Family) to boycott the meeting. And one "tea party" gathering refused to serve alcohol at its evening banquet, to show respect to the various Christian groups in attendance who oppose the use of alcohol (such as Southern Baptists); but that angered the libertarian conservatives who felt that their liberty to drink alcohol was being denied. The issue of marijuana legalization is one of the clearest points of conflict between the libertarian and social conservatives. Is there any way to reconcile the views of these two distinct elements of the "conservative" movement on the question of legalizing marijuana?

3. Barney Frank and Ron Paul are usually at the opposite extremes in the United States House of Representatives. Barney Frank is considered one of the most "liberal" members, and Ron Paul one of the most "conservative." Yet on the issue of legalizing marijuana, they are allies (though still a very small minority in the House of Representatives: Only three other members of

the House agreed to be cosponsors of their bill to eliminate federal laws against marijuana). Of the *other* issues considered in this book, which one do you think Barney Frank and Ron Paul would be most likely to *agree* on?

4. The debate over "freedom" is an ancient one that runs through philosophy, religion, politics, and many other areas of life. One prominent element of the debate concerns whether "real freedom" must involve choices that are rational and right. On one side are those who regard *genuine* freedom as the freedom of pursuing the right goal for the right reasons: Any other sort of "freedom" is mere "license"; it is false freedom that is unworthy of rational humans. In contrast are those who see *freedom* as the freedom to try anything, the freedom to make mistakes and take bad paths. This is a debate that also has a theological history: On one view, the angels enjoy the most perfect freedom, because they are always in the presence of God and thus never experience the slightest temptation to sin, but instead have an overwhelming desire to worship and—so far as possible—emulate God's perfection. On this view, of course, the notion of "fallen angels" who rebel against God is heresy, and clearly false. This view insists that perfect freedom is enslavement to God; you only have real freedom when you act in total and unquestioning obedience to God's perfect will. In the words of one popular hymn, the only way to be a good servant of God is to "trust and obey." On the other side of this theological debate is the view of Pico della Mirandola, a Renaissance writer who maintained that God's special and unique gift to humans was the power to *freely choose* to be either evil or virtuous, beastlike or godlike. The great Russian novelist, Fyodor Dostoyevsky, also celebrated the importance of free choice, even if the free choice is bad: "One's own free, unrestrained choice, one's own whim, be it the wildest, one's own fancy, sometimes worked up to a frenzy—that is the most advantageous advantage."

Which of these views of freedom do you find more plausible? Given the view *you* hold of freedom, can you find *anything* of value in the opposing view? To what degree is the debate over drug legalization a reflection of these conflicting views of freedom?

Additional Resources

Searching for Alternatives: Drug-Control Policy in the United States, edited by Melvyn B. Krauss and Edward P. Lazear (Stanford, CA: Hoover Institution Press, 1991), contains an excellent set of articles exploring competing views on drug policies. Another good collection, arranged as opposing positions on different aspects of the controversy over drug policies, is by Rod L. Evans and Irwin M. Berent, eds., *Drug Legalization: For and Against* (La Salle, IL: Open Court, 1992). A good set of essays, containing both pro and con views, is James A. Inciardi's *The Drug Legalization Debate* (Newbury Park, CA: Sage Publications, 1991); a more recent similar anthology is *Drug Legalization*, edited by Gale Editor (San Diego, CA: Greenhaven, 2010).

An interesting pair of opposing essays is Theodore Dalrymple's (a physician and psychiatrist who works in a British prison) "Don't Legalize Drugs," *City Journal*, 7, no. 2 (Spring 1997); and on the other side, Ethan A. Nadelmann's (professor of politics and public affairs at the Woodrow Wilson School of Public and International Affairs at Princeton University) "The Case for Legalization," *Public Interest* (Summer 1998). For a more extensive and detailed debate on the issue, see Doug Husak and Peter de Marneffe's *The Legalization of Drugs (For and Against)* (New York: Cambridge University Press, 2005).

The Cato Institute is a conservative think tank that takes views on many political issues. It generally supports minimizing the role of government, and thus opposes government interference in the choices of adults concerning what drugs they choose to take, and so favors drug legalization. A major paper by James Ostrowski, "Thinking about Drug Legalization," argues in favor of drug legalization, and can be found at www.cato.org/pubs/pas/pa121 .html. Ostrowski's paper, along with papers by Kurt L. Schmoke and several others, is followed by a number of brief essays (primarily but not exclusively by conservatives, such as Milton Friedman) that criticize drug prohibition, in David Boaz, ed., *The Crisis in Drug Prohibition* (Washington, DC.: The Cato Institute, 1991). In contrast, William Bennett, a "social values" conservative, vehemently opposes any move toward decriminalization of drugs, including marijuana; in a recent *CNN* piece ("Why Barney Frank and Ron Paul Are Wrong on Drug Legalization," June 30, 2011); he criticized the proposed legislation by Barney Frank and Ron Paul, insisting it "will only make things worse."

One of the best and most thorough arguments for legalizing drugs is offered by Douglas N. Husak in *Legalize This! The Case for Decriminalizing Drugs* (London: Verso, 2002). An excellent anthology presenting a variety of arguments for decriminalizing drugs (along with excellent essays on the history of the issue) is *Drugs and Society*, edited by Jefferson M. Fish (Lanham, MD: Rowman & Littlefield, 2006). A thoughtful brief book, leaning toward drug prohibition, is Philip Bean's *Legalising Drugs: Debates and Dilemmas* (Bristol, UK: Policy Press, 2010).

The Netherlands has adopted very liberal drug laws concerning marijuana, and so is often regarded as an interesting test of marijuana decriminalization. Though the situation in the Netherlands has generated controversy (the former U.S. drug czar, General Barry McCaffery, called it "an unmitigated disaster"), studies indicate that drug problems in the Netherlands are comparable to those in neighboring European countries with more severe laws, and the Netherlands has significantly fewer drug problems than the United States (lower rate of adult heroin addiction, lower rate of marijuana use among teens, much lower homicide rate, etc). For a more detailed examination of the Dutch experience, see Craig Reinarman, "The Dutch Example Shows That Liberal Drug Laws Can Be Beneficial," which can be found at www,cedri-uva.org/lib/reinarman.dutch .pdf, or in Scott Barbour, ed., *Drug Legalization: Current Controversies* (San Diego, CA: Greenhaven Press, 1999, 2000), pp. 102–108.

In 1999, the United States Congress Subcommittee on Criminal Justice, Drug Policy, and Human Resources, chaired by Representative John L. Mica, held a hearing on "Drug Legalization, Criminalization, and Harm Reduction." A number of papers were read into the record, both pro and con, and there was considerable discussion among the committee members and witnesses concerning drug legalization (though not surprisingly, the committee members were heavily against legalization; indeed, Representative Barr advocated that the committee should look into pursuing criminal charges against those who publicly advocate decriminalization of marijuana).

In June 2011, the *Report of the Global Commission on Drug Policy* was released. It advocates rethinking the "war on drugs" and the criminal approach to the drug issue, arguing that the criminalization approach is ineffective and very expensive, and causes great personal and social harm. The issues involved are examined carefully by an outstanding group of international leaders. The report is available online at http://www .globalcommissionondrugs.org/reports.

NORML is an advocacy group for the legalization of marijuana. Its website is at http://norml.org/.

The conservative journal, *National Review*, favors drug legalization; its editorial statement, along with the views of several other writers, can be found at www .nationalreview.com/12feb96/drug.html.

MYSEARCHLAB CONNECTIONS

A 1999 hearing on "Drug Legalization, Criminalization, and Harm Reduction," conducted by the United States Congress Subcommittee on Criminal Justice, Drug Policy, and Human Resources, can be found in its entirety at http://bulk.resource.org/gpo.gov /hearings/106h/63346.txt. The quite remarkable 2011 *Report of the Global Commission on Drug Policy* can be found online at http://www.globalcommisionondrugs.org/reports.

13

LEGACY ADMISSIONS

Chapter Outline

At many outstanding American universities across the country—from Harvard to Stanford, from the University of Virginia to Texas A&M—the number of qualified applicants far exceeds the number of students who can be admitted. Indeed, some Ivy League schools seem to take pride in the number of high school valedictorians who are denied admission: "We are such a superb university, and in such high demand, that even outstanding students often do not measure up to our admission standards." That top universities cannot accommodate many of their qualified applicants is unfortunate for the applicants who are denied admission, but so long as the admissions process is fair and unbiased, that is a sad fact of life which does not raise any special ethical issues. Recently, however, people have become aware of a long-standing practice at many of these universities that raises basic questions of fairness: The application competition is *not* a level playing field, because "legacy students" receive special consideration.

"Legacy students" are students whose close relatives (usually parents or grand-parents) are graduates of the university; for example, if Arthur's parents attended Harvard, then when Arthur applies for admission to Harvard, Arthur is given spe-cial consideration. Because he is a "legacy applicant," Arthur may gain admission to Harvard in preference to better qualified applicants whose parents did not attend

Harvard. No one denies this; to the contrary, Harvard (and many other schools) acknowledges and defends the practice. Some schools (such as Texas A&M) claim to have eliminated legacy considerations entirely, but that is a rare exception. In some selective schools, the number of legacy admissions approaches half of the incoming class. That does not imply that all of the legacy students were admitted *only* because they were legacy students. Legacy students are students whose parents (or other close relatives) attended an elite university. Thus the parents of those students were likely to have a stronger-than-average interest in education, and much more likely to have the financial resources to send their children to top private schools, hire special tutors to push up their children's SAT scores, and provide special opportunities for travel and exposure to the arts. Thus legacy students start with special educational advantages over most other students (students whose families did not attend elite universities and have significantly less money to invest in their children's early education), and so it would not be surprising if many of the legacy students have excellent academic records, and many of them might have been admitted even without the legacy boost. Furthermore, there is debate about how much boost is given to legacy applicants. Universities that acknowledge legacy admissions typically insist that the weight given to legacy is quite small; however, some people who have been involved in admissions at these universities report that legacy carries substantial weight, and that in many cases students whose academic records would not have qualified them for admission have been admitted as legacy students. When poorly qualified students are selected over much better students, there is often more to it than just mom or dad attending the school. If the parents (and perhaps grandparents) have a long history of making significant financial contributions to the school, the children may go on a special legacy list: If they can eat with a fork and have not committed any major felonies, those on that list gain admission.

But the number of legacy students admitted due to legacy is not the real issue: Much of that is in dispute because the secrecy involved in university admission processes makes it difficult to determine accurately all the details. What is not in dispute is the fact of legacy admissions: At almost all elite American universities, children of alumni are given special consideration. If you did not attend Harvard or Yale or the University of Virginia or the University of North Carolina, then when your children apply for admission to one of those schools, your children will be at a disadvantage: The admissions playing field will not be level.

For many years there was great controversy in the United States over "affirmative action" policies, particularly in the area of college and university admissions. Though there is significant disagreement about what was involved in affirmative action, the basic idea was this: If State University had a greater number of qualified applicants than it could admit, and a recognized group was significantly *under*represented in the State University student population, then some preference would be given to members of that underrepresented group in order to correct the imbalance. That is, if candidate A and candidate B *both* met the admission requirements for State University, and *both* seemed likely to succeed at the university, but candidate A was a member of an underrepresented group while B was not, then candidate A might be admitted ahead of candidate B even though candidate A's grades and test scores were slightly below those of candidate B. There have been many arguments, pro and con, about affirmative action. Those opposed say that it is unfair to penalize an individual student who *would* have been admitted—strictly on the basis of academic achievements—in order to correct a social wrong or a social problem. Those in favor of affirmative action emphasize the importance of having a diverse student body— a diversity that enhances the learning experience for all students—and also note that the student from the underrepresented group probably had to struggle harder to reach a level roughly comparable to that of the nonminority student (might have faced discrimination or perhaps studied in a weaker school and poorer school setting), and thus—having achieved almost as much while struggling against significant disadvantages—might well be the student with stronger abilities and greater potential. But whatever one thinks of the benefits or detriments of affirmative action, that is not the current topic. The issue here is a very different sort of "affirmative action," but one that has generated much less controversy.

Strawman Distortions

Affirmative action programs—in which persons belonging to underrepresented groups were given admission consideration in their college applications—have been very controversial. Legacy admissions programs have been much less controversial (partially because fewer people were aware of them), even though the number of students admitted as legacy applicants far exceeds the number admitted under affirmative action. Because legacy admissions programs have largely "flown under the radar," the issue has not generated as much heated controversy, and consequently the number of strawman distortions and ad hominem attacks has been smaller. There are not as many, but attacks do occur. Before we examine the real arguments for and against legacy admissions, it is important to set aside some of the strawman distortions.

One strawman distortion is that this issue is trivial: It involves only a tiny group of students who receive legacy preference, and so very few better qualified nonlegacy students are denied admission. That is not true, as legacy students are a significant percentage of admitted students in many schools (in some cases as much as half of the students admitted). But even if only a few people were treated unfairly, the issue would be important.

Another distortion is that college admissions are purely a private matter, and not an issue of public fairness. Even if it were true that this is an issue involving only private (and no public) funds or universities, it would remain an important moral issue (if someone is treated unfairly, that is an issue whether the institution is a private university or a public university, a private golf club or a public park). But it is not true. Many of the legacy schools are publicly supported universities (Virginia, North Carolina, and many other major flagship state universities) and even the private universities receive substantial public support (such as in research funds).

On the other side, legacy programs eliminate decisions based on merit and effort, and instead make selections through a secretive insider program. That is a distortion. No university admits all its students on the basis of legacy admissions; and except for the most extreme cases—when a student's family has made very substantial donations to the university—admissions are not based entirely on legacy (one admissions officer at an elite university described it thus: "Legacy considerations can heal the sick, but they can't raise the dead").

A final strawman distortion: Opponents of legacy admissions see no value in loyalty to one's alma mater. That is obviously false. Opponents of legacy admissions are as likely to feel deep affection and loyalty to the old home college as anyone else, and recognize the benefits that their college education gave them. What they deny is that anyone deserves special treatment based on that loyalty—special treatment that they regard as unfair. If you are a loyal citizen of your home village, it does not mean that your contracting firm should get special consideration for town construction projects: The contracts should go to the company best qualified to do the work. Likewise, I can be deeply loyal to the college I attended, without believing that my children should get special consideration when they apply for admission (special consideration that places other children at a special disadvantage).

What Is the Common Ground?

Many years ago, Dartmouth College (now Dartmouth University) faced financial difficulties that threatened to close the college. Many of its loyal alumni flocked to its support, grateful for the education they had received there, and dedicated to its long-term survival. As one of the supportive alumni, the great orator Daniel Webster, stated: "It is, sir, as I have said, a small college; and yet there are those who love it." Loyalty to one's college is legitimate: Your college education prepares you for a career, opens paths into the arts and literature, enhances your understanding of yourself and your world, and introduces you to some of your dearest friends. So whatever we think of legacy admissions, we can generally agree that there is nothing wrong and perhaps something admirable about loyalty to the colleges we attended.

Though we may disagree about what *counts* as fairness in a particular case, we agree that fairness is fundamentally important.

Finally, we generally agree that inherited privileges should be viewed with suspicion. Most of us are deeply opposed to inherited titles—such as king or duke—that are handed down from parents to children (without regard to the efforts or the talents of the children who inherit the rank): We would not want our Senate to be a House of Lords, in which the members hold office by inheriting a title from their parents. On the question of inherited *wealth,* there is greater disagreement (though many wealthy people worry that giving wealth to their children, who will become wealthy through no effort of their own, will have bad effects on the children—perhaps making them lazy or robbing them of any sense of accomplishment or purpose). In any case, most of us regard *inherited* wealth in a very different light from *earned* wealth; and many feel that there should be restrictions on inherited wealth. Where legacy admissions fit into this question of inheritance remains a debated question, but to the degree that it is based on *inheritance* rather than effort or actual accomplishment, it is subject to suspicion.

Arguments in Favor of Legacy Admissions

1. One argument offered in favor of legacy admissions is that they maintain special traditions: Rachel's great-grandfather, Reuben, went to Old Ivy, and his son, Reuben Jr.—Rachel's grandfather—followed in his father's footsteps; Rachel's mother, Rebecca, continued the pattern, and there she met her husband (whose father was a graduate of Old Ivy); and now Rachel wants to continue the family tradition, the fourth generation to attend Old Ivy. There is nothing wrong with such family traditions (so long as no one is pressured or coerced to continue the tradition). But if the tradition is being maintained at the expense

of unfairness to others (if there are others who are being unjustly deprived of admission because Rachel is admitted though not as well qualified), then the cost of maintaining tradition is paid in unfairness. And while this is a pleasant and in itself harmless tradition in Rachel's family, we should keep in mind that not all traditions are worth preserving: If Rachel wanted to maintain the tradition of operating a cotton plantation with slave labor, the fact that this is a multigeneration tradition in Rachel's family would not be a point in its favor.

2. Another argument in favor of legacy admissions is that students whose parents attended a school are often deeply committed to that school, long before they are high school seniors applying to colleges. They may have gone with their families to football games at their parents' alma mater, and those may be among their most cherished family memories. The first stuffy toy they can remember was a soft cuddly version of the college mascot. They have been singing the school fight song since they were in kindergarten. Going to that particular school is a deep-rooted family tradition, and failure to be admitted to that specific school feels like not just a personal failure, but as if one has let down the whole family. Nonlegacy students may place that particular school high on their lists of desirable schools, but there will almost certainly be a number of other schools that they consider equal or almost equal in desirability. Failure to be admitted to that particular school will be disappointing, but not the crushing disappointment that it may well be to a legacy student—and perhaps also to the parents of that legacy student, who had long cherished the idea of their child attending their beloved alma mater.

   It is of course disappointing when one does not gain admission to the school where mom and dad first met, and where you have attended tailgate parties before football games, and whose football jersey you have worn since preschool. That is balanced by the disappointment of a student who has worked diligently to qualify for admission but is denied admission because a less-qualified legacy admission student takes that slot. Certainly it will be a disappointment for the legacy student not admitted, but the disappointment should not be exaggerated; students who do not attend their parents' alma mater may well discover that some other school suits them just fine.

3. Some advocates of legacy admissions argue that legacy admissions are needed for university fund-raising. In fact, there is little evidence that legacy admissions are essential for effective fund-raising (few studies that have been done, but those studies have failed to establish any connection between university fund-raising and legacy admissions); but in any case, if the fund-raising is in support of elitism—to preserve a university that fosters special privileges for the wealthy and well-connected—it is not clear that the money is being raised for a good purpose. Furthermore, there are some forms of fund-raising that we consider fundamentally illegitimate. There is no objection to naming a building after a generous donor or placing a brick in a sidewalk of "honored friends of Home State University" or placing a plaque recognizing the generous support of a donor in refurbishing a laboratory. But although it would certainly raise a lot of money, we would not consider it legitimate fund-raising to offer Jimmy an A in calculus if Jimmy's family will donate $10,000 to the math library. And while there is no objection to naming the women's soccer field after a generous donor, it would not be acceptable to make Sarah the starting midfielder on the women's soccer team (replacing a more talented and harder working teammate) because Sarah's father donated $1 million to upgrade the soccer stadium. So even *if* legacy admissions are

important for fund-raising (and that is a disputed claim), it does not follow that such fund-raising through legacy admissions is legitimate. Obviously there are some forms of fund-raising that are *not* legitimate, and we would still have the question of whether legacy admissions fall into the legitimate or illegitimate category.

Arguments against Legacy Admissions

1. Legacy admissions are programs of special privilege for those who have already enjoyed special privileges. The question of whether colleges should give special consideration to students who have had to battle against significant *dis*advantages—such as racial discrimination, substandard schools, or severe poverty—is a question that has been the source of considerable debate. But whatever one thinks about that question, the idea of giving special consideration to students whose parents attended an elite college seems grossly unfair. Those parents are very likely to be comparatively wealthy and privileged, send their children to the best private or suburban schools, and provide all the advantages of tutors and private lessons and travel and computers. It is like taking all the contestants in a race, lining them up at the starting line, and then taking all the contestants who have inferior running shoes, the weakest coaching, the worst training facilities, and the poorest nutritional and health care histories and leaving them at the original starting line and then taking all the contestants with the best and lightest running shoes, the top coaches, superb training facilities, and excellent medical and nutritional support, and giving them a head start. Legacy admissions are sometimes characterized as "affirmative action for the privileged," and that seems an accurate description.

2. Legacy admissions perpetuate policies of racial and ethnic discrimination: If in the past blacks were excluded from the University of Virginia, or Jews were much less likely to be admitted to Harvard, then the legacy admissions programs at those schools extend such discrimination into the present day. Suppose that Gerald has just been admitted to the University of Virginia due to his legacy advantage. Of course Gerald's parents probably did not get into the University of Virginia because racist and ethnic discrimination eliminated many potential applicants; by the time Gerald's parents attended that school (thus giving Gerald a legacy advantage), such racial discrimination was outlawed. But that doesn't solve the problem: After all, Gerald's parents may have been admitted because—like Gerald—they were legacy students, due to the fact that *their* parents (Gerald's grandparents) attended the University of Virginia. But when Gerald's grandparents attended, it *was* a racially segregated university, and their attendance chances were enhanced by racist policies; and thus Gerald is now the beneficiary (through a line of legacy admission special treatment) of the racist policies that favored his grandparents.

3. Legacy admissions encourage permanent under- and overclasses based on inheritance rather than on merit. If there is a principle that is fundamental to American thought, it is that we are not a country of inherited rank and inherited privilege. No one is born with a hereditary title or a hereditary right to the best positions and leadership roles. To the extent that elite colleges offer greater opportunity for success, they betray that basic principle when they use legacy admissions. When positions of leadership go to those less qualified because they have been given special "credentials," this ultimately undermines the functioning of the entire society. This problem is exacerbated when we consider the notoriously lax-grading policies at many prestigious universities, in which a "B" is regarded almost as a failing grade; yet a degree from such a university still carries sufficient

prestige that it (in combination with the legacy student's family connections and wealth) propels the holder into positions of special leadership, for which the person is unqualified, or certainly not as well qualified as someone whose superior talents but lack of legacy influence resulted in inferior credentials. This promotes a system in which family legacy and connections—rather than genuine fortitude and ability—become major determinants of who holds positions of leadership in society, and that may cause harm to all members of the society as the quality of those in leadership positions declines.

Where Do We Stand?

Few people in our society believe that privileges granted to those who did not earn them are a good thing. One becomes a lord or duke or queen by birthright; we believe that one should become a senator, engineer, CEO, or physician not by birthright, but instead by talent and effort.

Everyone agrees that loyalty to an educational institution is good. But if one is giving to one's alma mater in expectation of a special benefit—the guaranteed admission of one's children—that falls in a different category than giving to one's alma mater from love of the school. If the "loyalty" to that school is actually a quid-pro-quo arrangement—"I donate money, you admit my kid"—then it is not a very admirable loyalty after all, and certainly not an act of generosity. Rather than a generous gift, it seems to fall under the category of bribery.

This is not an issue on which compromise is desirable: We'll admit fewer legacy students. That would be like a country club saying, "OK, we were wrong to totally exclude blacks; let's compromise: We'll admit just a few." If the discrimination is wrong, it is still wrong when it is done on a slightly smaller scale. So we should not seek compromise. We can, however, find common ground: In our society, we do not believe in inherited rank or privilege; we do believe in equal opportunity. When examined in that light, even those who benefit from legacy admissions may see the problems in such policies. They may also see the advantage to their own children of abolishing legacy privilege. It can hardly be regarded as a benefit to your children to encourage in them a sense of privilege: Even if I don't work and study, my spot in dad's school is guaranteed. Lazy and less-talented kids should have access to colleges; after all, they may be late bloomers. But it is wrong to give them special privileges, and give them slots that more talented and harder working students are denied (especially if that denial is tinged by racist or anti-Semitic legacy).

Finally, no matter how one feels about legacy admissions, everyone can agree that it is wrong to *claim* that a college admissions process is a level playing field when in fact it is not. Such deception leaves those who were not admitted—but who were in fact better qualified—with a sense that they did not "measure up," when in fact they certainly did. If you want to have a 1,600-meter race in which some of the participants get a 1,500-meter head start, that's fine; hold your race, and give out the prizes to the "winners." But you can't advertise the race as a fair contest, accept an application fee and require a substantial application package (with applicants required to write a special essay and fill out an extensive set of forms), and *then* give some racers a substantial head start, and celebrate the "winners" as superior racers and tell the losers that they did not win the awards because they were inferior runners. So *if* legacy-based admissions are to be allowed, at the very least that should be clear *before* students go through an expensive and time-consuming application process on the assumption that the competition is taking place on a level playing field. The secretive nature of the process is itself unfair, and particularly so if it hides an admissions process that is inherently unfair.

Questions for Reflection

1. Arnold is applying for admission to Old Ivy University (a prestigious and highly selective university); his father graduated from Old Ivy, and his father was admitted because he received special consideration as a legacy admission, because *his* father (Arnold's grandfather) was a graduate of Old Ivy. But when Arnold's grandfather was admitted (in 1936), Old Ivy did not accept any black or Jewish students, and so Arnold's grandfather benefited from a racist and anti-Semitic admission policy (had blacks and Jews been able to compete equally for admission in 1936, Arnold's grandfather might not have made the cut for admission). If Old Ivy now gives Arnold special consideration as a legacy student, is it perpetuating the racism and anti-Semitism that it practiced when Arnold's grandfather was an Old Ivy student?

2. Joe did not have a very distinguished college record; in fact, his grade point average was just barely high enough to allow him to graduate. On the LSAT (the Law School Admission Test), Joe scored in the bottom 5% of those taking the test. His qualifications would not get him anywhere close to being admitted to Home State University Law School, generally considered the top law school in the state. However, Joe's family has a large fortune, and Joe's father makes a contribution of several million dollars to Home State University Law School, enabling the school to endow several professorships at the law school and build an addition to the library. Though nothing is put in writing, the law school understands that this generous gift comes with strings attached: Joe is to be admitted for study at the law school. Because the law school can accept only a limited number of students, a much better qualified applicant is denied admission so that Joe can take a place in the entering class. Have the rights of the student denied admission (so that Joe can attend) been violated? Have the rights of *all* applicants to the law school been violated? Has the law school acted unethically? How would a utilitarian analyze this case? How would a virtue theorist analyze it? A social contract theorist?

3. Applications to highly selective colleges and universities take a lot of time and effort (applicants must write essays on assigned subjects, make sure that a wide range of material—from high school transcripts to reference letters—are sent), and the schools often charge a substantial application fee. In some of those schools, students who do *not* have a legacy preference are at a significant disadvantage. Do schools that give preference to legacy applicants have an obligation to provide that information to potential applicants?

4. Suppose a student invests time and money applying to a highly selective college, in which one-third of the admitted students are legacy admissions; that is, instead of 1,500 spots being available in the entering class and open for competition, there are only 1,000 (because 500 of those spots were taken by legacy students). The student files suit against the college, arguing that she entered the competition in the belief that she would be competing for one of 1,500 admission slots, when in fact only 1,000 were open to her. She argues that if she bought a lottery ticket for a lottery that advertised it was giving 1,500 prizes, but in fact 500 of those prizes were already given to relatives of the people running the lottery, then she would have been a victim of deceptive practices, and she should get her money back for her lottery ticket. In a similar manner, she should get her money back for her application, as well as financial compensation for the time and effort she invested in applying. If you were the judge in the case, would you rule for or against the student claim?

5. In 1945, Congress passed a law authorizing the president to make special appointments to West Point: The sons of those awarded the Medal of Honor could be appointed by the president to West Point—as many as the president chose to appoint. In effect, this gave a special hereditary privilege to sons of recipients of the Medal of Honor. As Carlton Larson writes (in a paper in the *Washington University Law Review*), this "is perhaps one of the starkest hereditary privileges

in modern American law." Solely because of the heroic acts of the father, his son gets special admission into the highly competitive West Point Academy. Is this a form of legacy admission? Would you vote for or against such a bill if you were a member of Congress?

Larson notes that in 1818 a bill was proposed concerning admission standards for West Point: The bill would have given admission preference to "the sons of officers and soldiers who were killed in battle or who died in the military service of the United States in the late war." The bill was harshly criticized and soundly defeated, on the grounds that it would "create a privileged order." What caused such a striking difference in attitude between 1818 and 1945?

Additional Resources

For detailed information on legacy admissions—their extent, where they occur, how much weight they carry—see Daniel Golden, *The Price of Admission* (New York: Three Rivers, 2006). Another interesting book on the subject is a collected volume of research on the subject, edited by Richard D. Kahlenberg, *Affirmative Action for the Rich: Legacy Preferences in College Admissions* (Washington, DC: Brookings Institution Press, 2010). Also by Richard D. Kahlenberg, see "10 Myths about Legacy Preferences in College Admissions," *Chronicle of Higher Education*, September 22, 2010.

A fascinating study of the history of legacy admissions (and attitudes toward hereditary privilege from the Revolutionary period to the present) is Carlton F. W. Larson's "Titles of Nobility, Hereditary Privilege, and the Unconstitutionality of Legacy Preferences in Public School Admissions," *Washington University Law Review*, 84 (2006): 1375–1440.

Among the sources discussing interesting aspects and instances of legacy admission (and other aspects of the college admission process), see Robert K. Fullinwider and Judith Lichtenberg, *Leveling the Playing Field: Justice, Politics, and College Admissions* (Lanham, MD: Rowman & Littlefield, 2004); Lani Guinier, "Admissions Rituals as Political Acts: Guardians at the Gates of Our Democratic Ideals," *Harvard Law Review*, 117 (2003); Jerome Karabel, *The Chosen: The Hidden History of Admission and Exclusion at Harvard, Yale, and Princeton* (New York: Houghton Mifflin Harcourt, 2005); and Mitchell L. Stevens, *Creating A Class: College Admissions and the Education of Elites* (Cambridge, MA: Harvard University Press, 2007).

MYSEARCHLAB CONNECTIONS

Richard D. Kahlenberg's excellent article on legacy admissions—"10 Myths about Legacy Preferences in College Admissions"—can be found at http://chronicle.com/article/10-Myths-About-Legacy/124561. Also online is an *Inside Higher Ed* article by Scott Jaschik, "Legacy of Bias," at http://www.insidehighered.com/news/2010/09/22/legacy. There is an interesting essay by Chris Peterson, an admissions counselor at MIT, who was upset at a report that MIT practices legacy admissions; Peterson makes very clear his own—and his institution's—principled rejection of any legacy considerations in decisions concerning who is admitted to MIT; the article can be found at http://mitadmissions.org/blogs /entry/just-to-be-clear-we-dont-do-legacy.

CHURCH AND STATE RELATIONS

Chapter Outline

Religion can be found in every human society, and controversies over religion are among the most intense. Indeed, some of the most brutal and extended wars have involved struggles between religious views: the Christian–Muslim struggles in the Middle Ages, the European wars between Protestants and Catholics, and the violent clashes between Hindus and Muslims in India and Pakistan. Religious differences were often the major cause of such conflicts. When other causes were involved, religious differences intensified the animosity. So it is not surprising that struggles concerning the proper role of religion *within* a country, and the appropriate relation between the church and the state, should be a major ongoing dispute. In Western countries, those disputes tend to focus on a few specific questions: Can the government legitimately support or encourage any religious views? That is, can the government legitimately favor one religious perspective over others, or any religious orientation whatsoever against those who reject all religious views (can the government legitimately favor belief in God over nonbelief)? Should government encourage or support specific religious practices or principles?

There are of course other very important questions related to religion and the state, particularly the question of *freedom* of religion: the freedom to practice any or no religion, in accordance with one's own choice, without pressure or coercion (so long as the practice of your religion does not harm others—you cannot include human sacrifice among the sacraments of your religion). That is an important issue, but—at least in the countries where people are likely to be reading this book—it is not a controversial one. Almost all of us are firmly committed to the basic principle that people should be free to worship (or not worship) as they choose. One reason for that commitment is our knowledge of the violent conflicts that emerge when one group attempts to impose its religious views on others. An even more basic reason is our realization of the fundamental importance that all of us attach to the liberty to make our own decisions—free of coercion—about our own religious beliefs (or nonbelief). Your views about basic religious questions—whether there is a God, the nature of God, the relation between God and humans, the nature of a good or virtuous life—are among your most important personal beliefs, and your views concerning such questions involve the most definitive elements of your character. Thus the right of religious liberty is widely regarded as one of the most basic human rights, recognized in the United States Bill of Rights, the Canadian Charter of Rights and Freedoms, and in Article 18 of the United Nations Universal Declaration of Human Rights (as follows):

> Everyone has the right to freedom of thought, conscience, and religion; this right includes freedom to change his religion or belief, and freedom, either alone or in community with others and in public or private, to manifest his religion or belief in teaching, practice, worship and observance.[1]

Basic religious freedom is obviously an important issue, but for almost all of us, it is a settled issue. We believe in religious freedom, freedom of worship, and freedom of belief. But controversies remain, and the most basic of those controversies is the question of the proper relation between religion and the government: the classic question of church and state.

It is sometimes said that the colonists came to North America in search of religious freedom. That's a nice story, but the truth is quite different. Certainly many colonists came to escape religious persecution, but not all came in search of religious freedom: Given the power, those who had been the victims of religious persecution were often eager to take their turn at persecuting. There were many instances of people being banished from a colony because they did not conform to the dominant religious beliefs, and several Quakers were hanged for their religious beliefs (including the remarkably courageous and knowledgeable Mary Dyer, who openly challenged the dominant Calvinist theology of the period by denying the doctrine of predestination and in 1660 was hanged in Boston Common). In many areas, Catholics were denied the right to hold office, or even to vote, well into the 19th century. Still, the horrors of religious persecution and religious wars, and the oppression of a state-supported church that was supported by taxes paid by everyone (including those who held different religious views), ultimately led to strong support for religious freedom.

You are free to worship (or not) as you wish, and to believe (or not) as you choose. You may certainly hold that your religion is the only true religion, and you may try—through sermon, song, and tract—to convert others to your true path. But you cannot interfere with the right of others to follow their own religious or nonreligious beliefs, and the government cannot support one (or any) religious view in preference to others. These are such basic principles that we may not spend much energy considering *why* we believe in them; but if we ask that question, it is not difficult to give an answer. I may feel a very deep commitment to my own religious (or atheistic) beliefs, and fervently wish that everyone would recognize the obvious truth of the beliefs I hold. I might even wish that those who are blind to the certain truth of my beliefs should be forbidden from proclaiming or following their mistaken paths, and I might like the idea of forcefully suppressing those competing false doctrines. But I realize that others hold different beliefs, and hold them with the same deep conviction that I do. When I consider how I would feel if they forcibly silenced my views, or forced me to swear allegiance to a religious view I regard as profoundly mistaken, or required me to support such a view with my tax money, then it is clear that I would think it unfair to be treated in such a manner. Simple consistency requires that I treat others as I would wish to be treated. Of course, because I believe that my beliefs are the only *true* beliefs, I might suppose that I would be doing others a favor by forcing them to acknowledge and support my beliefs, and freeing them from their mistaken path. But again, others might use the same justification for forcibly converting me from the beliefs I cherish. As John Stuart Mill noted, if my views are really true, then I should have nothing to fear from allowing them to be tested and challenged in the free marketplace of ideas; and by subjecting them to challenge, I keep my beliefs lively and vigorous, rather than having them decay into empty ritual—a common fate for religious beliefs that gain state support and are never challenged.

In the United States, the First Amendment to the Constitution—the first item in the Bill of Rights—forbids the government from any *establishment* of religion; and the basic interpretation of that amendment was given by Supreme Court Justice Hugo Black, in his majority opinion in the 1947 case of *Everson v. Ewing Township*:

> The "establishment of religion" clause of the First Amendment means at least this: Neither a state nor the Federal Government can set up a church. Neither can pass laws which aid one religion, aid all religions, or prefer one religion over another. Neither can force nor influence a person to go to or to remain away from church against his will or force him to profess a belief or disbelief in any religion. No person can be punished for entertaining or professing religious beliefs or disbeliefs, for church attendance or non-attendance. No tax in any amount, large or small, can be levied to support any religious activities or institutions, whatever they may be called, or whatever form they may adopt to teach or practice religion. Neither a state nor the Federal Government can, openly or secretly, participate in the affairs of any religious organizations or groups and vice versa.[2]

There are exceptions to the widespread belief in freedom of religion. Herman Cain (the very wealthy former CEO of Godfather's Pizza who sought the Republican nomination for president in 2012) stated that if a local community wanted to exclude a religious group from holding services or building a house of worship, then the community should have the right to impose such a ban. More specifically, Cain stated that if a local community wanted to exclude Muslims from building a mosque in the community (as occurred in a small city in Tennessee), then the local community should have the right to exclude such religious groups (Cain did not take a position on whether a predominantly Jewish community could legitimately exclude Christian churches or whether a predominantly Catholic community could exclude Protestant churches or whether a predominantly atheistic community could exclude all churches). Obviously there are some people who share Cain's position (or his original position—after widespread criticism, Cain reversed his earlier view and endorsed the right of all citizens to freedom of worship). But most people in our society share a basic belief in religious freedom, including the freedom of minority groups to worship as they please. That, after all, is what we mean by saying that people have a basic *right* to religious freedom: It is not something that you can be deprived of, even if the majority do not like your religious beliefs.

Although belief in religious freedom is widely shared, that does not eliminate controversies concerning the relation between church and state. There remain deeply divisive questions about what *counts* as state support of religion: Do religious rituals in public schools count as state support of religion? Does a Nativity scene or a Star of David on a public building imply state support of a specific religious view? If a public school building is open for community activities, must the school also allow the building to be used for religious services? Can student fees paid at a public university be used to support a religious publication? Can a religious view of human origins be taught in public schools, as an alternative to widely accepted scientific views? All of these questions spark deep controversies, and raise genuine and difficult questions.

Strawman Distortions

Strawman attacks seem to flare up whenever church–state questions arise. For example, those who are *opposed* to religious displays in public places (such as postings of the Ten Commandments in courthouses or displays of Nativity scenes in public parks) or to religious ceremonies (of prayer or Bible reading) in public schools are often accused of wanting to *ban* religion. In fact, people who actually want to ban religion are hard to find in our society. There are some who see religion as stupid superstition, and wish religion would wither away; but that is very different from wishing to ban it. After all, there are probably various things you don't like, and perhaps even believe are stupid—royal weddings, paintings of Elvis on black velvet, fried Hostess Twinkies, 8 O'Clock Classes—that you do not claim should be banned. Sam Harris and Richard Dawkins are perhaps the most vocal contemporary opponents of religious belief, but they have no wish to ban religious arguments, religious practices, or religious belief. Many of those who oppose any state support of religion are themselves deeply and sincerely religious, and believe that allowing the state to become involved in promoting religious beliefs turns religion into something cheap, or at best something formal and meaningless. Dropping quarters emblazoned with "In God We Trust" into a parking meter is hardly an inspiring religious experience, and few people feel closer to the divine when droning "one nation, under God," or when putting down the beer and peanuts to sing "God bless America" during the seventh-inning stretch. Religious beliefs and religious experiences are intensely personal matters, and turning them into formal state-sponsored recitations can deprive them of life and meaning. Thus, many who are deeply religious—and who certainly do not wish to ban religious belief or religious practices—oppose state-sponsored religious rites, fearing that such practices will devalue and demean authentic religious experiences. Finally, there are many who oppose state-sponsored religious practices because they believe that religion is an intensely private matter. Perhaps they take seriously the teachings of Jesus, that one should not make a show of one's religious beliefs, but instead pursue one's religious practices quietly and privately:

> When thou prayest, thou shalt not be as the hypocrites are: for they love to pray standing in the synagogues and in the corners of the streets, that they may be seen of men . . . ; But thou, when thou prayest, enter into thy closet, and when thou has shut thy door, pray to thy Father which is in secret. (Matthew 6:5–6)[3]

In short, those who oppose all state support of religion come in many varieties and from many perspectives, but it would be very difficult to find among them *anyone* who wishes to ban religious practices. Indeed, even those who are repulsed by religion and would love to see it die away are *not* eager to place any sort of *ban* on religion. There would be no better way of breathing life and fire and zeal into religious groups than by threatening to ban religion. The most tepid believers who attend services only on high holy days would immediately be out in force, waving banners and proclaiming their dedication to the religious tradition that is under threat.

A common but silly strawman claim is that those who want a strict separation of church and state want to "ban prayer in public school." That is obviously false. If a child wishes to pray for divine assistance during a math test, or say grace before lunch, the child is free to do so; and if a few students wish to clasp hands and quietly pray before lunch, they have every right to do that. However, the school cannot do anything to *officially* endorse or encourage religious belief (a teacher cannot lead the children in saying grace and the principal cannot lead a prayer before the start of school or read a religious text over the loudspeaker at the close of the school day). Furthermore, students—and teachers—are free to wear a cross, a *kippah*, a headscarf, or ashes from Ash Wednesday. (If your religion requires that you wear a curved ceremonial sword, then we have problems.)

On the other side, there *are* those who want a state religion, enforced by the state: That is certainly the goal of the Taliban, in its areas of Afghanistan; and it is the position favored by the leaders of the Iranian Revolution. There are also a few Christian groups who would like to make the United States into a theocracy; you can find their writings as part of the Dominionist movement (be forewarned, if you seek out some examples on the internet: Some of the members of this group—but certainly not all—are virulently racist, and you may be disgusted by some of the writings you discover). These are people who believe that the United States was founded as a Christian nation and that "Biblical law" should govern the country (they favor, for example, very severe measures toward anyone found guilty of sex outside of marriage), and that all officeholders should be required to pass very strict religious standards (only Christians would be allowed to hold office, and only a select group of Christians would qualify). Such people do exist, but obviously most of the people who favor some state recognition and support of religion do not hold such views.

Somewhat more common are those who want some elements of their religious beliefs taught in the public schools. Typically they want public school children to be taught that the structure of the universe—and particularly the origin of humans—was the creation of God, and that God designed humans and the universe for a specific purpose. (This is largely an American phenomenon; few people in Canada or Australia or England, or anywhere in Europe, would favor such a policy.) These views are put forward as "creation science" (sometimes presented as "intelligent design theory") and thus as a scientific theory and not a *religious* intervention in the public schools at all; but such claims are difficult to take seriously. The proposed creation science model follows no principles of scientific method. It is not falsifiable, it makes no testable predictions, and it violates the principle of simplicity (Occam's razor); and it is put forward by groups with the avowed goal of bringing a particular view of God (God as a purposeful Creator) into public schools. As noted by Judge John E. Jones III (the judge in the Dover, Pennsylvania, case in which the local school board required that biology courses include the "theory of intelligent design" as an alternative to the evolutionary account), the intelligent design account "violates the centuries-old ground rules of science."

Perhaps the major problem with teaching the Biblical creation story as science is not that it is bad science, but that it is bad religion. Treating the story as a factual account of the origins of the solar system and of humans deprives the account of its much deeper spiritual lesson: We are all brothers and sisters, we are equals under God, and we should treat one another as part of a caring family. That deep spiritual ideal is lost when the account is treated as a biology or geology textbook.

Less extreme—and more typical of the people who favor some state support of religion—are those who want to allow some modest form of prayer in school, and the traditional singing of Christmas carols by school choirs, and perhaps a Nativity scene and a Jewish menorah in a public park. That may or may not be a good idea; but it is certainly an idea that is worthy of serious honest discussion. Honest discussion is not encouraged by strawman attacks that portray efforts to place a Nativity scene on the courthouse lawn as the first step in forcing all citizens to practice Christianity, and opposition to such displays as attacks on freedom of worship.

What Is the Common Ground?

Though there is profound disagreement concerning the details, we generally agree with the basic principle of religious freedom: the freedom to worship and believe (or not) as we freely choose. We agree that religious material may be presented in public places with public funding, so long as it is not done to promote a specific religious view. For example, few would object to Handel's *Messiah*, or to a state-supported exhibit of the religious paintings of Rembrandt, or a state-supported tour of some of Michelangelo's religious themed sculptures, or government support of the exquisite Muslim-themed calligraphy from the court of Suleiman the Magnificent. These are clearly presented for esthetic rather than religious purposes. And we generally agree that the government should neither promote nor oppose any religious (or antireligious) view.

Arguments in Favor of Strict Church–State Separation

Should a public high school be allowed to have public prayer, broadcast over the loudspeakers, before a football game? (If teammates *voluntarily* pray in the locker room before the game or after making a touchdown or for the swift recovery of an injured friend, that is not an issue; the question is whether there should be public prayer sponsored by the school.) Should a large plaque bearing the Ten Commandments be placed on the wall of a public courthouse? Should a Nativity scene be allowed on public property in front of the town hall? What are the arguments *against* such displays and ceremonies?

1. When religious displays are placed in public places—places that are supposedly the property of *all* people in a democratic society—they imply that these are expressions of beliefs shared by *all citizens*. Thus the displays attribute beliefs they do *not* hold to many citizens, who are made uncomfortable by the implication that as citizens they *should* hold those views and that anyone not sharing those beliefs is not a full member of the community. If you suppose that such displays as the Ten Commandments—several of which endorse a very specific religious view—are of no real significance and people should not be disturbed by their presence, imagine walking into the county courthouse to find emblazoned on the wall a statement of belief in paganism, or perhaps a strong

endorsement of atheism. Most Christians and Jews and Muslims would find that disturbing, and feel that they are perhaps unwelcome outsiders in this government building, and even unwelcome as citizens of this country. It is not surprising, then, that many U.S. citizens—agnostics and atheists, but also Hindus, Wiccans, followers of Native American religions, Baha'is, and many others—are disturbed by religious statements that are presented as government-endorsed but with which they disagree.

Perhaps some of these displays were not placed there with the *intent* of making others feel like outsiders (though they may have that result); however, some courthouse displays of the Ten Commandments have been placed for the specific purpose of endorsing a specific religious view. For example, when Alabama Supreme Court Justice Roy Moore had a prominent display of the Ten Commandments placed on the courthouse grounds, his avowed purpose was to endorse the Judeo-Christian tradition of belief, and to make clear that *his* court adhered to those religious principles. An even more striking example of using public religious statements for the *exclusion* of nonbelievers is the addition of "under God" (following "one nation") in the Pledge of Allegiance. The words were added at the height of McCarthyism and the House Un-American Activities Committee witch hunt for "communists in the government." They were added with the explicit purpose of making it clear that atheists were not welcome in the United States. In short, public displays and public rituals *can* have the purpose of endorsing a specific religious view, and treating any citizen not endorsing that view as an outsider.

It is tempting to say that (as in the case of Santa Fe, Texas) so long as everyone in the community is comfortable with school prayer and Bible reading, and prayer before football games and graduations, then there is no harm in simply letting it continue. The problem is that if religious belief and religious practices are that deeply entrenched and widely favored, it becomes terribly difficult for anyone uncomfortable with the religious practices to speak up; and—as was the case in Santa Fe—anyone who does express concern over the practice runs the risk of ostracism, and even verbal and physical abuse. By continuing the practice, one sends a clear signal that "outsiders" are not welcome. That is not a signal that should be sent to any American citizen in any American community.

2. The second argument against displaying religious symbols on public property is offered by many who fervently *believe* in the religious views displayed. Turning elements of religious devotion into government-approved displays destroys much of the deep religious significance of those religious symbols. If one regards the birth of Jesus as a uniquely wonderful event for all the world, then reducing that to something that is government-endorsed cheapens it, reduces it to the level of a government ceremony, and robs it of much of its spiritual meaning. If one sees the Ten Commandments as God's special covenant (either with a chosen people or with all humans), then treating them as an element of a government-approved creed turns them into something secular: an attempt at claiming divine approval for a particular human-constructed legal or governmental system.

In one of his shows, Stephen Colbert invited Congressman Lynn Westmoreland—who had cosponsored a bill to place the Ten Commandments in both the Senate and House chambers—to visit his program. The Congressman eagerly displayed his deep devotion to the Ten Commandments, and his commitment to placing them in public places. Stephen Colbert expressed his enthusiasm for the project (satirically), and then asked the Congressman to use this opportunity to acquaint the television audience with the Ten Commandments: Would the Congressman please run down the list of the Ten Commandments, so everyone in the television audience could be reminded of them and their importance? Unfortunately, the Congressman—though he stumbled around for several minutes—could recall only three of the commandments: "don't lie, don't steal, don't murder"; though his press secretary later claimed that Congressman Westmoreland could actually recall seven of them. Obviously for Congressman Westmoreland the Ten Commandments had lost any status as divine law (he could not be bothered to learn what they are); rather, they functioned as a political prop, to claim that this particular Congressman was on "God's side," and that therefore the Congressman had the divine stamp of approval. When religious symbols and beliefs become part of political campaigns and political posturing, any deep religious meaning of those symbols is soon eroded away. One might propose as a general rule: If you want to keep your religious symbols strong and alive, keep them out of the public square and out of the hands of politicians.

Arguments to Allow Some State Support for Religion

1. One argument for *allowing* religious themes and religious symbols into the public sphere is closely related to the last argument for keeping them *out* of government spaces and processes. This is the argument that these symbols have become such a common part of the culture that they have lost their religious significance and become secularized, so that they no longer count as a government endorsement of religion. Christmas is deeply embedded in the national culture and heritage, to the point that it has become a *secular* holiday (like Labor Day or the Fourth of July). Christmas trees, tinsel angels on lamp posts, strings of lights, Nativity scenes, Santa Claus with his reindeer—these no longer have spiritual significance, but have become thoroughly secularized, and thus are not offensive to the principle of church–state separation. Placing a Christmas tree and a Nativity scene at the county courthouse is no more an endorsement of religion than the shopping mall announcement of "only six more shopping days 'till Christmas' " is a call to prayer.

In response to this argument, it is by no means clear that a Nativity scene is quite comparable to a Christmas tree or an illuminated Santa and reindeer. But if in fact the Nativity scene has been emptied of all spiritual significance and rendered purely secular (like an American flag), then that would perhaps be a reason for Christians to want such displays *removed* from public display, in hopes that they may regain some of their lost spiritual significance. If you think of a ritualistic opening prayer you may have heard—such as the Senate chaplain's opening prayer for sessions of the Senate or a prayer over the loudspeaker before a football game or a prayer prior to a graduation ceremony (the Supreme Court has ruled against such prayers in public school ceremonies, but they still occur in some places)—then it is very doubtful that you received any spiritual blessing or spiritual uplift from those prayers. To the contrary, they typically seem an empty exercise, even less inspiring than the ritual singing of the national anthem. So this argument faces a tough dilemma: If the religious symbol retains its spiritual significance, then it has no place in the public sphere, because it would count as a government endorsement of a specific religion. If the symbol has become thoroughly secularized and is now devoid of religious significance, then (for people who value the symbols as spiritually significant) that is a good reason for keeping religious symbols *out* of the public sphere and out of government clutches in order to preserve their spiritual power.

2. A second argument for allowing religious symbols and practices into the public or governmental sphere is based on their importance as shared symbols that help to unite a large and diverse country. They serve as a means of maintaining valuable cultural practices and traditions that give the country its identity and unity, and help to inspire common goals and values in our diverse population.

There is no doubt that religious symbols and rituals can promote unity among followers of that religion. All religions have sacred rites and rituals, typically including songs and ritual chants as well as special celebrations, often including dancing or other forms of ritual motion (kneeling or perhaps making the sign of the cross). All of these are important in creating bonds among the followers of a particular religious tradition. But using such symbols and rituals to promote unity in proudly diverse cultures such as that of Canada or the United States seems a hopeless cause. The public display and endorsement of a specifically Christian symbol will not promote harmony, but discord: discord not only between Christians and those of other faiths (or no faith), but also among the multitude of Christian denominations (and as the history of Ireland makes clear, discord between different Christian groups can be quite bitter indeed). Furthermore, there are plenty of nonreligious symbols as well as other means for use in forging a sense of national unity: national flags and national anthems, shared principles (such as commitment to freedom of religion), and shared accomplishments (such as putting a man on the Moon or conquering a specific disease or guaranteeing health care for *all* citizens). And if one insists on the importance of religious symbols for this purpose, it is clear that there is no shortage of places—from churches to private homes to billboards—for the prominent display of such symbols.

Where Do We Stand?

We generally agree (there are some extreme exceptions) that we do not want the state establishing a religion, or favoring a particular religion. That would infringe on one of our most cherished liberties and undercut our basic principle of the state being neutral on questions of individual values and choices. Furthermore, most of us are concerned that when politicians and the government "show their support" for a religious view, it cheapens religion and deprives it of much of its strength and worth. Religious views are often a major catalyst in the *challenge* to state policies, as in the civil rights and abolitionist movements. When a politician kicks off a campaign with a highly publicized "prayer service," clearly the goal is political gain rather than spiritual awakening. We also agree that we do not want the state infringing on the free exercise of religion (except when necessary to protect others: If your religion requires human sacrifice, then that religious practice will not be allowed). No matter how misguided the majority may think a religious view, minority religious groups should enjoy freedom to practice their religion as they wish.

Questions for Reflection

1. In the United States, the government recognizes a number of federal holidays, some of which (such as Christmas) are of special significance to Christianity. Is that showing special support and preference for one religion over others?

2. A disputed question is the right of parents to raise their children in accordance with their religious views. For the most part, we allow this with almost no restrictions: If you wish to teach your children that evolution is false, and

that the world was created just a few thousand years ago, you are welcome to do so (whether you have the right to impose such religious teachings on other children in public schools is of course a very different matter). But what if your religion demands the handling of lethal vipers? Generally, you are free to do so—just as others are free to expose themselves to risk by riding motorcycles or cliff diving. But you are not free to subject your children to the risks of handling poisonous snakes: Endangering the health and life of children, who are not of sufficient maturity to make their own decisions in the matter, is unacceptable (though you may endeavor to teach them your religious views, in the hope that they will choose to become snake-handling adults).

Perhaps the most debated question of this sort is the question of whether parents whose religious views forbid most forms of medical treatment (particularly blood transfusions) can deny life-saving medical treatment to their children. In the case of adults, this is a settled question: If you choose not to have medical treatment—even if your doctors caution that a simple medical procedure (such as a blood transfusion) will save your life, and refusing the treatment will soon result in death—that is entirely your choice, whether motivated by religious or other reasons. But should parents be allowed to make such choices for their children? Should parents who are Jehovah's Witnesses be allowed to refuse life-saving blood transfusion for their children, on religious grounds? Should parents be allowed to deny all medical treatment to a very sick child, relying instead on prayer? In a number of cases, such decisions have resulted in the deaths of children. In the United States, 18 states have laws exempting parents from criminal prosecution if they deny medical treatment to their children on religious grounds. (These laws were passed rather quietly, after intense lobbying; most people in those states are unaware of the laws, and most legislators are wary of offending the small but vocal group who support such laws). In some ways, these laws seem inconsistent with our larger outlook. After all, in the Judeo-Christian Biblical tradition, it is required that children who blaspheme or show disrespect to their parents be killed; but there is no question that a parent who kills a child who "shows disrespect" will be prosecuted for murder. Very few of us believe that the state cannot legitimately restrict religious practices that call for the killing of children. Is it legitimate for the state to interfere in religious practices—such as rejecting all medical treatment and relying exclusively on prayer—that will result in the deaths of children?

3. There are fringe religious groups and churches in the United States that believe in and teach very ugly doctrines of racial hatred, claiming that those of African descent are "mud people" and cursed by God. Vile as those views are, most of us believe that people have a right to practice and even promote such religions of hatred and prejudice (so long as they do not actually involve harming others or calling for their harm: You can preach that a group is cursed by God, but you cannot incite your congregation to harm that group—though sometimes the line between the two is difficult to draw). Does respecting the freedom of religion of such groups extend to allowing them to teach their children their doctrines of prejudice and hate? Could the state legitimately interfere when such teachings are transmitted to children?

4. U.S. presidents have traditionally proclaimed an annual "national day of prayer." Is that a violation of the principle of separation of church and state? If the president instead called for a "national day of atheism," would believers find that offensive? Are the two cases analogous?

5. Since "under God" was added to the Pledge of Allegiance, there has been controversy over whether this is an illegitimate government endorsement of a religious view (it certainly asserts the existence of God, and affirms a specific view of God: that God does not simply set everything in motion and leave it to run, but takes a special interest in what happens—at least what happens to this nation—and may

intervene to give aid and protection). The question that often arises is whether this is specific enough to be offensive to those who do not believe in God or in that view of God; or is this instead such a modest generic statement that no one should be offended by it? If you are Christian—and you have school-age children whom you wish to raise as Christians—would you be disturbed if instead of "one nation, under God," we substituted "one nation, that proudly makes its own way with no need of help from any god"? Is that a legitimate comparison?

6. Prior to prayers, many Muslims perform a cleansing ritual of foot washing. University students (especially commuter students) often do not have a convenient place for this cleansing ritual. Several public universities have installed foot-washing basins in a number of restrooms to accommodate the needs of their Muslim students. Part of the concern was safety: Students using wash basins sometimes slipped, and at least one student was seriously injured in a fall.

Some people have objected that installing foot-washing basins promotes the practice of a particular religion. A representative of Americans United for Separation of Church and State stated: "I don't think the Constitution permits you buying an item or building a facility used exclusively by one religious group." A spokesman for the Council on American-Islamic Relations disagreed: "It's not a promotion of a particular faith. People aren't saying, 'Oh, become a Muslim so you can use this faucet.' It's an accommodation of existing students" (Redden, 2007).[4]

Are the universities that install foot basins providing a legitimate service to their student body, or is this an illegitimate state support of religious practices?

7. At Grand Canyon National Park, there are three large bronze plaques at some of the most scenic and popular sites in the park. The plaques were placed there some 50 years ago by the Evangelical Sisterhood of Mary, with the avowed purpose of honoring God. Each plaque contains a passage from the Bible;

one reads "Sing unto God, sing praises to his name"; another is "All the earth shall worship thee, and shall sing unto thee"; the third contains "O Lord, how manifold are thy works! in wisdom has thou made them all: the earth is full of thy riches." Does the presence of such plaques in a public park violate the principle of church–state separation?

8. Suppose that in Chicago there is an exquisitely beautiful church—splendid wood carvings throughout depicting various Biblical stories, jewel-like stained glass of extraordinary brilliance, and a stone architecture of wonderful grace. It continues to function as a house of worship for a small Christian denomination, whose membership has dwindled over the years. When the church was built, in the early 1800s, this denomination was large and wealthy, and its members spared no expense—bringing in the best stonemasons, glassmakers, and woodcarvers—to make their sanctuary beautiful; but now the church has few members and little money. The congregation cannot afford the upkeep on the church, and the church is falling into disrepair. A member of the state legislature proposes that the state provide funds to restore the building, clean and restore the stained glass, and make some needed repairs to the wooden sculptures. The legislator insists that her motive is preserving a beautiful historical building that might otherwise decay beyond repair and be lost. Another legislator argues against providing such funds, on the grounds that it would support the house of worship of a particular religion, and that state funds should not be used for such purposes. If you were in the legislature, how would you vote? Would your vote be different if the church were *never* opened to the public? If the church were regularly open to the public, and it was frequently visited by tourists as well as art and architecture classes from local universities?

9. In Australia, there is an enormous red rock that rises straight out of the plains of the desert. The British colonists who came to Australia called it "Ayers Rock," because Ayer apparently was the

first British explorer to see the rock. The native peoples of Australia call the rock Uluru, and their ancestors, of course, were quite familiar with the magnificent rock long before British explorers and colonists arrived in Australia. For most Australians, and for most of the tourists who venture deep into the outback to see the famous rock, it is a striking natural object of remarkable beauty; and—although it poses some hazards—many visitors enjoy the challenge of climbing to the top of the rock. For the native population of Australia, however, the rock has a very different significance: It is a sacred site, of great spiritual importance; and they regard climbing the rock as a violation of its sacred status. For these people, climbing the rock for "fun" or a "physical challenge" would be analogous to someone going to the old temple wall of the Jerusalem Temple—the famous "wailing wall"—and using it as a wall for racquet ball; or playing water polo at the site in the Jordan River where John is believed to have baptized Jesus. If you were a visitor to Ayers Rock, would you think it acceptable to climb the rock? Should the Australian government ban people from climbing the rock?

10. Many Muslim women in the United States and Canada wear headscarves (*hijab*) in public, including at school, and it rarely raises any questions or objections. In France, however, wearing of headscarves has become a very controversial issue indeed, especially since they were banned by law from state schools, starting in 2004. There are many different and conflicting views on the significance of a woman wearing a headscarf, and those conflicting views can be found among Muslims and non-Muslims alike. Traditionally, the headscarf signifies modesty, regarded as an important Muslim virtue by both men and women: Neither men nor women should flaunt their physical attractiveness (and this is only one element of a general insistence on modesty—one should be modest concerning one's wealth, status, intellect, and athletic ability). Thus many Muslims (including many Muslim women) regard wearing a hijab as a

symbol of gender *equality*. On the other hand, there are also many people (both Muslim and non-Muslim) who regard the headscarf as a symbol of the oppression of women, of treating women as inferior and as property, and as something forced upon women. Still other Muslim women regard the hijab as a proud and freely chosen symbol of their Muslim identity, part of their personal identity.

When the French banned the wearing of headscarves in public (government-operated) schools, their primary justification was the preservation of a *secular* state, in which one has complete freedom to practice any religion (or to reject all religion) in the private sphere—in one's home or church or club—but not to promote religious views in public areas such as schools. Thus the government banned the wearing of any large visible religious symbol by students in school, including not only headscarves but also kippahs, turbans, large crosses or Stars of David, and clothing (such as t-shirts with slogans) promoting a religious or antireligious theme. Is such a school dress code a legitimate restriction on promoting religious views in public schools, or an illegitimate infringement on freedom of religious practice?

11. Joline was celebrating her 21st birthday with friends at a local tavern, and unfortunately she celebrated a bit too much. She hadn't realized quite how much alcohol she had consumed until she was driving home and was pulled over by a state trooper. The breathalyzer showed that she was clearly over the legal limit, and she was arrested for driving under the influence. Since Joline had a clean record until this occasion, the judge fined her a substantial sum and then offered her an option: She could spend the next four weekends in the county jail, or she could attend and fully participate in a special Alcoholics Anonymous program (one night each week for the next 12 weeks) for those found guilty of driving under the influence. Joline happily chose the AA program over a dreaded jail sentence, and dutifully showed up for her first AA meeting. To her surprise, Joline discovered

that the AA meeting was deeply religious: Participants were required to acknowledge a higher power—God—and acknowledge their complete dependence on God. Joline, a fervent atheist, refused to participate; the leader of the AA meeting reported to the judge that Joline had refused to participate in the program, and the judge called Joline back into court and sentenced her to four weekends in jail. Joline (through her lawyer) appealed her sentence, on the grounds that this sentence was an unfair violation of the principle of separation of church and state. In her appeal, Joline's lawyer made the following argument:

> There is certainly no requirement that the state provide a non-incarceration alternative to those guilty of driving under the influence. It would be perfectly legitimate for the state to sentence all offenders to jail. It is also legitimate for the state to set up alternatives, as it has done in this case: a special treatment program substituted for jail time. But what is *not* legitimate is for the state to set up a program—such as A. A.—that is

designed for those who believe in God, but provide no alternative for those who reject belief in God. That is giving special treatment to believers, and that is a policy that is prohibited by the First Amendment guarantee of freedom of religion and of equal treatment to all without regard to religious belief.

If you were the appeals court judge in this case, how would you rule?

12. In several national parks (for example, Capitol Reef in Utah), there are rock carvings and rock paintings (petroglyphs) from past centuries that have religious significance, and often are still regarded as of great religious importance by contemporary Native American groups. These are carefully protected and preserved. Many people who insist on protecting these Native American religious symbols would be strongly opposed to placing Christian or Jewish or Muslim religious plaques in the parks. Is there any inconsistency between carefully preserving the former and prohibiting the latter?

Additional Resources

An interesting and clearly written book on landmark U.S. court cases dealing with church–state issues is Peter Irons's *God on Trial* (New York: Viking Penguin, 2007). This is a book that has been praised by advocates on both sides of the issues. For more on the key U.S. Supreme Court cases related to this issue, go to www.oyez.org (it contains audio recordings of the oral arguments before the Supreme Court, which are often very interesting, and is an excellent guide to categories of cases and the written opinions of both the majority and minority). Robert S. Alley, ed., *The Constitution & Religion: Leading Supreme Court Cases on Church and State* (Amherst, NY: Prometheus, 1999) is a good collection of key Supreme Court cases on the relation between religion and the state. Forrest Church has pulled together an excellent collection of the original writings of the Founding Fathers of the United States concerning the relation between religion and the state: *The Separation of Church and State: Writings on a Fundamental Freedom by America's Founders* (Boston, MA: Beacon Press, 2011).

On the constitutional issues raised by church–state questions, a book which argues for strict church–state separation is Isaac Krammick and R. Laurence Moore's *The Godless Constitution: A Moral Defense of the Secular State* (New York: W. W. Norton, updated edition published in 2005); and on the other side of the issue, Daniel Dreisbach's *Thomas Jefferson and the Wall of Separation between Church and State* (New York: New York University Press, 2002).

Derek H. Davis is the editor of a collection of essays by leading scholars on church–state issues: *The Oxford Handbook of Church and State in the United States* (New York: Oxford University Press, 2010). An interesting and readable book that ultimately suggests a middle ground approach is Noah Feldman's *Divided by God: America's Church-State Problem—and What We Should Do about It* (New York: Farrar, Straus and Giroux, 2006).

For information on the Christian "Dominionist" movement—and the views of those who believe the United States should be a Christian nation—see Sara

Diamond's *Roads to Dominion: Right-Wing Movements and Political Power in the United States* (New York: Guilford Press, 1995); Frederick Clarkson's *Eternal Hostility: The Struggle between Theocracy and Democracy* (Monroe, ME: Common Courage Press, 1997); and Kevin Phillips's *American Theocracy: The Perils and Politics of Radical Religion, Oil, and Borrowed Money in the 21st Century* (New York: Viking, 2006).

The issue of teaching evolution in schools has an enormous literature. Edwin J. Larson has written two excellent books related to the subject: *Summer for the Gods* (Cambridge, MA: Harvard University Press, 1997), a Pulitzer Prize–winning history of the Scopes trial and the continuing controversy; and more broadly on the subject, *Trial and Error: The American Controversy over Creation and Evolution* (New York: Oxford University Press, 3rd ed., 2003). Kenneth R. Miller, *Finding Darwin's God: A Scientist's Search for Common Ground between God and Evolution* (New York: HarperCollins, 1999), is a cell biologist at Brown University, who argues for the compatibility of religious belief and Darwinian evolution.

On the web, religioustolerance.org is an excellent site for a variety of topics, and is particularly good on church–state issues; go to http://www.religioustolerance.org/const_am.htm, and (for material on prayer in public schools) to http://www.religioustolerance.org/ps_pray.htm. The Pew Forum on Religion & Public Life, at pewforum.org, is excellent on recent court cases concerning church and state; go to http://pewforum.org/Topics/Issues/Church-State-Law/. www.au.org is the site for Americans United, a group that supports separation of church and state; it has good material on current events and relevant news stories.

Endnotes

1. Article 18, Universal Declaration of Human Rights (United Nations, 1948)
2. Everson v. Ewing Township, Supreme Court of the U.S., 1947
3. Matthew 6, 5–6
4. Elizabeth Redden, "One Contested Sink," April 13, 2007, Inside Higher Education

MYSEARCHLAB CONNECTIONS

Go to www.religioustolerance.org for excellent material on church–state issues (and a variety of other topics). There have been many fascinating and important U.S. Supreme Court cases on church–state relations (often struggling over the interpretation of the "establishment clause" and the "free exercise" clause in the First Amendment to the Constitution: "Congress shall make no law respecting an establishment of religion, or prohibiting the free exercise thereof"). The following cases (including the majority and minority opinions, as well as the very interesting oral arguments) can be found at www.oyez.org. An important case in which the Court adopted the standard that the state cannot become "excessively entangled" with religion is *Lemon v. Kurtzman*, 1971. *Zelman v. Simmons-Harris* (2002) concerned government aid vouchers for students attending private religious schools. One of the most interesting and controversial decisions was *Engel v. Vitale*, 1962, which ruled against mandatory school prayer. Other important Supreme Court decisions concerning school prayer are *Wallace v. Jaffree*, 1985; *Lee v. Weisman*, 1992; and *Santa Fe Independent School District v. Doe*, 2000. Supreme Court decisions on public religious displays include *Lynch v. Donnelly*, 1984; *Allegheny County v. Greater Pittsburgh ACLU*, 1989; *Van Orden v. Perry*, 2005; and *McCreary County v. ACLU of Kentucky*, 2005 (the 2005 cases deal with displays of the Ten Commandments). For some very interesting cases decided by the Supreme Court of Canada, go to http://www.scc-csc.gc.ca/decisions/index-eng.asp (in the website of the Supreme Court of Canada), and look up cases by year; see *R v. Big M Drug Mart*, 1985; *Syndicat Northcrest v. Amselem*, 2004; and *Multani v. Commission scolaire Marguerite-Bourgeoys*, 2006 (the last one is a particularly interesting case concerning the wearing of a dagger that is part of Sikh religious devotion). Also, see the entry on "Religion and Political Theory" in the *Stanford Encyclopedia of Philosophy*, at plato.stanford.edu.

PATRIOTISM

Chapter Outline

BREATHES there the man with soul so dead,
Who never to himself hath said,
"This is my own, my native land!"
Whose heart hath ne'er within him burn'd
As home his footsteps he hath turn'd
From wandering on a foreign strand?
If such there breathe, go, mark him well;
For him no Minstrel raptures swell;
High though his titles, proud his name,
Boundless his wealth as wish can claim;
Despite those titles, power, and pelf,
The wretch, concentred all in self,
Living, shall forfeit fair renown,

And, doubly dying, shall go down

To the vile dust from whence he sprung,

Unwept, unhonour'd, and unsung.[1]

    Sir Walter Scott

The love of one's country . . . is in many cases no more than the love of an ass for its stall.[2]

J. B. Zimmermann

Perhaps the most contentious contemporary issue is abortion, but *patriotism* may be the question on which it is hardest to find common ground. Certainly it would be difficult to reconcile J. B. Zimmermann with Sir Walter Scott. Patriotism as an ethical issue does not come up quite as often or as directly as does abortion: If a woman wishes to have an abortion, then she must directly confront the issue of laws restricting or banning abortion. But if Alice is a fervent patriot, then she can attend patriotic rallies on Independence Day, wear a flag pin on her lapel, and fly a flag on her front lawn; and Barbara, who believes patriotism is more a problem than a virtue, can simply avoid such activities. Still, there are some cases where the issue becomes more personal and more difficult to bypass. One area is in the contents of public school textbooks, particularly history books. Should the focus be on the most positive aspects of U.S. history, such as the inspiring Declaration of Independence, the struggle to defeat Nazism, the efforts to help rebuild Europe following World War II, the medical advances by researchers such as Jonas Salk (that all but eliminated the dreadful threat of polio), and the accomplishments of U.S. scientists in the exploration of space and the understanding of physics? Or should there be a more balanced history, including the attractive as well as the less attractive elements of our history: the fact that the United States retained slavery long after other Western nations had abolished it, the "trail of tears" and other abuses of Native Americans, the notorious Tuskegee "experiment" in which poor black men were denied treatment for venereal disease so the progression of their illnesses and deaths might be "observed," the prolonged internment of U.S. citizens of Japanese descent during World War II, and the brutal racist lynchings that continued through the middle of the 20th century. That is a question that confronts everyone, but especially the parents of school-age children.

The patriotism question is also unavoidable in times of war, particularly when there is a draft. During the Vietnam conflict, some people took the view that (as the country song says) "It wasn't me who started that old crazy Asian war, but I was proud to go and do my patriotic chore."[3] That is, even if the war is crazy, and wrong, so long as my country declares war, I'll fight on behalf of my country: I'll *proudly* do "my patriotic chore." Others believed that it would be wrong to support their country in a war they considered morally wrong. But either way, when young people were being *drafted* into the armed forces and sent to fight in Vietnam, they were directly and personally confronted with the issue.

So what can we make of patriotism? Is it a noble virtue or dangerous vice? Before examining that question, we must first consider a prior question: What *is* patriotism?

In most of the issues considered earlier, there was little confusion over what was at issue. For example, on the question of capital punishment, the question is whether it is ever legitimate to take the life of someone who commits a terrible crime. There may be differences over when (if ever) capital punishment is justified (should an accidental murder committed during the course of a robbery be eligible for the death penalty?); but there is no question about what the death penalty *is*. The same is true of the abortion controversy: There are certainly disagreements about when (if ever) abortion is justified, but there is no dispute over what abortion *is* (though of course there may be dispute about the words used in describing it—"unborn child" or "fetus"). But on the subject of patriotism, one of the first questions concerns exactly what patriotism *is*. That is a controversial but important question: Until we are clear about exactly what we *mean* by *patriotism*, we may simply talk past one another. If Jane claims patriotism is a great virtue, while Julia regards patriotism as a dangerous vice, it may be that they have a basic moral disagreement; but it is also possible that they have a deep moral *agreement*, but mean very different things by patriotism. So before we plunge into a debate about patriotism, it is essential to be clear on what *patriotism* means.

Our concern is a very practical moral issue that is the source of deep and troubling divisions, and it is important that we deal with that specific controversy. When examining that controversy, we are debating patriotism in its most ordinary meaning: special allegiance to one's country. If you are a citizen of Canada or the United States or Mexico or Brazil, do you have a special obligation to your country and its people? Do you as a citizen have an obligation to *support* your country, no matter what? (For example, many people say that as an American citizen, you have every right to debate American policies and criticize the programs of your country; but once America is at *war*, then all criticisms must stop, and all true patriots and good American citizens must unite in supporting the war effort.) Is it *right* to give special allegiance to one's own country and fellow citizens, in preference to the citizens of other nations? Or is special allegiance to one's own country and its citizens a distortion of genuine moral behavior, which requires that we treat all persons equally (on this view, it is just as important for a Canadian to feed a hungry person in Bangladesh as it is to provide food for a hungry person in Toronto). So we'll use the term in what seems to be the most ordinary sense. Patriotism is special affection for one's country, a sense of special obligation to one's country and one's fellow citizens; and by *country* we'll mean the country in which one is a citizen. A Texan may have a special affection for Texas, but if the Texan is *patriotic*, then the patriotism must be toward the United States. There may be special problems if one feels allegiance to an area that wishes to claim *independence* from the larger country (for example, Basque separatists, or those in Quebec who wish Quebec to be independent of Canada, or—in the 18th century American colonies—those British citizens who wanted independence from England); but those are special questions that we can set aside as we discuss the general question of patriotism and its status as a virtue or a vice.

If we say that patriotism is a special allegiance or commitment to one's country, that still leaves difficult questions. Does patriotism mean that you support your country *no matter what*? If so, then patriotism is certainly not a virtue. Suppose your country adopted policies similar to those of Nazi Germany: goals of genocide, world domination, and enslavement of "inferior peoples." In that case, it would be profoundly wrong to support your country and its policies. There are a few people who assert "my country, right or wrong"; but that means giving up your status as a free autonomous person, and renouncing your own independent moral judgments in favor of judgments made by others: by your fellow citizens or by the leaders of your country. Such mindless allegiance to a king or a country is not something that most of us would find attractive, or even morally acceptable. "You should never criticize your country in time of war." To the contrary, if your country is engaged in an unjust imperialist war, then you probably have a moral obligation to criticize your country's behavior. Abraham Lincoln believed the war against Mexico was an imperialist attack designed to take a vast section of Mexico into the United States (and to make matters worse, extend slavery into that section where slavery had been abolished). Lincoln fiercely criticized his country during wartime, together with Henry David Thoreau and many other American citizens. Indeed, Thoreau insisted that it was morally wrong for an American citizen *not* to criticize what he considered an unjust war of aggression.

This is simply one element of a larger point: If you are an autonomous moral being, then you cannot accept anything or anyone as the absolute unquestionable authority on moral issues, whether that authority is a political leader, a country, or a religious teacher. Of course you *can* do that; in fact, many people have done so. But you cannot do that and remain an autonomous self-governing person. And the dangers of doing so are obvious. Think of those who gave up their own moral deliberation and unquestioningly followed Hitler, or the unfortunate people who blindly followed Jim Jones to a mass suicide at Jonestown. But even if you give absolute and unquestioning allegiance to a leader who is genuinely admirable, in doing so you lose your status as a self-directed deliberative moral being. It cannot be considered an act of virtue to deprive oneself of moral deliberation and moral standing. That does not mean, of course, that you cannot seek the guidance of religious teachers; nor does it mean that you cannot greatly admire and even seek to emulate great moral examples (such as Bishop Desmond Tutu). But it does mean that *you* must be the final judge of that individual's moral guidance: You take Desmond Tutu as an important moral guide because you have evaluated him and his teachings and found them to give good moral direction; you do *not* conclude that they *must* be good moral teachings simply because Desmond Tutu taught them. And if—as an autonomous moral person— you support your country, it must be because through your own moral deliberation you have judged your country to be pursuing morally legitimate goals.

There is another problem with mindless unconditional support of one's country: Such blind patriotism is often used for particularly vile ends. Because this sort of patriotism blocks careful examination of policies and their justification—this is the act of my country, so it *must* be right—it is easily called into service to support wars of aggression and policies that cannot withstand honest scrutiny. Whatever one thinks of patriotism as a virtue or vice, there is no doubt that it is sometimes used to justify horrific policies. The more fervent the patriotic outcry, the less likely that anyone will question what is proposed in the name of patriotism. Doubts and dissenters can be silenced by accusations of treason: If you are not with us, you are a traitor. That is not a wholesome atmosphere for careful critical deliberate examination of a government plan or policy.

So if patriotism is a virtue, it cannot mean that you support your country *no matter what*. That form of patriotism—sometimes called *extreme* patriotism—has little or nothing to recommend it, except to those who find it a useful tool for manipulating public opinion.

Under extreme patriotism, you must either make yourself a moral nonentity, deny all your own autonomous moral judgments, and count whatever your country does as right; or you must deny your own reflective critical judgment and delude yourself that your country is in fact always morally right (and thus you must blind yourself to your country's flaws and moral shortcomings). No morally acceptable view can require that you reject either your freedom of judgment or your rationality. When the soldiers of my country are at war,

I must support them and their efforts no matter what: That would be extreme patriotism. It would imply that Japanese patriots had an obligation to support Japanese troops in their brutal treatment of the citizens of Nanking, that no American could legitimately criticize the invasion of Grenada or the attack on Iraq, and that no patriotic German could object to the brutal treatment of the Poles or the Russians in the German invasion of those countries.

So if we are looking at the real issue, and not a strawman, we are not considering extreme patriotism. If patriotism implies that anyone who was a German citizen in 1942 was obligated to support the moral horrors of Nazism, then patriotism is not a view that can be counted as morally acceptable, much less morally virtuous. Perhaps, then, real patriotism means that you support the *ideals* of your country. That is certainly a more attractive position, but it's not clear that it is a form of *patriotism*. James Otis was one of the leaders of the American Revolution. He was apparently the person who first used the phrase that became a slogan of the Revolution: "Taxation without representation is tyranny." Another famous saying often attributed to Otis (actually, it was his motto): "Where liberty is, there is my country." That is a noble sentiment, worthy of being a motto. But it is very different from saying "My country, no matter what." To the contrary, according to this principle, if the United States was *not* a country that promoted liberty, then Otis would not claim it as his own (and obviously no country that embraced slavery could actually count itself as a country that promoted liberty). And if some other country *also* embraced liberty, then that country would be as much his *own* country as his native land. Thus when examined carefully, this principle is closer to *cosmopolitanism* than to traditional patriotism. According to the cosmopolitan view, we should be citizens of the *world*, rather than giving special allegiance to any particular country. On this view, we should embrace moral principles and work to promote those principles. Any country that embraces and promotes those principles we should support, and any country that opposes them we should oppose. Accidents of birth do not establish right or wrong.

Extreme patriotism—blind support for one's country, no matter what—is a morally blind and morally bankrupt position. But there is a more plausible version of patriotism that competes with strict cosmopolitanism. In contrast to "My country, right or wrong," moderate patriots say: "My country, when she is right to be kept right, when she is wrong to be reformed." Do you have a special obligation to make sure your country is doing right? Yes; after all, you are supporting that country through your work and your taxes; you are facilitating the acts of your country, whether right or wrong. So this *moderate* form of patriotism holds that you do have special obligations to your country and your compatriots, and particularly an obligation to prevent your country from doing morally bad acts; but you do *not* have an obligation to support it when it promotes bad policies and engages in unjust acts. Is this moderate form of patriotism virtuous? Is it obligatory?

As a moral view, extreme patriotism is a nonstarter. The essential question is whether *moderate* patriotism is preferable to a *cosmopolitan* view (in which we regard ourselves as "citizens of the world," with obligations to other persons as well as to the moral principles we cherish, but with no special obligation to a specific country). Perhaps the best statement of the cosmopolitan view was expressed by George Santayana, a Spanish philosopher who spent most of his academic career at Harvard: "To me, it seems a dreadful indignity to have a soul controlled by geography."[4] On the cosmopolitan view, I am first of all a citizen of the *world*; I happen to have been born in Spain, or the United States, or Pakistan, or Australia; but that accident of birth gives me no special reason to value one patch of ground rather than another. I am a citizen of country X, and so long as that country follows morally legitimate policies, I will support it. When it goes astray, I shall strive to correct it. But I have no special obligation to correct the wrongs of my country (any more than the wrongs of any other country). For cosmopolitans, I *certainly* have no obligation to support my country when it engages in wrongdoing. So, is cosmopolitanism better than moderate patriotism? Is moderate patriotism morally legitimate?

Strawman Distortions

The most obvious strawman distortion in the examination of patriotism is the claim that if you criticize your country (or its leaders), you do not support your country; or, even more extreme, you hate your country. That would disqualify almost every thoughtful citizen of any country from being a patriot, for no country is perfect, and no country is above criticism. On the other hand, those who are patriots—at least those who are moderate patriots—do *not* support their country and its policies "no matter what," and it is a strawman distortion to accuse moderate patriots of such abandonment of their moral scruples. To claim that patriots believe they should support their country even if it adopts Nazism is to set up an extreme patriotism strawman.

What Is the Common Ground?

What all sides can agree on is that we have a special obligation to push our country toward morally legitimate behavior. We are part of the country, and we participate in any illegitimate benefits it gains by unjust acts. By our taxes and support, we facilitate the behavior—good or bad—of our country. So there is a special obligation to one's country (especially for those in a democracy): an obligation to monitor its acts, and try to prevent it from doing wrong. As Igor Primoratz argues, "we have reason to develop and exercise a special concern for the moral identity and integrity of our country. By doing so, we will be attending to an important aspect of our own moral identity and integrity."

Second, we all agree that no morally legitimate form of patriotism can require that we support our country "no matter what." If your country promotes genocide, or engages in a war of imperialist aggression, or practices slavery, then supporting such policies is morally wrong, and your status as a citizen does not justify support of such policies.

Arguments in Favor of Moderate Patriotism

1. One of the most common arguments in favor of moderate patriotism is that special obligations to our country are based on *gratitude* for the benefits given by the country: its legacy of law, social support, education, and workable institutions. This does not require that the country be perfect or that its virtues be exaggerated nor its defects be hidden. But unless the country is monstrous toward its citizens—as Guatemala and El Salvador and the Soviet Union (under Stalin) and Germany (under Hitler) were for many years, carrying out mass killings of their own citizens and leaving almost all citizens in a state of constant fear—most citizens have gained significant benefits from citizenship in the country: protection from attack by foreign forces, a decent level of internal order, and support of educational and health care programs that benefit individual citizens. Very few of us believe that we are citizens of *perfect* countries; indeed, most of us would acknowledge some significant flaws in the country in which we live. Still, most of us would agree that we

have received benefits from our country (even if we believe we have not received our fair share of those benefits, we have received *some* benefits); and because we have received those benefits, we have an obligation to the country that was our benefactor. The basis of this is a reciprocity obligation: Because the country has provided us with benefits, we owe it some degree of support in return.

If we assume that there is a reciprocity obligation toward our country, the question remains of exactly what that obligation involves. Perhaps it involves following the laws of that country (so long as the laws are not themselves morally wrong, such as the fugitive slave law) and paying a fair share of taxes. But does it require something more, such as special devotion to that country? You were born into Canada as a Canadian citizen, protected by the Canadian justice system, provided health care in Canada's excellent system of universal health care, educated in good public schools and an excellent publicly supported Canadian university. Now you are deciding whether to stay in Canada, or move to France and apply for French citizenship. Would you be doing anything *wrong* in leaving Canada and living the rest of your life in France? Would you be failing in your obligation to your home country that nurtured you?

Though some may disagree, most of us would see nothing wrong in a young Canadian emigrating to France; indeed, if you are considering moving to another country after you graduate (perhaps you spent a semester abroad, and found the country where you studied particularly appealing), you probably do not consider that a *moral* issue at all. If so, then it is difficult to support the idea that you have a special obligation to the country of your birth. Still, reciprocity does carry some weight. Family members of a hungry South Carolina child may have fought in defense of my safety, or paid taxes to support the medical research that saved my life or the life of my mother; and since we seem to have a special obligation to help those who have in the past helped us, that might explain some degree of special obligation to our fellow citizens. But *most* medical advances—including those that have benefited me and my family—were discovered by people who do not happen to be citizens of my country. So reciprocity would hardly seem to stop at the border.

2. There is a second argument for moderate patriotism: We need shared commitment in order to undertake large projects, and in order to make sacrifices for the good of everyone in the country. Of course we should be concerned for people in all corners of the globe, but it is not easy to motivate sacrifices for others, especially those outside our community and family. One way of doing so is to extend the sense of community to a larger group. That is still difficult. Many Americans seem to feel little concern for fellow Americans who are impoverished, and persuading Germans and Belgians that they are now part of one unified Europe, and so they should feel special concern for the problems in financially troubled parts of Europe such as Greece and Spain, has proved to be a profound challenge. But the point is that a sense of national unity may help in that difficult project: It is good to help those in poverty who are our fellow citizens, and that is positive even if it would be better still to help the impoverished in other countries as well. Certainly we ought to do more for the hungry child in Somalia; but that does not change the fact that if ties of citizenship can persuade us to do more for the hungry child in Mississippi, that is a positive result. "Every child born in America should have enough to eat, should have decent medical care, should have an education that gives him or her the genuine opportunity to make the most of his or her talents and abilities." Not every American would support that assertion; there are those, after all, who believe

that if children go hungry or lack medical care, that's their (and their parents') tough luck. But the principle that *every* American child should have a genuine opportunity to succeed (and children without education, food, or health care are denied that opportunity) inspires most Americans to willingly make some sacrifices in order to live up to that ideal. And for *most* people, feeding hungry children is a positive result.

The real questions arise when we push the question one step further: Why should we stop at the border? It's important to me that children in Maine, Iowa, and Arizona be well-fed; but shouldn't it be *just* as important that children in Guatemala, Pakistan, and Nigeria are well-fed? If a child is hungry, what difference does it make if that child is in South Carolina rather than Somalia?

3. An especially interesting argument for moderate patriotism is based on the importance of our *country* in our understanding of who we are. Even if we often disagree with the policies of our country, part of our *identity* is in being a citizen of that country. We want to be part of something larger than ourselves that accomplishes major goals: building a transcontinental railroad or putting a man on the moon. We want an identity that extends beyond our immediate ends and mortal span. An important element of my personal narrative may involve playing a small part in an enormous enterprise: the defeat of Nazism, the forging of a new nation, and the overthrow of a tyrannical government. Not all of these things require patriotism, of course; it is possible to join in a variety of united ongoing enterprises. Those active in the long struggle for civil rights certainly have a sense of being part of a large, lengthy, and worthwhile enterprise. When steel workers overcame powerful opposition to form a successful union, they became part of a positive movement to which their individual efforts contributed. On a lesser scale, the extended community of dedicated fans who cheer for a favorite football team—and celebrate its history and hope for its future—may give a sense of belonging to a larger and continuing shared enterprise. But being part of a country, and identifying as a citizen of that country—even when acknowledging the flaws in the country's historical record—is one way that many people give larger meaning and significance to their lives and efforts. We are painfully aware of our own mortal limits. As citizens of a country that will endure beyond our own mortal spans, and in our efforts to sustain and improve that country, our lives may have some greater and longer lasting significance. Devotion to our country is one important way of accomplishing that, and that identification may encourage the mutual sacrifices necessary for achievement of difficult goals. Allegiance to larger groups—not limited to countries or nation-states, but certainly including those—is one of the ties that most humans regard as an important element of a rich and satisfying life.

Arguments against Moderate Patriotism (in Favor of Cosmopolitanism)

1. The basic argument against any form of patriotism (obviously against extreme patriotism, but even against the much more modest moderate patriotism) is that it is arbitrary. As moral agents and moral actors, it shouldn't matter whether a person happens to have been born in Brooklyn or Madrid, Kabul or Mumbai, Cairo in Egypt or Cairo in Illinois. In our concern for and relations with others, the accident of their

birth is surely an irrelevant consideration. A hungry child in Somalia has the same claim on our concern as a hungry child in Seattle. If one side is fighting to defend slavery and the other side to abolish slavery, then the only morally legitimate side is the abolitionist side, whether you happen to have been born in Maine or in Virginia. If the country of your birth is waging a war of aggression against its neighbor, then the accident of your birth is no justification for supporting the aggressive country. "Where liberty is, there is my country": That was the motto of James Otis, a leader in the American Revolution; and though Otis is regarded as an American patriot, his real allegiance was to principles (such as the principle of the right of individual liberty), and his struggle was to promote those principles. As a British citizen, Otis was willing to fight against Britain when he believed that Britain was violating those principles.

In response to this arbitrariness argument, some people claim that such universal inclusiveness is a noble ideal, but that it is an ideal that human animals are incapable of reaching. Given our nature as social beings and the reality of our social bonds, the strongest inclination to help others is toward our family, and then our immediate community, and then to others with whom we share special bonds (such as being compatriots). An abstract concern for "all human beings" is an ideal more suitable for angels than human social animals. In response to this, it seems clear that some people move beyond such limited concerns, and feel genuine concern for those beyond our communities and borders. Disasters such as tsunamis and earthquakes often prompt outpourings of aid from around the world—from strangers who could not find the stricken region on a map, and are certainly not fellow citizens. However, some fear there may be a price for aiming at perfectly abstract universality: Rather than promoting generosity to all, it may lessen generosity to those who are part of "our country" by taking away the special sense of community some feel for their fellow citizens. Ideally our concern for our fellow citizens should be a springboard to expand our concern to those beyond our borders; whether that expansion actually occurs—except in special conditions of disaster, or among a few exceptional individuals—is a difficult question.

2. A second argument against moderate patriotism is that patriotism tends to exaggerate the goods of the country and hide its flaws. It thus gives us a false perspective and makes it less likely that we will recognize and correct our country's faults. People sometimes say that no patriot should *criticize* his or her country during wartime, but if American patriots follow that principle, they will have few opportunities for constructive criticism: Between the Vietnam War, the attacks on Grenada and Panama, the first Gulf war, and a war in Afghanistan that has stretched over the past decade, there have been few times in the last half century when America was not at war. Patriots sometimes treat wartime criticisms of one's country or its leaders as "giving aid and comfort to the enemy"; indeed, internal critics of the United States—especially during the long periods of war—have often been called traitors. Without honest examination and criticism of a country and its policies, the country cannot confront and correct its flaws. Obviously that blindness is an element of extreme patriotism, but even moderate patriotism may not be the best atmosphere for careful critical examination.

3. A third criticism of patriotism is that it too easily swings toward militarism and attacks on an outgroup. One of the easiest ways of forging group identity is by means of an *outgroup*: Ohio State would not be quite so distinctive without Michigan, the University of North Carolina would not be the same without Duke, and the Red Sox nation needs the Yankees. That can lead to serious problems. Politicians know that one way of

distracting their citizens from the problems that they are not fixing (or perhaps that they are causing) is by setting up a threatening enemy: Anyone who challenges our policies must be in the service of that enemy.

Wag the Dog—a 1997 film starring Dustin Hoffman, Robert De Niro, Anne Heche, Willie Nelson, and Woody Harrelson—is the story of an election campaign in desperate trouble. The president is running for reelection, the election is only a few days away, the president has recently had a sexual escapade with an underage girl, the press is starting to close in on that story, and the president's campaign manager is desperate to come up with something that will distract the attention of the country until after the election. The campaign manager enlists an enterprising Hollywood producer who conjures up a fake war in Albania, complete with a beautiful young woman fleeing the fighting with her kitten, and frightened refugees saved by the heroic intervention of American troops. There is extensive news coverage with dramatic film of the war, daring rescues, returning American war heroes, even patriotic songs written for this specific war: a nonexistent war created for crass political purposes. It's a remarkably funny film, but it leaves a lump in your stomach. It sounds too much like other wars that were fought for similarly selfish political purposes, and in which people actually died. When the United States wanted to maintain control of countries in Latin America (El Salvador, Guatemala, and Nicaragua) for the benefit of U.S. corporations (such as AT&T and United Fruit Company), it was convenient to have a powerful enemy—the Soviet Union—so that when the people of those countries rebelled against oppressive governments, the United States could suppress those revolutions and claim that it was defending the United States against Soviet aggression and communist conspiracies. Obviously this is not a necessary consequence of *moderate* patriotism; but so long as hatred and fear of an enemy is an effective means of promoting support for a group, it will be a constant temptation and danger.

Where Do We Stand?

Can we find common ground between the moderate patriot and the cosmopolitan? Yes. In the 19th century, the United States adopted horrific policies in its treatment of Native Americans, and Belgians treated the Africans of the Congo brutally; in the 20th century, Germany carried out an official program of mass murder, while Japan treated the residents of defeated Chinese cities with extraordinary cruelty. In all these cases—and it would be easy to cite many more, from the ancient to the contemporary—countries adopted and carried out policies that were terribly wrong. If you were a citizen of one of those countries, and you supported those activities of *your country*, then you did something morally wrong. We can agree on that, whether we are patriots or cosmopolitans. In the mid-19th century, the *official policy* of the United States required that all U.S. citizens aid in the capture and return of any escaped slaves. Patriot or not, anyone who participated in such acts committed a grave moral wrong.

What else can we agree on, both moderate patriots and cosmopolitans? Certainly we can agree that patriotism can be a very dangerous emotion, leading to wars that are unnecessary and unjustified. That is not to say that war is never justified—that's a very different issue. But patriotic fervor has sometimes led to wars that were totally *un*justified, resulting in terrible suffering for vast numbers of people. Perhaps we can also agree that patriotism—at least sometimes—produces positive results. Patriotism inspired programs to "put the first man on the Moon," to build a transcontinental railroad, to conquer polio; and it sometimes moves people to sacrifice some of their own goods in order to help less fortunate fellow citizens. In addition, patriotism can sometimes inspire people to strive to live up to the highest ideals of their country: At least part of what moved many people in the struggle to abolish slavery was the obvious and profound conflict between slavery and the ideals of freedom expressed in the Declaration of Independence; and that same discomfort prompted widespread support for the civil rights movement. It didn't always work, of course; many patriotic Americans opposed minority voting rights. But even if we do not always live up to the high ideals expressed in the documents and monuments of our country, those ideals may sometimes have a positive effect. And since many worthwhile projects demand strong cooperation and at least some degree of shared sacrifice—whether the project is the construction of the transcontinental railroad or the abolition of slavery—the unity and sacrifice that patriotism sometimes promotes can be of benefit. Whether the benefits outweigh the problems is a question on which you will have to reach your own conclusion.

Questions for Reflection

1. Thomas Paine—the great champion of the American Revolution, who wrote inspiring pamphlets that stirred the spirits of the American soldiers in the darkest period when victory against the British seemed most unlikely—left America a few years after the success of the American Revolution, moving to France and encouraging revolutionary forces against the royalists. Paine was deeply devoted to the ideals of freedom, and supported efforts to gain freedom, whether by English or Americans or French. Was Paine an American patriot?

2. In the U.S. Civil War, it was well-known that brother fought against brother, son against father, friend against friend. Could a patriot from Virginia fight for the Union? Could a patriot from Virginia fight against the Union? Could a patriot from New York fight for the Confederacy (believing this to be a war of aggression, sincerely though wrongly believing that states have the right to allow slavery)? Does the fact that a Virginian fighting for the Union would be fighting to abolish slavery, while a New Yorker fighting for the Confederacy would be fighting to keep slavery, have any impact on the question of whether they can be patriots?

3. Germany did abysmal things during World War II: treatment of the Jews and of many others, brutality toward the Russians, harsh repressive measures toward occupied countries, and abominable treatment of prisoners of war. Would there be *anything* virtuous in remaining loyally patriotic toward the German mother country during that war?

4. If there were a revolution, and your country became something very different (no longer a democracy, say), would patriotism require that you maintain allegiance to that country?

5. During the Mexican war, when the United States invaded Mexico, Henry David Thoreau refused to pay a tax that was specifically passed to fund the war effort. Was that an act of patriotism?

6. For many people, there is no uglier word than *traitor*. But why is that? Is it because betraying your country is such a naturally vile thing? Or is it because we must struggle to make betrayal of a country seem vile, and so we emphasize and exaggerate the awfulness of such acts?

7. "If I had to choose between betraying my country and betraying my friend, I hope I should have the guts to betray my country." This was the view of the novelist E. M. Forster.[5] Do you find it admirable, or despicable?

8. Was George Washington a British traitor?

9. Horace: "Noble and fitting it is to die for one's country." Bertrand Russell: "Patriotism

is the willingness to kill and be killed for trivial reasons." Is there any common ground between the views of Horace and Russell?

10. During the Vietnam War era, Daniel Ellsberg made public some secret government documents concerning the Vietnam War: documents revealing that the U.S. government had been misleading its citizens about the conduct and progress of the war, claiming that the war effort was much more successful than it in fact was. Ellsberg clearly violated federal law by releasing the papers, but it was also clear that he had acted as a matter of conscience, at great personal risk, with no intent to betray his country (but instead believing he was upholding the basic principles of his country), and with no personal financial motive. He believed that in a democracy, it is wrong for the government to lie to its citizens: When citizens are not told the truth about government activity, the government is no longer a government "by the people, of the people, and for the people." Was Ellsberg a traitor or a patriot?

11. During World War II, several Germans (including German officers) plotted to assassinate Hitler; were they patriots, or traitors? If two people disagree on that question, what are the opposing views of patriotism that they are likely to hold?

12. The story of the San Patricio Brigade is little known in the United States, though its soldiers are regarded as heroes in Mexico. The San Patricio Brigade was made up of Irish immigrants to the United States who had arrived in the United States in the early 19th century not long before the U.S. invasion of Mexico. The Irish immigrants of that period were often quite poor (they were usually fleeing famine in Ireland), there was widespread prejudice against the impoverished Irish immigrants, and they were often despised and mistreated. A number of these immigrants had served in the British military and were well-trained soldiers; being desperate for work, they signed up when the U.S. Army was recruiting soldiers for the war against Mexico. They were treated brutally in the army (subjected to severe flogging and other forms of torture and humiliation for minor offenses). As they marched into Mexico with the U.S. Army, many of these Irish soldiers began to have doubts about fighting against Mexico. The Mexicans they encountered treated them with respect and friendship, in contrast to the brutal treatment they received from their U.S. officers. The Irish soldiers were Roman Catholics, like the Mexicans whose country they were invading (the other U.S. soldiers and officers were almost exclusively Protestant); and many of the Irish soldiers began to feel they had more in common with the people they were attacking than with the soldiers in their own army. Furthermore, the Irish soldiers began to doubt the justice of the invasion. In fact, opposition to the Mexican War and doubts about its legitimacy were widespread in the United States (as a member of Congress, Abraham Lincoln condemned it; Henry David Thoreau went to jail rather than pay a tax to support it; both Ulysses Grant and Robert E. Lee expressed doubts about the justice of the invasion, though they were officers in the U.S. Army of invasion), and many people—including many of the Irish soldiers—regarded the war as an act of imperialist aggression. Eventually many of the Irish soldiers concluded that they were fighting on the wrong side. Many deserted, and a large group of those joined the Mexican Army. The U.S. deserters who joined the Mexican Army made up a special unit, with their own battle flag: the San Patricio Brigade. All of them realized that if captured by U.S. forces, they would be executed. They fought courageously and desperately, and in fact were one of the most effective units in the Mexican Army. Most were killed in battle, but some were captured; of those who were captured, most were hanged; some were branded (with a hot branding iron, just below the right eye), and ultimately released (most of those remained in Mexico). The U.S. records of the San Patricio Brigade—and the story of their fight against the United States—were sealed

for over a century, and not released to historians until 1975. Were the members of the San Patricio Brigade U.S. traitors? Mexican patriots? Both? Neither?

13. Every country has events in its history of which it is not proud: events that run directly contrary to the image it cherishes of itself. For example, the United States cherishes its self-image as a "cradle of democracy," and a "beacon of liberty." These are certainly wonderful ideals, and it is perfectly legitimate for the citizens of the United States to seek to inspire their children to cherish those ideals. Unfortunately, the United States has a history that falls far short of those ideals, and sometimes seems to mock them. We may cherish the image of the United States as a "cradle of democracy" and a champion of freedom; but in fact, the United States permitted slavery long after it had been abolished in Europe. Far from being a democracy at its origin, the United States permitted only a small minority of its residents—white male property owners—the privilege of voting. Perhaps even worse, the United States has a history of supporting brutal dictatorships (such as in El Salvador, Guatemala, and Haiti) and undermining emerging democracies (as in Nicaragua and Argentina). Almost everyone agrees that it is worthwhile to acquaint our children with the ideals cherished by the nation, and to encourage their devotion to those ideals; to what extent is it good (or bad) to explain to children the ways in which the country has failed to live up to (or even betrayed) those ideals?

Additional Resources

An outstanding collection of articles is edited by Igor Primoratz, *Patriotism* (Amherst, NY: Humanity Books, 2002), including important articles by Alasdair MacIntyre and Igor Primoratz. Another excellent anthology is by N. Miscevic, *Nationalism and Ethnic Conflict: Philosophical Perspectives* (Chicago and LaSalle, IL: Open Court, 2000); Robert McKim and Jeff McMahan, eds., *The Morality of Nationalism* (Oxford: Oxford University Press, 1997), contains a number of worthwhile essays.

An interesting defense of moderate patriotism is offered in a very readable book by Stephen Nathanson, *Patriotism, Morality, and Peace* (Lanham, MD: Rowman & Littlefield, 1993). Yael Tamir's *Liberal Nationalism* (Princeton, NJ: Princeton University Press, 1993) is an intriguing effort to reconcile nationalism with liberalism.

Joshua Cohen is the editor of *For Love of Country: Debating the Limits of Patriotism* (Boston: Beacon Press, 1996). The book starts with an essay by Martha C. Nussbaum in which she argues for replacing our limited national and patriotic loyalties with a broader and more cosmopolitan perspective that emphasizes allegiance to principle rather than country. Following Nussbaum's essay are responses by 16 distinguished writers, and the book concludes with Nussbaum's reply. A profound but disturbing essay, "Reverend Wright and My Father: Reflections on Blacks and Patriotism," can be found in Randall Kennedy's recent book, *The Persistence of the Color Line: Racial Politics and the Obama Presidency* (New York: Pantheon, 2011).

Nationalism is an issue that obviously has close connections with questions concerning patriotism. For a contemporary defense of nationalism, see David Miller, *On Nationality* (Oxford: Oxford University Press, 1995).

Garrett Wallace Brown and David Held are the editors of an excellent anthology covering major cosmopolitan views as well as critics of cosmopolitanism: *The Cosmopolitan Reader* (Cambridge UK: Polity Press, 2010). Kok-Chor Tan's *Justice without Borders: Cosmopolitanism, Nationalism, and Patriotism* (Cambridge UK: Cambridge University Press, 2004) is a subtle examination of the relations among nationalism, patriotism, and cosmopolitanism. Kwame Anthony Appiah, *Cosmopolitanism: Ethics in a World of Strangers* (New York: Norton, 2006), provides a fascinating history of the cosmopolitan view in a graceful and accessible book. Seyla Benhabib, *Another Cosmopolitanism* (New York: Oxford University Press, 2006), explores cosmopolitan ideals and potential conflicts with other values; the book includes commentaries, together with Benhabib's response.

An issue that often arises in connection with questions of patriotism is whether our schools should strive to instill patriotism in our children; in particular, should we teach the history of our country with special emphasis on the positive elements of its history and the noble principles it espouses, or should we include all the blemishes and shortcomings? Should we remember the Alamo, and forget the imperialist attack on Mexico to expand the American empire? Should we note that in our Declaration of Independence we championed the principle that all men are created equal, and ignore the fact that the United States continued to hold slaves long after most other countries had abolished slavery? Should we teach about the Boston Massacre, but ignore the massacre at Wounded Knee? The controversy over what should be included in—and omitted from—our history textbooks is covered in the popular press and debated in the journals. An excellent collection of articles on this question is edited by Robert K. Fullinwider, *Public Education in a Multicultural Society: Policy, Theory, Critique* (Cambridge: Cambridge University Press, 1996). Recent interesting essays on the issue are by David Archard, "Should We Teach Patriotism?" *Studies in Philosophy and Education*, 18, 1999: 157–173, which argues against teaching patriotism; and by John White supporting teaching for patriotism in "Patriotism without Obligation," *Journal of Philosophy of Education*, 35, no. 1, 2001: 141–151. An excellent study of the long struggle over what should be included in American history textbooks is John Moreau's *School Book Nation: Conflicts over American History Textbooks from the Civil War to the Present* (Ann Arbor: University of Michigan Press, 2003). An excellent and very readable book exploring the heated contemporary debate over how history should be taught to elementary and high school students is Gary B. Nash, Charlotte Crabtree, and Ross E. Dunn's *History on Trial: Culture Wars and the Teaching of the Past* (New York: Random House, 1997). For international perspectives on the question of history education, see Irene Nakou and Isabel Barca, eds., *Contemporary Public Debates over History Education* (Charlotte, NC: Information Age Publishing, 2010); it covers 14 different areas of the world. Stuart J. Foster and Keith A. Crawford, *What Shall We Tell the Children? International Perspectives on School History Textbooks* (Charlotte, NC: Information Age Publishing, 2006), emphasize the deep cultural conflicts over what the society values, as played out in controversies over history texts. Robert Trivers, a distinguished biologist, includes a powerful chapter on "False Historical Narratives" in his fascinating book, *The Folly of Fools* (New York: Basic Books, 2011). For a history of the United States quite different from the one you read in school, take a look at Howard Zinn's *A People's History of the United States* (New York: HarperCollins, 2003).

Endnotes

1. Sir Walter Scott
2. J.B. Zimmermann, quoted in S. Nathanson, Patriotism, Morality, and Peace (Lanham MD Rowman & Littlefield, 1993).
3. "Ruby, Don't Take Your Love to Town" written by Mel Tillis
4. George Santayana, The Life of Reason, 1905
5. E.M. Forster, "What I Believe," The Nation, July 16, 1938.

MYSEARCHLAB CONNECTIONS

See the entries for "Patriotism," "Cosmopolitanism," and "Nationalism" in the *Stanford Encyclopedia of Philosophy*, at plato.stanford.edu.

16

Free Speech or Speech Codes?

Chapter Outline

Almost everyone believes in free speech. It is a basic right, guaranteed by the United States Bill of Rights, the Canadian Charter of Rights and Freedoms, and the Universal Declaration of Human Rights of the United Nations. Everyone should be free to support and argue for almost any idea, from Tea Party efforts to dramatically cut government regulation and government aid programs to the Occupy Wall Street push for a major reorientation of our economic system. Both fascists and communists—and all political views in between—have every right to present and promote their views. Both atheists and fundamentalists should be free to argue for their perspectives. "I hate what you say, but I will defend to the death your right to say it." That is a view almost all of us would endorse. Not everyone agrees, of course; there are those who would ban certain religious views, and ban criticism of favored religious traditions. But for most of us, the basic right of free speech is not a divisive issue. And it is important to keep that in mind: As we examine differences of opinion related to the question of free speech, it is important to remember that we share a basic foundation of broad agreement.

During the Inquisition, heretics were tortured and executed for promoting ideas that were in conflict with Catholic orthodoxy (Galileo spent his later years under house arrest, and under threat of torture, for writing in favor of the Copernican theory; Galileo was comparatively lucky, for others were burned at the stake for speaking in favor of that view). In the American colonies of New England, several people were hanged for speaking against the prevailing Calvinist version of Christianity. Not so long ago in the United States, people lost their jobs and some were imprisoned for supporting communist views. Still, though we do not always live up to our principles concerning freedom of speech, it is a broadly shared principle.

There are places where free speech is severely restricted; for example, there are a number of countries in which expressing skepticism concerning the dominant religious views is forbidden; in some cases, it may even be punishable by death. But in the United States, Canada, Europe, Australia, and New Zealand, the basic right to champion or challenge any religious or political view is broadly accepted. The problematic cases concern what is known as "hate speech": speech using racial or ethnic slurs, speech that demeans on the basis of gender or sexual orientation or religious belief. In France, ethnic and racial slurs can be treated as criminal acts; this usually happens only in extreme cases, such as the highly publicized case of fashion designer John Galliano, who in 2011 was convicted by a French court on charges of making public insults for reasons of religion, race, or ethnicity. Galliano was convicted of spewing racist and anti-Semitic insults on two occasions in a Parisian bar, and was fined (he could have been sentenced to prison).

When hate speech is forbidden, that does not mean that claims and arguments are blocked. One can still argue that a particular racial or ethnic group is inferior, that all men are worthless, that women are commanded by God to be submissive to men, or that homosexuality is a moral abomination. Such views may be vile and stupid and bigoted, but most people who believe in free speech believe that people have the right to express and support even nasty, stupid opinions (though some European countries do place restrictions on the expression of views that are regarded as particularly insulting to specific groups). The key issue is not whether bigots can express and argue for their vile positions, but whether such bigots should be allowed to demean others by hurling racial or ethnic or homophobic slurs. Of course such words are not always used as hate speech; in many cases, a group that has been the target of hate speech will appropriate some of the hate terms to describe themselves when talking *within* the group—doing so may take some of the sting out of such words, and also promotes a sense of in-group solidarity. But there is an obvious difference between people of a common racial or ethnic group using a term among their close friends, and persons outside the group using the same term as a vicious and demeaning insult.

The general debate over hate speech codes often pits those who emphasize the value of unfettered free speech against those concerned to protect the rights and opportunities of minority groups; and in the U.S. courts, this conflict often plays out as a tension between the First Amendment right of free speech and the Fourteenth Amendment right of equal protection under the law. The U.S. Supreme Court has consistently ruled that no speech should be restricted for its ideological content (including hate speech and hate posters or banners or songs); however, the Court does allow some restrictions on "fighting words" and on speech aimed at threatening or intimidating. In *Virginia v. Black* (2003), a majority of the Court ruled that the state of Virginia could legitimately prohibit cross-burning—when used for the purpose of intimidation—because of its notorious history as a "particularly virulent form of intimidation" that has a "long and pernicious history as a signal of impending violence." Outside the United States, most Western countries have much stronger hate speech laws. In the United Kingdom, the Public Order Act of 1986 made incitement to racial hatred an offense punishable by up to seven years imprisonment. In 2001, the Council of Europe adopted a measure (rejected by the United States) criminalizing internet hate speech; it prohibits "any written material, any image or any other representation of ideas or theories, which advocates, promotes or incites hatred, discrimination or violence, against any individual or group of individuals, based on race, colour, descent or national or ethnic origin, as well as religion if used as pretext for any of these factors."

In the United States, the question of free speech currently centers on campus "speech codes." There is no question that racial and ethnic and gender and sexual orientation slurs can create a hostile atmosphere, and can make the academic environment very unpleasant for those who are verbally attacked. Furthermore, the stereotyped thinking promoted by such bigoted labels hardly encourages careful critical thinking. The case for banning hate speech from the campus can be supported on two distinct educational grounds. One, that hate speech creates an atmosphere hostile to many students and thus impairs the learning environment, and two, that the stereotypical thinking encouraged by such language is inimical to careful open-minded critical thinking, which universities strive to promote. On the other hand, colleges and universities cherish their rich tradition of free speech, where even the most unpopular ideas can be presented and championed, and open argument and free exploration of ideas are regarded as cornerstones of the academic environment.

Strawman Distortions

No one is suggesting that even the vilest and stupidest claims and arguments should be banned. The question is whether slurs and derogatory comments should be allowed. It is a strawman distortion to suggest that those who favor campus speech codes believe that some ideas and beliefs should be off-limits to challenge. Those who favor speech codes want to ban hate words such as racial slurs, not the free expression of ideas and arguments. Furthermore, those who favor campus speech codes that ban hate speech agree that there is *value* in absolutely unlimited free speech; however, they believe that there are other goods—such as tolerance, and creating a welcoming and safe campus environment for groups that often feel threatened and unwelcome—which are even more valuable than absolute free speech.

On the other hand, even the fiercest opponents of campus speech codes agree that threats and harassment are unacceptable in any setting, and certainly have no place on college campuses. Opponents of campus speech codes agree that acts of verbal harassment and intimidation—in which hate speech may be used—should not be tolerated. It is one thing to refuse to ban even vile racist slurs; but when a group of white students follow a black student across campus shouting racist comments, or when someone repeatedly phones a gay person to make homophobic insults, that is a threatening act of harassment and intimidation, which should be subject to college disciplinary action or even criminal charges. And obviously it would be a gross strawman distortion to suggest that those who oppose campus speech codes are giving their *approval* of racism or ethnic hatred or any other form of bigotry. Opponents of campus speech codes believe that everyone should have freedom of speech, and that such freedom must allow all speech. They agree that racist slurs are vile and despicable, but insist that freedom of speech includes freedom for even the nastiest speech.

What Is the Common Ground?

Belittling others is wrong; racial and ethnic discrimination and prejudice is wrong. You do not believe that it is morally acceptable to abuse or discriminate against people on the basis of their gender or ethnic group; but if you do, then we are not likely to find any common ground. I sincerely hope you have the good fortune to overcome such biases. No doubt the most effective means of doing so is to actually get to know people of the group you despise—you may very well find yourself becoming friends with and even admiring some of the people you once reviled. There is no better way to enrich your life than by having a wide range of friends, including friends of varying backgrounds and interests and ethnic groups. Perhaps the second best way of overcoming prejudice—perhaps the prejudice that you grew up with in your family or community—is to take a close look at older adults who have held onto their deep prejudices all through their lives: Observe the narrowness of their perspectives and their obsession with the prejudices that seem to control and define them, and ask yourself if you really want to be like that. But it is unlikely that any *argument* will cut through your prejudice. In any case, if you genuinely approve of your own deeply prejudiced and biased value system, then it is doubtful that we can discover any common ground for discussion. That doesn't mean that you must be absolutely free of all prejudice to meet on common ground; that is a wonderful ideal, but perhaps few people reach it. But even if you harbor some prejudices from the community in which you grew up, you recognize that your prejudiced attitude is a flaw, not a virtue; and you are working to overcome it, as best you can.

We also value open inquiry, the free expression of ideas and arguments and views and theories, the insistence that no question is off-limits, no opinion is ruled out of order without a hearing. These values of respecting diversity and protecting free speech can come into conflict; but it is important to remember that this is not a conflict between *opposing* values, but rather a question of different weighting of values we all consider important and worthwhile: the value of free speech and the value of tolerance. The differences on this question can be intense. It is important to keep in mind that we have much more agreement than disagreement on this question.

Arguments in Favor of Unrestricted Free Speech

1. Free speech is not always purely rational; it may also be expressive. *Uncle Tom's Cabin* was not an *argument*, but it had a profound effect on many people, making vivid to them the horrors of slavery. "Protect life" and "preserve choice" are not arguments, but they are important expressions of views, and we would not want to ban them; that is, we would not want to ban them if we believe in freedom of speech and the freedom to express your ideas and beliefs and feelings. The spewing out of racial hatred that one finds at Klan or Nazi rallies is stupid and disgusting. But free speech means free speech, including freedom to express stupid vile beliefs and ideas, even if these are couched in terms of disgusting ethnic slurs. Indeed, it is the ugly speech that poses the question, since no one is interested in banning arguments for or expressions of the views they find attractive. "But their 'arguments' are stupid, baseless, without any redeeming content or intelligent analysis; they just vomit out vile stupid slurs; if we ban *that*, we won't be restricting intelligent argument." But that takes us down the road of deciding whether speech is intelligent or not, and banning speech we judge below the mark.

Judging the quality of speech is something we want to do for ourselves, not have government or other authorities do it for us. The price of genuinely free speech is allowing even nasty ignorant speech to have a free voice.

2. If we ban racist and homophobic speech, we do not deal with the underlying problem. In fact, we may even exacerbate it, when those who hold bigoted views are driven underground, and then find like-minded people—and on the internet, they are easy to find—who intensify and reinforce these views. Indeed, those holding the most extreme positions are likely to gain the largest following. By banning such speech, we may give those who hold deep prejudices a sense of being excluded and persecuted, and drive them together into groups that become even more toxic and hate-filled in their united sense of being outcasts who are treated—and silenced—unjustly.

3. Banning hate speech hides the problem, and thus avoids making serious efforts to deal with the deeper prejudices and ignorance of which hate speech is the ugly symptom. When hate speech is silenced, the hatred does not go away; instead it may go deeper, and fester. It is true that hate speech is hurtful to those who are its target; but that is because prejudice and bias and hatred are hurtful. Instead of banning hate speech, the college community should invest the time and energy and courage to confront the real problem, and take *effective* measures to combat and reduce prejudice (including helping those who *are* prejudiced—and who are themselves often bitter and marginalized and resentful—to deal with the problems at the root of their prejudices). Genuinely effective measures would include changing the curriculum to be more inclusive of the perspectives and accomplishments and cultures of those other than the dominant societal group, actively increasing diversity of both students and faculty, and providing counseling to help those who are enmeshed in their prejudices as well as those who are victims of prejudice. Speech codes are a quick and easy way of pretending to deal with the problem, or of hiding the problem, but without making the commitment and investment to genuinely deal with the problem.

4. Banning speech tends to work in favor of the strongest groups, not the weakest minorities. Powerful groups often use speech codes to suppress the voices of minority groups who are speaking out against oppression and mistreatment. Those who have suffered from prejudiced treatment are often passionate about the mistreatment they have endured; thus their speech on the subject is often emotional and confrontational, and in the heat of expressing their grievances they may use language that is insulting to the groups they regard as their oppressors, and may thus run afoul of speech codes. Being in positions of power, dominant groups are often better positioned to make use of speech code violation charges than are minorities.

Arguments in Favor of Speech Codes

1. An interesting and innovative argument for banning hate speech is based on the claim that hate speech is an inaccurate characterization of what is being banned. Hate speech is more than just speech; by its very nature, it is an *act*, indeed an act of delivering a *threat*.

The question is, does hate speech actually constitute a threat? There is no question that hate speech is often one element of a threat: When a group confronts a target of its prejudiced hatred, and chases that person calling out racist slogans or surrounds and taunts that person, then that is an act of threat and intimidation and harassment that is certainly more than speech. But the question is whether hate speech *in itself* is a threat, whether hate speech falls into a special category of *automatically* expressing a threat whenever it is used. When a student in a classroom uses a racial slur in referring to a classmate, or in the course of class discussion (suppose in the course of seminar discussion a student refers to Albert Einstein using an anti-Semitic slur, or to Martin Luther King using a racial epithet, or to Oscar Wilde using a homophobic slur), does that in itself constitute a *threat* to Jewish or black or gay students in the class? The line between viciously racist speech and threatening speech is not always easy to draw; perhaps—so this argument goes—that is because there is no line to draw. The U.S. Supreme Court has generally ruled that hate speech is not in itself a threat, and thus cannot be—as threats *can* be and are—banned. However, the Court ruled in 2003 that in some circumstances burning a cross—a traditional symbol of the Ku Klux Klan, often placed as a warning or threat to those it targeted—was a form of speech that expressed ideas (despicable ideas, but ideas and thus protected by free speech principles), but that it *also* was the overt expression of a *threat*, and could thus be banned. So at least some forms of speech (counting speech broadly, as including symbolic acts such as cross-burning) *can* be threats. Whether *all* forms of hate speech fall into that category is the challenging question for this argument in favor of banning hate speech.

2. Hate speech poisons the atmosphere, and deprives us of space for genuine discussion; and it marginalizes or even excludes some from the discussion. That is the key point emphasized in this book: If we want to have genuine discussions of our differences, productive arguments about controversial positions, and positive steps toward workable solutions, then ad hominem attacks and strawman distortions must be carefully avoided. Still, it is one thing to be aware of the genuine harm caused by hate speech (harm to intelligent discussion and inquiry, and harm to those who are its targets), and quite another to *ban* hate speech. We should certainly work to prevent hate speech, and strive to educate everyone about its harms; but it does not follow that it should be *banned* by speech codes.

3. Hate speech hurts, demeans, and excludes. It is easy for those who have enjoyed privileged status to proclaim the importance of permitting all forms of speech; but they have never felt the sting of verbal taunts that challenge one's worth and dignity, taunts that are used to exclude from the group as well as from participation in discussion. Hate speech makes people feel unwelcome, and it is often directed at those who have traditionally been underrepresented on college campuses, and who are thus already less confident of being welcomed and included. It may be difficult for those who have never felt marginalized—who have never felt the pain of hate attacks while being a vulnerable minority—to recognize the hurt and insecurity such attacks can cause. If you are a Christian in the United States, then you may well be offended by a cartoon that ridicules Jesus, but you will hardly feel threatened by it. But if you are a Muslim in the United States, a cartoon ridiculing the Prophet Muhammad will be felt quite differently: not only as offensive, but also as a personal attack implying that Muslims are unwelcome and unwanted in this country.

4. By banning hate speech, we make clear our basic values of inclusiveness and rejection of prejudice. When a college or a country bans hate speech, it makes a very important statement of its basic inclusiveness values, and its disgust with those who would foster prejudice and hatred. That strong and publicly enforced statement of values sends a clear signal to those who have been the victims of prejudice that they are welcomed and respected in this community; and it sends a clear signal to those who hold prejudices that their views and values are regarded with disgust by the larger community.

Where Do We Stand?

Though the controversy over free speech versus codes against hate speech is often intense, for most of us—whichever side of the debate we favor—there is much more common than disputed ground. With few exceptions, all of us agree on the importance of free speech—especially the importance of free speech and open debate on college and university campuses, where no idea or argument should be ineligible for debate and discussion. In fact, even countries that ban hate speech—such as England, Sweden, France, and Canada—stress in their governmental principles the importance of the right of free speech. Thus the French Declaration of the Rights of Man and of the Citizen declares that "The free communication of thoughts and opinions is one of the most precious rights of mankind"; the Canadian Charter of Rights and Freedoms states that among the fundamental freedoms are "freedom of thought, belief, opinion and expression." But those countries do not regard freedom of speech, important as it is, as an *absolute* freedom; rather, they believe that it can, in very special cases, be trumped by other important rights (including the right not to be demeaned by hate speech) and by other vital interests (such as the interest in preventing the promotion of racial, ethnic, and religious hatred, which can lead to violence against minority groups). Those on the other side (who believe freedom of speech is so basic and essential that even hate speech must be tolerated) *agree* that hate speech is vile, and that stirring up hatred against persons on the basis of their race, religion, ethnicity, gender, or sexual orientation is a terrible wrong. Indeed, almost everyone *agrees* that free speech is a very valuable right *and* that hate speech is terrible. The *differences* in their views are real and important, but those differences should not obscure the very important basic *agreements* between the competing sides.

Perhaps the key differences between them are two. First, advocates of free speech who oppose banning even vile hate speech believe that free speech must be carefully guarded against any restrictions based on content: Once we allow such restrictions, then more restrictions are likely to follow, and there is danger of free speech being gradually eroded away. Those who want to ban hate speech, in contrast, are confident that hate speech restrictions can be made without threatening the basic principle and the basic value of free speech. Second, while both sides *agree* that racial and ethnic and homophobic and religious bias is a serious problem, and that promotion of such hatred and bias is a serious wrong, they *disagree* on the best way to combat hate speech, as well as the prejudices it promotes and from which it grows. Those who want to ban hate speech believe that such a ban is the most effective means of blocking hate speech, and of expressing disgust with hate speech and combating prejudice: When a college (or a country) bans hate speech, it makes a clear statement that it regards such racist speech and prejudiced attitudes as so vile and disgusting that they have no place on the campus (or in the country). From the other perspective, those who reject bans on hate speech believe that such bans are *not* the most effective way of combating prejudice: The ban on hate speech drives the hate speech and the hatred itself underground, but does not confront it, does not really deal with it or take effective steps to make clear *why* it is vile and destructive, and makes no effort to help those expressing or feeling such prejudices to overcome their problems. It is not easy to counsel and convert those who are locked into racist or ethnic prejudice; but silencing them avoids even trying. The basic difference then is not over the vileness of such prejudice-based hate speech, but instead over the best means of opposing and reducing it. In the heat of disagreements over free speech and campus speech codes, it is easy to focus on the genuine differences, but it is important to remember that the agreements are even deeper than the differences.

Questions for Reflection

1. We run into problems when some voices can drown out others. The oil and natural gas industries spend many millions advertising how environmentally friendly their industries are, and how good they are for the economy. Their voices are so well-financed that they tend to drown out those who are concerned about fracking, the dangers of offshore drilling, the environmental risks posed by pipelines, the environmental and health damages caused by burning fossil fuels, and the major environmental damage caused by extracting oil from oil sands. If we value free speech, there is no doubt that these enormously wealthy industries, with yearly and even quarterly profits in the billions of dollars, should be able to give their arguments and express their views. Does genuine free speech require "equal time" for those with opposing views, or at least *some* comparable opportunity to make their views known?

2. "Fringe" candidates are not invited to debates. Obviously we don't want every kook who claims he or she is a candidate for president cluttering up the stage; on the other hand, the only ones who are allowed on the stage are those with well-funded campaigns (Herman Cain could appear in the debates, because he had substantial wealth, notwithstanding the fact that he was grossly unprepared for a presidential candidacy). How would you solve this?

3. The U.S. Supreme Court has ruled that in some circumstances cross-burning is not protected speech, because it is actually a threat. Flag-burning may be almost as vile to some people, but flag-burning is not associated with acts of violence: You may feel profoundly angry and disgusted at someone who burns a flag in protest, but the flag burner is obviously posing no physical threat to you; on the other hand, cross-burning has traditionally been associated with brutal physical attacks and murder, and a burning cross might very well be regarded—and intended—as a threat against racial or ethnic groups. Is there any other form of speech that might also be regarded as more of a threat than merely being speech, and thus subject to ban? For example, book burning has a long association with attacks on those who wrote or who favor the book (the burning of books was often regarded by the book burners as a substitute for a desired attack on the unavailable author; sometimes books were burned prior to burning their author). What about hanging in effigy? What about shouted slurs against homosexuals, which strike fear because they are often followed by physical attack?

4. Minorities are often in vulnerable positions, much more vulnerable than are majorities. In the United States, ridiculing the Pope is offensive; ridiculing the Prophet is even more offensive, because it is directed at a vulnerable minority population, which feels threatened and marginalized much more easily (of course one should be able to criticize the *views* of either the Pope or the Prophet; but that is a different matter). Should there be special protection for those in vulnerable minorities?

5. Denying the holocaust is a criminal offense in many European countries. Certainly denial of the holocaust is stupid, and to many it is hurtful, and it is often associated with extreme anti-Semitism. Still, it may seem strange to single out holocaust denial—of all the possible stupid and vile views—for special criminal penalties. After all, the Inquisition—in which heretics and "witches" were tortured and executed—was also horrific, but it is not a criminal offense to deny that the Inquisition occurred. Slavery was a horrific wrong, but denying the existence of slavery is not criminalized. But of course the holocaust is comparatively recent—there are people who were imprisoned in the death camps who are still alive, as well as persons who participated in various ways in the mass murder of Jews and others regarded as "undesirables" by the Nazis. In addition to being recent, Europe is the very place where the holocaust occurred. And finally, the holocaust—with its systematic mass murder efforts at genocide—stands out

as one of the singularly evil events of modern history. Do those special factors justify the special free speech restriction against denial of the holocaust? Are there any special *disadvantages* to not allowing people to argue that the holocaust did not occur?

6. A fan yelling racial slurs at a basketball game will be escorted out, and may be denied future admission. Very few people oppose that policy. If a student voices racist, sexist, ethnic, or sexual orientation slurs during a class, should the same policy apply? Should the classroom policy be stricter, less strict, or the same as that in the athletic arena?

7. The internet has made possible the easy dissemination of hate speech of all sorts, as well as making it possible for racists and bigots to find one another and organize into groups. In Europe, there is an internet ban on hate speech, and on any speech that promotes racial or ethnic hatred. Is that a good idea, or no?

Additional Resources

Andrew Altman (professor of philosophy at Georgia State University) offers strong arguments in favor of campus speech codes; see "Liberalism and Campus Hate Speech: A Philosophical Examination," *Ethics*, 103 (January 1993), and "Equality and Expression: The Radical Paradox," *Social Philosophy and Policy*, 21, no. 2 (July 2004): 1–22. For a clear statement of the case against campus codes, see Jonathan Rauch (who writes for the *Economist*): *The Kindly Inquisitors: The New Attacks on Free Thought* (Chicago: University of Chicago Press, 1993), and "In Defense of Prejudice: Why Incendiary Speech Must Be Protected," *Harper's Magazine* (May 1995).

An excellent book on the subject, which includes examination of key court cases as well as essays from a variety of perspectives, is edited by Milton Heumann and Thomas W. Church, *Hate Speech on Campus: Cases, Case Studies, and Commentary* (Boston: Northeastern University Press, 1997). Judith Wagner DeCew, "Free Speech and Offensive Expression," *Social Philosophy and Policy*, 21, no. 2 (July 2004): 81–100, addresses both legal and ethical issues. Cass R. Sunstein, *Democracy and the Problem of Free Speech* (New York: The Free Press, 1993), offers a thoughtful study of a variety of issues related to free speech. Timothy C. Shiell, *Campus Hate Speech on Trial* (Lawrence, KS: University Press of Kansas, 1998), develops a detailed and fair account of both the development of campus speech codes and the court cases surrounding them.

The American Civil Liberties Union (ACLU) has consistently opposed restrictions on speech, even when the speaker is advocating positions that most regard as vile. An excellent statement of its position can be found in an ACLU briefing paper, "Hate Speech on Campus," at archive.aclu.org /library/pbp16.html; see also its home site at www.aclu.org.

Speaking of Race, Speaking of Sex: Hate Speech, Civil Rights, and Civil Liberties (New York: New York University Press, 1995), by Henry Louis Gates, Jr., Anthony Griffin, Donald Lively, and Nadine Strasssen, is a strong collection of essays in defense of free speech and opposing speech codes; the introduction, by Ira Glasser, is a clear overview of the general argument for free speech.

Some of the most eloquent defenders of codes banning hate speech have been advocates of a legal perspective called "Critical Race Theory." For an excellent collection of papers within this viewpoint, see Mari J. Matsuda, Charles R. Lawrence III, Richard Delgado, and Kimberlé Williams Crenshaw, *Words That Wound: Critical Race Theory, Assaultive Speech, and the First Amendment* (Boulder, CO: Westview Press, 1993). Mari J. Matsuda's "Public Response to Racist Speech: Considering the Victim's Story" is reprinted in the collection, and is particularly strong in bringing to life the experience of victims of hate speech.

W. Bradley Wendel, in "'Certain Fundamental Truths': A Dialectic on Negative and Positive Liberty in Hate-Speech Cases," *Law and Contemporary Problems* 65 (Spring 2002): 33–85, offers a very interesting and readable dialogue on both legal and ethical issues related to hate speech. See also Martin P. Golding, *Free Speech on Campus* (Lanham, MD: Rowman & Littlefield, 2000).

MySearchLab Connections

The website for the First Amendment Center, at http://www.firstamendmentcenter.org, contains a wealth of material on contemporary issues related to freedom of speech, freedom of the press, and freedom of religion. Go to the *Ethics Updates* website at http://ethics .sandiego.edu, and under "Ethical Theory" click on "Rights Theories," scroll down to the NPR "Talk of the Nation" recordings; the "Kids and Free Speech" program is excellent. One of the most important free speech rulings by the Supreme Court of Canada is *R. v. Zundel*, 1992, in which the Court ruled that even the vile, false, and stupid speech of a holocaust denier is protected by the Canadian Charter of Rights and Freedoms; the case can be found at http://www.scc-csc.gc.ca/decisions/index-eng.asp (in the website of the Supreme Court of Canada); look up cases for 1992. The U.S. Supreme Court has generally been very protective of free speech (though it is not quite so insistent on protecting the speech rights of high school students). In *Snyder v. Phelps*, 2011, the Court ruled (by an eight-to-one majority) that members of the Westboro Baptist Church have the right to demonstrate outside the funerals of U.S. soldiers killed in action. Almost everyone despises the actions of the Westboro group: They carry signs saying "thank God for dead soldiers," proclaiming that "God hates you," celebrating the deaths of soldiers, and viciously attacking gays and lesbians. While there may not be many things agreed upon by both the left and the right in the United States, both agree that the behavior of the Westboro Baptist Church demonstrators is repulsive. But in keeping with a long tradition, the Court ruled that even stupid, hateful, vile speech is protected by the Constitution. In *Virginia v. Black*, 2003, the Court ruled that while the First Amendment right of free speech is vitally important and must be protected, certain forms of "speech"—such as cross-burning—may be illegal because they are a form of illegal intimidation that pose a direct threat of violence. In *Tinker v. Des Moines Independent Community School District*, 1969, the Court ruled that the rights of students to protest (in this case, by wearing black arm bands to protest the Vietnam War) must be protected unless the protests cause "substantial interference with school discipline or the rights of others" (which the wearing of arm bands did not). However, in a fiercely debated case (decided by a five-to-four margin) the Court upheld the suspension of a student who displayed a banner saying "BONG HITS FOR JESUS" at a school sponsored rally that took place outside the school grounds (*Morse v. Frederick*, 2007). All the U.S. Supreme Court cases can be found at www.oyez.org.

17

CORPORATE RESPONSIBILITY

Chapter Outline

A business is in business to make money; so long as it maximizes profits, stays within the law, and does not cheat its employees or customers, it is fulfilling its obligations.

A business is a citizen of the community. It must make a profit to survive, but it also has obligations to the community and country—and world—in which it exists; a corporation has obligations not only to its stockholders, but to others as well.

These are two basically different views concerning the moral obligations of businesses. On one side, the key obligation of corporations is to make profits for their investors and stockholders. On the other side, businesses—like individuals—have obligations that go beyond pure self-interest. *Both* sides of this debate agree that businesses have an obligation to follow basic moral principles: not lying or cheating or engaging in fraudulent behavior. But on the former view, the business of a business is to make a profit for its investors and stockholders, and beyond that it has no moral obligations to anyone other than following the basic moral rules that forbid lying and cheating and coercing; it must follow the rules of the game, but it has no obligation beyond that obligation of minimal decency. On the latter view, businesses have an obligation not to lie and cheat, just as you and I do; but just as we also have moral obligations to help others and contribute to the good of our community, so also do businesses.

Both sides agree concerning the *negative* obligations of businesses: Businesses should not lie, cheat, steal, endanger others, or break the law. The interesting questions come in the area of *positive* obligations. We generally believe that individuals have at least *some* obligation to help others. (Not everyone agrees; but most of us agree that if we see a child is drowning in a flood-swollen stream, we have at least an obligation to call 9-1-1, probably an obligation to throw the child a rope, and perhaps even an obligation to go to considerable trouble and even some risk to save the child's life. The range and scope of the obligation may be disputed, but few would deny that we have at least *some* obligation.)

In fact, most businesses consider it "good business" to provide positive help, and they often publicize their efforts: They make special "charitable contributions" when their customers buy a car during a special month-long promotion, they sponsor Little League teams, or they contribute to supporting a ballet company. In many such cases, the "sacrifice" made by the business is not a sacrifice at all: The pizza parlor that sponsors a Little League team gets advertising, as well as hordes of ravenous children and their parents stopping by for postgame pizza parties. The automobile company is attempting to increase its sales, as well as enhance its image. That is not to deny that some of these may be genuinely generous acts, with positive motives; but many are far from being self-sacrificing. The really difficult questions arise outside the glare of publicity: "Our manufacturing plant is releasing high levels of carbon into the atmosphere; we are within the legal limits, but by installing a new scrubbing device, we could reduce our carbon emissions significantly, with less damage to the environment. The new scrubbing device is expensive, and retrofitting the emission system will also cost money. Installing the device will not bankrupt the company, and will not put the company at risk (our profits are quite substantial), but it will reduce our profits. *Should* we install the new scrubber? Are we morally *obligated* to install the new scrubber?" Bank of America imposed a new fee on those who use its debit cards; it was legal, though certainly not justified by any additional costs (the use of debit cards actually reduced its processing costs). Bank of America was not driven to the added fee by desperate need for more income. Was this charge wrong? (It stopped because it received terrible publicity, and many customers were moving their bank deposits elsewhere; not because of any moral considerations.)

Sometimes it is suggested that business is amoral: Its only concern is to turn a profit, and "all's fair in love and war" and also in business. But obviously every enterprise, business or otherwise, that has an impact on others also has moral implications; and business has an enormous impact on the lives of all of us. Business decisions can literally ruin the lives of many people—taking their life savings, depriving them of meaningful work, and polluting their communities. The business decision of Ford Motor Company to sell cars with dangerously defective gas tanks, which resulted in a number of people being burned to death and others suffering terrible debilitating burns, had a deadly impact on many individuals and a tragic impact on many families. Like all human endeavors, business is— for better or worse—an enterprise with profound moral issues and implications.

Strawman Distortions

Very few people believe that a business or corporation can or should devote itself entirely and exclusively to doing moral good; it must, if it is to remain in business, make a profit. So it is a strawman distortion to claim that the demand for corporate responsibility is a demand that businesses sacrifice all concern for profitability in the interests of promoting the public good. On the other side, consider those who believe that the focus of business must be on making a profit, and that businesses should not seek the public good at the expense of any reduction in profits: Those who hold this view do *not* believe that businesses have no moral obligations. To the contrary, they believe that businesses have an obligation to follow the law and to follow all the standard moral principles that almost all of us value: Businesses must not lie to their customers, or cheat their employees, or endanger the life or health of others, or break the law, and so on. So it is a *strawman* to suggest that on this view businesses would be amoral and follow no moral principles whatsoever.

What Is the Common Ground?

We all agree on some basic points, and most would agree on some others. Most of us agree that it is legitimate for a company to pursue profits. Some strict Marxists would disagree, insisting that profits are money that is stolen from the workers. But most believe that there is nothing wrong in itself with the pursuit of profit; indeed, some people even think that there is something morally exemplary in the pursuit of maximum profit—but that goes too far for most. What almost all of us agree on is that the legitimate pursuit of profit does *not* trump all other concerns. During the American Civil War, some clothing manufacturers made enormous profits by selling inferior uniforms and inferior quality boots and shoes to the military; the clothing and boots soon fell apart, and the soldiers suffered. The profits on such sales were huge, and fortunes were made, but the profits were *not* legitimate. A few years ago a pharmacy owner diluted some expensive medications, and then sold them at full price. The drugs were less effective, and as a result, some patients were slow in recovering, and others died. The pharmacist increased profits, but the manner of doing so was morally and legally wrong. Some companies collected waste oil, containing high levels of lead and mercury and other heavy metals, and accepted payment for disposing of these hazardous oil wastes in ways that would minimize pollution (through burning the wastes in special high-temperature rotary kiln incinerators); but instead of actually disposing of the polluted oil in a rotary kiln incinerator, they sold the polluted oil to the owners and managers of large apartment and office buildings in metropolitan areas, and the polluted oil was burned as fuel oil—while the high levels of lead and mercury were released into the air for the city dwellers to breathe, resulting in increased rates of serious and even fatal illness. Those who collected and sold the oil made a fortune (and often they got away with it: They were charging much less than legitimate hazardous waste companies for taking away the polluted oil, and they were charging the building operators much less than they would have to pay for clean oil, so everyone was making money—and the citizens who were breathing the polluted air, and suffering respiratory diseases and increased risk of cancer, were none the wiser). But anyone who thinks that is a *legitimate* means of increasing profits is a moral monster.

So we agree that businesses have an obligation to operate within the laws and regulations (often they do not, but that does not change the fact that they have that obligation; just as a father who does not pay child support for his children still has an *obligation*—both legal and moral—to do so). Furthermore, we agree that in business one has an obligation to follow the same basic principles of morality that apply to all human activities: Don't cheat, don't lie, don't steal, and don't harm others. When a business runs a false or misleading advertisement—advertising Listerine as effective in preventing colds, advertising Anacin as a special combination pain reliever (when in fact the only pain-relieving ingredient in

Anacin is aspirin), promoting a drug for a certain disease even when the company knows that the drug is useless for that purpose, advertising Head-On as an effective pain reliever (when in fact it is simply water with a few ingredients to give it a strong scent and a slightly different consistency)—then it has violated the basic moral principle that we learn in childhood, and that is fundamental to maintaining trust and cooperation and mutual respect: Tell the truth; don't lie or deceive. The fact that you are engaged in business does not exempt you from the basic moral principles that are essential in human relationships. Even Milton Friedman—the most vigorous advocate of the view that corporations and other businesses have no positive obligation other than maximizing profits—agrees that businesses have an obligation to follow both the law and basic moral principles.

Arguments against Corporate Responsibility

1. Businesses/corporations are in business to make profits, and they have that obligation to their investors. If their investors wish to contribute funds for charitable purposes, that is their choice; but the business in which they invest has no right to give away funds that should be distributed as profits to shareholders: Profits are not their money to give. This is the classic argument against corporate responsibility; it was made famous by the economist, Milton Friedman. (Of course if you, Betty, are the sole owner of "Betty's Pretty Good Pizza," then there is no problem with you providing free pizza for a homeless shelter or a charity fund-raiser, or contributing money from your pizza shop profits to sponsor a community soccer team; you have no investors who are entitled to a share of your profits.)

This argument has some force. I am a stockholder in your company, and thus I am entitled to my fair share of the company profits. If you decide to distribute some of those profits as charitable donations, or reduce the profits by installing pollution control devices beyond those that are legally required, then you are spending money that is rightfully *mine*. The ways in which you are spending that money may be good, but it is not your money to spend. If I decide to donate some of my stock dividends to charity or spend my money reducing pollution, that is *my* choice, not yours to make for me.

There are two possible replies to this argument. First, there is an underlying assumption in the argument that stockholders are only interested in increasing dividends, and that assumption is questionable. Obviously investors are interested in making a return on their investment, but most investors are not as obsessed with maximizing income as this argument suggests. Investors have other interests as well, including interests in a healthy environment and a well-functioning community. Thus many investors may find it quite reasonable for corporations to seek less than maximum profits in order to achieve important social goals: Not all goods that benefit investors are strictly monetary. Second, even *if* we suppose that investors are concerned only with increasing profits and thus increasing the return on their investments, it may be the case that when corporations invest in social goods they are actually maximizing their own profits. A manufacturing corporation that spends extra money on pollution control—beyond what is legally required—may enhance its reputation as a responsible reliable company and thus makes its products more attractive to consumers as well as attracting and retaining more dedicated and satisfied employees. For example, many Fortune 500 companies provide domestic partner insurance benefits to their employees, even though they are not required to do so; but that enhances their images as progressive companies that care for their employees, and thus aids them in recruiting talented young workers. When a company makes a special effort to improve conditions in its community, or reduce pollution, or provide better working conditions and benefits to its employees, the company may create a better image, and thus attract more customers and investors as well as recruiting and keeping more talented workers, thus providing greater long-term dividends for their stockholders.

2. If corporations confine themselves to pursuit of profit, that will produce maximum efficiency. Every company will strive (within legal limits) to maximize its profits, the weaker and less efficient companies will be weeded out while the most effective businesses will prosper, and the overall economy will run at peak efficiency. Under such competitive conditions, the "invisible hand" of economic power will insure that everyone prospers.

That's an appealing myth, but the reality has rarely matched the myth: The Great Depression and the 2008 collapse of the financial markets are among the most obvious problems for this optimistic story. In a global economy, the problems with this story are even more evident. When global corporations can swiftly and easily move resources not only around the country but around the world, having every company seek maximum profits (with minimum regulation) may yield enormous short-term profits, but at the cost of widespread economic misery and long-term economic disaster. Small companies cannot compete with the enormous economic power of large corporations—which can demand huge discounts from manufacturers and suppliers that smaller companies are denied, and can lobby local, state, and national governments for special benefits and tax breaks that smaller companies do not receive. Communities are desperate to attract the jobs and investments that large corporations can provide by locating a manufacturing plant or distribution center in their town; thus communities compete against one another to offer the most attractive deal to the corporation: deals that exempt the corporation from paying local taxes for a number of years, that provide upgraded highways and improved infrastructure in the vicinity of the new manufacturing center, perhaps even offering special reduced rates on water supply and on waste management. The state that is competing for such industries may pass laws (such as "right to work" laws) that prevent workers from organizing for higher wages and better working conditions, and thus drive down the cost of labor. When the company has been at that location for a decade, and its special privileges are about to expire, the company can threaten to move elsewhere if the special benefits are not renewed; and indeed, it may well move elsewhere in any case—perhaps to another country where environmental regulations are less stringent and thus costs of manufacturing are less, and where workers' wages and governmental standards for worker safety are even lower. The abandoned community is left with enormous debt and a large investment in highways that are now unused, along with a large number of newly unemployed workers who now—rather than paying taxes to support the community—are in need of government services. All of these factors may produce great wealth, but that wealth becomes concentrated in fewer and fewer hands, and eventually a large market economy can no longer function (luxury goods have a ready market, but the great mass of ordinary citizens cannot afford the houses and furniture and appliances that drive a market economy).

3. The most interesting argument against corporations making contributions to social goods is that such contributions are an abuse of the corporation's power. In a democracy, questions concerning major social issues (such as levels of pollution control, efforts to stop discrimination, and the level of obligation to provide jobs) are major issues, and

they should be decided by the voters, or by the people elected by the voters. Corporation officers are *not* elected by the people; and when corporations make social decisions that are not required by law, that gives corporations too much power, and it is a power that is illegitimate in a democracy.

There is no question that multinational corporations have enormous power—many major corporations have more income and greater wealth than the entire gross national product of a number of countries. *If* corporations actually refrained from influencing social and governmental policy, this argument might have greater force. But in fact a number of industries—energy companies are perhaps the most obvious—are deeply involved in the regulatory process for their own industries. For example, the oil industry does enormous lobbying in favor of drilling in deep ocean water and other environmentally sensitive areas, limiting safety regulations for oil rigs, increasing levels of allowable pollution, lowering worker safety standards and relaxing their enforcement, and establishing tax breaks for their industries—just to name the most obvious. They also do massive advertising to influence public opinion (e.g., the massive advertising by the natural gas companies to convince the public of the safety of extracting oil from shale fields by means of "fracking," by oil companies to convince the public of the critical need for drilling in environmentally fragile areas, by the coal industry to oppose stricter standards on pollution control, and by pharmaceutical companies to ease the requirements on drug testing); they fund candidates who support their interests; and they set up and support citizens' groups to influence public opinion and to exert pressure on legislators (some of these are grassroots groups of genuine citizens who support views that the corporations favor; others are "astroturf" groups that appear to be run by private citizens but are in fact funded by corporations and operated by company-appointed public relations firms masquerading as groups of concerned citizens). There may be good reasons—in a country that aspires to function as a democracy—to greatly restrict or even ban large corporations from exerting such massive influence on elections and on elected officials; but that is another question. In any case, the argument that corporations should not promote social goods (such as fighting discrimination through their hiring programs or operating by stricter environmental standards than the law requires or refusing to buy or sell lumber from endangered rain forests or refusing to sell tobacco products in their stores) is a hollow argument, when in fact corporations are investing enormous resources in lobbying, advertising, and electoral efforts to influence government legislation and regulation. The stark reality is that corporations have a massive influence on social issues through their lobbying, public issue advertising, and support for specific candidates for local, state, and national office. It would be very strange to suggest that it is somehow a corruption of the democratic process when one company sets higher and more costly standards of pollution control than the government requires, while other companies are spending massive amounts to prevent stricter environmental regulations (e.g., auto companies striving to prevent stricter emission standards and the petroleum industry fighting tighter regulation of offshore drilling) and to relax restrictions already in place (such as restrictions on drilling or building pipelines through environmentally sensitive areas).

Arguments in Favor of Corporate Responsibility

1. The most basic and widely accepted argument for corporate responsibility—for corporate contributions to the public good—is a simple one: It's good business. As noted in answer to the first argument *against* corporate social responsibility, businesses—from

mom and pop pizza parlors to multinational corporations—have long since discovered the benefits (the monetary benefits) from contributing to social goods. When Betty's Pizza sponsors a soccer team in the local youth league, the restaurant improves its community image, gains positive advertising when the kids wear soccer jerseys emblazoned with "Betty's Pizza," and sells lots of pizza to hungry young soccer players and their families: a very nice return on a modest investment. Betty may sponsor the team out of her sincere devotion to children and because of her genuine belief in the positive physical and social effects on the children; but whatever her motives, Betty soon learns that the money she donates to support youth soccer is a good business investment. When a major corporation provides domestic partner benefits even though it is not required by law to do so, the directors of the corporation may do so because they genuinely believe that discrimination against gay and lesbian couples is a moral and social wrong; but the corporation also gains goodwill in the gay and lesbian community (with its significant purchasing power) as well as a progressive image that improves the corporation's chances of hiring talented young professionals. When a manufacturing company sets very strict standards for pollution control, its reputation for quality control is enhanced, and its products become more attractive to consumers (especially environmentally concerned customers). Even if such corporate social investments are costly in the short term, they may well return long-term profits.

2. The first reason for corporations to make social investments is that it is often to their own benefit. In those cases, it is a win-win situation. If the local symphony orchestra can convince a commercial airline that by making a substantial tax-deductible donation to the orchestra, the airline will greatly enhance its image as a socially responsible company, and will be listed prominently in every concert program, and the affluent orchestra goers will be more disposed to choose that airline for their next trip, then everyone comes out ahead: The community gains support for its orchestra, and the airline gains enough customers to more than offset the cost of the contribution.

   The second reason in support of corporate responsibility is much broader, and attempts to justify corporate social responsibility *beyond* the level that would contribute to corporate profits. This is an argument that corporations *should* support social goods even when such support cuts into their profits. When a corporation in Pittsburgh makes a substantial profit, obviously much of that profit is the result of its own effective efforts: the quality of its production facilities, the expertise of its design department, the creativity of its marketing staff, and the careful planning of its management. But the corporation's efforts are by no means the only factor enabling the corporation to turn a profit. In addition, there is the city and regional infrastructure—highways, bridges, airports, railroad lines, and the locks that make the area rivers navigable for commerce—essential to the operations of the corporation; the higher education programs at the University of Pittsburgh and Carnegie-Mellon and the Penn State system (and throughout the country) that trained the highly skilled workers and managers that made the company successful; the public schools and technical colleges that prepared the many employees—from truck drivers to maintenance personnel—essential for the basic functioning of the corporation, and prepared others for higher educational training; the well-enforced tradition of basic integrity among city and state workers, which allowed the corporation to do its work without the necessity of bribing public officials; the police force and fire departments that protected corporation property as well as its employees; a medical system to protect the health of employees; and the area cultural and recreational facilities that make the area a desirable place for valued employees to live. No doubt you could think of many other factors that have been essential conditions for the corporation's success, and to which a wide range of community members—both current and past—have made vital contributions. According to this argument, all of those community members are *stakeholders* in the corporate profits, just as the corporate stockholders are. The corporation can legitimately claim a profit for its achievements, but the multitude of other people—not employed by the corporation—who laid the essential foundation for the corporation's success are also entitled to share in the corporate profits. If the company is a pharmaceutical company, its work is based on generations of dedicated efforts by scientists and researchers and doctors and research subjects who built the great body of scientific knowledge that makes possible the corporation's profitable new research results. On this view, the corporation has an *obligation* to give back to the community: an obligation that is just as strong as the obligation to its employees and stockholders.

Where Do We Stand?

Corporations have a responsibility to do no harm. Packaging junk bonds and selling them to unsuspecting investors as blue chip investments is deceitful and harmful. Selling a car that the manufacturer knows to have an exploding gas tank that is likely to cause deaths is wrong, notwithstanding the fact that it maximized profits. Pharmaceutical companies maximized profits when they marketed antidepressants to adolescents after their research showed that those drugs significantly increased the likelihood of adolescent suicide, but those profits were wrongfully gained. When a major pharmaceutical company promoted a useless medicine for an off-label purpose, it was fined billions of dollars, but profited much more than the fine; the fine could be written off as just a cost of doing business—the company's profits were billions of dollars more than its fine—but what the company was doing was wrong. Causing environmental damage that results in cancers is wrong, even if you never get caught and what you do is within the limits of the law. That is not to say that corporations must be absolutely perfect, and never pose risks. When you drive to school, you damage the atmosphere and pose a risk to pedestrians; but that is quite different from speeding through a school zone at 70 mph. When you manufacture a car, it is always possible to make the car safer; you could design your car like a stock car, in which drivers often walk away from high-speed crashes with just a few bumps and scratches; but at some point, the process becomes too expensive. Drawing the line precisely may be difficult; but just as there is a difference between night and day though we may have a hard time drawing an exact moment (that's why we have the concept of twilight), there is a clear difference between cutting corners in ways that pose unacceptable risks and economizing in a responsible manner.

If a corporation pursues a policy that you would think wrong if you adopted it for your own benefit, or that you would think wrong as an "impartial spectator," then it is still wrong if the corporation does it on behalf of its stockholders. If you are a corporate officer, you have an obligation to the stockholders who have invested in your company in hopes of making a return on their investments; but that obligation to your stockholders does *not* legitimize cheating or harming others in order to maximize profits. You have an obligation to support your children; that does not mean that you have the right to rob a liquor store in order to buy a bicycle for your kid. These are settled points, on which almost all of us would agree. The more difficult questions arise when we consider *positive* obligations of businesses and corporations. If we confine the questions to cases in which businesses can "do themselves good" while doing good for the community—for example, by helping a local community college set up a new training program that will provide well-trained local talent for skilled jobs the corporation needs to fill—then there is still no controversy. But if we push further, into questions of whether a corporation has an obligation to aid its society and community in ways that do *not* increase its profits, then the questions get tougher. Most people—with the exception of doctrinaire disciples of Milton Friedman—would agree businesses have at least some modest obligation to contribute, to reciprocate the many benefits the business has received from both present and past members of the community. At the other extreme, no one would require that a business bankrupt itself in order to aid the community. The actual degree and limits of business/corporate social responsibility remain a question on which there is significant and genuine disagreement. Even so, the areas of agreement are at least as worth noting as the remaining areas of disagreement. Friedman is the classical advocate for the view that the *only* positive obligation of business is to make a profit; but even Friedman would *agree* that all businesses have a strong moral obligation not to harm or endanger others, to play by the rules and regulations (it is wrong to bribe a government official in order to win a contract, and it is wrong to hack into another company's computer system in order to steal trade secrets or disrupt a competitor's shipping schedule), and to be honest in dealings with both employees and the public. And today, there are very few companies that do not devote at least some resources and efforts for the benefit of the community. They may well want to reap long-term monetary benefits for their good works, and they certainly are eager to publicize their generosity ("for every touchdown scored by the Elephants, Queezy Chemicals will donate $100 to fighting childhood leukemia"); still, whatever their motives and level of generosity, a visible commitment to the good of the community is important to most businesses and corporations.

Questions for Reflection

1. Corporation X moves a factory into Springfield because it is offered a fabulous deal. Then after the tax break is over, it gets a better offer, leaving Springfield with the enormous costs of highways and infrastructure. Is this a legitimate business practice?

2. Is it legitimate for a company to play one city (or state) off against another? In 2011, Sears claimed that it was considering moving its corporate headquarters from Chicago to Columbus, Ohio. Sears entered into discussions with Ohio to consider relocating there, and Ohio offered $400 million in incentives and tax breaks to coax Sears to make the move. Illinois, under threat of losing a large company and a large employer, offered Sears a 15-year incentive plan of some $275 million if it would stay. Most analysts believed that the company never really had any plans to move to Ohio, but instead used the Ohio offer as leverage to extract a better deal from Illinois. Economics professor Edward Hill (quoted in a December 14 article in the *Cleveland Plain Dealer*) put it bluntly: "Sears should give 10 percent to Ohio as a thank you gift. . . . It's clear they were after financing. It was a shakedown for money." There is no question that the process was legal, and it is certainly not unusual. Was Sears engaged in a morally legitimate business practice?

3. Your pro baseball team has been supported by the folks of Metropolis for half a century. When the team was losing, the fans still bought tickets

and came to the games. The city built the team a nice new stadium about 20 years ago. It's still a very nice stadium, though there are a few in the league that are even better, with more rows of expensive loges. The tax base for Metropolis is down right now—a couple of major industries have gone bankrupt—but the team is still well-supported and is making a steady profit for you, the owner. Another city, Megalopolis, wants a pro baseball team, and is offering to build a fabulous new stadium *and* give you all the money from the parking concession. Clearly you would make more money in Megalopolis. You're already quite wealthy, of course, but you would still like to have more money. Would it be morally wrong to move the team to Megalopolis?

Suppose that you are not owner, but CEO; the team is owned by a corporation, with many investors; would that change anything? Would it be wrong for you to make less than optimum profit by keeping the team in Metropolis?

4. There are several perfectly legal companies that specialize in "remixing" the waste products from various industries, to bring those waste products under legal pollution limits and allow them to be used for fuel. Here's how it works. Your manufacturing firm, X, uses solvents to clean the residue from its metal-working process; the solvent waste product contains 10 parts/million of mercury. The regulations (let us suppose) say that if the solvent contains 6 or less parts/million of mercury, it can be burned for fuel in your plant. Being able to burn your waste solvent would be great: You could save money on fuel costs, and you also avoid the high costs of disposing of the polluted solvents. Unfortunately, your solvents are too high in mercury, so you can't use them for fuel. Down the highway is another manufacturing firm, Y, that also uses solvents for cleaning; its production process leaves no mercury in the solvents, but does leave 10 parts/million of lead. Like its manufacturing neighbor X, it can't legally burn its waste solvent, because you are only allowed to use the solvents for fuel if they contain 6 or less parts/million of lead. But the waste solvents from company X contain no lead,

just as the waste solvent from Y contains no mercury. Now along comes Company Z, a re-mixing company: It takes 10 tons of waste from company X, mixes it with 10 tons of waste from Company Y, and look what happens: The resulting 20 tons of waste now contains only 5 parts/million of mercury and 5 parts/million of lead; both the lead and the mercury levels have been cut in half (because the volume is doubled), and so it is legal for both companies to burn the resulting mix for fuel, which they do. Of course when they burn the polluted fuel, exactly the same amount of mercury and lead are being released into the atmosphere and into the air we breathe—but by mixing the wastes from both companies, the levels are reduced to under the legal limits (the waste fuel burned by Company X will now contain 5 parts/million of *both* mercury and lead, rather than 10 parts/million mercury; and the waste fuel burned by Company Y will likewise contain 5 parts/million of *both* mercury and lead, rather than 10 parts/million lead). This is a perfectly legal and very profitable business. Is it ethically legitimate?

6. You are the owner and manager of a small private computer software company that has been producing business software products for 25 years. You don't publish any of the blockbuster big programs, but you produce a steady stream of software products that have sold well, and your software company has turned a solid profit that has allowed you to live quite comfortably (no yachts or private jets, but a very nice primary residence, a small condo at a beautiful Colorado ski area, and another small condo just outside Palm Beach). Your company has some 20 employees, including 5 programmers who have worked for the company for an average of 20 years each, and who have been excellent workers. You pay them decently, a little above market average, and you provide a health care plan and a small pension, as well as a paid vacation. In short, your programmers certainly are not getting rich, but they can sustain a decent middle-class way of life for themselves and their families.

At a trade association meeting, you run into an old friend who also owns a small software company (specializing in computer games); your friend tells you that he has laid off all his programmers, and now has the programming done by a firm in South Korea: the Korean firm does a great job, the internet makes sending files between North America and South Korea as easy as sending them to the office down the hall, and your friend's software company has cut its programming costs by 75%. The Korean programming firm has a booth at the trade association meeting, and when you talk to its representative you discover that indeed, you could cut your programming costs by 75% by firing your programmers and sending the work to the programming firm in South Korea. You know that if you lay off your five programmers—all of whom are in their early 50s, not financially in a position to retire, and not likely to find work that will pay anything like the salaries they are now making—they will suffer financially, while you will gain significantly: you would certainly be able to trade up to larger and nicer ski and beach condos, for example. Would it be legitimate to fire your programmers?

Suppose that instead of a privately owned business, you have incorporated, and sold stock in your software company. If you lay off the programmers, the profits will be higher and the stock dividends larger; does that change anything?

Suppose that all of your competitors have now switched to having their programming done overseas, and they are able to sell their software for a somewhat lower price, and you are now at a competitive disadvantage. There is no danger of your company going bankrupt, but profits have declined by about 10%. Would that make a difference?

7. In 1998, the president of Harman Mining Company filed a civil lawsuit against A. T. Massey Coal Company, claiming that Massey had fraudulently canceled a contract with Harman, thus forcing Harman into bankruptcy. In 2002, a West Virginia jury found in favor of Harman, awarding

damages of $50 million. Massey appealed the case to the West Virginia Supreme Court of Appeals. While the case was making its way to that court, there was an election for a seat on the West Virginia Supreme Court of Appeals. An incumbent Supreme Court justice, Warren McGraw, was challenged by Brent Benjamin. Massey's CEO, Don Blankenship, set up a special "non-profit corporation" named "And for the Sake of the Kids"; and through that organization Blankenship funneled over $3 million to campaign in favor of Benjamin and to run negative campaign ads against McGraw. This was an enormous sum for a West Virginia Supreme Court election, and in fact made up more than half of all the money spent on Benjamin's campaign. Benjamin won the election. In 2007, when the case finally came before the West Virginia Supreme Court, the court ruled three to two in favor of *overturning* the $50 million judgment against Massey, with Benjamin casting the deciding vote to overturn the jury verdict. The investment by Blankenship in Benjamin's campaign for a West Virginia Supreme Court seat certainly paid dividends for Massey. Was that a legitimate business investment? Would Milton Friedman have approved? (This case went to the U.S. Supreme Court, which ruled in 2009—by a five-to-four majority—that Benjamin should have recused himself from the case, and not been involved in the Court's judgment of the case: *Caperton v. A. T. Massey Coal Co.*, 129 S. Ct. 2252.)

8. Many U.S. military contracts—for example, for new fighter aircraft or a new shoulder-fired missile—are awarded without bids. Because the military hardware is often top secret, the United States does not want other countries involved in manufacturing the military hardware and gaining access to military secrets, and frequently there is only one U.S. company that has the capacity to design and manufacture the highly technical military hardware. When these contracts are awarded, they are typically given as "cost plus" contracts; that is, if your company gets the contract to

manufacture 20 new top secret fighter jets, the Pentagon will pay you your costs for the project *plus* a percentage over your costs (usually between 10% and 15%) as your profit. So if you have a cost plus 10% contract to manufacture the jet fighters, and your *cost* for each fighter is $10 billion, then the government will reimburse you the $10 billion and add another billion (the plus 10%) as your profit. Of course if the cost for designing and manufacturing each fighter is $20 billion, then you double your profits. You don't need a major in accounting to realize that the higher the cost of producing each fighter, the more profit you will make.

Since designing and manufacturing a new fighter jet is an enormous project, your company will not do all the work; instead, some aspects of the work will be farmed out to subcontractors. One of the subcontracted jobs will be manufacturing seats for the fighter pilots. Two companies have made proposals to manufacture the seats. The seats will obviously be expensive, because they have to be carefully designed to fit the interior and keep the pilot comfortable as well as within easy reach of all the instruments; they must be adjustable for pilots of different heights; and they must be ejectable (in case the plane is damaged and the pilot must escape). Company A will build the seats for $500,000 each; the seats will be perfectly functional and comfortable and attractive. Company B will build the seats for $1,000,000 each; basically they are identical to the seats that Company A is proposing—they work just as well, and are equally comfortable—but most people find them slightly more attractive (the leather is a slightly more attractive shade of tan). If you go with Company A, the cost of the 20 fighters will be reduced by $10 million; if you go with Company B, the fighter jets will cost $10 million more, and your company *profit* will be increased by $1 million. You know that if you give the contract to Company B, no one will ever complain; you are not doing anything illegal (you are not taking a bribe from Company B in order to select them). Some members of the Senate Military Appropriations Committee might notice that the cost for the seats seems a little high. But both your company and many of the individual corporate officers are making substantial contributions to senators and members of Congress, so they won't raise any objections. Besides, if anyone raises questions, you have an easy reply: Aren't the men and women who fly our fighter jets and risk their lives protecting our freedom entitled to work in attractive settings? The taxpayers will take a hit—but when you spread it around among the millions of taxpayers, they won't even be aware of it. Is this a legitimate means of maximizing company profits?

Additional Resources

The classical source for the view that the only obligation of a corporation is to maximize profit for its investors is Milton Friedman's *Capitalism and Freedom* (Chicago: University of Chicago Press, 1962). An early statement of the corporate social responsibility view was by Howard R. Bowen, *Social Responsibilities of the Businessman* (New York: Harper & Brothers, 1953). A good account of the development of the corporate social responsibility perspective can be found in Morrell Heald, *The Social Responsibilities of Business: Company and Community, 1900–1960* (Cleveland, OH: Case Western Reserve University Press, 1970).

A good textbook study of corporate social responsibility is Michael Blowfied and Alan Murray's *Corporate Responsibility*, 2nd ed. (New York: Oxford University Press, 2011). C. K. Prahald and Michael E. Porter, eds., *Harvard Business Review on Corporate Responsibility* (Cambridge, MA: Harvard Business Press, 2003) is a good collection of papers on corporate social responsibility.

Jeffrey Hollender and Bill Breen's *The Responsibility Revolution: How the Next Generation of Business Will Win* (Hoboken, NJ: Jossey-Bass, 2010) is a book on how businesses can be more successful by acting responsibly for the society and the environment. C. B. Bhattacharya, Sankar Sen, and Daniel Kurschan, *Leveraging Corporate Responsibility: The Stakeholder Route to Maximizing Business and Social Value* (New York: Cambridge University Press, 2011) focus on the full range of those to whom corporations owe responsibility.

In K. Ravi Raman and Ronnie D. Lipschutz, eds., *Corporate Social Responsibility: Comparative Critiques* (Basingstoke, UK: Palgrave Macmillan, 2010), scholars from around the world and various perspectives take a critical look at corporate social responsibility. Dinah Rajak's *In Good Company: An Anatomy of Corporate Social Responsibility* (Stanford, CA: Stanford University Press, 2011) is a fascinating and carefully researched book that takes a more skeptical stance on some aspects of the corporate social responsibility model. David Vogel's *The Market for Virtue: The Potential and Limits of Corporate Social Responsibility* (Washington, DC: Brookings Institution Press, 2005) is a clear look at the limits of the corporate social responsibility model. In *Corporate Social Responsibility: The Good, the Bad, and the Ugly* (Cheltenham, UK: Edward Elgar Publishing, 2009), Bobby Banerjee develops a powerful critique of much of the corporate social responsibility movement, arguing that there is a basic conflict between the profit and social responsibility motives.

Though there is no question that many of the corporate investments in corporate social responsibility are of genuine benefit to the public, in some cases the contributions go to fake citizens groups that are actually constructed and funded by a corporation in order to promote corporate profits at the expense of public welfare, while appearing to be "grassroots" citizens groups in support of some public good (these fake grassroots groups are sometimes called "astroturf" groups). For example, a company that is polluting may set up and then contribute to an astroturf group that campaigns for pollution controls that are weaker than needed; or a company that is promoting tobacco use among children (in order to create more nicotine addicts at an early age) may set up an astroturf group to "prevent underage use of tobacco," in hopes that voluntary contributions to a group supposedly discouraging underage tobacco use—but actually *promoting* such use, by presenting tobacco use as an *adult* pleasure that is not for *children*—will persuade the government not to set up stricter laws regulating the sale of tobacco. For a fascinating but depressing look at some of that activity, see John Stauber and Sheldon Rampton, *Toxic Sludge is Good for You!* (Monroe, ME: Common Courage Press, 1995).

The Markkula Center of Applied Ethics at Santa Clara University has an excellent website, providing interesting cases, good articles, and many links; go to www.scu.edu/ethics. Corporate Watch provides information on various companies and on a number of business ethics issues, at www.corpwatch.org. Sourcewatch at www.sourcewatch.org has interesting material on a wide variety of issues; for a deeply skeptical perspective on corporate social responsibility, go to the site and search corporate social responsibility.

MYSEARCHLAB CONNECTIONS

See the entry for "Business Ethics" in the *Stanford Encyclopedia of Philosophy*, at plato.stanford.edu. A wide variety of excellent material can be found at www.scu.edu/ethics, the website of the Markkula Center of Applied Ethics at Santa Clara University.

Index